OXFORD MEDIEVAL TEXTS

General Editors
J. W. BINNS   D. D'AVRAY
M. S. KEMPSHALL   R. C. LOVE

BYRHTFERTH OF RAMSEY
HISTORIA REGVM

Byrhtferth of Ramsey

HISTORIA REGVM

EDITED AND TRANSLATED BY
MICHAEL LAPIDGE

CLARENDON PRESS · OXFORD

Great Clarendon Street, Oxford, OX2 6DP,
United Kingdom

Oxford University Press is a department of the University of Oxford.
It furthers the University's objective of excellence in research, scholarship,
and education by publishing worldwide. Oxford is a registered trade mark of
Oxford University Press in the UK and in certain other countries

© Michael Lapidge 2022

The moral rights of the author have been asserted

First Edition published in 2022

Impression: 1

All rights reserved. No part of this publication may be reproduced, stored in
a retrieval system, or transmitted, in any form or by any means, without the
prior permission in writing of Oxford University Press, or as expressly permitted
by law, by licence or under terms agreed with the appropriate reprographics
rights organization. Enquiries concerning reproduction outside the scope of the
above should be sent to the Rights Department, Oxford University Press, at the
address above

You must not circulate this work in any other form
and you must impose this same condition on any acquirer

Published in the United States of America by Oxford University Press
198 Madison Avenue, New York, NY 10016, United States of America

British Library Cataloguing in Publication Data

Data available

Library of Congress Control Number: 2022935837

ISBN 978–0–19–284970–0

Printed and bound by
CPI Group (UK) Ltd, Croydon, CR0 4YY

Links to third party websites are provided by Oxford in good faith and
for information only. Oxford disclaims any responsibility for the materials
contained in any third party website referenced in this work.

PREFACE

During the past generation, Byrhtferth of Ramsey (d. *c.*1020) has emerged as one of the major authors of late Anglo-Saxon England. Like Bede before him, he is now recognized as the author of computistical writings, notably a *Computus* and an accompanying handbook, which he called his *Enchiridion*, intended to explain the complexities of that difficult science, as well as of saints' Lives, in particular a *Vita S. Oswaldi*, the Life of Oswald, bishop of Worcester (961–92) and archbishop of York (971–92) and founder of Ramsey Abbey, and a *Vita S. Ecgwini*, the Life of an early eighth-century bishop of Worcester who was the founder of Evesham Abbey. But—again like Bede—Byrhtferth was also a historian, and in recent times he has been recognized as the author of a history of the Anglo-Saxon kingdoms, from the earliest times up to the reign of King Alfred (d. 899). This historical work, the *Historia regum*, has not hitherto attracted a modern critical edition, and the present work is intended to supply that want.

Byrhtferth's *Historia regum* has not been preserved as an independent text, but survives as the first component of a large historical compilation by the early twelfth-century historian Symeon of Durham, a compilation which is itself preserved uniquely in a single manuscript, now Cambridge, Corpus Christi College 139, dating from the third quarter of the twelfth century. In 2013 David Rollason and I proposed to the editors of OMT a joint edition of Symeon's work as it is preserved in the Corpus manuscript, the intention being that I would be primarily responsible for the edition of the parts of Symeon's historical compilation which had earlier been composed by Byrhtferth, with David taking primary responsibility for the remainder of Symeon's work. We worked for a number of years in fruitful collaboration, but eventually we realized—what we should perhaps have realized from the outset—that our editorial approaches were incompatible: my intention was to reconstruct Byrhtferth's text as a work of the late tenth century, by (for example) removing from the text those passages which were manifestly later interpolations into Byrhtferth's original work, and restoring the original spellings of Anglo-Saxon names, whereas David's concern was to present the edition of a twelfth-century Durham compilation, incorporating all the accretions and interpolations which the work had acquired in the two centuries following Byrhtferth's original composition. We therefore agreed, entirely

vi PREFACE

amicably, to pursue our editorial aims independently, by asking the Delegates of OUP to reconsider our original proposal of 2013 as a proposal for two separate editions. The *Historia regum* of Byrhtferth of Ramsey, therefore, is the subject of the present volume; David Rollason's edition of Symeon of Durham, *Historia de regibus Anglorum et Dacorum*, will follow in due course in a separate (and much larger) volume.

My first obligation is to express my warmest thanks to David Rollason for years of discussion of the text as preserved in the Corpus manuscript, for commenting in detail on an earlier version of the present edition, and especially for persuading me to pay closer attention to the contributions of the later annotators of CCCC 139. David d'Avray (on behalf of the OMT editors) dealt masterfully with the divorce proceedings which led to the separation of the proposed Byrhtferth and Symeon volumes and their adoption by the Delegates of OUP. Joanna Story supplied me with a number of valuable references to secondary literature. I owe a long-standing debt to the late Peter Hunter Blair, who was my Cambridge colleague in the Department of Anglo-Saxon, Norse, and Celtic in the early 1970s, and whom I used to meet regularly for coffee following our lectures; during these coffee-breaks we frequently discussed the *Historia regum*, and he listened sympathetically to my arguments that the original author was Byrhtferth (following his death in 1982 I was privileged to inherit his heavily annotated copy of Arnold's Rolls Series edition of Symeon, which has been beside me during many years' work on the present edition). And finally I am grateful, as always, for the attentive care which Rosalind Love (on behalf of the OMT editors) devoted to the book, and to her many valuable suggestions for its improvement, and to the equally attentive care which Bonnie Blackburn, as copy-editor, devoted to the volume's layout and presentation.

M. L.

January 2022

CONTENTS

ABBREVIATIONS	ix
INTRODUCTION	xiii
I. Byrhtferth of Ramsey	xiii
II. Cambridge, Corpus Christi College 139	xvii
III. The Authorship of the First Four Sections	xxi
IV. Byrhtferth of Ramsey and the First Four Sections	xxiii
V. The Sources of the *Historia Regum*	xliii
VI. The Transmission of the *Historia Regum*	lxxvi
VII. Previous Editions	lxxxi
VIII. Editorial Procedures	lxxxvi
HISTORIA REGVM	I
PART I	2
PART II	22
PART III	58
PART IV	118
APPENDICES	
1. The Annals 888–957	171
2. The Hexham Interpolations	183
BIBLIOGRAPHY	191
INDEX OF QUOTATIONS AND ALLUSIONS	201
GENERAL INDEX	205

ABBREVIATIONS

ALL i, ii

M. Lapidge, *Anglo-Latin Literature 600–899* (London, 1996) [i]; *Anglo-Latin Literature 900–1066* (London, 1993) [ii]

ASC

The Anglo-Saxon Chronicle: ed. C. Plummer and J. Earle, *Two of the Saxon Chronicles Parallel* (2 vols.; Oxford, 1892–9); trans. D. Whitelock, *The Anglo-Saxon Chronicle: A Revised Translation* (London, 1961)

Bede, *HE*, ed. Colgrave and Mynors

Bede's Ecclesiastical History of the English People, ed. B. Colgrave and R. A. B. Mynors (OMT, 1969; rev. repr. 1991)

Bede, *HE*, ed. Lapidge

Bede, *Historia ecclesiastica gentis Anglorum*, ed. M. Lapidge; trans. P. Chiesa, *Beda: Storia degli inglesi* (2 vols.; Milan, 2008–10)

Bede, *VBOH*

Venerabilis Baedae Opera Historica, ed. C. Plummer (2 vols.; Oxford, 1896)

BHL

[Bollandists], *Bibliotheca Hagiographica Latina* (2 vols.; Brussels, 1899–1901, with supplements, 1911, 1986) [cited by item number]

BL

The British Library, London

BnF

Bibliothèque nationale de France, Paris

BodL

The Bodleian Library, Oxford

Byrhtferth, *Comp. proem.*

The *proemium* to Byrhtferth, *Computus*: ed. P. S. Baker and M. Lapidge in *Byrhtferth's Enchiridion* (Early English Text Society, s.s. xv; Oxford, 1995), pp. 375–9

— *Ench.*

Byrhtferth's Enchiridion, ed. P. S. Baker and M. Lapidge (Early English Text Society, s.s. xv; Oxford, 1995), pp. 2–248

— *HR*

—— *Historia regum*, ed. below, pp. 1–169

— *VSE*

—— *Vita S. Ecgwini*, ed. M. Lapidge in *Byrhtferth of Ramsey: The Lives of St Oswald and St Ecgwine* (OMT, 2009), pp. 205–303

— *VSO*

—— *Vita S. Oswaldi*, ed. M. Lapidge in *Byrhtferth of Ramsey: The Lives of St Oswald and St Ecgwine* (OMT, 2009), pp. 1–203

ABBREVIATIONS

CCCC	Corpus Christi College, Cambridge
CL	Cathedral Library
CPL	*Clavis Patrum Latinorum*, ed. E. Dekkers and A. Gaar (3rd edn.; Steenbrugge, 1995) [cited by item number]
CSEL	Corpus Scriptorum Ecclesiasticorum Latinorum (Vienna, 1866 –)
DEPN	E. Ekwall, *The Concise Oxford Dictionary of English Place-Names* (4th edn., Oxford, 1960)
DMLBS	*Dictionary of Medieval Latin from British Sources*, ed. R. E. Latham, D. R. Howlett, R. K. Ashdowne, *et al.* (Oxford, 1975–2013)
EHD i	*English Historical Documents*, i. *c.500–1042*, ed. D. Whitelock (2nd edn., London, 1979)
HE Continuatio (I)	'Continuations', in Bede, *HE*, ed. Colgrave and Mynors, pp. 572–3; ed. J. Story in 'After Bede: Continuing the *Ecclesiastical History*', in S. Baxter, C. Karkov, J. L. Nelson, and D. Pelteret, eds., *Early Medieval Studies in Memory of Patrick Wormald* (Aldershot, 2009), pp. 165–84, at 183
HE Continuatio (II)	'Continuations', in Bede, *HE*, ed. Colgrave and Mynors, pp. 572–7
HSC	*Historia de Sancto Cuthberto: A History of Saint Cuthbert and a Record of his Patrimony*, ed. T. Johnson South (Anglo-Saxon Texts, iii; Woodbridge, 2002)
ICL	*Initia Carminum Latinorum saeculo undecimo antiquiorum*, ed. D. Schaller and E. Könsgen (Göttingen, 1977)
LDE	*Symeon of Durham: Libellus de Exordio atque Procursu istius hoc est Dunhelmensis Ecclesie*, ed. D. Rollason (OMT, 2000)
LHS	M. Leumann, J. B. Hofmann, and A. Szantyr, *Lateinische Grammatik* (2 vols.; Munich, 1965–71)
LVD	*Liber Vitae of Durham*, ed. H. Sweet in *The Oldest English Texts* (Early English Text Society, lxxxiii; London, 1885), pp. 153–66
Mansi, *Concilia*	J. D. Mansi, *Sacrorum Conciliorum Nova et Amplissima Collectio* (31 vols., Florence, 1759–98)
MGH	Monumenta Germaniae Historica
—— *AA*	—— *Auctores Antiquissimi*
—— *Epist.*	—— *Epistolae (in quarto)*

ABBREVIATIONS

—— *Ep. sel.*	—— *Epistolae selectae* (*in octavo*)
—— *PLAC*	—— *Poetae Latini Aevi Carolini*
—— *SS*	—— *Scriptores* (*in folio*)
—— *SS rer. Germ.*	—— *Scriptores rerum Germanicarum* (*in octavo*)
ODB	*Oxford Dictionary of Byzantium*, ed. A. P. Kazhdan *et al.* (3 vols., Oxford, 1991)
ODNB	*The Oxford Dictionary of National Biography*, ed. H. C. G. Matthew and B. Harrison (60 vols.; Oxford, 2004)
OLD	*Oxford Latin Dictionary*, ed. P. W. Glare (Oxford, 1968–82)
OMT	Oxford Medieval Texts
PASE	*The Prosopography of Anglo-Saxon England:* <www.pase.ac.uk>
PL	Patrologia Latina, ed. J.-P. Migne (Paris, 1844–64)
'Ramsey Annals'	C. R. Hart, 'The Ramsey Computus', *English Historical Review*, lxxxv (1970), 29–44, at 38–44
SChr	Sources chrétiennes (Paris, 1941–)
WB Ency.	*The Wiley Blackwell Encyclopedia of Anglo-Saxon England*, ed. M. Lapidge, J. Blair, S. Keynes, and D. Scragg (2nd edn.; Oxford, 2014)

INTRODUCTION

BYRHTFERTH OF RAMSEY

BYRHTFERTH OF RAMSEY is one of the most prolific, but also idio-syncratic authors of the Anglo-Saxon period, whose surviving corpus of writings includes works in both Latin and Old English. The fenland monastery of Ramsey was founded in 966 by Oswald, bishop of Worcester (961–92), on land granted by Æthelwine, the wealthy ealdorman of East Anglia, who became Ramsey's lay patron; a century later its endowment had grown to the point that it was the tenth richest abbey in England.[1] In his earlier life, during the 950s, Oswald had spent time overseas at the Benedictine monastery of Fleury, which housed the remains of St Benedict himself; as a result of Oswald's experience at Fleury, Ramsey too was dedicated to St Benedict. Fleury was immensely wealthy, and housed the largest library in Europe; significantly, one of the most learned of Fleury's monks, Abbo, spent two years (985–7) at Ramsey, at the invitation of Oswald, whom he had known at Fleury. While at Ramsey, Abbo taught the monks of the fledgling monastery the principles of ecclesiastical computus[2] and the intricacies of Latin metre.[3] He also composed at Ramsey his *Passio S. Eadmundi*, an account of the murder of Edmund, king of East Anglia, by the Danes in 869.[4] Abbo brought with him to Ramsey a number of Latin works previously unknown in Anglo-Saxon England (for example, Macrobius, *Comm. in Somnium Scipionis*) as well as the text of his own *Computus*, copies of which survive in various English manuscripts.

---

[1] For the early history of Ramsey, see *Byrhtferth, The Lives*, ed. Lapidge, pp. xv–xxix.

[2] On the distinguishing characteristics of Abbo's *computus*, see *Byrhtferth's Enchiridion*, ed. Baker and Lapidge, pp. xlii–xlv. An Abbonian *computus* is printed in PL xc. 727–820; for the manuscripts which transmit this work, not yet adequately edited, see Bourgain, 'Abbo Floriacensis abb.', pp. 18–20. Another work of Abbo which is relevant to his knowledge of computus is his commentary on the *Calculus* of Victorius of Aquitaine, in Peden (ed.), *Abbo of Fleury and Ramsey*, pp. 63–131; on this, see Bourgain, 'Abbo Floriacensis abb.', pp. 12–13.

[3] Abbo's *Quaestiones grammaticales* were composed at the prompting of, and dedicated to, his 'beloved English brothers, especially those in the monastery of St Benedict [i.e. Ramsey]' (*Dilectissimis in Christo Angligenis fratribus, maximeque in monasterio sancti patris Benedicti*): *Abbo Floriacensis Quaestiones Grammaticales*, ed. A. Guerreau-Jalabert (Paris, 1982), pp. 209–75; the quotation is from p. 209.

[4] *BHL* 2392; in *Three Lives of English Saints*, ed. Winterbottom, pp. 67–87.

xiv INTRODUCTION

Byrhtferth entered the monastery of Ramsey, possibly as an oblate, soon after its foundation, perhaps *c*.970. He may thus have been still in his teens during Abbo's sojourn at Ramsey; whatever his precise age at the time, Byrhtferth became a devoted pupil of the great European master. It was possibly at Abbo's instigation that Byrhtferth began assembling passages from earlier computistical and philosophical writings (including Macrobius, *Comm. in Somnium Scipionis*) in order to elucidate the complexities of two of Bede's writings, *De natura rerum* and *De temporum ratione*. This *collectaneum* or compendium of excerpts from earlier writings is transmitted as the *Glossae Bridferti Ramesiensis in Bedam*; no manuscript of the work survives, but it was printed from a now lost manuscript by Johann Herwagen in 1563.[5] Again, at Abbo's instigation (probably), Byrhtferth compiled his own ecclesiastical *Computus*, consisting of tables used to calculate the date of Easter and other movable feasts of the liturgical year, mnemonic poems encapsulating the rules by which these dates are calculated, a calendar, diagrams of the earth, the planets, etc.; this compilation serves in turn as prefatory to a corpus of other relevant computistical writings, including Bede, *De temporibus*, *De natura rerum*, *De temporum ratione*, and Helperic, *De computo*. Byrhtferth's *Computus*, which has never been printed in full,[6] is preserved in three twelfth-century English manuscripts; in one of these (Oxford, St John's College, 17 [Thorney, AD 1110–11]) it is preceded by a diagram of 'the physical and physiological fours' compiled by Byrhtferth which bears the legend 'hanc figuram edidit Bryhtferð monachus Rameseiensis cenobii de concordia mensium atque elementorum' (fo. 7ᵛ), followed by a preface in Byrhtferth's own name: 'Proemium Brihtferthi Rameseiensis cenobii monachi'.[7] At the end of the Preface, Byrhtferth refers reverently to the writings and learning of Abbo: 'constant Abbonis sophistę dicta, alumpni Benedicti

---

[5] See Gorman, 'The glosses of Bede's *De temporum ratione* attributed to Byrhtferth of Ramsey'; Lapidge, 'Byrhtferth of Ramsey and the *Glossae Bridferti in Bedam*'; and Byrhtferth, *The Lives*, ed. Lapidge, pp. xxxiii–xxxvi. The *Glossae Bridferti Ramesiensis in Bedam* are edited in *Opera Bedae*, ed. Herwagen, i. 164–81 [on *De temporum ratione*, c. 1], i. 182–4 [on *De temporum ratione*, c. 4], ii. 1–49 [on *De natura rerum*, cc. 1–22, 25–7, 29–31, 36], ii. 49–173 [on *De temporum ratione*, cc. 2–3, 5–64]; the *Glossae Bridferti* as printed by Herwagen are repr. PL xc. 186–254 [on *De natura rerum*, cc. 1–22, 25–7, 29–31, 36], 297–518 [on *De temporum ratione*, cc. 2–3, 5–64], 685–95 [on *De temporum ratione*, c. 1], 700–2 [on *De temporum ratione*, c. 4].

[6] The contents of Byrhtferth's *Computus* are fully catalogued, and many items (including the calendar) printed, in *Byrhtferth's Enchiridion*, ed. Baker and Lapidge, pp. 373–427.

[7] Ibid. p. 375. Byrhtferth's name is also encoded in some pictograms and ogams placed at the centre of his diagram of the physical and physiological fours in St Johns 17 (fo. 7ᵛ); see Sims-Williams, 'Byrhtferth's ogam signature'.

BYRHTFERTH OF RAMSEY

patris, per cuius beniuolentiam percepimus huius rei intelligentiam necnon aliarum rerum peritiam'.[8] There is, therefore, no doubt that this computus in the three twelfth-century English manuscripts is the work of Byrhtferth of Ramsey.

Byrhtferth was well aware that the science of computus was complex and difficult. Part of his responsibilities as a monk of Ramsey included giving instruction in this difficult subject to younger monks (novices, presumably) of the abbey, as well as to secular clergy (*clerici*) of the neighbourhood, whose training apparently involved some, perhaps elementary understanding of computus—at the least, an understanding of the principles by which the date of Easter was to be calculated each year. In order to facilitate his teaching duties, Byrhtferth composed a handbook on the subject of ecclesiastical computus and—with his penchant for learned vocabulary—typically called it his *Enchiridion* ('handbook'), a work partly in Latin (for the benefit of the young monks), partly in English (for the benefit of the secular clergy). The *Enchiridion* consists of four parts, of which the first two treat computistical procedures, the third treats grammatical terminology, and the fourth consists of a sort of dictionary of the numerological meanings of numbers from 1 to 20, plus 40, 60, 100, and 1000. There is no doubt that the *Enchiridion* is the work of Byrhtferth, for he names himself six times during the course of the work:

Byrhtferðus ipse scripsit bene, beneque docet ille suis discipulis (ii. 1, lines 438–9: 'Byrhtferth himself writes well, and teaches well his pupils')

swylce Byrhtferð ðus cweðe (ii. 1, line 488: 'as Byrhtferth thus says')

Oratio patris Byrhtferði (iii. 2, line 2: 'the prayer of father Byrhtferth', followed by the quotation of two lines from Arator, *Historia apostolica*)

swylce frater Byrhtferð þus cweðe (iii. 3, lines 95–6: 'as brother Byrhtferth thus says')

nu togeare, þa Brihtferð writere þis awrat, synd feowertyne epactas and Ianuarius hæfð nigon rihtinga (iii. 2, lines 111–13: 'Now in this year, when the writer Byrhtferth wrote this, there are fourteen epacts and January has nine regulars')

Byrhtferð mæssepreost stent on þam twelftan stede æfter þam biscope Eadnoðe (iii. 2, lines 198–200: 'Byrhtferth the mass-priest stands in the twelfth position, after Bishop Eadnoth')

---

[8] Ibid. pp. 375–9, at 379: 'writings of the scholar Abbo, an alumnus of St Benedict [i.e. Fleury], through whose kindness I received my understanding of this subject [the computus] as well as my knowledge of other things'. There is an earlier edition of Byrhtferth's *Comp. proem.* or 'Preface' by Forsey, 'Byrhtferth's *Preface*'.

xvi INTRODUCTION

From these various self-references, there can be no doubt that the author of the *Enchiridion* was Byrhtferth, nor is there any doubt that he was a priest and monk at Ramsey.[9] The reference to a year in which there are fourteen epacts and January has nine regulars (quoted above) indicates unambiguously that this sentence of the *Enchiridion* was composed in AD 1011. It is the one and only verifiable date in the career of Byrhtferth.

I have set out fully the evidence for Byrhtferth's authorship of the *Computus* and the *Enchiridion*, because understanding of the flamboyant Latin of these two works is fundamental to identifying further literary production of this idiosyncratic author. In 1929 Samuel J. Crawford, who was at that time at work on an edition of Byrhtferth's *Enchiridion*, identified the characteristic features of Byrhtferth's Latin style in a work which was known to have been composed at Ramsey *c*.1000, but was then treated as anonymous (since the unique manuscript carries no attribution of authorship): the *Vita S. Oswaldi*, a Life of Bishop Oswald of Worcester, the founder of Ramsey Abbey.[10] In the light of Crawford's helpful analysis of Byrhtferth's Latin style, I was able in 1975 to attribute another early eleventh-century saint's Life, transmitted anonymously alongside the *Vita S. Oswaldi* in the one surviving manuscript, to Byrhtferth: the *Vita S. Ecgwini*, the Life of an early eighth-century bishop of Worcester who was the founder of Evesham Abbey.[11] These two saints' Lives were subsequently edited as the work of Byrhtferth of Ramsey,[12] with full analysis of the distinctive, indeed idiosyncratic Latin style in which they are couched. It is on the basis of this fuller understanding of Byrhtferth's Latin style that it is possible to identify him as the author of the *Historia regum* edited here.[13] But before turning to analysis of the Latinity of the *Historia regum*, and arguments for attributing the work to Byrhtferth, it is necessary to understand the context in which it has been preserved.

---

[9] *Enchiridion* i. 1. 157–8: 'Þas þing we gemetton on Ramesige þurh Godes miltsigendan gife,' 'We found these things [i.e. understanding of computus] at Ramsey through God's merciful bounty.'

[10] Crawford, 'Byrhtferth of Ramsey and the anonymous Life of St Oswald'.

[11] Lapidge, 'The hermeneutic style', pp. 90–4 [= *ALL* ii. 128–32]; and Lapidge, 'Byrhtferth and the *Vita S. Ecgwini*'.

[12] Byrhtferth, *The Lives*, ed. Lapidge.

[13] The four parts of this work edited here are preserved as a component of a larger work by Symeon of Durham, and have no separate title (or rubric) in the principal surviving manuscript of Symeon's work. The title '*Historia regum*' which I use throughout is editorial, and is intended to provide an appropriate indication of the contents of the four parts of Byrhtferth's work, as will become clear from subsequent discussion.

CAMBRIDGE, CORPUS CHRISTI COLLEGE 139

CCCC 139 is a large compendium of historical writings that may well be the most important surviving source for the history of northern England in the period up until the twelfth century. It consists of 180 folios (plus two flyleaves and four end-leaves) in large quarto format (304 × 214 mm), written in double columns, thirty-five or thirty-six lines to the page.[14] A *terminus post quem* for the writing of the manuscript can be deduced from two of its contents: a rhythmical poem on the defeat and death of Somerled (fo. 133[r–v]) in 1164 (inc. 'Dauid rege mortis lege clauso in sarcofago'), and another poem, in hexameters this time, on the death of Malcolm IV of Scotland (fo. 165[vb]), which took place in 1165 (inc. 'Cur sic, care, taces? Pro me loquitur mea uita'). From these two poems it is clear that the manuscript must have been written in the third quarter of the twelfth century, and a date of *c*.1170 has reasonably been suggested.[15] Some earlier scholars argued that the manuscript was written at Hexham,[16] others that it was written at Sawley in West Yorkshire (it bears an erased *ex libris* datable to *c*.1200 on fo. ii[r]: *Liber sancte Marie de Salleia*).[17] More recently, however, convincing arguments have been made that the manuscript was in fact written at Durham and only subsequently owned at Sawley, a Cistercian monastery which had close links with Durham. Joanna Story demonstrated conclusively that the brief chronicle on fos. 48[r]–50[v] was copied directly from a Durham manuscript, now Durham, CL, B. IV. 25, fos. 3[r]–5[v].[18] Bernard Meehan showed that the copy of the *Historia Brittonum* on fos. 168[v]–178[v] was used to correct a copy of the same text in Durham, CL, B. II. 35 (s. xii[2]) at Durham itself, and that the chronicle of Regino of Prüm on fos. 17[r]–35[v] was copied from yet another Durham manuscript, now CL, C. IV. 15 (s. xii in.).[19] The sum of this evidence indicates that CCCC 139 was written at Durham *c*.1170, but was subsequently owned at Sawley.

[14] James, *Descriptive Catalogue*, i. 317–23. Excellent digitized images of the manuscript are available at <https://parker-stanford-edu.ezp.lib.cam.ac.uk>.

[15] Baker, 'Scissors and paste', pp. 96–8, suggests the outer limits of 1164 and 1175; Hunter Blair, 'Some observations', pp. 70–1, proposes *c*.1170.

[16] James (following Theodor Mommsen), *Descriptive Catalogue*, i. 323; H. S. Offler, 'Hexham and the *Historia Regum*', *Transactions of the Architectural and Archaeological Society of Durham and Northumberland*, n.s. ii (1970), 51–62.

[17] Hunter Blair, 'Some observations', p. 118; Dumville, 'The Corpus Christi "Nennius"', p. 369.

[18] Story, 'Symeon as annalist', pp. 203–7.

[19] Meehan, 'Durham twelfth-century manuscripts', pp. 440–2.

xviii   INTRODUCTION

As we have seen, CCCC 139 is a large compendium of historical texts containing, inter alia, extracts from the *Chronicon* of Regino of Prüm (fos. 17^r–35^v), Richard of Hexham, *De gestis regis Stephani et de bello Standardii* (fos. 36^r–46^r), and a tract *De obsessione Dunelmi* (fos. 50^r–51^r). However, the principal component of this historical compendium is Symeon of Durham, *Historia de regibus Anglorum et Dacorum* (fos. 51^v–129^v), which covers the period from 732 and the death of Bede (735) to 1129. In the manuscript this work is followed by a continuation of Symeon's composition by John, prior of Hexham, entitled *Historia Iohannis prioris Haugustaldensis ecclesie .xxv. annorum* (fos. 129^v–147^r), which treats the years 1130–53. Symeon's *Historia de regibus* is preceded by a rubric (fo. 51vb) which identifies him as the precentor of Durham:

Incipit historia sancte et suauis memorie Symeonis monachi et precentoris ecclesie sancti Cuthberti Dunelmi de regibus Anglorum et Dacorum et creberrimis bellis, rapinis, et incendiis eorum post obitum uenerabilis Bede presbyteri fere usque ad obitum regis primi Henrici filii Willelmi nothi qui Angliam adquisiuit, id est .cccc. .xxix. annorum et .iiii. mensium.

The work is concluded by a rubric in similar phrasing on fo. 129rb:

Explicit historia suauis et sancte memorie Symeonis monachi et precentoris ecclesie sancti Cuthberti Dunelmi, annorum .cccc. .xxix. et mensium quattuor.

Peter Hunter Blair convincingly demonstrated that these rubrics (*incipit* and *explicit*) were composed in 1164,[20] and indicate that the copying of Symeon's *Historia de regibus* had been completed—at Durham—by September 1164 (i.e. 429 years and four months after the death of Bede at the end of May 735).

The past generation has seen enormous advances in our knowledge of Symeon, principally through research led by David Rollason and several of his colleagues in Durham.[21] In light of this research, it may now confidently be stated that Symeon was a monk of northern French (possibly Norman) origin who came to Durham in the employ of Bishop William of Saint-Calais (1081–96), who in 1083 re-established Durham as a Benedictine house and at approximately the same time initiated construction of the magnificent cathedral which survives to

---

[20] Hunter Blair, 'Some observations', pp. 77–8.

[21] See the essays in Rollason, Harvey, and Prestwich, eds., *Anglo-Norman Durham*, esp. those by Alan Piper, 'The Durham Cantor's book' (pp. 79–92) and Michael Gullick, 'The scribes of the Durham Cantor's book' (pp. 93–109), plus all the essays in Rollason, ed., *Symeon of Durham*, and (more briefly), Rollason, 'Symeon of Durham and the community of Durham'.

CAMBRIDGE, CORPUS CHRISTI COLLEGE 139 xix

this day as one of the glories of English (Anglo-Norman) architecture.[22] In his role as precentor, Symeon would have been responsible for maintaining Durham's martyrology, that is, the record of saints and their feast days, which were commemorated annually by the community. In light of this presumed responsibility, attention has been drawn by Alan Piper and Michael Gullick to a surviving Durham copy of Usuard's *Martyrologium*, which has been annotated throughout in a distinctive Anglo-Norman hand datable to the last decade of the eleventh century: Durham, CL, B. IV. 24.[23] Given the date of the annotations, it has been concluded, not unreasonably, that the hand of the martyrology scribe is that of Symeon himself. Furthermore, as precentor, Symeon was responsible for the cathedral library, and Michael Gullick has been able to identify a substantial corpus of manuscripts either written or annotated by Symeon of Durham which testify impressively to his activities as scribe and librarian.[24]

Where these manuscripts can be dated, they show that Symeon was active as a scribe and librarian during the period from the 1090s to 1129. During this time he assembled at Durham an impressive collection of historical writings concerned with English, especially Northumbrian history; his study of these writings resulted in his major historical work, the *Libellus de exordio et processu istius, hoc est Dunhelmensis, ecclesie* (referred to hereafter as *LDE*), composed during the years 1104 and 1107/9.[25] The date of his death is unknown, but must have occurred soon after 1129. His other major work, the *Historia de regibus Anglorum et Dacorum*, was the product of his last years, and was possibly left unfinished at the time of his death.[26]

Symeon's *Historia de regibus* is itself a composite text, and we may best begin by listing its several components as they are preserved in CCCC 139:

   (i) the kingdom of Kent from 616 onwards; martyrdom of the royal Kentish princes Æthelred and Æthelberht (fos. 52ra–54vb);

  (ii) the kingdom of Northumbria from its foundation; the monastery of Monkwearmouth–Jarrow and its illustrious alumnus, Bede (fos. 54vb–60ra);

---

[22] See Aird, 'An absent friend: The career of Bishop William of Saint-Calais'.

[23] Piper, 'The Durham Cantor's book'; Gullick, 'The scribes of the Durham Cantor's book'.

[24] Gullick, 'The hand of Symeon of Durham'. Gullick lists more than forty manuscripts which contain Symeon's handwriting.

[25] *Symeon of Durham: Libellus de exordio*, ed. Rollason.

[26] Thus Rollason, 'Symeon's contribution', p. 10.

XX INTRODUCTION

(iii) the kingdoms of Northumbria and Mercia: annals for the period 732–801 (fos. 60ra–68rb);

(iv) the kingdom of Wessex, 802–87: the career of King Alfred (fos. 68rb–75ra);

(v) annals 888–957 (fos. 75ra–76ra);

(vi) excerpts from bk. ii of William of Malmesbury, *Gesta regum* (fos. 76ra–76vb);[27]

(vii) excerpts from John of Worcester, *Chronica*, for the years 848–1118 (fos. 77ra–122va);[28]

(viii) annals 1119–29 (fos. 122va–129va).

It will be clear from even this brief listing of contents that Symeon's *Historia de regibus* is not a coherent piece of historical writing. It assembles excerpts from many earlier works—and not all these sources are listed here[29]—without any attempt to integrate them or to eliminate repetitions and contradictions, of which there are many. Thomas Arnold, the nineteenth-century editor of Symeon's historical works, commented that the '*Historia Dunelmensis Ecclesiae* [i.e. the *LDE*], written when he was in middle life and full of energy, is an original work; the *Historia* [*de regibus*] is not'.[30] Nevertheless, many of the sources laid under contribution by Symeon contain historical information not found elsewhere, and therefore have unique value. Our concern is with one of these sources, the first four sections (nos. i–iv in the list above), which treat the history of the English kingdoms from 732 until 887.

---

[27] The excerpts from William may be found in the edition of R. A. B. Mynors, R. M. Thomson and M. Winterbottom, William of Malmesbury, *Gesta Regum Anglorum. The History of English Kings*, vol. i (OMT, 1998), pp. 250–4 (ii. 154–5), 406 (ii. 221), 384–6 (ii. 207), and 414–16 (ii. 226–7), respectively.

[28] The excerpts from John of Worcester form a very substantial part of Symeon's *Historia de regibus* (they occupy pp. 98–253 of Thomas Arnold's edition, *Symeonis Monachi Opera Omnia*). For the most part they are reproduced verbatim from John's *Chronica*. Thus, Symeon's annals for 948 to 1066 (Arnold, pp. 98–185) correspond to *The Chronicle of John of Worcester*, ed. Darlington and McGurk, ii: *The Annals from 450 to 1066* (OMT, 1995), pp. 260–606, with omissions and additions; those for 1067 to 1118 (Arnold, pp. 185–253) correspond to *The Chronicle of John of Worcester*, iii: *The Annals from 1067 to 1140*, pp. 4–144, with omissions and additions. Many of the earlier entries (up to 887) in John's *Chronica* were copied directly from Asser, *Vita Ælfredi*, so there is considerable overlap and repetition between the annals for 848–87 in item (vii) of Symeon's *Historia de regibus*, and those which he had previously incorporated under no. (iv), above.

[29] For example, against 884 (Arnold, pp. 115–17), Symeon incorporated the account of John Scottus Eriugena from William of Malmesbury, *Gesta pontificum Anglorum*, ed. Winterbottom, v. 240, pp. 586–8).

[30] *Symeonis Monachi Opera Omnia*, ed. Arnold, ii, pp. xx–xxi.

THE AUTHORSHIP OF THE FIRST FOUR SECTIONS

Anyone who reads these four early sections (i–iv) of Symeon's *Historia de regibus* will be struck immediately by the pompous, inflated verbosity of the Latin—sentences blown up with polysyllabic adjectives and adverbs, rare and unusual words of all sorts, Graecisms among them, ostentatious quotations from classical poets, especially Boethius, wordplay, especially polyptoton of various kinds, protracted rhetorical questions, and so on. This feature of these early sections was remarked by most previous editors of Symeon. John Sharpe, in his preface to Henry Petrie's edition of Symeon in the *Monumenta Historica Britannica* of 1848, noted that 'the bulk of the first Chronicle, that is to say, the passion of Ethelred and Ethelbert [i.e. no. (i)], the Genealogy of the Northumbrian Kings [i.e. no. (ii)], the Annals to the year 803 [i.e. no. (iii)] and the excerpts from Asser [i.e. no. (iv)], are all in a style *ridiculously inflated*' (my italics);[31] of no. (iv), in particular, he observes that Asser's Life of Alfred is 'often amplified in a strangely inflated manner'.[32] He deduced that these four parts were written 'long before Simeon's time'.[33] Twenty years later John Hodgson-Hinde prefaced his edition of Symeon's work by noting the 'grandiloquent phraseology' of the *passio* of Ethelbert and Ethelred [i.e. no. (i)],[34] a work which, in his opinion, 'was written long before the age of Symeon',[35] and he went on to suggest that the style of the *passio* influenced the author of what he called Part I of Symeon's work, the history from 732 to 957 [i.e. nos. (ii)–(iv), plus (v) above], with their 'laboured and ambitious style'.[36] He concluded that these parts were 'far anterior to the age of Symeon, whatever part he may possibly have taken in reducing them to their present form'.[37] In his view, all these early sections [i.e. parts (i)–(iv), plus (v)] had once 'formed the collections of an anonymous student in the reign of Edward the Confessor'.[38]

---

[31] *Monumenta Historica Britannica*, ed. Petrie and Sharpe, p. 88.
[32] Ibid. p. 87.
[33] Ibid. p. 89.
[34] *Symeonis Dunelmensis Opera*, ed. Hodgson-Hinde, p. xxiii.
[35] Ibid. p. x.
[36] Ibid. p. xi.
[37] Ibid. p. xiv.
[38] Ibid. Hodgson-Hinde's dating of all these sections to the reign of Edward the Confessor (1042–66) is based on the final annal-entry in section (v), the annals for 888–957. I shall argue that section (v) is distinct from the four previous sections (i–iv), and is not the work of the same author: see below, Appendix I, pp. 171–82.

xxii INTRODUCTION

Seventeen years later, Thomas Arnold, in his edition of Symeon's works for the Rolls Series (1882–5), developed further the arguments of his predecessors regarding the authorship of the early sections of the *Historia de regibus*. In particular, Arnold assigned the composition of those sections to a period somewhat earlier than the reign of Edward the Confessor: 'I am persuaded that the more attentively any experienced person may study the curious document between pages 14 and 94 of this volume [i.e. parts (ii)–(iv), plus (v), as far as the annal for 957], the more firmly will he be convinced that it is a composition of the 10th, not the 11th century.'[39] Arnold's attention was drawn in particular to the frequent mentions of St Cuthbert in part (v), the annals for 888–957 [i.e. those printed as Appendix I, below], from which he deduced that 'the writer was certainly a monk or servant of St Cuthbert', and hence Arnold referred to the author of all five early sections as the 'Cuthbertine'.[40] But although the association with St Cuthbert is, in my view, irrelevant to the authorship of the first four sections, Arnold's assessment of their Latin style was uncannily prescient:

Let the reader look at pp. 14, 31, 55, 76, 84, and remark the curious way in which illustrative scraps of metre are cited from Boethius (pp. 14, 65, 67 etc.); then let him read some pages of the Life of St Oswald of York, written by a Ramsey monk of the late 10th century [i.e. Byrhtferth, *VSO*]; he will feel, I think, that both works belong to nearly the same period, the same grade of culture.[41]

These nineteenth-century editors rightly noted the distinctive, flamboyant style of the first four sections of Symeon's work, and rightly concluded that they must have been composed in a period earlier than the twelfth century, possibly in the tenth. They did not, however, undertake detailed analysis of the Latin style of these early sections: their conclusions, however justified, remain impressionistic only. A first attempt to identify the stylistic features which made these sections stand out from the remainder of Symeon's work was made by Peter Hunter Blair in 1963, who noted the following: the use of variegated

---

[39] *Symeonis Monachi Opera Omnia*, ed. Arnold, ii, p. xxv.

[40] Ibid. p. xvii. Arnold was referring to the annals for 899, 925, and 934 (pp. 92–3 of his edition). For reasons set out below, these references to St Cuthbert in the annals for 888–957 have no bearing on the authorship, or place of origin, of the first four sections, whose composition I regard as entirely separate from that of section (v); see below, Appendix I, pp. 171–82.

[41] *Symeonis Monachi Opera Omnia*, ed. Arnold, ii, p. xvii.

BYRHTFERTH AND THE FIRST FOUR SECTIONS   xxiii

expressions and 'bombastic circumlocutions' to describe the death of individuals; the use of 'three verbs in immediate succession to one another' (by which he means asyndeton); the use of superlatives; and a few striking set phrases (e.g. *bellicosis... uiris, bellica uirtute*).[42] In his view these features confirm the impression expressed by the nineteenth-century editors, that the early sections 'bear the imprint of one and the same writer'.[43] Hunter Blair made no attempt to identify this writer, but he concluded his article by observing that 'In the end judgement will perhaps rest upon opinions about its latinity and here one looks for parallels neither to the lucidity of Bede's Latin nor to the simple style used by the northern historians of the twelfth and thirteenth centuries.'[44]

Forty years ago I attempted to answer the question posed by Peter Hunter Blair, by providing a detailed analysis of the language of the first four sections of Symeon's work, and showing how the various features of Byrhtferth's language (as witnessed in the Proemium to his *Computus* and in the Latin sections of his *Enchiridion*, as well as in his two saints' Lives, *VSO* and *VSE*) were likewise characteristic of the first four sections, and furthermore that various stylistic 'tics' of Byrhtferth's authentic writings—repetition of certain favourite formulas and quotations from earlier writers, for example—were also to be found in these early sections.[45] During the intervening years, modern editions of Byrhtferth's writings—notably the Proemium to the *Computus*, the *Enchiridion*, and the two saints' Lives—have become available, so it is appropriate to restate the evidence on which my earlier conclusion was based, namely that Byrhtferth is the author of these four sections. Inevitably, editorial work on these texts during the past decades has brought further examples of links between Byrhtferth's writings and the *HR* to light, so that what follows is an expanded treatment of the evidence first presented in 1982.

BYRHTFERTH OF RAMSEY AND THE FIRST
FOUR SECTIONS

The following analysis of the Latin of the first four sections of Symeon's work treats the following subjects: vocabulary, repeated phrases,

[42] Hunter Blair, 'Some observations', pp. 96–9; see also pp. 114–15.
[43] Ibid. p. 114.
[44] Ibid. p. 118.
[45] Lapidge, 'Byrhtferth of Ramsey and the early sections of the *Historia Regum*'.

xxiv INTRODUCTION

irrelevant digressions, rhetorical constructions, and favourite quotations; where these same features are found in Byrhtferth's Latin writings (*Comp. proem.*, *Ench.*, *VSO*, *VSE*), I have given references.

i. Vocabulary

I begin with one of the most striking features of the vocabulary, namely the penchant for polysyllabic adjectives and adverbs declined in the superlative (for sake of consistency I cite all examples in the masculine nominative singular form of the adjective). I list all such adjectives which occur in the first four sections (as listed above)—which henceforth I shall refer to as the *Historia regum* (*HR*)—of Symeon's larger work; those words which are also used in other writings by Byrhtferth are highlighted in bold.[46]

Adjectives (and adverbs) construed in the superlative

acerrimus (i. 5, iv. 11), amarissimus (iv. 1), aptissimus (i. 2), audacissimus (iv. 14), **beatissimus** (ii. 3, ii. 20, iii. 22; *VSO* i. 3, ii. 1, ii. 2, ii. 4, iv. 8, iv. 14, iv. 21, v. 16, v. 22; *VSE* iii. 1, iii. 2), bellicosissimus (iii. 16), **benignissimus** (iii. 28, iv. 15; *VSO* iii. 12, v. 12; *VSE* i. 13, iii. 5), carissimus (iv. 6), **celerrimus** (i. 5; *VSO* ii. 4 [*bis*]), Christianissimus (ii. 2), citissimus (i. 3, i. 6), **clarissimus** (i. 3; *Comp. proem.* 4), **clementissimus** (iv. 5; *VSO* iv. 16; *VSE* iv. 8, iv. 10), creberrimus (i. 6), decentissimus (i. 2, i. 9), deuotissimus (i. 8, iv. 10, iv. 15), **dignissimus** (iii. 20, iv. 6; *Ench.* i. 2. 204, iv. 1. 272, iv. 1. 180, iv. 1. 310, iv. 1. 329; *VSO Prol.* [*bis*], i. 8, ii. 2, ii. 4, ii. 5, iii. 5, iii. 11, iv. 6, iv. 8 [*bis*], v. 7, v. 8, v. 11 [*ter*], v. 16, v. 18; *VSE* iii. 3, iii. 4, iv. 5), **dilectissimus** (iv. 10, iv. 13, iv. 16; *VSO* ii. 5, iv. 9, v. 8, v. 18, v. 21; *VSE* iii. 3, iv. 5), dirissimus (iii. 22), **durissimus** (iv. 11, iv. 14; *VSO* i. 4, iv. 10, v. 4; *VSE* ii. 4), elegantissimus (iv. 15), **famosissimus** (i. 6, iii. 14, iv. 1, iv. 3, iv. 15; *VSE* iii. 3, iv. 11), **firmissimus** (iii. 29; *VSO* iv. 4), **fortissimus** (ii. 2, iii. 23, iv. 10 [*bis*], iv. 13; *VSO* ii. 8, v. 4, v. 5; *VSE* iv. 1), gloriosissimus (i. 1, iii. 11, iii. 18), **gratissimus** (i. 3; *VSE* iv. 10), grauissimus (iii. 10, iii. 16), hypocrissimus (iv. 1), indignissimus (iv. 15), iniquissimus (i. 5, i. 8), insignissimus (iv. 7), inuictissimus (iii. 15), **iustissimus** (i. 2; *VSO* iv. 21), largissimus (i. 3), **limpidissimus** (ii. 9; *Comp. proem.* 24; *VSO* ii. 3), munitissimus (iii. 15, iv. 17), **nequissimus** (i. 5, iv. 1; *VSO* v. 11; *VSE* iv. 8), **nobilissimus** (iii. 15, iv. 1; *Ench.* iv. 1. 124), paenitissimus (iii. 27), **piissimus** (i. 8, iv. 16; *VSO Prol.*, ii. 2, ii. 3, iii. 12),

---

[46] This list of polysyllabic adjectives and adverbs may be compared with that compiled for the two saints' Lives (Byrhtferth, *The Lives*, ed. Lapidge, pp. xlvi–xlvii).

BYRHTFERTH AND THE FIRST FOUR SECTIONS   xxv

potentissimus (iv. 2), **praestantissimus** (iv. 11; *VSO* ii. 3, iii. 2, iv. 7; *VSE* iv. 8), **pretiosissimus** (i. 6; *Ench.* i. 1. 141, iv. 1. 237), promptissimus (iv. 10), prudentissimus (i. 3), **pulcherrimus** (i. 3, i. 6; *VSO* ii. 3), purissimus (iii. 15), **rectissimus** (i. 2; *VSO* ii. 8), **reuerentissimus** (ii. 1, ii. 8, ii. 20; *Ench.* iv. 1. 327; *VSO Prol.*, iii. 5, iv. 6, v. 9; *VSE* iii. 3, iii. 4, iv. 5, iv. 6), **sacratissimus** (i. 2, i. 10; *Ench.* iv. 1. 198), **sanctissimus** (i. 1, i. 2, i. 5, i. 9, ii. 14, ii. 17, iii. 6, iii. 20, iii. 28, iv. 8, iv. 15 [*bis*]; *Ench.* iv. 1. 362; *VSO* i. 3, iii. 11, iv. 2, iv. 12, iv. 16, v. 14; *VSE* iii. 3, iii. 7, iv. 12), **sapientissimus** (iv. 16, iv. 18; *VSO* iv. 7), serenissimus (i. 2, i. 3), sollertissimus (i. 2, iii. 6), spurcissimus (i. 10), strenuissimus (iii. 6), tenerrimus (i. 2), **teterrimus** (i. 3; *VSO* iv. 17, v. 7; *VSE* i. 2, i. 12, iii. 7), utilissimus (ii. 11).

Adjectives in -alis

caducalis (i. 2), ceruicalis (ii. 11), **episcopalis** (i. 2; *Ench.* iv. 1. 245; *VSE* i. 8), magistralis (i. 2), **magnalis** (i. 6; *VSO* i. 3), nocurnalis (i. 5), praecordialis (i. 2), **regalis** (i. 3, i. 6, iii. 23; *Ench.* iv. 1. 90, iv. 1. 195; *VSO* iii. 11, iv. 7 [*bis*], v. 1; *VSE* i. 8, iii. 2 [*bis*], iii. 5, iv. 11).

Adjectives in -bilis

acceptabilis (iii. 26; *VSO* v. 16), execrabilis (iv. 1), **flebilis** (iv. 1; *Ench.* iv. 1. 269), habitabilis (iv. 16), honorabilis (i. 6, i. 8), incomparabilis (iii. 10, iv. 6), **inedicibilis** (i. 10, iii. 16, iii. 20, iv. 16; *Ench.* iv. 1. 22; *VSO Prol.*, i. 3, iii. 7, iv. 8, iv. 20, v. 21; *VSE* i. 3, i. 14, ii. 12, iv. 11), **inenarrabilis** (iii. 27; *VSO* ii. 5; *VSE* iv. 11), ineuincibilis (i. 2), inexterminabilis (ii. 11), **inmarcescibilis** (i. 9; *Ench.* iv. 1. 325), innumerabilis (iv. 1), instabilis (iii. 14), inuincibilis (iv. 13), irrationabilis (iv. 1), lacrimabilis (ii. 11), miserabilis (iii. 22, iii. 25, iv. 1), perseuerabilis (i. 3), **praeamabilis** (iv. 1; *VSO* v. 3), **rationabilis** (iii. 25; *VSO* iv. 6, v. 1, v. 12), stabilis (i. 3), **terribilis** (iv. 8, iv. 13; *VSO* iii. 10; *VSE* iv. 3), uigorabilis (i. 3).

Adverbs in -iter

amabiliter (iv. 5), annualiter (iv. 18), **atrociter** (iv. 8; *VSE* iv. 9), **breuiter** (i. 8; *VSO* iii. 4, iii. 14, iv. 10, v. 1, v. 3; *VSE Epil.*), **crudeliter** (iii. 27, iv. 7; *VSO* iv. 18), **digniter** (i. 10; *Ench.* iv. 1. 48; *VSO* i. 1, i. 4, i. 6, ii. 7, iii. 2, iii. 14, iii. 19, iv. 5, iv. 19; *VSE* i. 13, iii. 2, iii. 3, iv. 9), **duriter** (iii. 27; *VSO* iv. 18; *VSE* iv. 9), **eneruiter** (iv. 14; *Comp. proem.* 79; *VSO* ii. 6; *VSE* i. 9), firmiter (iv. 10; *VSO* ii. 7, iii. 2, v. 3), fortiter (iv. 12; *VSO* v. 4), **honorabiliter** (iv. 5; *VSO* iv. 19), hostiliter (iv. 7), **immisericorditer** (iii. 19, iii. 25; *VSE* iv. 10), **inedicibiliter** (iii. 25 [*bis*]; *VSO* ii. 5, iii. 6, v. 3; *VSE Epil.*), inenarrabiliter (iii. 26),

xxvi INTRODUCTION

infatigabiliter (iv. 13), irrationabiliter (iv. 1), **memoriter** (iv. 6; *VSO* iii. 2, iii. 7), **mirabiliter** (iii. 9, iii. 21; *Ench.* i. 1. 79; *VSO* iii. 3, iii. 4, iii. 16, v. 5; *VSE* i. 1, i. 11), miserabiliter (iii. 21, iv. 1), **muliebriter** (iv. 5; *VSO* ii. 8; *VSE* iv. 2), naturaliter (i. 2), **nequiter** (iii. 9, iv. 1; *VSE* iv. 10), **pleniter** (i. 3, i. 5; *VSO* iii. 2, iii. 3, v. 8; *VSE* iv. 8), **regaliter** (iii. 25, iii. 28; *VSO* iii. 9, iii. 10, iv. 11; *VSE* i. 2, iv. 11), **sollemniter** (iii. 17; *VSO* i. 5, v. 7, v. 11 [*bis*]; *VSE* iv. 8), suauiter (iii. 25), **sublimiter** (iii. 18; *Ench.* iv. 1. 367), uenerabiliter (iii. 24), **uiriliter** (iv. 3, iv. 8, iv. 9, iv. 10, iv. 15; *VSO* i. 4, iii. 12, v. 5 [*bis*]; *VSE* i. 9 [*bis*]), uituperabiliter (iv. 1).

Agentive nouns in -or

bellator (iv. 15, iv. 18), **defensor** (iii. 28, iv. 15; *VSO* i. 1, iv. 11, iv. 14 [*bis*], v. 15), interemptor (i. 4, iii. 19), interfector (iii. 25, iii. 27), patrator (ii. 12), persecutor (i. 4, i. 10), praedecessor (ii. 13, iii. 18), raptor (iv. 9), remunerator (i. 2), susceptor (iii. 28).[47]

Diminutives

ciuitatula (iv. 15), **gerulus** (i. 8; *VSO* v. 2), **puerulus** (iv. 15; *VSO* v. 7), riuulus (ii. 17), scientiola (i. 3), scintillula (i. 14), **sententiola** (i. 3; *VSO* iii. 4), **seruulus** (iv. 1; *VSO Prol.*), **tyrunculus** (i. 3; *Comp. proem.* 29).

Graecisms

agonista [ἀγωνιστής, 'a combatant'] (i. 4; *Ench.* iv. 1. 350; *VSO* ii. 7, ii. 5; *VSE* ii. 4), **brauium** [βραβεῖον, 'prize in the games'] (iii. 16; *Comp. proem.* 33), **caraxare** [from χαράσσω, 'to sharpen', 'to engrave', hence 'to write'] (ii. 16; *Ench.* iv. 1. 36; *VSE* i. 14), chrisma [χρῖσμα, 'anointing'] (i. 2), **clima** (κλίμα, 'a region'] (iii. 22; *Ench.* iv. 1. 56; *VSE Epil.*, iii. 5, iv. 1, iv. 7), **diadema** [διάδημα, 'a band or fillet'] (iii. 23, iv. 2; *Ench.* iv. 1. 90; *VSO* ii. 4, iv. 6, iv. 7; *VSE* ii. 2, iii. 5, iv. 11), epinicion [ἐπινίκιον, 'a triumph'] (ii. 9, iii. 14; *Ench.* iv. 1. 395–6), exenia [ξείνια (n. pl.), 'gifts'] (i. 4), historiographus [ἱστοριογράφος, 'writer of history'] (ii. 2, iii. 11, iii. 15), monas [μονάς, 'a unit, monad'] (i. 2, iv. 13), **onoma** [ὄνομα, 'name'] (i. 2, iv. 7; *Ench.* iv. 1. 40; *VSO* i. 4, i. 8; *VSE* iii. 1), pentecontarchos [πεντηκοντάρχος, 'captain of fifty

---

[47] The lack of consistent overlap between *HR* and the writings of Byrhtferth in respect of agentive nouns in *-or* is no doubt to be explained in terms of the very different subject matter of the writings: the *HR* is mostly concerned with war, murder, and conquest, the saints' Lives with saintliness and miracles.

BYRHTFERTH AND THE FIRST FOUR SECTIONS   xxvii

men'] (iv. 16), platoma [correctly *platumma*, from Greek πλάτυμμα, 'flat cake', hence 'a tablet on which an inscription is inscribed'] (iii. 23).[48]

Poeticisms

The first four sections of *HR* include numerous words which are characteristic of the poetic register in Latin; these include a number of what are called 'poetic compounds', that is to say, bipartite tetrasyllabic words made up of two disyllables, together constituting a choriamb (– ◡ ◡ –). The first of the two elements will typically derive from a noun or adjective (*alti-*, *armi-*, *auri-*, *belli-*, etc.); the second element will typically be deverbative (*-fluus*, *-loquus*, *-potens*, *-sonus*, *-volus*, etc., as well as *-fer* and *-ger* declined in oblique cases).[49] Examples in the *HR* include *aequiloquus (iv. 14), **armipotens** (iii. 28, iv. 7, iv. 15; *VSO* iii. 10; *VSE* iii. 4), bellipotens (iv. 3), ignicomus (i. 3), imbrifer(us) (iii. 30), **magnificus** (iii. 6; *VSO Prol.*, i. 3, v. 10), **mortifer(us)** (i. 3; *VSO* iii. 6), multimodis [adv.] (i. 2), pestifer(us) (i. 3), **salutifer(us)** (iii. 27; *VSO* ii. 7, ii. 8, iii. 8, v. 14), **ueridicus** (iii. 1, iii. 11; *VSO* i. 1), ueriloquus (ii. 3, ii. 17). Also belonging to the poetic register are nouns terminating in *-amen*, construed in abl. sg. or nom./acc. pl. so as to constitute a ready-made dactyl (such compounds are characteristic of Latin poetry from Ovid onwards): **certamen** (i. 2, iii. 3, iv. 10; *VSO* ii. 7, iii. 2, iv. 7; *VSE* ii. 3, iv. 5, iv. 10), **conamen** (i. 3; *VSO* i. 4, ii. 6), gestamen (i. 6), libramen (i. 3), **moderamen** (ii. 6; *VSO* ii. 2; *VSE* iv. 8), sinuamen (i. 3), temptamen (iv. 7).

Solecisms

The early sections of *HR* include three words which are unattested elsewhere, and are possibly coinages by the author, or perhaps simply mistakes: aequilocus (iv. 14, for aequiloquus?), hypocrissimus (iv. 1), and paenitissimus (iii. 27). Each of these words is discussed in the notes accompanying the relevant chapters in question.

The use of these superlative adjectives and adverbs imparts to the work a heightened, almost hysterical tone: a saint is not merely *beatus*, but *beatissimus*, never simply *sanctus* but always *sanctissimus*. It is difficult to say whether these superlative forms were used so frequently

---

[48] To this list of Graecisms should be added *aristerium* (from ἀσκητήριον, 'monastery'): *HR* i. 7, *VSO* ii. 4, ii. 9, iii. 14, iii. 18, *VSE* ii. 12 (and see note in Byrhtferth, *The Lives*, ed. Lapidge, pp. 38–9, n. 28) as well as *hypocrissima* (from ὑπόκρισις, 'hypocrisy'): *HR* iv. 1, from an otherwise unattested adjective *hypocrissus?

[49] See Lapidge, 'Poetic compounds in Late Latin'.

xxviii INTRODUCTION

because they had lost the emphatic power such forms originally had and meant no more than the corresponding positive forms.

ii. Repeated Phrases

Throughout the *HR* (i.e. the first four sections reproduced in Symeon's *Historia de regibus*) are found phrases which are used repeatedly by Byrhtferth, to the point that they become in effect clichés:

ad ordinem narrationis redeamus ['let us return to the sequence of our narration'] (*HR* ii. 9: 'redeamus ad ordinem narrationis'; iii. 22: 'ad ordinem reuertamur narrationis'; iii. 26: 'ad historiae nostrae narrationem redeamus'); also *VSO* i. 2 ('ad ordinem... redeamus proprie relationis'), iii. 14 ('ad uiam nostri sermonis redeamus'), iv. 11 ('paulatim digressi sumus; sed redeamus ad uiam'), v. 8 ('nunc ad propria redeamus'); *VSE* i. 11 ('nunc igitur redeamus ad ordinem narrationis'), i. 14 ('nunc autem stilus reuertatur scriptoris ad ordinem narrationis').

annus iubeleus ['year of the Jubilee'] (*HR* i. 2: 'uirgines corpore sancto tenerrimi septenis dierum curriculis, ut septem septies augmentatis et monade supposito, singularis in praesenti uita acquirerent fructum iubelei, hoc est annum aeternae felicitatis'; ii. 12: 'ut dignus existeret sancta sanctorum intrare, iubeleique anni remissionem percipere'); cf. *HR* iii. 19: 'mercedem iubelei anni percipiendo', and also *VSO* i. 6: 'concupiscens... sumere ab eo iubelei anni remissionem').[50]

armipotens rex ['king mighty in arms'] (*HR* iv. 7, iv. 10, iv. 15; cf. iii. 28: 'armipotens imperator'); also *VSO* iii. 10; *VSE* iii. 4.

aurora diei illucescente ['with the dawn of day breaking'] (*HR* i. 5); also *VSE* ii. 12 ('illucescente aurora sequentis diei').

caelestis regni gaudia ['the joys of the heavenly kingdom'] (*HR* i. 1: 'aeterna caelestis regni subiit gaudia'); also *VSO* iv. 21; *VSE Epil.*, and cf. *VSO* ii. 1 ('aeternae felicitatis gaudia'), iii. 13 ('ad gaudia Paradisi'), v. 6 ('ad etheree lucis gaudia'); *VSE* iii. 6 ('ad caeli gaudia').[51]

---

[50] The word *iubeleus* occurs in Lev. 15: 10, and means simply 'the year of jubilee, the fiftieth year'. However, Byrhtferth interpreted the number 50 as signifying the Day of Judgement, since this is the meaning of the second fiftieth psalm (*Ench.* iv. 1. 385–90: 'Alter uero quinquagesimus psalmus de ultimo die affatur iudicii'). Accordingly, *annus iubeleus* means for Byrhtferth the year, and hence the day, of final judgement; the passage to heaven can therefore be described as 'receiving the remission of the year of jubilee'. This idiosyncratic, indeed distinctively Byrhtferthian use of the expression *annus iubeleus* is repeated twice in the *HR*.

[51] For the phrase *caelestis regni gaudia*, cf. Cassiodorus, *Expositio psalmorum I–LXX*, lxvii. 7: 'ad gaudia regni caelestis eleuauit' (CCSL xcvii. 588); Gregory, *Hom. in Hiezechielem* ii. 8: 'caelestis regni gaudia rimatur' (CCSL cxlii. 338); Bede, prose *Vita S. Cudbercti*, cc. 34 ('ad

BYRHTFERTH AND THE FIRST FOUR SECTIONS   xxix

cordis penetralia ['depths of the heart'] (*HR* iv. 6); also *VSO* ii. 1 ('sitiebant ipsius penetralia cordis').[52]

cordis tripudio ['heartfelt joy'] (*HR* iv. 13: 'immenso cordis tripudio'; cf. iv. 11: 'inmenso repletus est tripudio'); also *VSO* i. 4 ('ingredientes cum tripudio cordis'), iv. 16 ('cum tripudio cordis ambulauit nobiscum').[53]

densi uepres ['thick brambles'] (*HR* iv. 5: 'per latibula densarum ueprium'); also *VSE* ii. 7 ('densis uepribus plenus'), ii. 9 ('in densis uepribus').

fortuna arridente ['with Fortune smiling'] (*HR* iv. 5, iv. 11; cf. ii. 19: 'arridente pace'); also *VSO* i. 2, v. 11, *VSE* iii. 3.[54]

Gregorianus concentus ['Gregorian chant'] (*HR* iii. 21 ('cum Gregorianis concentibus'; cf. i. 4: 'Gregoriano...organo'); also *VSO* iv. 18 ('Gregorianus concentus...auditus est').

hac illac ['here (and) there'] (*HR* iii. 22, iv. 6, iv. 10, iv. 14 [*bis*]); also *VSO* iv. 8; *VSE* ii. 9, ii. 11, iv. 9.[55]

illud scholastici ['that (saying) of the scholar'] (*HR* iv. 9, iv. 16); also *VSO Prol.*, ii. 7; *VSE* i. 10; cf. *illud psalmigraphi* (*VSO* i. 2, iv. 12; *VSE* ii. 2), *illud centesimi...psalmi* (*VSO* i. 1), *illud Ecclesiastes* (*VSO* iv. 8), *illud dignissimi Bede* (*VSO* iv. 8).

---

gaudia regni coelestis ferri'), 39 ('ad gaudia regni coelestis'); and Bede, *HE* ii. 5, iv. 2, with discussion in Byrhtferth, *The Lives*, ed. Lapidge, p. 144, n. 189.

[52] The words *penetralia cordis* are a poetic phrase apparently first used by Juvencus, *Euangelia* iv. 7; but cf. also Damasus, *Epigrammata* i. 4, xi. 5, and Aldhelm, *Carmen de uirginitate* 1620. Exactly similar in sense is Byrhtferth's use of the expression *cordis secreta* (*VSO* i. 4, which also derives from Juvencus: *Euangelia* i. 304, ii. 488, and iii. 146).

[53] To judge from the electronic databases, the phrase *cordis tripudio* is not found in classical or patristic Latin; for an occurrence in an Anglo-Saxon charter roughly contemporary with Byrhtferth, see Byrhtferth, *The Lives*, ed. Lapidge, p. 21, n. 69. Closely related is the expression *mentis tripudio* (*VSO* i. 5, *VSE* i. 13).

[54] The phrase derives ultimately from Juvenal, *Sat.* vi. 605–6 ('stat Fortuna improba noctu / arridens'). Whether the use of this single phrase is sufficient to establish that Byrhtferth had read Juvenal is unclear (cf. Lapidge, *The Anglo-Saxon Library*, p. 124, n. 137); possibly, as I suggest there, the phrase was a *façon de parler* devised by Abbo (whose knowledge of Juvenal was thorough), and picked up by Byrhtferth without having read Juvenal for himself; cf. Byrhtferth, *The Lives*, ed. Lapidge, p. 14, n. 36.

[55] The archaic formulation *hac ... illac* is atttested in the ancient dramatists, such as Plautus (*Asinaria* 741–2, *Rudens* 213) and Terence (*Eunuchus* 105, *Heauton timorumenos* 512), but was also used by poets of the Augustan age and later, such as Ovid (*Met.* iv. 360, *Heroides* x. 83). Cf. also the comment of Donatus, *Ars maior* (ed. Holtz, *Donat*, p. 642), and *TLL* vi/3, cols. 2746–9, where it is noted that the phrase is used *saepissime apud poetas, scaenicos et epicos*, but more rarely in prose (*rarius in prosa oratione*). The use of this archaic expression is another example of intentional poeticism.

INTRODUCTION

in exordio huius operis ['at the beginning of this work'] (*HR* i. 1: 'in exordio nostrae historiae'; ii. 1: 'in exordio huius operis'); also *Ench.* iv. 1. 3: 'in exordio uenerabili huius exigui operis'.[56]

infra cordis cubicula ['in the depths of the heart'] (*HR* iv. 10); also *VSO* iii. 9.[57]

libet / placet inserere ['it is fitting to insert'] (*HR* i. 1: 'in exordio nostrae historiae placet inserere'; ii. 3: 'libet huic nostro operi inserere'; iv. 8: 'libet aliqua historiae nostrae inserere'); also *Ench.* iv. 1. 103: 'placet huic operi nostro figuram adicere', iv. 2. 11: 'libet hic aliqua curtim inserere', *VSO* i. 3: 'que placuit hic inserere'; iii. 19: 'in fine huius modici operis placet inserere'; iv. 10: 'hic inserere breuiter placet'; v. 8: 'uersus...hoc in loco placet inserere'; v. 9: 'quorum nomina hic inserere curauimus'; *VSE* i. 14: 'nos uero hanc epistolam huic loco inserere nolumus'.

limina apostolorum ['the thresholds of the apostles'] (*HR* ii. 5: 'profectus est...ad limina sanctorum apostolorum'; ibid.: 'ad limina principis apostolorum profectus est'); also *VSO* i. 4 ('ad limina pretiosorum apostolorum peruenire desiderabat'), iv. 5 ('ad limina sanctorum properaret apostolorum'; ibid.: 'ad sanctorum limina peruenit gaudens apostolorum'), *VSE* i. 13 ('ad sanctorum limina peruenit gaudens apostolorum'), iii. 3 ('ad sancta limina apostolorum pretiosorum...uenissemus').[58]

obsecro scientibus oneri non sit ['I beg that it not be a burden to knowledgeable persons'] (*HR* ii. 16: 'de quorum positione strictim nescientes instruere, obsecro scientibus oneri non sit'); also *Ench.* iv. 1. 399–400: 'de millenario strictim loquamur, scientes obsecrans ut oneri non sit quod ignorantibus placet traducere'; *VSE* i. 6: 'sic paulatim libet pandere ignotis, ut notis non sit oneri quod ignorantibus manifestari delectat'.[59]

peramplius et perfectius ['more thoroughly and completely'] (*HR* ii. 20); also *Ench.* i. 2. 144.

---

[56] Cf. also *VSE Epil.* ('pars huius exigui operis') and i. 14 ('in calce huius exigui operis').

[57] The phrase was apparently adapted by Byrhtferth from an earlier source: cf. Augustine, *Enarrationes in psalmos* [Ps. xxxv] (CCSL xxxviii. 325); Caesarius of Arles, *Sermones*, xc. 3: 'intus in cubiculo cordis tui' (CCSL ciii. 371); and Aldhelm, *Ep.* vi [*ad Sigegytham*]: 'ex intimo cordis cubiculo' (ed. Ehwald, p. 497); and see Byrhtferth, *The Lives*, ed. Lapidge, p. 71, n. 92.

[58] This phrase, much used by Byrhtferth, was probably taken from Bede: either *Historia abbatum*, c. 2: 'apostolorum limina Romam uenire disponens', c. 21: 'ad limina beatorum apostolorum tendens' (Bede, *VBOH* i. 365, 385; *Abbots of Wearmouth and Jarrow*, ed. Grocock and Wood, pp. 24, 70 respectively), or *HE* v. 19. 3 (ed. Lapidge, ii. 412; ed. Mynors, trans. Colgrave, p. 518).

[59] The notion is expressed by Byrhtferth, in slightly different form, at *Ench.* i. 1. 137–40: 'Et idcirco hoc silentio non pretermittam: hoc est, plurima pandere ignotis libet et non silere propter scientiam philosophorum.'

BYRHTFERTH AND THE FIRST FOUR SECTIONS   xxxi

post spatium exigui temporis ['after a brief space of time'] (*HR* iii. 15: 'post spatium exigui temporis'; iii. 23: 'post exigui temporis spatium'); also *VSO* v. 21 ('post spatium exigui temporis').

regali diademate ['with royal diadem'] (*HR* iii. 23); also *Ench.* iv. 1. 90; *VSE* iii. 5.

regni fastigia ['the summit of the realm'] (*HR* i. 4: 'usurpare praesument tui regni fastigia'; ii. 2: 'regni fastigia'; cf. iii. 14: 'totius regni monarchiam et Francorum fastigium populorum'); also *VSO* iii. 6 ('precellunt...ipsius regni fastigium'), v. 4 ('consecratus est rex...ad regni fastigium').[60]

Romulea urbs ['the Romulean city' i.e. 'Rome'] (*HR* iii. 28: 'Romuleae urbis moenia ingreditur'; cf. iv. 5: 'Romuleas adire sedes'); also *VSO* i. 4 ('ad locum...Romulee urbis'), iv. 1 ('egregii Romulee urbis Gregorii patris executor'); *VSE Epil.* ('custodis...Romulee urbis'), ibid. ('reuersus est a Romulee urbis moeniis'), i. 12 ('ad urbis Romulee moenia'), i. 13 ('patris Romulee urbis'), ibid. ('decus Romulee urbis'), ii. 1 ('de Romulea urbe'), iii. 3 ('Romulee urbis adiit moenia'), iii. 5 (Romulee urbis adiit moenia'), iii. 5 ('Romulee urbis moenia adire').[61]

sagaci ingenio ['with shrewd intelligence'] (*HR* iv. 18); cf. the expression *sagaci mente*, which is frequent in Byrhtferth (*VSO* iii. 7, iv. 17; *VSE Epil.*, i. 9).

salsi maris ['of the salt sea'] (*HR* ii. 6: 'maris salsi gurgites'); also *VSO* iii. 4 ('cumque salsi maris enormem pontum pertransirent').[62]

sceptro redimitus ['adorned with the sceptre'] (*HR* iv. 2: 'maximo sceptro redimitus'; cf. i. 3: 'munificentia regali redimitus'); cf. *VSO* i. 7 ('redimitus pontificali dignitate'); *VSE* iii. 5 ('regali diademate ornatus sceptroque redimitus'), iv. 11 ('diademate redimitus').

sicut finis...probauit euentus ['as the outcome (of his life) established'] (*HR* iv. 8: 'sicut finis eius sanctissimae uitae probauit euentus'); also *VSO* ii. 1 ('sicut postea rei probauit euentus'), iii. 2 ('sicut finis sue gloriose uite demonstrauit euentus'); *VSE* i. 8 ('sicut finis sue uite demonstrauit euentus').

subthronizatus solio ['enthroned on the throne'] (*HR* iii. 21: 'regni solio est subthronizatus'; cf. iv. 17: 'in regia...potestate subthronizatus');

---

[60] For the possible liturgical origin of the phrase *regni fastigium*, see Byrhtferth, *The Lives*, ed. Lapidge, pp. 63–4, n. 53.

[61] The phrase may ultimately derive from Paulinus of Nola, *Carm.* xix. 483, or from Bede, *HE* v. 7 ('urbem Romuleam uidit': the epitaph of King Ceadwalla), or from Alcuin, *Carm.* i. 1458.

[62] The phrase *salsi maris* is surprisingly rare; an occurrence in Cassiodorus, *Expositio psalmorum* lxxvii. 29 (*CCSL* xcviii. 719) is noted in Byrhtferth, *The Lives*, ed. Lapidge, p. 56, n. 20.

xxxii INTRODUCTION

also *VSO* v. 1 ('subthronizatus regali culmine'), ibid. ('subthronizatus in edito solio'), v. 12 ('subthronizatus in meditullio... conuentionis'); *VSE* i. 10 ('subthronizatus in solio').[63]

ueloci cursu ['with a swift passage'] (*HR* iv. 7: 'direxit et nuntios ueloci cursu ad Ælfredum'); also *VSO* i. 4 ('ueloci cursu').[64]

uice regiminis ['vice regency'] (*HR* iii. 12); also *VSO* iv. 19.

urbana facundia ['urbane eloquence'] (*HR* iv. 16: 'quis urbana facundia suffultus'); also *VSO* iii. 14 ('urbana fretus facundia'); *VSE Epil.* ('urbana fretus eloquentia').[65]

It will be seen that these expressions are employed by Byrhtferth almost as formulas, to be recycled almost at will.

iii. Irrelevant Digressions

Byrhtferth had the habit of frequently wandering from his subject matter, often to include digressions of material which had a particular interest for him. I illustrate this propensity by discussing four such digressions as they are found in the *Historia regum*: solar and lunar eclipses; the movement of tides; concern with the Four Cardinal Virtues; and the iniquities of secular clerics. The concerns expressed in these digressions are well attested in Byrhtferth's other writings.

Alongside the usual record of deaths and murders, medieval annalists in all countries were in the habit of recording occurrences of astronomical and meteorological phenomena, including eclipses of the sun and the moon. At one point of Part III, possibly prompted by the mention of a lunar eclipse in *HE Continuatio* (II), s.a. 752, Byrhtferth records the occurrence of a lunar eclipse on 31 July of that year (*HR* iii. 8). In his pedantic, schoolmasterly way, Byrhtferth then stops to explain to ignorant readers what a lunar eclipse is: 'Because this event has been mentioned, it is appropriate to explain to the ignorant what an eclipse is, namely a "defect" or "deficiency" of the moon' (iii. 8). He begins his explanation by quoting the definition of a lunar eclipse given in Isidore's *Etymologiae* (iii. 59), and then, for good measure, goes on to explain that a 'deficiency' of the sun (i.e. a *solar* eclipse) usually happens at the beginning of a lunar cycle, quoting here from Bede's

---

[63] The word *subthronizatus* is exceptionally rare in Latin texts earlier than the 10th c., according to the electronic databases, but it is found in Anglo-Saxon charters of the 10th c. drafted by the royal scribe known as 'Dunstan B': see Byrhtferth, *The Lives*, ed. Lapidge, p. 146, n. 1.

[64] The phrase *ueloci cursu* is possibly taken from Gregory, *Moralia in Iob*, vii. 30. 45: 'ueloci cursu fugere uitam peccatoris' (CCSL cxliii. 368).

[65] Byrhtferth derived this phrase from Aldhelm, prose *De uirginitate*, c. 20: 'quis urbana verborum facundia fretus enarrare sufficiat' (*Opera*, ed. Ehwald, p. 250).

BYRHTFERTH AND THE FIRST FOUR SECTIONS xxxiii

De temporum ratione, c. 27 (who in turn was quoting from Pliny the Elder's *Naturalis historia*, ii. 56). Byrhtferth was thoroughly familiar with Bede's discussion of solar and lunar eclipses, because in his *Glossae in Bedam* he compiled an extensive collection of *testimonia* to illustrate c. 27 of *De temporum ratione* (including a lengthy quotation of Pliny, *Naturalis historia*).[66]

Still in Part III of the *Historia regum*, Byrhtferth mentions against the year 793 that Ealdorman Sicga (who had killed King Ælfwald) was buried at Lindisfarne; and later in the same chapter he goes on to record the famous sack of Lindisfarne by the Vikings in that year. But before treating the Vikings' depredation, the mention of Lindisfarne reminds him that Lindisfarne is an island which, at high tide, is cut off from the mainland, whereupon he launches into an explanation of tidal movements and lunar influence, drawn once again from Bede, this time from both *De natura rerum*, c. 39, and *De temporum ratione*, c. 29. Once again, Byrhtferth in his *Glossae in Bedam* had compiled a small corpus of *testimonia* in order to illustrate the content of this chapter of *De temporum ratione* (though not, so it would seem, to c. 39 of *De natura rerum*);[67] and both these works of Bede were included by Byrhtferth in his compendium of computistical texts as it is preserved in Oxford, St John's College 17.[68]

At a point in Part IV of the *Historia regum*, Plegmund, archbishop of Canterbury, is said to have been endowed with 'the four columns', that is, the Four Cardinal Virtues of justice, wisdom, temperance, and courage: 'Plegmundus archiepiscopus...praeditus bis binis columnis, iustitiae uidelicet, prudentiae, temperantiae, fortitudinis' (*HR* iv. 15). This is a verbose way of saying that Plegmund was wise and just; but instead of producing such a simple statement, the author felt compelled to refer to the Four Cardinal Virtues. Reference to these Four Cardinal Virtues is a recurrent feature of Byrhtferth's writings:

---

[66] Byrhtferth's *glossae* to this chapter of *De temporum ratione* (entitled *De magnitudine vel defectu solis et lunae*) are most conveniently read in PL xc. 411–20 (reprinted from Herwagen's edition of 1563); among the *testimonia* quoted here are Isidore, *De natura rerum*; the *Homiliae* of Haymo of Auxerre; Martianus Capella, *De nuptiis Philologiae et Mercurii*; Macrobius, *Comm. in Somnium Scipionis*; and the passage from Pliny the Elder, *Naturalis historia*, mentioned by Bede (PL xc. 416–17).

[67] Byrhtferth seems to have omitted *De natura rerum*, c. 39 (entitled *De aestu oceani*) from his *Glossae in Bedam*; his *glossae* to *De temporum ratione*, c. 29 (entitled *De concordia maris et lunae*) are most conveniently read in PL xc. 422–4.

[68] Oxford, St John's College 17, fos. 62^r–65^r (*De natura rerum*) and 65^v–123^r (*De temporum ratione*, including the *Chronica maiora*); see *Byrhtferth's Enchiridion*, ed. Baker and Lapidge, p. liv.

xxxiv INTRODUCTION

Ench. iv. 1. 37–9 ('Quaternarius perfectus est numerus et quattuor uirtutibus exornatus: iustitia uidelicet, temperantia, fortitudine, prudentia'), *Ench.* iv. 1. 234–6 ('pretiosissime uero uirtutes sunt... quaterne—iustitia, fortitudo, temperantia et prudentia');[69] *VSO* iii. 8 ('resplenduit prudentia Eadnoð uenerandus sacerdos, qui temperantiam atque iustitiam necne fortitudinem concupiuit nobili indagine percipere'); cf. *VSE* i. 9 ('bis binas uirtutes conicere mente sagaci potuisset').

At an earlier point of the *Historia regum*, during the description of the learning of King Alfred, there occurs a striking and unprompted outburst against clerics: 'O clerici, attendite et uidete regem in sinu librum deferre die noctuque; uos uero nec legem Dei scitis nec scire uultis' (*HR* iv. 6). There is no context in the work for such an outburst. However, its tenor may be better appreciated by comparing several similar outbursts in passages of the *Enchiridion*, where Byrhtferth—evidently charged with the thankless task of instructing idle clerics—repeatedly upbraids them: 'Exterminant huius modi nonnulli clerici imperiti (heu, pro dolor!) qui non habere desiderant philacteria sua; uerbi gratia, ordinem quem susceperunt in gremio matris ecclesie non seruant, nec in doctrina sancte meditationis persistunt' (*Ench.* i. 3. 2–5);[70] 'Quoniam sermo iste ad desides congruit clericos, ammonemus, pacis reuerentia, eos ut discant que ignorant et postmodum doceant ceteris que didicerint' (*Ench.* i. 4. 4–5);[71] 'cepi cordetenus ruminare pauca ex plurimis, quali medicamine possem clericis proficere ut alee ludos relaxarent et huius artis notitiam haberent' (*Ench.* i. 4. 9–11);[72] 'libet hic aliqua curtim inserere, ut habeant minus indocti clerici horum mysteriorum ueritatem quam sequi ualeant absque fuco mendacii'

---

[69] Byrhtferth refers again to the Four Cardinal Virtues in the so-called 'Postscript' to his *Enchiridion* (ibid. p. 244, lines 26–36; in Old English). For the origin of the concept of the Four Cardinal Virtues in Greek and Latin literature, and its recurrence in patristic authors, esp. Ambrose and Martin of Braga, and Gregory the Great and Bede, see *Byrhtferth's Enchiridion*, pp. 340–1 (comm. ad iv. 1. 37–9).

[70] *Byrhtferth's Enchiridion*, ed. Baker and Lapidge, p. 46: 'Some ignorant clerics, alas, who do not want to keep their philacteries with them make a mess of calculations of this sort; in a word, they do not preserve the discipline they received in the bosom of Mother Church, nor do they persevere in the pursuit of holy wisdom.'

[71] Ibid. p. 52: 'Because this discussion is pertinent to lazy clerics, let us urge them, begging their pardons, to learn those things they are ignorant of, and thereafter teach to others what they have learned.'

[72] Ibid.: 'I began inwardly to ruminate on a few things among many concerning what medicine I might apply to the clerics so that they would ease up on the dice-playing and acquire some knowledge of this science.'

BYRHTFERTH AND THE FIRST FOUR SECTIONS   XXXV

(*Ench.* iv. 2. 11–13).[73] The contempt for clerics which pervades the *Enchiridion* is also found in Byrhtferth's *Vita S. Oswaldi*, in a passage describing King Edgar's expulsion of secular clerics from the Old Minster, Winchester: 'Clericos perosos habuit; nostri habitus uiros (sicut diximus) honorauit, abiectis ex cenobiis clericorum neniis.'[74] Byrhtferth's contempt for secular clerics—derived, apparently, from bitter daily experience—gives point to his express approbation of King Edgar's expulsion of clerics from the Old Minster. The same contempt will be seen to underlie the otherwise unmotivated outburst against clerics in the description of King Alfred's pious behaviour in *HR* iv. 6, as quoted above.

iv. Rhetorical Constructions

The syntax of the first four parts of the *Historia regum* is embellished by various rhetorical devices or tropes. We know that Byrhtferth was thoroughly familiar with the employment of rhetorical tropes, because he devotes a substantial portion of his *Enchiridion* to the subject (*Ench.* iii. 3. 21–143, under the rubric DE SCHEMATIBVS). Much of Byrhtferth's discussion is derived from Bede, *De schematibus et tropis*, with amplifications taken from the commentary on the same work of Bede by Remigius of Auxerre. Several rhetorical tropes are used repeatedly throughout the *Historia regum*; these same tropes characterize Byrhtferth's Latin prose. I discuss five such tropes: hyperbaton; polyptoton; paronomasia; asyndeton; and erotema.

Hyperbaton refers in essence to any departure from the natural order of words; in studies of Latin prose style it is used more specifically to describe the artistic separation of an adjective from its noun.[75] Hyperbaton is particularly frequent in Latin verse (where the need to separate adjective and noun is often determined by metrical exigencies), and it is possible that the use of hyperbaton in a prose writer represents striving for poeticism. Certainly hyperbaton is pervasive in the first four parts of the *Historia regum*; an example may be found in nearly every sentence. For convenience I cite some examples from Part

---

[73] Ibid. p. 232: 'it is appropriate briefly to insert a few remarks here, so that less well-trained clerics may possess the truth of these mysteries and follow them without the deception of falsehood'.

[74] Byrhtferth, *The Lives*, ed. Lapidge, p. 74: 'He [King Edgar] held clerics in contempt; he honoured men of our order, as I have said, once the trifles of the clerics had been cast out of the monasteries.'

[75] LHS ii. 689–94; see also the important studies by Adams, 'A type of hyperbaton in Latin prose', pp. 1–16; Winterbottom, 'A "Celtic" hyperbaton?'; and esp. Wright, 'Gildas's prose style', pp. 117–28.

xxxvi INTRODUCTION

I (the *passio* of SS. Æthelred and Æthelberht), since in this part the *HR* author was arguably composing freely (whereas in the following parts he was heavily reliant on earlier authors: Bede in Part II, previous annals in Part III, Asser in Part IV). The simplest form of hyperbaton occurs when an adjective is separated from its noun by a dependent noun (this schema may be represented as aBA, where lower case 'a' represents the adjective, upper case 'A' the noun with which it agrees, and 'B' the dependent noun), as in the following examples:

> **aBA**
> post peractum uitae cursum (i. 2)
> breui notationis serie (i. 2)
> nullo turbinum fluctu (i. 3)
> nullis discordiarum angoribus (i. 3)
> immitis fraudulentorum... saeuitia (i. 3)
> gratissima pietatis cura (i. 3)
> cernua innocentium colla (i. 3)
> in honestis subselliorum locis (i. 4)
> ad nocturnales matutinorum hymnos (i. 5)

A more complex form of hyperbaton occurs when one pair of adjective + noun frames a second pair of adjective + noun, denoted by abBA, as follows:

> **abBA**
> bini regalis stirpis filii (i. 2)
> in herili caelestis regis palatio (i. 2)
> insignium illustri cura uirtutum (i. 2)
> ignicomis mortiferae uexationis furiis (i. 3)
> clarissimorum tuae dignitatis successurorum (i. 3)
> ex assistentibus tuae celsitudinis loquor tyrunculis (i. 3)
> perquisita directi ominis scientiola (i. 3)
> Gregoriano potitis dulcis armoniae organo (i. 4)
> ascito tanti criminis auctore (i. 5)

A variant of abBA occurs when the framing pair of adjective + noun encloses a noun + adjective (rather than adjective + noun) sequence, denoted by aBbA:

> **aBbA**
> sine accuratis disciplinae magistralis loquamur eloquentiis (i. 2)
> in coenoso mentis impiae uolutabro (i. 3)
> largissima regnorum... subiacentium sinuamina (i. 3)
> miro potentiae suae miraculo (i. 6)

BYRHTFERTH AND THE FIRST FOUR SECTIONS xxxvii

Finally, the most striking kind of hyperbaton occurs when the adjective + noun pairs are interwoven with each other, so that adjective follows adjective and noun follows noun (the adjective pairs sometimes separated from the noun pairs by a verb), denoted abAB:

abAB
sanctioris rectissimum aequitatis culmen (i. 2)
indeficientis praecordialibus orationis compti priuilegiis (i. 2)
sordidarum scabenti deturpatus meditationum prurigine (i. 3)
pretiosa uero tantorum membra agonistarum (i. 4)

It would be tiresome (and unnecessary) to list every example of these kinds of hyperbata in the *Historia regum*; suffice it to say that hyperbaton is the most commonly occurring rhetorical device in all four parts of the text, although its prevalence has been illustrated only from the first few chapters of Part I.

Polyptoton may be defined as the repetition of distinct, but etymologically related forms of a word.[76] Byrhtferth himself, following Bede (and Remigius) defines polyptoton in his *Enchiridion* as the repetition of the same words 'with many (different) case endings' (*Ench.* iii. 3. 104–9), which is simply the etymological meaning of *poly* + *ptoton*; but he will also have been familiar with the more useful definition of polyptoton given in Isidore's *Etymologiae*.[77] The following examples are found in *HR*: 'uidere autem uideor' (i. 3), 'contra insurgentes gentes exsurgeret' (iii. 28), 'tenuitque...potenti uigore sui potentatus' (iii. 24), 'regionum regna regaliter regebat' (iv. 3), 'gestas gestantem' (iv. 6), 'munitione arcis muniti' (iv. 7), 'principum princeps' (iv. 14), 'cum magna nutritorum atque nutricum diligentia sunt nutriti' (iv. 15). There would be little point in listing all the examples of polyptoton which are found in the writings of Byrhtferth, but the following will show that his delight in this rhetorical device is strikingly similar to that found in the *Historia regum*: 'scrutanti scrutinio scrutemur' (*Ench.* iv. 1. 76–7); 'rex...iura regni regaliter protegens' (*VSO* iii. 10); 'subdidit ergo se rex regi regum' (*VSO* iv. 4); 'desiderio desideraui' (*VSO*

---

[76] LHS ii. 707–8.

[77] Isidore defines polyptoton as the employment of one word in different cases (*Etym.* i. 36. 17), and cites by way of illustration a line of Persius: 'ex nihilo nihilum, ad nihilum nil posse reuerti' (*Sat.* iii. 84). In his discussion of polyptoton in the *Enchiridion* (*Ench.* iii. 3. 104–9), Byrhtferth quotes this same line from Persius (ibid. line 99). See also discussion in Byrhtferth, *The Lives*, ed. Lapidge, p. lix, where the suggestion is made that the use of polyptoton may be another aspect of Byrhtferth's poeticism, inasmuch as polyptoton is a characteristic feature of classical Latin poetry (for which, see Wills, *Repetition in Latin Poetry*, pp. 189–268).

xxxviii INTRODUCTION

v. 12), 'propria uisitatione infernum uisitando' (*VSE* i. 1), 'precibus placitis placatus' (*VSE* iii. 3), 'qui exspoliari desiderat sanctum, ipse despoliatus sit a sancto' (*VSE* iv. 10).

Paronomasia is related in some ways to polyptoton, except that in this case the wordplay is between similar sounding, but etymologically unrelated words: what in English is called a pun.[78] In his discussion of rhetorical devices in the *Enchiridion*, Byrhtferth illustrates paronomasia by pairing the words *amans* ('loving') and *amens* ('mad').[79] But in this discussion he also cited an example of what might more accurately be classified as polyptoton, namely the words *semens, sementis*, and *seminarium*, all of which derive from the same root and are etymologically related.[80] Several examples of paronomasia in the *Historia regum* conform to Byrhtferth's more elastic definition of paronomasia: 'absente regis praesentia' (i. 3); 'laedentes grauiter laeserunt' (iii. 23); and, speaking of God, 'quia respicit omnia solus, uerum possumus dicere solem' (iii. 27), where the wordplay is on the similar sounding, but etymologically distinct words *solus* and *sol*. In his saints' Lives, Byrhtferth uses exactly similar examples of paronomasia. Thus, in describing Abbo's great eloquence, Byrhtferth emphasizes his point by punning on the similarity in sound between *facundia* ('eloquence') and *fecunditas* ('abundance'): 'doctoris phylosophie facundiam et facundie fecunditatem gnarus lector potest intelligi' (*VSO* v. 8). Similarly, at one point in the Life of St Ecgwine, he describes a leader in the sinful city of Babylon as being 'as full of vices as Pharaoh was of riches', where the pun is on *uitiis / diuitiis*: 'tam plenus erat uitiis sicut pharao diuitiis' (*VSE* iv. 3).

Asyndeton is the stringing together of words in the same grammatical class and case without the use of connectives.[81] There are numerous examples of asyndeton in the *Historia regum* (it will be recalled that this is one of the stylistic features which led Peter Hunter Blair to argue that the early sections of the work were by one tenth-century Anglo-Latin author): 'fundauit perfecit rexit' (ii. 13); 'occiditur sepelitur obliuiscitur' (iii. 15); 'uallatus confortatus glorificatus' (iii. 16); 'discurrentes praedantes mordentes interficientes' (iii. 22, describing the Viking attacks on Lindisfarne); 'quassauit perdidit contriuit' (iii. 23); 'adorat ditat exornat' (iii. 28); 'turbati sunt, admirati

---

[78] LHS ii. 709–14.

[79] *Ench.* iii. 3. 70–85, at 71.

[80] Ibid. line 73.

[81] See LHS ii. 828–31. Byrhtferth himself does not discuss asyndeton among the *schemata* in his *Enchiridion*; but he does describe its opposite, namely polysyndeton, as 'speech which is adorned with many conjunctions' (*Ench.* iii. 3. 113–16).

BYRHTFERTH AND THE FIRST FOUR SECTIONS xxxix

sunt, commoti sunt' (iv. 10). Similar use of asyndeton is found throughout Byrhtferth's writings, but two examples may suffice: 'emicuit floruit percrebruit incanduit' (*VSO* iii. 6, describing St Benedict); 'expellantur deiciantur derideantur suspendantur colligentur uerberentur' (*VSO* iv. 12, describing the expulsion of monks from monasteries during the 'anti-monastic reaction').

Erotema is a rhetorical question, a device used for particular emphasis.[82] In the *Historia regum* (and in Byrhtferth), such questions take a predictable form: 'as to how great was such-and-such, who shall say?'[83] The interrogative pronouns and the verbs of saying may vary somewhat, but the construction is invariable. In the *Historia regum* the following examples occur: 'Quot uero... diuina uolumina, quantas... reliquias attulit, quis annunciet?' (ii. 6); 'Qualiter dilatauit regni sui imperia... quis urbana facundia suffultus possit labiis exultationis edicere?' (iv. 16); 'sancta quoque loca qualiter ditauit ornamentis..., quis enuntiet?' (iv. 16); 'quanta munera suis episcopis contulit, quis enarret?' (iv. 16). With these examples, compare the many occurrences of the same type of question in Byrhtferth: 'quam gloriosum habitaculum... praebuit, quis poterit digne perscrutari?' (*VSO* i. 5); 'quanta summus pater contulit, quis cuncta expediet?' (*VSO* ii. 3); 'qualibus illud monasterium ornamentis ditauit,... quis expediet?' (*VSO* iv. 15); 'quam gloriose incitauit principes,... quis urbanitate fretus possit edicere?' (*VSO* v. 5); 'quam sollempniter suscepti sunt presules,... quis digne expediet?' (*VSO* v. 11); 'quam nobiliter aeditui ornauerunt,... quis annuntiet?' (*VSO* v. 11); 'quot lacrimas... emisit, quis expediet?' (*VSO* v. 21); 'quis urbana fretus eloquentia potest pleniter inuestigare?' (*VSE Epil.*); 'quantus resplenduit fulgor, quis... potest edicere?' (*VSE* i. 2); 'quam prudenter columbe simplicitatem retinuit,... qualis stilus pronuntiet?' (*VSE* i. 9); 'quantum se humiliauerit, quis millenis poterit uerbis explicare?' (*VSE* i. 10); 'quomodo alter... consolatus est, quis digno fauore pronuntiet?' (*VSE* i. 13); 'quanta letitia... ardebat,... quis explicet? Quis adnuntiet? Quis rite enarret?' (*VSE* iv. 10).

v. Favourite Quotations

The sources of the first four sections are discussed in detail below (pp. xliii–lxxvi); here I mention some idiosyncratic quotations shared by

---

[82] Cf. LHS ii. 457–60, and 467.

[83] The model for this type of rhetorical question appears to have been Aldhelm, prose *De uirginitate*, c. 20: 'quantum profeticae dignitatis gratia enituerit ..., quis urbana verborum facundia fretus enarrare sufficiat?' (*Opera*, ed. Ehwald, p. 250).

xl INTRODUCTION

Byrthferth and the author of the *Historia regum*. Four such quotations are in question: a phrase adapted from a verse in the book of Job; a poem on annals and seasons attributed to Bede (inc. 'Me legat annales'), followed by a distich beginning 'Hos claros uersus'; some lines from the 'Metrical Calendar of Ramsey'; and a two-line quotation borrowed from the *Historia apostolica* of the sixth-century Italian poet Arator.

The book of Job

At one point in the book of Job, the author expresses the fervent wish that the sinner and his sins pass into the excessive heat of Hell: 'ad nimium calorem transeat ab aquis nivium et usque ad inferos peccatum illius' (Job 24: 19: 'May his sin pass from the snow waters to excessive heat, and even as far as Hell'). This biblical quotation provides the germ of a line in the *Historia regum*: 'transibunt animae de poenis niuium' ('their souls shall pass from the pains of snows'),[84] where the author has made the sinners' souls (*animae*) the subject of the sentence, and has altered the biblical subjunctive to future indicative plural (*transibunt*). The point of the alterations is illustrated nicely by a similar quotation found in each of Byrhtferth's saints' Lives: 'transibunt animae de aquis niuium ad aquas nimium' (*VSO* iv. 20), and again, 'transibunt anime de aquis niuium ad aquas nimium' (*VSE* i. 12): 'their souls shall pass from snow waters to waters excessively'. From these two sentences it may be seen that the Byrhtferthian adaptation of the verse from Job is almost identical to, and helps to inform, the quotation in the *Historia regum*. This suggests that if the quotation there had been completed by the scribe, it would probably have concluded with the words *ad aquas nimium*. The idiosyncratic alteration of biblical *transeat…peccatum* to *transibunt animae* indicates that these quotations are from the same pen.

'Me legat annales'

The twelve-line poem in question (inc. 'Me legat, annales cupiat qui noscere menses') is found in a number of English and Continental manuscripts, usually attributed to Bede (although the attribution is extremely doubtful, given that the poem is a simple rehash of hexameters borrowed from Dracontius).[85] The same poem is quoted in full at

---

[84] As copied by the original scribe of C, the quotation was left incomplete at *niuium*; a later scribe in C (my C²) completed the sentence by adding the words 'ad calorem nimium'—a clear indication that the scribe recognized the quotation from Job. But it is not possible to know how the sentence was completed in the original text of the *Historia regum*.

[85] *Bede's Latin Poetry*, ed. Lapidge, pp. 515–17.

BYRHTFERTH AND THE FIRST FOUR SECTIONS xli

HR ii. 15, where it is followed immediately by two lines describing the attribution of the poem to Bede:

> Hos claros uersus uenerabilis edidit auctor
> Beda sacer, multum nitido sermone coruscus.

It is significant, therefore, that when this twelve-line poem is quoted in Byrhtferth's (unprinted) *Computus* as preserved in Oxford, St John's College 17, fo. 14ʳ, the poem is preceded by the same two lines attributing the poem to Bede.[86] I have suggested elsewhere that this distich was very probably composed by Byrhtferth himself;[87] in any case, its presence in the *Historia regum*, in a context very similar to that in Byrhtferth's *Computus*, is a striking link with Byrhtferth.

The 'Metrical Calendar of Ramsey'

At one point of his narrative (*HR* iii. 24), the *HR* author relates that in 797 Eanbald, having received the pallium, was confirmed as archbishop of York on 8 Sept. of that year, that is to say, on the feast of the Nativity of the Virgin—'confirmatus est .vi. idus Septembris, qua die celebratur solempnitas, id est, Natiuitas sanctae Mariae, de qua poeta ait'—and then quotes the following two lines:

> Splendet honore dies, est in quo uirgo Maria
> stirpe Dauid regis procedens, edita mundo.

The source of these two lines has baffled earlier editors;[88] but in fact the two lines derive from a metrical calendar which has been interpolated into the computistical calendar which forms part of Byrhtferth's *Computus*, as preserved in Oxford, St John's College 17, fos. 16ʳ–21ᵛ,[89] and which I edited for the first time as the 'Metrical Calendar of Ramsey'.[90] The verses in question are on fo. 20ʳ of St John's 17, as follows:

> Splendet honore dies summo quo uirgo Maria
> stirpe Dauid regis procedens, edita mundo.[91]

---

[86] Ibid. p. 515; and see *Byrhtferth's Enchiridion*, ed. Baker and Lapidge, p. 384.

[87] Byrhtferth, *The Lives*, ed. Lapidge, p. xliii.

[88] *Symeonis Monachi Opera Omnia*, ed. Arnold, ii. 58, n. b: 'The authorship of these lines … might perhaps be discovered by means of a patient perusal of Juvencus, Sedulius, Fortunatus, St. Aldhelm, and other Christian poets. The time that I have been able to give to the search has hitherto proved fruitless.'

[89] The calendar, with the verses interpolated, is printed in *Byrhtferth's Enchiridion*, ed. Baker and Lapidge, pp. 391–415.

[90] 'A tenth-century metrical calendar from Ramsey', pp. 363–6 [= *ALL* ii. 380–3].

[91] Ibid. p. 365 [= *ALL* ii. 380]. The minor variant *est in* for *summo* is probably the result of quotation from memory.

xlii INTRODUCTION

Now it is surely significant that Byrhtferth quotes lines from the 'Metrical Calendar of Ramsey' (MCR) on three occasions in his *Vita S. Oswaldi*:

Qua die colebatur festiuitas de qua poeta cecinit ita: 'Bis binis <passus colitur Baptista Iohannes>.' (*VSO* iii. 17 [MCR 91])

aduenit optabilis utrisque dies (qui est .vi. Id. Nouembris) in qua colitur horum sollempnitas sanctorum de quibus cecinit poeticus uersus: 'Quattuor hi sancti roseis sertis coronati.' (*VSO* v. 11 [MCR 112])

De quo poeta ait, 'Aula Dei patuit Osuualdo pridie Martis, / pontifici summo alta petendo poli.' (*VSO* v. 17 [MCR 32–3])

The fact that Byrhtferth interpolated the 'Metrical Calendar of Ramsey' into the computistical calendar in his *Computus* and that he then quoted from this metrical calendar on three occasions in his *Vita S. Oswaldi*, suggests that he may have been the author of the 'Metrical Calendar of Ramsey'. That the author of the *Historia regum* should also quote from this poem—which does not appear to have been known outside Ramsey—strengthens the impression that Byrhtferth is the author of the *Historia regum*.

Arator

Several times in his *Enchiridion* Byrhtferth quotes two lines from Arator, *Historia apostolica*, as follows:

> spiritus alme, ueni! sine te non diceris umquam;
> munera da linguae qui das in munere linguas.[92]

Byrhtferth employs these two lines as a kind of personal prayer, to ask the Holy Spirit's continuing support of his writing; they are used in particular at points of transition from one major part of a work to another. Thus, he quotes them to mark the transition from Part II to Part III of his *Enchiridion* (*Ench.* ii. 3. 265–6), and a second time in the same work as he steels himself to launch into a detailed exposition of Paschal reckoning (*Ench.* iii. 2); here he describes the lines as his personal prayer, and even provides an (Old) English translation:

> Oratio patris Byrhtferði:
> Spiritus alme, ueni. Sine te non diceris umquam;
> munera da lingue, qui das <in> munere linguas.
>
> Cum nu, halig gast. Butan þe bis<t> þu gewurðod;
> Gyf þine gyfe þære tungan, þe þu gyfst gyfe on gereorde.[93]

---

[92] *Historia apostolica*, ed. McKinlay, i. 226–7 (CSEL lxxii. 25): 'Come, kindly Spirit! Without Your support You can never be described; grant the bounties of speech, You Who have the gift of tongues.'

[93] *Byrhtferth's Enchiridion*, ed. Baker and Lapidge, p. 136.

THE SOURCES OF THE *HISTORIA REGVM*   xliii

Similarly, as he prepares to describe the life of St Ecgwine, in the *epilogus* of his *Vita S. Ecgwini*, he quotes the two lines again and describes them as the *exordium meae orationis* (*VSE Epil.*).[94] It cannot be a matter of coincidence that the *HR* author, as he concludes Part II of his work on Bede's writings and prepares to deal with the unwieldy annalistic material of Part III, quotes this very same 'prayer of Father Byrhtferth', as Byrhtferth calls it:

nos uero ad negotium sollerti cura, Christi clementia succurrente, peragemus, sic orando:

> spiritus alme, ueni, sine te non diceris umquam;
> munera da linguae, qui das in munere linguas. (*HR* ii. 20)

There could not be a clearer indication that the first four parts of the *Historia regum* are the composition of Byrhtferth of Ramsey.

THE SOURCES OF THE *HISTORIA REGVM*

Part I

Byrhtferth begins his *Historia regum* with the kingdom of Kent. The first chapter (*HR* i. 1) provides a genealogy of the early kings of Kent, from Æthelberht (d. 616) onwards. This material is taken verbatim from Bede, *HE* ii. 5. 1–2 (ed. Lapidge, i. 196–200; ed. Colgrave and Mynors, p. 148). In the material quoted here from Bede there are no variant readings which might give some indication of the nature of the manuscript of the *HE* from which Byrhtferth was copying.

After this preliminary chapter concerning the early kings of Kent, the remainder of Part I (*HR* i. 2–10) is taken up with the murder of two princes of the Kentish royal family, named Æthelred and Æthelberht. The remains of these Kentish princes—who were murdered at some point during the reign of King Ecgberht (664–73)—were preserved at Wakering in Essex. From the later (post-Byrhtferthian) *Passio SS. Ethelredi et Ethelbricti* (*BHL* 2641–2), we learn that, in the late tenth century, the remains of SS. Æthelred and Æthelberht lay buried at Wakering in a small minster church[95] on an estate belonging to Æthelwine, ealdorman of East Anglia: 'inclito duce Ethelwino (in

---

[94] Byrhtferth, *The Lives*, ed. Lapidge, p. 208.

[95] In the post-Byrhtferthian *Passio SS. Ethelredi et Ethelbricti*, this minster church is described as a 'church of that same estate which is called Wakering, which is served lazily by a few uninterested priests': 'ecclesia eiusdem uille que uocatur Wakerynga, cui inseruiebant segniter pauci incuriosi presbiteri' (ed. Rollason, *The Mildrith Legend*, p. 103).

xliv INTRODUCTION

cuius uilla reperti sunt tumulati)'.[96] Ealdorman Æthelwine was the founder and lay patron of Ramsey; unsurprisingly, he arranged for the remains of the two princely martyrs to be translated from Wakering to Ramsey: 'exempti sunt [*scil.* the martyrs' remains] a fratribus monasterii Ramesige et transuecti ad idem cenobium, quod isdem comes construxerat, cooperante sancte recordationis domno Oswaldo archipresule'.[97] The translation apparently took place *c*.990.[98] It is described as follows in the thirteenth-century *Liber benefactorum* of Ramsey Abbey:

Sub eadem tempestate duo gemelli fratres Athelredus atque Athelbritus, ex ingenuo antiquorum regum stemmate oriundi et... innocenter iugulati, apud villam venerabilis aldermanni, Wacheringe nomine, antiquitus habebantur in ecclesia consepulti. Quos quum pietas divina martyrii gloria sublimatos nonnullis signorum indiciis declarasset, visum est eidem aldermanno minus eis ibidem honoris et reverentiae quam deceret exhiberi, eorumque pignora fecit cum devotione condecenti Ramesiam transferri, ecclesiam ipsam et omnium donationum suarum consummationem duarum pretiosarum gemmarum illustratione perornans.[99]

Once they had been translated to Ramsey, their remains were housed in a single urn ('utrosque spacium unius urne continuit') and—so it would appear—Byrhtferth, at that point Ramsey's foremost scholar, was put to the task of composing the *passio* of these two (originally Kentish) martyrs. The resulting *Passio SS. Æthelredi et Æthelberhti* (*BHL* 2643), presumably composed for the occasion of the martyrs' translation to Ramsey, or soon afterwards, was subsequently incorporated entire by Byrhtferth into Part I of his *Historia regum* (*HR* i. 2–10); it does not survive independently of the *Historia regum*.

The source(s) on which Byrhtferth drew for his *passio* cannot be stated precisely, because the source-text in question has not survived.

[96] Ibid. p. 102.
[97] Ibid.
[98] The *Passio SS. Ethelredi et Ethelbricti* states (ibid.) that the translation took place during the reign of King Æthelred, hence post 978, and was orchestrated by Ealdorman Æthelwine, who died in 992; the outer dating *termini* for the translation are therefore 978×992.
[99] *Chronicon Abbatiae Rameseiensis*, ed. Macray, p. 55: 'At this same time [*scil.* the ealdormanry of Æthelwine (962–92)] two twin brothers, Æthelred and Æthelberht, born of the noble stock of ancient kings and ... innocently murdered, had long since been buried in a church on an estate of the venerable ealdorman, named Wakering. Since the divine Mercy had declared through certain miracles that they had been elevated through the glory of martyrdom, it seemed to this same ealdorman that less honour and reverence was being accorded to them there than was fitting, and he had their remains translated to Ramsey with appropriate devotion, adorning the church itself [Ramsey] and the fulfilment of all his donations by the splendour of these two precious jewels.'

THE SOURCES OF THE *HISTORIA REGVM*   xlv

The outlines of this source-text must be reconstructed from various other surviving texts, all of them later in date than Byrhtferth himself. These other texts include the aforementioned *Passio SS. Ethelredi et Ethelbricti* (*BHL* 2641–2), apparently composed at Ramsey, and uniquely preserved in Oxford, BodL, Bodley 285 (?Ramsey, s. xiii in.), fos. 116–21;[100] a treatise entitled 'Resting-Places of English Saints' ('Þa halgan þe on Angelcynne restað'),[101] preserved in London, BL, Stowe 944, fos. 6–61 (New Minster, Winchester, AD 1031),[102] fos. 34^v–39^r, the first part of which is a separate document concerning the royal saints of Kent (fos. 34^v–36^v); the *Vita S. Mildrethae* (*BHL* 5960), composed in the 1090s by Goscelin of Saint-Bertin, then a monk of St Augustine's, Canterbury, preserved in seven English manuscripts, four of which date from the early twelfth century;[103] a fragmentary text in Old English, the end of which has been truncated, in London, BL, Cotton Caligula A. xiv (s. xi med.), fos. 121^v–124^v;[104] and a recently discovered *Vita S. Eadburgae* (*BHL* 2384a) by the secular canon known to hagiographers from the first initial of his name, B. (to be discussed more fully below). The focus of these texts is not on SS. Æthelred and Æthelberht, but on their sister Eormenburg, also called Domneua, the foundress and abbess of the church of Minster-in-Thanet, and her daughter Mildrith, who succeeded her as abbess. As a group, these texts are said to transmit what has been called 'the Mildrith Legend' (the name was

---

[100] Ed. in Rollason, *The Mildrith Legend*, pp. 90–104. In addition to this account of the two martyrs who were translated to Ramsey by Ealdorman Æthelwine, Bodley 285 also preserves a copy of Goscelin's *Inventio, translatio et miracula S. Ivonis* (*BHL* 4622–3; ed. PL clv. 81–9 + *Chronicon abbatiae Rameseiensis*, ed. Macray, pp. lix–lxxxiv; see Love, 'Goscelinus Sancti Bertini mon.', pp. 239–42), the account of an originally Persian saint whose remains were discovered near Ramsey and translated there in 1002. Goscelin composed his account of the discovery and translation of St Ivo during the abbacy of Herbert Losinga (hence 1087×1090/1), to whom his work is dedicated. It is the presence of these two texts—one concerning the martyrs Æthelred and Æthelberht, the other concerning St Ivo—which suggests that Bodley 285 was written at Ramsey; see Ker, *Medieval Manuscripts in British Libraries*, ii, p. 89. For St Ivo, see also below, p. lxxvi, n. 179.

[101] *Die Heiligen Englands*, ed. Liebermann, pp. 1–6; also ed. Birch in *Liber Vitae: Register and Martyrology of New Minster and Hyde Abbey, Winchester*, pp. 83–7.

[102] Listed (with bibliography) by Gneuss and Lapidge, *Anglo-Saxon Manuscripts*, no. 500; ed. in facsimile by S. Keynes, *The Liber Vitae of the New Minster and Hyde Abbey Winchester*, with description of the text of the 'Resting-Places' at p. 100.

[103] Rollason, *The Mildrith Legend*, pp. 108–43; for discussion of the manuscripts and transmission, see Love, 'Goscelinus Sancti Bertini mon.', pp. 245, 248–9.

[104] *Leechdoms, Wortcunning and Starcraft of Early England*, ed. O. Cockayne (Rolls Series; 3 vols.; London, 1864–6), ii. 422–8. On the manuscript, see Gneuss and Lapidge, *Anglo-Saxon Manuscripts*, no. 310.

xlvi INTRODUCTION

first used by David Rollason).[105] The (lost) source-text from which these various versions derive was arguably composed at Thanet in the early eighth century, after the death of Mildrith herself, which occurred sometime between 737/8 and 748.[106]

The first four texts which transmit the 'Mildrith legend', and which have been discussed by David Rollason and others, are all later in date than the period of Byrhtferth's scholarly activity. However, there is another text relevant to Byrhtferth and his account of SS. Æthelberht and Æthelred which dates from the archbishopric of Ælfric and is thus contemporary with Byrhtferth's scholarly activity, namely the *Vita S. Eadburgae*. This *Vita* is made up of three parts, the first of which is preserved anonymously in a single fourteenth-century English manuscript, now Gotha, Forschungsbibliothek, I. 81, fos. 185ᵛ–188ᵛ.[107] The first part of the text bears the rubric: *Incipit Vita sanctorum Æthelredi et Æthelberti martyrum et sanctarum uirginum Miltrudis et Edburgis Idus Decembris*. The Latin of the *Vita S. Eadburgae* is highly distinctive, and Rosalind Love has advanced powerful arguments for identifying the anonymous author with the secular canon known only by the first initial of his name—B.—who was active at Canterbury under the patronage of Archbishop Ælfric (995–1005), and is best known as the author of the earliest *Vita S. Dunstani* (*BHL* 2342).[108] Love's argument is based on similarities in Latin style between the *Vita S. Eadburgae* and B.'s *Vita S. Dunstani*—shared phraseology and vocabulary, some of it idiosyncratic in the extreme, some of it based on Greek, and much of it unattested elsewhere and presumably coined by the author.[109] We know that Byrhtferth very probably visited Canterbury at about this time, because in his *Vita S. Oswaldi* he at one point quotes

---

[105] Rollason, *The Mildrith Legend*, pp. 15–31, who lists and describes all surviving witnesses to the 'legend', including the first four of the texts mentioned here; the *Vita S. Eadburgae* was unknown to Rollason, since it was edited for the first time by Rosalind Love in 2019 ('St Eadburh of Lyminge and her hagiographer').

[106] The attribution of the original (lost) text to Thanet is argued persuasively by Hollis, 'The Minster-in-Thanet foundation story', who sees 'the Mildrith legend' as 'the dynastic legend of a royal *Eigenkloster*, which relates how the founder-abbess gained the monastery's land and left it to her daughter' (p. 44). Rollason (*The Mildrith Legend*, p. 16) had earlier argued that the original text was composed at Wakering. In my view, the Wakering material was interpolated into the Thanet material by Byrhtferth himself, and has no bearing on the origin of the lost source-text. See below, pp. xlix–l.

[107] The *Vita S. Eadburgae* has been impeccably edited by Rosalind Love, 'St Eadburh of Lyminge', pp. 374–408, with the part of the text relevant to the Kentish princes Æthelberht and Æthelred at pp. 374–84.

[108] *The Early Lives of St Dunstan*, ed. Winterbottom and Lapidge, pp. 2–108.

[109] Love, 'St Eadburh of Lyminge', pp. 343–56.

THE SOURCES OF THE *HISTORIA REGVM*   xlvii

a passage of B.'s *Vita S. Dunstani* which is attested uniquely in a manuscript written and preserved at Canterbury,[110] implying that he must
have visited Canterbury and seen the manuscript there. While visiting
Canterbury, he could also have seen a copy of B.'s *Vita S. Eadburgae*;
indeed it is even possible that, during his visit, Byrhtferth met B. in
person.[111]

In any case, there is sound evidence that Byrhtferth was familiar
with B.'s *Vita S. Eadburgae*. In his *Historia regum* (i. 4, below), he
describes the inappropriate silence—in lieu of the liturgical perform-
ance of the last rites—which attended the murder of SS. Æthelberht
and Æthelred as follows:

Porro nullo eis indulto fletus suspirio, <u>nullo decem cordarum reboante officio</u>,
non hymnorum pulcherrrimo Ambrosiano titulo, <u>nec Gregoriano potitis dulcis armoniae organo</u>, non defuere summae deitatis cum multiplicis <munere>
uirtutis exenia.[112]

This sentence is strikingly similar to B.'s account in his *Vita S. Eadburgae*
of what attended the death of the two Kentish princes—not the last
rites consisting of the psalms of David and Gregorian chant, but the
noisy revelry of the murderers:

Non laudum condigna cantica, <u>non Dauitica decem cordarum psalmodia</u>, non
clara lampadum lumina, <u>non Gregoriana pro interemptorum requie commen-
damina</u>, sed illicita ibi perstrepebant carnificum conuiuia.[113]

The similarity of sentence structure and wording (emphasized by
underlining) makes it difficult not to think that Byrhtferth was influenced here by the older man's presentation of the martyrs' death and
the absence of the liturgical celebration which was the martyrs' due.

In other respects, Byrhtferth's account of the Kentish princes'
martyrdom echoes the first part of B.'s *Vita S. Eadburgae*; but the
emphasis in each is inevitably different. B. mentions the site of the
martyrdom as Eastry (3.1), but obviously has no need to mention
the subsequent translation to Wakering, which in all likelihood is

---

[110] *Vita S. Oswaldi* v. 6 (ed. Lapidge in Byrhtferth, *VSO*, pp. 158–9, with n. 66, as well as
discussion ibid. p. lxxix). The manuscript of B.'s *Vita S. Dunstani* from which Byrhtferth
appears to be quoting is London, BL, Cotton Cleopatra B. xiii, on which, see Gneuss and
Lapidge, *Anglo-Saxon Manuscripts*, no. 323.

[111] Note that Byrhtferth and B. are entirely distinct persons, each with an individual and
idiosyncratic style of writing Latin. An erroneous identification of the two by Jean Mabillon
misled generations of scholars.

[112] See below, p. 10.

[113] *Vita S. Eadburgae* 2.1 (ed. Love, 'St Eadburh of Lyminge', p. 374).

xlviii INTRODUCTION

Byrhtferth's fabrication. In B.'s account of the foundation of Thanet, he relates that King Ecgberht summoned Eormenburg/Domneua to him, and gave her eighty hides of land in expiation of his murder of her two brothers; but he makes no mention of her hind (*cerua*) and the way in which the monastic estate was demarcated. Byrhtferth, for his part, does not mention that the estate demarcated by the hind consisted of eighty hides, because his principal focus is on Wakering, not Thanet, and he only mentions the demarcation of the Thanet estate in order to provide a context for the death of Thunor (an event which is not mentioned by B.). It is clear, in short, that both authors were adapting a pre-existing foundation legend to their individual purposes.

We may now return to the narrative of the foundation of Thanet, and the role played in that foundation by the sister of the two murdered princes. It seems clear, from comparison of the surviving witnesses, that the principal character in the 'Mildrith legend' was the princes' sister Domneua, or (in some versions) Domne Eafe, the apparent alias of a woman named Eormenburg (*HR* i. 8: 'Eormenburga uel Domneua nomine'). In the early charters of Minster-in-Thanet, the name of the founding abbess is given as Eabbe or Æbbe (the latter being simply a spelling of the former name).[114] This Eabbe was the recipient of royal grants recorded in charters dated from 689 to 697;[115] her daughter Mildrith, who succeeded her as abbess, was the recipient of charters between 724 and 737/8;[116] and Mildrith's successor Eadburg is first recorded as the recipient of a royal grant in 748.[117] The charters do not enable us to assign precise dates to the abbacies of Eabbe and her daughter Mildrith, but it would seem that Eabbe had probably died by 700 or soon after, and that Mildrith ruled as abbess through the 720s and 730s, and died at some time between 738 and 748.

The parents of the three siblings—Æthelred, Æthelberht, and Eormenburg/Eabbe—were Eormenred, who was the elder brother of

---

[114] Eabbe (or Æbbe) is apparently a hypocoristic form of Eormenburg. I suggest that the name Eabbe was subsequently combined with Latin *Domina*, so that *Dom(i)na* + *Eabbe* became *Domnefa* or *Domneua*, 'Lady Eabbe'. The alteration in spelling of bilabial b with labiodental f is well attested in early Old English orthography (Campbell, *Old English Grammar*, p. 179 [§444]).

[115] *Charters of St Augustine's Abbey ... and Minster-in-Thanet*, ed. Kelly, nos. 40 (dated 689), 41 (*c*.690), 42 (690), 43 (*c*.690), 44 (694), and 46 (697).

[116] Kelly, ibid. nos. 47 (for 724), 48 (for 727), 49 (for 733?), and 50 (for 737/8). A charter in favour of Mildrith (no. 45), dated to 696—when, on the evidence of charters cited in the previous note, Eabbe was still abbess—is regarded by Kelly as an 'outright fabrication' (p. 158).

[117] Kelly, ibid. no. 51 (for 748).

THE SOURCES OF THE *HISTORIA REGVM*   xlix

King Earconberht of Kent (640–64),[118] and a woman named Oslafa, otherwise unknown (indeed Eormenred the father is known only from these Kentish sources: he is nowhere mentioned by Bede, who discusses King Earconberht, his younger brother, at *HE* iii. 8. 1 and iv. 1. 1). The father of Eormenred and Earconberht was Eadbald, king of Kent (616–40). What is not clear is why, on Eadbald's death in 640, the throne passed to Earconberht, the younger son, rather than to Eormenred, the elder. And then when Earconberht died, he passed the Kentish throne to his son Ecgberht, who reigned from 664 to 673. Ecgberht's claim to the throne might have seemed precarious to some, given the presence of the two æthelings, his cousins, Æthelred and Æthelberht, the sons of Eormenred, the elder brother on whom the kingship might naturally have devolved. According to the 'Mildrith legend', a wicked councillor named Thunor played on Ecgberht's anxieties (*HR* i. 4), and apparently received royal permission to dispose of these potential rivals to his throne. Æthelred and Æthelberht were accordingly murdered by Thunor at the royal estate of Eastry in Kent, as Byrhtferth relates (*HR* i. 6).

Thus far, Byrhtferth was following the narrative which he inherited from the lost text of the 'Mildrith legend'. But if the two princes were murdered at Eastry in Kent, how did their remains come to be preserved at Wakering in Essex? None of the sources of the 'Mildrith legend'—with the exception of Byrhtferth's *Historia regum* and the anonymous Ramsey *Passio SS. Ethelredi et Ethelbricti*, which takes its account of the murder from Byrhtferth—mentions Wakering. In order to make his narrative relevant to Ramsey, which had recently acquired the relics of the two Kentish princes, Wakering—from which their relics had been translated to Ramsey—needed to figure significantly. Byrhtferth accordingly refashioned the inherited narrative to explain that, after the two princes had been murdered at the royal estate of Eastry, and their bodies had been revealed by a divine column of light (*HR* i. 5), it was suggested by those present that they be translated to Christ Church, Canterbury (*HR* i. 6: 'delata in urbem Cantiae, Christi sepelirentur in monasterio'). But—miraculously—the bodies could not be moved. Next, it was proposed that they be taken to St Augustine's, Canterbury; but again, they could not be moved. Several other

---

[118] The sources of the 'Mildrith legend' make it clear that King Eadbald (616–40) had two sons, Eormenred and Earconberht. By the normal operation of primogeniture, Eadbald's throne should have passed to the elder son (Eormenred), not to Earconberht. This oddity of succession was one of the reasons for the instability of the Kentish throne, and for the anxieties of Ecgberht, who succeeded his father Earconberht in 664.

INTRODUCTION

possible locations were mooted, without result. In the end, it was suggested that they should be taken to 'the very famous minster called Wakering' (*HR* i. 6: 'ad famosissimum gestarentur monasterium Wacrinense'). Once this suggestion had been made, the bodies could easily be moved; and so they were translated to the minster at Wakering, where they were given burial behind the main altar, where over the course of many years their remains were the cause of many miracles. Byrhtferth proposed to narrate two of these miracles (*HR* i. 6: miracles 'de quibus duo posterorum notitiae nunc propalare praesenti sermone decreuimus'), but in fact only supplied one, the miracle of the stolen sheep (i. 7).[119] In any case, it is clear that the account of the translation from Eastry to Wakering, when seen against other narratives of the 'Mildrith legend', is a pious fiction invented by Byrhtferth himself. And if a modern reader should think Byrhtferth incapable of inventing a pious fiction such as this, a cursory reading of the *Vita S. Ecgwini* should remove all doubt.

At this point Byrhtferth's narrative returns to Domneua, the murdered princes' sister (*HR* i. 8–10). According to Byrhtferth, and to other sources of the legend, Domneua apparently played on Ecgberht's guilty conscience, and asked from the king—as a sort of *wergild*, perhaps—a grant of land in Thanet on which to establish a minster church. The amount of land in question was left to Domneua's discretion. She proposed that the boundaries of the land should be demarcated by her pet hind. While the hind was proceeding to mark out the eventual boundaries, Thunor reproached the king for allowing a stupid animal to decide so important a matter, whereupon Thunor was struck dead by a divine lightning bolt (*HR* i. 8). The place of his death was marked by a burial mound, thereafter called *Thunreshleaw*.[120] The territory thus demarcated became the endowment of Minster-in-Thanet, over which Domneua presided as first abbess and where she introduced seventy virgins who had been consecrated by Archbishop Deusdedit (*HR* i. 9: 'ecclesiam ... constituit, cum septuaginta sanctimonialibus a sancto archiepiscopo Deusdedit consecratis, inibique

---

[119] It is possible that Symeon of Durham simply omitted to copy the second miracle; but it is equally possible that Byrhtferth forgot to supply it (no second miracle is recorded in the later Ramsey *Passio SS. Ethelredi et Ethelbricti*, whose author reproduces the first sheep-stealing miracle virtually verbatim from Byrhtferth).

[120] Burial mounds often figure in the bounds of land grants recorded in Anglo-Saxon charters, a useful point made by Hollis ('The Minster-in-Thanet foundation story', pp. 51–2).

THE SOURCES OF THE *HISTORIA REGVM* li

consecrauit').[121] At her death, she was succeeded as abbess by her daughter Mildrith, who had been trained overseas in ecclesiastical discipline (*HR* i. 9: 'ecclesiasticis in transmarinis partibus disciplinis eruditam'),[122] and whose sanctity was revealed through a number of miracles, of which Byrhtferth narrates one, in which an angel in the shape of a dove landed on her head while she was sleeping in order to protect her from evil spirits (*HR* i. 10).[123]

It will be seen that the 'Mildrith legend' was essentially a foundation story concerning Minster-in-Thanet, and that, in order to make it relevant to a Ramsey audience, Byrhtferth needed to adapt the inherited material concerning Thanet in Kent to explain how the bodies of the murdered princes came to be preserved on an estate in Essex belonging to Æthelwine, the founder and lay patron of Ramsey. The most significant intervention by Byrhtferth in the inherited 'Mildrith legend' was evidently his account of the miraculous transfer of the martyrs' bodies from Eastry to Wakering, but he altered the inherited material in other ways. For example, all remaining texts of the 'Mildrith legend' treat a large cast of characters related in some way to the royal Kentish house (Eormengyth, another sister of Æthelred, Æthelberht, and Domneua; two additional daughters of Domneua, named Mildburg and Mildgith; Seaxburg, wife of King Earconberht, who bore him Werburg; and many more): Byrhtferth eliminated all these other royal persons so as to focus his narrative exclusively on SS. Æthelred and Æthelberht and their sister Domneua. His lengthy description of Thunor is evidently his own contribution to the legend, as is Thunor's lengthy speech to King Ecgberht counselling the removal of the two princes (*HR* i. 3). The verbose amplification of what is essentially a very small narrative core is

---

[121] There is a chronological problem with Byrhtferth's statement that the seventy virgins had been consecrated by Deusdedit, who was archbishop of Canterbury from 655 to 664—a generation earlier than the abbacy of Domneua, which, as we have seen, apparently fell sometime in the 690s. Awareness of the chronological difficulties led some authors of texts preserving the 'Mildrith legend' to substitute Archbishop Theodore (668–90) for Deusdedit (which is not an entirely satisfactory resolution of the problem); among these texts is B.'s *Vita S. Eadburgae* (c. 10), in which B. states that Mildthryth took the veil of holy orders at the hand of Archbishop Theodore, along with seventy other virgins (*una cum aliis septuaginta uirginibus*: ed. Love, 'St Eadburh of Lyminge', p. 380).

[122] In the *Vita S. Eadburgae* (cc. 7–8), B. describes Mildthryth's period of study in Gaul: 'Quam [*scil.* Mildthrytham] gloriosa genitrix ad Gallias usque destinauit' (ed. Love, 'St Eadburh of Lyminge', p. 378).

[123] Byrhtferth clearly took this miracle from the source-text of the 'Mildrith legend' which he was following, for the same miracle is narrated by B. in his *Vita S. Eadburgae* c. 14 (ed. Love, 'St Eadburh of Lyminge', p. 382) and by Goscelin in his *Vita S. Mildrethae*, c. 25 (ed. Rollason, *The Mildrith Legend*, p. 138).

lii INTRODUCTION

entirely characteristic of Byrhtferth, and the same techniques of invention and amplification will be seen to characterize his later essays in hagiography, the *Vita S. Oswaldi* and the *Vita S. Ecgwini*.

Part II

In Part II, Byrhtferth turns from Kent to Northumbria, and begins by providing a regnal list of Northumbrian kings, from Ida (d. 559/60) to Ceolwulf, to whom Bede dedicated his *Historia ecclesiastica*.

HR ii. 2. The Northumbrian regnal list on which Byrhtferth drew was similar (but not identical) to that in the so-called 'Moore Memoranda', which were added to the copy of Bede's *Historia ecclesiastica* in the 'Moore' manuscript now in Cambridge (Cambridge, UL, Kk. 5. 16, fo. 128ᵛ).[124] Information from these *memoranda* is supplemented, for the kings from Æthelfrith to Ceolwulf, by reference to Bede *HE* i. 34, ii. 2, ii. 5, and ii. 9.

HR ii. 3–14. With the history of Northumbrian kings serving as a sort of framework, Byrhtferth turns his attention to the twin monasteries of Monkwearmouth and Jarrow, basing himself here on Bede's *Historia abbatum* (*CPL* 1378; *BHL* 8968), from which he quotes extensively and usually verbatim, which allows certain deductions to be made about the nature of the text from which he was quoting. The *Historia abbatum* is preserved in eleven manuscripts, all of them English, and some dating from as early as the tenth century.[125] The earliest surviving manuscript of the *Historia abbatum* is now London, BL, Harley 3020, fos. 1–34 (Glastonbury or St Augustine's, Canterbury, s. x/xi; provenance Glastonbury),[126] a manuscript contemporary with the lifetime of Byrhtferth. Several variant readings in the text of the *Historia abbatum* as quoted by Byrhtferth are recorded uniquely in Harley 3020:

HR ii. 4 [= Bede, *Historia abbatum* i. 1]: Despexit militiam cum corruptibili donatiuo terrestrem, ut uero regi <u>militans</u> regnum in superna felicitate mereretur habere perpetuum.[127]   <u>militans</u> *Harley 3020*; militare *all other MSS*

---

[124] The 'Moore Memoranda' are ed. Hunter Blair, 'The *Moore Memoranda*', p. 246. On the manuscript, see Gneuss and Lapidge, *Anglo-Saxon Manuscripts*, no. 25.

[125] Bede, *VBOH*, ed. Plummer, i. 364–78 (who knew only eight of the surviving witnesses), and by Grocock and Wood in *Abbots*, pp. 21–75; for the transmission, see Lapidge, 'Beda Venerabilis', pp. 74–7, with stemma at p. 76, followed by Grocock and Wood in *Abbots*, pp. ci–cxiii, with stemma at p. cxii, qualified in certain important respects by Winterbottom, 'The text and transmission of some Bedan texts', pp. 449–54.

[126] Gneuss and Lapidge, *Anglo-Saxon Manuscripts*, no. 433; the argument for an origin in Glastonbury was made by Carley, 'More pre-Conquest manuscripts from Glastonbury Abbey', esp. pp. 268–76 and 279–81.

[127] Plummer, *VBOH* i. 365; Grocock and Wood in *Abbots*, p. 24.

THE SOURCES OF THE *HISTORIA REGVM*   liii

HR ii. 6 [= Bede, *Historia abbatum* i. 4]: monasterium… facere praeciperet, ad ostium fluminis Viuri ad laeuam.[128]

> ad laeuam *Harley 3020 (and Durham, CL, B. II. 35)*; ad aquilonem *all other MSS*

HR ii. 11 [= Bede, *Historia abbatum* i. 13]: tanta eos namque affecit infirmitas carnis, ut perficeretur uirtus Christi in eis; cum uero quadam die desideratus eis, se inuicem… uidere et alloqui.[129]

> desideratus *Harley 3020*; desiderantibus *all other MSS*

These three striking variants might suggest that Byrhtferth was quoting Bede directly from Harley 3020; but there are difficulties with this inference. There is no evidence that Harley 3020—which has associations with St Augustine's and Glastonbury—was ever at Ramsey. And there are passages in Byrhtferth's quotations from the *Historia abbatum* which contain variant readings attested neither in Harley 3020 nor in any other surviving manuscript of Bede's work. For example, in Byrhtferth's quotation of *Historia abbatum* i. 1, in the phrase 'regnum in superna felicitate mereretur habere perpetuum' (*HR* i. 4, quoted above), all manuscripts of Bede read *ciuitate*, not *felicitate*; and in his quotation of *Historia abbatum* i. 8, in the phrase 'gloriabatur se singularem per omnia seruare disciplinam' (*HR* ii. 9), all manuscripts of Bede's work read here *regularem*, not *singularem*. If any weight is to be placed on these variants—and they are not simply to be regarded as Byrhtferth's penchant for verbal variety—it would suggest that he was quoting from a close but lost relative of Harley 3020, not from Harley 3020 itself.

HR ii. 15. After discussing at considerable length the monastery of Monkwearmouth–Jarrow and its abbots, Byrhtferth comes at last to the writings of Bede. Given his own scholarly interest in computus, and in the annalistic structure of his *Historia regum*, it is not surprising that he should begin by quoting a poem on the subject, a poem which, in his opinion, had been composed by Bede himself. The poem in question (inc. 'Me legat, annales cupiat qui noscere menses') is a bland comment on the transience of time and the seasons, and has no value whatsoever for computistical reckoning. It is preserved in a substantial number of manuscripts, Continental as well as English, dating from the ninth century onwards, and is most unlikely to be a genuine composition by Bede, since it is in effect a *cento* of lines quoted from

---

[128] Plummer, *VBOH* i. 368; Grocock and Wood in *Abbots*, p. 32.
[129] Plummer, *VBOH* i. 376; Grocock and Wood in *Abbots*, p. 50.

liv INTRODUCTION

Dracontius.[130] Byrhtferth had earlier included this poem in his *Computus*;[131] it was accompanied there, as here, by a hexameter distich describing Bede's authorship of the poem:

> Hos claros uersus uenerabilis edidit auctor
> Beda sacer, multum nitido sermone coruscans.

It is reasonable to suppose that this distich was composed by Byrhtferth himself.

HR ii. 16. While still discussing Bede, Byrhtferth next inserts the entire text of Bede's *Versus de die iudicii* (*CPL* 1370), under the title— possibly supplied by Byrhtferth himself—*Lamentatio Bedae presbyteri*.[132] The *Versus de die iudicii* were a very popular school-text, especially in late Anglo-Saxon England,[133] and are preserved in more than forty manuscripts. A substantial number of textual variants in the transmission makes it possible to identify several distinct manuscript classes.[134] These include a class of manuscripts which circulated largely in England and which preserve in the poem's final lines Bede's personal dedication to Bishop Acca (a); and a second class (β) largely represented by Continental manuscripts, from which the final lines of dedication to Acca have been removed (the identity of a Northumbrian bishop apparently being deemed to be of no interest to a Continental audience). The suppression of the final lines of the poem (156–63) left it with what was felt to be too abrupt an ending; so someone, somewhere on the Continent, composed a filler-line, metrically unworthy of Bede, to conclude the poem; manuscripts with this additional line (line 155) form a subgroup (γ) of the Continental class β manuscripts.

It is clear that the text of the *Versus de die iudicii* available to Byrhtferth at Ramsey belonged to class a, the English class of witnesses.[135] This

---

[130] Ed. most recently by Lapidge in *Bede's Latin Poetry*, pp. 515–17, on the basis of six manuscripts.

[131] See *Byrhtferth's Enchiridion*, ed. Baker and Lapidge, p. 384, on Oxford, St John's College 17, fo. 14^r.

[132] *Bede's Latin Poetry*, ed. Lapidge, pp. 158–79.

[133] See Lendinara, 'The *Versus de die iudicii*'.

[134] Lapidge, 'Beda Venerabilis', pp. 131–7; *Bede's Latin Poetry*, ed. Lapidge, pp. 56–66.

[135] Interestingly, when Byrhtferth had occasion to quote extensively from the *Versus de die iudicii* in his (later) *Vita S. Ecgwini*, the manuscript from which he was quoting belonged to the amended Continental subgroup γ, not to the English class a. I have argued that, when Byrhtferth composed his *Vita S. Ecgwini*, he was resident not at Ramsey but at Evesham, the implication being that he no longer had access to the copy of the poem which he had used at Ramsey in composing his *Historia regum*, and that the copy available for his use at Evesham

THE SOURCES OF THE *HISTORIA REGVM*   lv

can be demonstrated clearly from the following variants in the poem as quoted by Byrhtferth:

> quassatos nec uult <u>animos</u> infringere dextra (25)[136]
> animos α; calamos βγ

> et stupet adtonito simul impia <u>turma</u> timore (86)
> turma α; turba βγ

> quae superant sensus cunctorum et dicta <u>uiuorum</u> (92)[137]
> uiuorum α; uirorum βγ

> sed pax et pietas, bonitas, opulentia <u>regnant</u> (135)
> regnant α; rerum β; regnum γ

In addition to these distinctive α-variants, the text of Bede's poem as quoted by Byrhtferth in the *Historia regum* omits line 155, which, as stated above, is a feature of the subgroup γ of Continental manuscripts.[138] Byrhtferth, then, had access at Ramsey to a copy of the English (α) redaction of Bede's *Versus de die iudicii*; but although a number of Anglo-Saxon manuscripts of this redaction survive, none of them is identical in every respect to the text as quoted by Byrhtferth.

HR ii. 18. This chapter was copied by Byrhtferth from Bede, *HE* v. 23. 3.[139] It includes the following sentence concerning the death of Berhtwald, archbishop of Canterbury: 'Anno Dominicae incarnationis .dccxxxii., Byrhtpaldus archiepiscopus longa consumptus aetate, defunctus est die .v. Iduum Ianuariarum.' In manuscripts of the

---

belonged to the Continental subgroup γ. See Byrhtferth, *The Lives*, ed. Lapidge, p. 226 with n. 56.

[136] The point of the variant *animos / calamos*—the words are indistinguishable in terms of their metrical quantity—is that the verse is based on a passage of Isaiah 42: 3 ('calamum quassatum non conteret'), so that, if the allusion to Isaiah is to be foregrounded, the line as preserved in the Continental manuscripts (βγ)—'quassatos nec uult <u>calamos</u> infringere dextra' ('nor does He wish to snap off broken reeds with His right hand')—may well represent what Bede originally wrote. However, the reading *animos* transmitted by the English group of manuscripts (α) makes explicit the tropological sense which is no doubt present in *calamos*—'nor does He wish to snap off shaken <u>minds</u> with His right hand'—could equally well be what Bede wrote. See discussion in *Bede's Latin Poetry*, ed. Lapidge, pp. 57–8.

[137] In this case the reading *uiuorum* transmitted by the English (α) manuscripts presents a metrical error, for the first syllable of the word is required by position to be short, whereas the first syllable of *ũiuorum* is naturally long. The first syllable of the variant *uĩrorum*, preserved in the Continental manuscripts βγ, is naturally short, and scans correctly in position.

[138] Although the version of the poem copied by Byrhtferth omitted line 155, a later corrector of CCCC 139 at Durham, the scribe I designate C², added line 155 in the margin of C, which implies that the manuscript of Bede's *Versus de die iudicii* available at Durham in the late twelfth century belonged to the Continental subgroup γ.

[139] *HE*, ed. Lapidge, ii. 468; ed. Colgrave and Mynors, p. 558.

lvi INTRODUCTION

Northumbrian redaction of the *HE* (LMB), including the 'Moore Bede' and the 'Leningrad Bede', the day of Berhtwald's death was wrongly given as 13 January ('die Iduum Ianuariarum'); in manuscripts of the Southumbrian or Canterbury redaction (CKO), this error was corrected from local knowledge by supplying *.v.* before *Iduum*.[140] This evidence suggests unequivocally that Byrhtferth's text of the *HE* was a manuscript of the Southumbrian redaction.

HR ii. 19. This long chapter was copied by Byrhtferth from Bede, *HE* v. 23. 4–6.[141] The quoted passage contains no significant textual variants.

HR ii. 20. The description of Bede's life is taken from c. 25 (of Book v) of Bede's *Historia ecclesiastica*, as Byrhtferth himself acknowledges: let the reader 'legat capitulum .xxv. historiae Anglorum gentis'; but note that Byrhtferth has altered Bede's first person verbs to third person, as befits a narrative. The final two hexameters of *HR* ii. 20 are quoted from Arator, *Historia apostolica* i. 226–7—a favourite quotation of Byrhtferth (see above, pp. xlii–xliii).

Part III

Part III consists of a series of annal-entries, dating from 732 to 801. The sources for these entries cannot be established precisely. Scholars have previously assumed that the author (here identified as Byrhtferth) was simply reproducing a single set of annals for those years, compiled probably at York; hence Part III is sometimes referred to as 'the York Annals'.[142] Close attention to the sources of individual entries in Part III suggests instead that it was compiled from a number of individual, pre-existing collections of annals, some of them now lost.[143] These

---

[140] See discussion by Lapidge in *Beda: Storia*, ii. 721, and by Hunter Blair, 'Some observations', p. 86.

[141] *HE*, ed. Lapidge, ii. 468–70; ed. Colgrave and Mynors, pp. 558–60.

[142] For example, Arnold, in *Symeonis Monachi Opera Omnia*, ii, p. xviii: 'For the first 70 years of his period he used the ancient Northumbrian Chronicle, the existence of which was detected ... by Dr Stubbs' (*scil.* in *Chronica Magistri Rogeri de Houedene*, i, p. xxix); Hunter Blair, 'Some observations', pp. 86–99, esp. 87: 'there can be no doubt that this part of the *Historia Regum* has preserved what is basically an eighth-century chronicle'; followed by Lapidge, 'Byrhtferth of Ramsey and the early sections', p. 115 [= *ALL* ii. 335]: '[Part III] is basically a chronicle for the years 732–802. Because this chronicle contains much information about York and Northumbria which is not found elsewhere, it has been plausibly suggested that it is based on a set of annals originally compiled at York (or in the vicinity of York) in the early ninth century.'

[143] There is a reflex of the annals assembled by Byrhtferth in Part III in the so-called 'Ramsey Annals', which are preserved in Oxford, St John's 17 (Thorney, AD 1110–11), fos. 139ʳ–143ᵛ + London, BL, Cotton Nero C. vii, fos. 80ʳ–84ᵛ. The 'Ramsey Annals' are ed. in Hart, 'The Ramsey Computus', pp. 38–44; for the years 733–800 (at pp. 41–2) the skeletal

THE SOURCES OF THE *HISTORIA REGVM*   lvii

sources include two separate and independent annalistic continuations of Bede's *HE*, one for the years 731 to 734 (*Continuatio* [I]), the other for the years 732 (731 being the date at which Bede completed his *HE* and sent it to King Ceolwulf) to 766, the year in which Archbishop Ecgberht of York, King Ceolwulf's cousin, died (*Continuatio* [II]); a set of vernacular annals resembling,[144] but not identical to, the 'northern recension' of the *Anglo-Saxon Chronicle* (represented by MSS DE);[145] and a set of Continental annals treating the rise of Charlemagne and the Carolingian dynasty, similar to, but not identical to, the *Annales regni Francorum* or 'Royal Frankish Annals', known from Continental manuscripts, but not preserved in any English witness. These various annal collections were evidently available at Ramsey *c*.1000; but how they got there is unknown. It is perhaps worth remarking that at least two of the collections—*HE Continuatio* (II) and the Continental annals—have undeniable links with York, and that Oswald, the founder of Ramsey, was archbishop of York. Possibly it was through the agency of Oswald that these texts were acquired by Ramsey's library.

In combining these various distinct annalistic sources so as to make a continuous narrative, Byrhtferth deserves the respect of modern historians, for his procedure is the same as theirs. In addition to these anonymous annal collections, Byrhtferth also drew at various points in Part III on Bede's *HE*. But there are many annalistic entries in Part III which have no correlate in other sources, annalistic or otherwise, and for which Byrhtferth is the sole witness. It is for this reason that his

---

entries in these 'Ramsey Annals' often parallel entries in *HR* Part III, and have been signalled where appropriate in the accompanying notes below. Hart's arguments that Oxford, St John's 17 was written at Ramsey between 1083 and 1092 are nonsense, and could have been avoided if he had looked carefully at the entries on fo. 29ᵛ concerning Gunther, abbot of Thorney (1085–1112); for the Thorney origin of the manuscript, see instead N. R. Ker, *Catalogue of Manuscripts containing Anglo-Saxon* (Oxford, 1957), p. 435 (no. 360), and Lapidge, 'A tenth-century metrical calendar', pp. 348–9 [= *ALL* ii. 365–6].

[144] Byrhtferth seems to refer to these (lost) vernacular annals as the 'historia uel cronica huius patriae' (*HR* iii. 7).

[145] See *The Anglo-Saxon Chronicle*, trans. Whitelock, p. xiv: 'Brit. Mus. Cott. Tiber. B. iv, cited as "D", and Laud Misc. 636 in the Bodleian Library, cited as "E", must also be linked together. Both differ from the versions hitherto discussed in their inclusion in the early part of the Chronicle of much material of northern interest, drawn from Bede and from northern annals which were also available to the author of the twelfth-century work *The History of the Kings* which is ascribed to Simeon of Durham.' The manuscript preserving the D-version (BL, Cotton Tiberius B. iv: see Gneuss and Lapidge, *Anglo-Saxon Manuscripts*, no. 372) was written somewhere in the West Midlands (Worcester?) in the mid- or late eleventh century; that preserving the E-version (Oxford, BodL, Laud Misc. 636) was written at Peterborough in the early twelfth century (s. xii in.). Whitelock concluded (ibid.): 'I have little doubt that the common archetype from which both are derived was compiled at York.'

lviii INTRODUCTION

Historia regum is a valuable source for eighth-century Anglo-Saxon, especially Northumbrian history.

HR iii. 1. The first two sentences of this chapter, concerning Archbishops Berhtwald and Tatwine, are taken from Bede, *HE* v. 24. 1 (ed. Lapidge, ii. 478; ed. Colgrave and Mynors, p. 566). But thereafter, as Byrhtferth passes beyond the chronological limit of Bede's *HE*, he is obliged to rely on different, post-Bedan sources. In the first instance, in *HR* iii. 1–12 (for the years 732–66), Byrhtferth drew on annalistic continuations of Bede's *HE* which are found in a number of manuscripts of Bede's great work. Two such continuations are in question: *HE Continuatio* (I) is a brief set of four annal-entries for the years 731–4 (two of which record astronomical events) which were added to fo. 128^r of the 'Moore Manuscript' (Cambridge, UL, Kk. 5. 16) following the prayer which Bede placed at the end of the *HE* ('Teque deprecor, bone Iesu ... ante faciem tuam');[146] *HE Continuatio* (II) is a more extensive set of nineteen annal-entries, for the years 732 to 766, which is preserved in a number of Continental manuscripts of the *HE*, all dating from the twelfth century or later, but, oddly, not in any manuscript written in England.[147] As Joanna Story has pointed out, the years 732 and 766 define the length of the archiepiscopate of Ecgberht, who was archbishop of York during those years, and who was the cousin of King Ceolwulf, the dedicatee of Bede's *HE*.[148] Although these two continuations of the *HE* are distinct and apparently had different origins, it seems clear that both of them were available to Byrhtferth in Ramsey in the late tenth century, perhaps in separate copies of Bede's *HE*.

In the present chapter (*HR* iii. 1), the sentence stating that King Ceolwulf 'was captured, tonsured, and restored to his kingdom' ('rex

---

[146] The four annal-entries which make up *HE Continuatio* (I) are edited from the 'Moore Manuscript' by Colgrave and Mynors, p. 572, and by Joanna Story, 'After Bede', pp. 183-4. Story argues that these four entries were composed by Bede himself, and were added to (some) manuscripts of the *HE* after the formal completion (and dedication to Ceolwulf) of the work in 731: ibid. pp. 172-4.

[147] *HE Continuatio* (II) is printed by Colgrave and Mynors, pp. 572-7, on the basis of eight manuscripts written in either Germany or the Netherlands between the twelfth and sixteenth centuries. Three more Continental manuscripts (one of the twelfth, two of the fifteenth century) were identified by Joshua Westgard; see discussion of these nineteen annal-entries by Story, 'After Bede', pp. 177-83.

[148] Story, 'After Bede', p. 180: 'This arrangement [*scil.* the chronological extension from 732 to 766] is unlikely to be a coincidence and may indicate that the *Continuatio* was composed at a centre that both favoured Ecgberht's dynasty and promoted the archiepiscopal community at York. It may also imply that the *Continuatio* was considered a "finished" text, beginning and ending with references to Archbishop Ecgberht, before it was exported to the Continent.... The completion and export of a York-focused chronicle shortly after 766 is entirely plausible in this immediate historical context.'

THE SOURCES OF THE *HISTORIA REGVM*　　lix

captus, attonsus, et remissus est in regnum') is taken from *HE Continuatio* (I), as is the statement that Bishop Acca was expelled from his episcopal see ('Acca episcopus eodem anno de sua sede est fugatus'). The following sentence concerning the death of Bishop Cyneberht of Lindsey, however, derives from *HE Continuatio* (II). The murder of Alric and Esc is found in no other source.

HR iii. 2. The statement that Tatwine, archbishop of Canterbury, received the pallium in 733, and then ordained Bishops Aluuig and Sigfrid, is taken verbatim from *HE Continuatio* (II). The following statement, concerning the solar eclipse on 14 August, however, is taken verbatim from *HE Continuatio* (I): 'Anno .dccxxxiii. eclipsis facta est solis .xviii. kal. Sept. circa horam diei tertiam, ita ut pene totus orbis quasi nigerrimo et horrendo scuto uideretur esse coopertus.'[149]

HR iii. 3. The first sentence concerning the eclipse of 734 and the report of the death of Archbishop Tatwine in that year are taken from *HE Continuatio* (I) (ed. Colgrave and Mynors, p. 572; ed. Story, 'After Bede', p. 183). The list of archbishops of Canterbury, from Augustine to Berhtwald, apparently derives from an episcopal list in which the archbishops were given in a numbered sequence (several such lists are preserved in Anglo-Saxon manuscripts, but it is not possible to identify which of these lists Byrhtferth was consulting). The final sentence of the chapter, concerning the ordination of Bishop Frithuberht of Hexham, was suggested by an entry in *HE Continuatio* (II) (ed. Colgrave and Mynors, p. 572), which does not, however, specify Frithuberht's see. This implies that Byrhtferth may have had access to a fuller version of *HE Continuatio* (II) than what has survived in the later Continental manuscripts of these annals printed by Colgrave and Mynors.

HR iii. 4. The first annal-entry in this chapter, for 735, concerning Nothelm of Canterbury, Ecgberht of York, and the death of Bede, was taken verbatim from *HE Continuatio* (II) (ed. Colgrave and Mynors, p. 572), but the following two entries, for 736 and 737, are not found in either of the *HE Continuationes*, and the final entry in this chapter,

---

[149] Ed. Colgrave and Mynors, p. 572; ed. Story, 'After Bede', p. 183. As stated above, *HE Continuatio* (I) is preserved solely in the 'Moore Bede' (Cambridge, UL, Kk. 5. 16), but this manuscript cannot have been Byrhtferth's source, for two reasons: first, the reading *scuto* describing the appearance of the eclipse in Byrhtferth is given (erroneously) as *sicut* in the 'Moore Bede'; and secondly, the 'Moore Bede' had already been taken from England to the Continent by the late eighth or early ninth century, when a brief tract *De consanguinitate* was added in Continental Caroline minuscule on fo. 128[v].

lx INTRODUCTION

concerning Swæfberht of the East Saxons, is not found in any source other than Byrhtferth.

HR iii. 5. The deaths of King Æthelheard and Archbishop Nothelm, given by Byrhtferth against the year 739, are recorded against 740 in *HE Continuatio* (II), but not the information that Cuthred, Æthelheard's brother, succeeded to the West Saxon throne—information which is found s.a. 740 in the *Anglo-Saxon Chronicle* (trans. Whitelock, p. 29). The death of Aldwulf, bishop of Rochester, is not recorded in either of these sources, however. The final entry in this chapter, concerning the death of Æthelwald, bishop of Lindisfarne and the successor of Cynewulf, is found both in *HE Continuatio* (II) against 740 (ed. Colgrave and Mynors, p. 574), as in Byrhtferth, and in *ASC*, but against 737, wrongly for 740 (trans. Whitelock, p. 29).

HR iii. 6. This entire chapter on Bishop Acca is taken nearly verbatim from Bede, *HE* v. 20. 2 (ed. Lapidge, ii. 430; ed. Colgrave and Mynors, pp. 530–2).

HR iii. 7. The statement that Arnwine was killed in 740 has an approximate parallel in *HE Continuatio* (II), s.a. 740: 'Arnuuini et Eadbertus interempti' (ed. Colgrave and Mynors, p. 574). But Byrhtferth's statement that Arnwine was the son of Eadwulf is found nowhere else. The following sentences concerning Archbishop Cuthberht and Dunn, bishop of Rochester, are paralleled in *ASC* s.a. 740 (trans. Whitelock, p. 29), but without the information that Cuthberht was the eleventh archbishop of Canterbury or that Dunn succeeded Aldwulf—information possibly derived by Byrhtferth from an episcopal list like the one laid under contribution at *HR* iii. 3 above. The fire at York in 741 is mentioned in *ASC* s.a. 741 (trans. Whitelock, p. 29); the fiery flashes in the air seen in 745, but never before witnessed by men of that age ('uisi sunt in aere ictus ignei quales numquam ante mortales illius aeui uiderunt') are possibly the shooting stars mentioned against 744 in the *Anglo-Saxon Chronicle* (trans. Whitelock, p. 30). Byrhtferth's next statement in this chapter betrays confusion about the identity of a bishop of York named Wilfrid, who, 'some people say' (*ut quidam referunt*), died in this year (i.e. 745), 'but I say that before Bede had finished his *Historia*, he [Wilfrid] was translated from this world to the lofty realms of the eternal vision' ('nos uero dicimus quod priusquam Beda suam historiam explicuisset, translatus est ex hoc mundo ad celsitudinem aeternae uisionis'). Byrhtferth has confused the first Bishop Wilfrid, who died at Oundle in 710 (as Bede relates in *HE* v. 19. 14), with the second Wilfrid, who was bishop of York from 714 to 732, and

THE SOURCES OF THE *HISTORIA REGVM*   lxi

died in 745.[150] The final statement in this chapter, concerning the death of Ingwald, bishop of London, is taken from *HE Continuatio* (II) (ed. Colgrave and Mynors, p. 574). The remaining two obits—of an unnamed bishop of the Hwicce,[151] and Abbot Herebald—are not mentioned in any of the annalistic sources which Byrhtferth was using.

HR iii. 8. The first entries in this chapter, concerning the death of Ælfwald, king of the East Angles, and the capture of Bishop Cynewulf are not recorded in either *HE Continuatio* (II) or in *ASC*. Offa, the son of Aldfrith, is not known from any other source, but the insurrection of Cuthred, king of the West Saxons, against King Æthelbald of Mercia is taken verbatim from *HE Continuatio* (II), s.a. 750 (ed. Colgrave and Mynors, p. 574). The remainder of the chapter is taken up with description of a lunar eclipse, which Byrhtferth assigns to 31 July 752. No eclipse is recorded against that date in Byrhtferth's known annalistic sources; but *HE Continuatio* (II) records an eclipse of the moon against 24 January 753 (ed. Colgrave and Mynors, p. 574). However, the dates are so different that two separate lunar eclipses may well be in question (in which case the source of Byrhtferth's information is unknown). Byrhtferth's subsequent definition of a lunar eclipse is taken from Isidore, *Etymologiae* iii. 58–9, separated by an irrelevant definition of a solar eclipse which Byrhtferth implies is taken from Pliny (*inquit Plinius*, where the reference is to Pliny's *Naturalis historia* ii. 56), but in fact derives from Bede, *De temporum ratione*, c. 27. This chapter closes with a report of the martyrdom of Boniface and fifty-three companions in 754, in wording very similar to that in *HE Continuatio* (II), s.a. 754 (ed. Colgrave and Mynors, p. 574).

HR iii. 9. The first statement, concerning the death of Cuthred, king of the West Saxons, in 755, and the succession of Sigeberht, is paralleled by a statement in *ASC* (trans. Whitelock, p. 30), where it is assigned to the year 756. The following discussion of the siege of Dumbarton, and the role of King Eadberht in that siege, is found in no other source. The following entries concerning the death of King Æthelbald and the expulsion of Beornred by King Offa in 757, and the

---

[150] Symeon of Durham apparently reproduced Byrhtferth's confused statement without alteration, and thus it was transcribed by the main scribe of CCCC 139; but a later corrector of the manuscript (my C²) attempted to remove the error by writing *ille primus Wilfridus* over *translatus sit*; see the app. crit. to this passage.

[151] Byrhtferth did not realize that the bishop of the Hwicce in question was none other than Wilfrid (II), who apparently held the sees of Worcester and York in plurality, as Bishop Oswald was to do in Byrhtferth's own day.

lxii INTRODUCTION

tonsure of Eadberht, king of Northumbria, in 758, have very close parallels in *HE Continuatio* (II) (ed. Colgrave and Mynors, p. 574).

HR iii. 10. The events of this chapter, concerning Æthelwald Moll and the death of Onust, king of the Picts, are recorded in *HE Continuatio* (II), s.aa. 759 and 761 (ed. Colgrave and Mynors, pp. 574–6), with some of this detail also found in the northern recension of *ASC*, s.a. 761 (trans. Whitelock, p. 32). But other details, for example the marriage of Æthelwald Moll and Queen Æthelthryth, are found in no other source.

HR iii. 11. The chapter begins by recording the death of Ceolwulf, formerly king of Northumbria, but at that time a monk at Lindisfarne, in 764. Bede had dedicated his *Historia ecclesiastica* to Ceolwulf, and Byrhtferth quotes Bede's words of dedication from the *Praefatio* of the *HE*. His quotation contains one striking variant: 'et nunc ad scribendum ac plenius ex tempore meditaturum transmitto'. The only manuscript containing this variant (*meditaturum* for *meditandum* in all other manuscripts) is London, BL, Cotton Tiberius C. ii, a manuscript probably written at St Augustine's, Canterbury, in the second quarter of the ninth century.[152] Either Byrhtferth had access to Cotton Tiberius C. ii or he was quoting from a lost congener. The subsequent entries in the chapter, concerning the destruction of several monasteries by fire, and the death of Abbot Freoholm, are not recorded in any other source. The final entry, concerning the death of Bishop Frithuwald of Whithorn, is paralleled in *ASC*, s.a. 763 (trans. Whitelock, p. 32).

HR iii. 12. The earlier entries in this chapter, pertaining to 765 and 766, have parallels both in *HE Continuatio* (II) (ed. Colgrave and Mynors, p. 576: Alchred, Ecgberht) and in *ASC* D(E), s.aa. 765, 766 (trans. Whitelock, p. 32). The death of Archbishop Ecgberht in 766 is the final entry in *HE Continuatio* (II). Henceforth, Byrhtferth was obliged to draw on other annalistic sources.

HR iii. 13. Much of the information in this chapter (e.g. the burning of Catterick by the 'tyrant' Earnred) is not found elsewhere. The death of King Eadberht in 768 is recorded in the 'northern recension' (MSS. D(E)) of the *Anglo-Saxon Chronicle* (trans. Whitelock, p. 33). Similarly, the notice of the death of Pippin in 768 appears to derive from a Carolingian set of annals related to (but not identical to) the so-called 'Royal Frankish Annals'. It is possible that a copy (now lost) of these annals was acquired by York through the agency of Alcuin, who had

---

[152] See Bede, *HE*, ed. Lapidge, i. 6 *ad app. crit.* The significance of the variant was previously remarked by Hunter Blair, 'Some observations', pp. 90–1. On the manuscript, see Gneuss and Lapidge, *Anglo-Saxon Manuscripts*, no. 377.

THE SOURCES OF THE *HISTORIA REGVM*

lxiii

returned to York from Charlemagne's court for three years (790–3), and thereafter remained in contact with his former home, as a number of letters in Alcuin's correspondence, sent from the Continent to various recipients in Northumbria, clearly attests. Other information in this chapter (e.g. the consecration of Aluberht as bishop of the Old Saxons, the death of the anchorite Echha at Crayke) seems likewise to derive from York sources.

HR iii. 14. Much of the information in this chapter too is not found elsewhere (e.g. the deaths of Sigbald and Ecgric in 771, the deaths of Pictel and Swithwulf in 772), but the death of Carloman, the succession of Charlemagne, and Charlemagne's invasion of the continental Saxons are all recorded in the 'Royal Frankish Annals', a version of which may have been available at York through contact with Alcuin (see above). The death of Wulfhæth, abbot of Beverley, in 773, and the receipt of the pallium by Ælberht, archbishop of York (and Alcuin's mentor), are not known from any other source, but presumably derive somehow from York.

HR iii. 15. The information contained in this chapter is paralleled in various sources: the notice concerning King Alchred being driven into exile is also found in *ASC* D(E), s.a. 774, as is the report concerning Æthelwald Moll's son; the notice concerning the Pictish king Ciniod (Cynoth) was arguably taken from an unidentified Pictish source (the spelling *Cynoth* indicates a Pictish rather than an Irish annalistic source, in which the name would have been spelled *Cináed*); a report concerning Charlemagne's siege of Pavia is contained in the 'Royal Frankish Annals'; and the note about the hand of St Oswald is from Bede, *HE* iii. 12. 3, as Byrhtferth states (*sicut narrat Beda historiographus huius gentis*). Other information in this chapter (e.g. the reports concerning Ealdorman Eadwulf (s.a. 774) and Abbot Ebbi (s.a. 775)) has no known source.

HR iii. 16. The detailed notice of Charlemagne's campaign against the Saxons is paralleled in the 'Royal Frankish Annals', but Byrhtferth's report contains information not found in that source (e.g. the mention of the *prouincia Bohuueri*), which suggests that he had access to a fuller version of these Carolingian annals than what has survived in Continental manuscripts. The entries concerning Pechtwine and Whithorn (s.a. 777), and Æthelbald and Heardberht together with Ælfwald (s.a. 778), have parallels in *ASC* D(E), s.aa. 777, 778 (trans. Whitelock, p. 34).

HR iii. 17. The three events recorded against 780 by Byrhtferth (the burning of Ealdorman Beorn, the death of Archbishop Æthelberht of York, and the resignation of Bishop Cynewulf of Lindisfarne) correspond to entries in *ASC* D(E), s.aa. 779 and 780 (trans. Whitelock, p. 34).

lxiv INTRODUCTION

HR iii. 18. The numerous entries in this chapter are paralleled for the most part in *ASC* D(E) s.aa. 780 (Tilberht), 782 (Werburh), 786 (Botwine; Cyneheard and Cynewulf; the papal legation) (trans. Whitelock, pp. 34–5). Only the notice concerning the consecration of Ealdwulf is not recorded in *ASC*.

HR iii. 20. Most of the entries in this chapter are paralleled in *ASC* D(E), s.aa. 787 and 788 (trans. Whitelock, p. 35). Byrhtferth supplies a few details not found in *ASC*, such as the fact that Abbot Alberht of Ripon was succeeded by Sigred (this succession is recorded in no other source).

HR iii. 21. Some of the entries in this long chapter have parallels in *ASC* D(E), s.aa. 790, 791, and 792 (trans. Whitelock, p. 36), but Byrhtferth's account also contains various pieces of information not found elsewhere (e.g. the murder of Ælfwald's two sons by King Æthelred). Alcuin's letter on image-worship, mentioned s.a. 792, has been lost, as has the *liber synodalis*, which was apparently an account of the Acts of the Second Council of Nicaea (787) sent by Charlemagne to Northumbria (and arguably brought to York by Alcuin when he spent three years there (790–3)).

HR iii. 22. The first few entries in this chapter (concerning the fiery portents and Ealdorman Sicga) are paralleled in *ASC* D(E), s.a. 793. The mention of Lindisfarne, which is separated from the mainland at high tide, prompts from Byrhtferth a digression on high and low (flood and ebb) tides, drawn from Bede, *De natura rerum*, c. 39, and *De temporum ratione*, c. 29. The description of Cuthbert's retreat on Farne Island is from Bede, *HE* iiii. 26. 1–3. On the verse quotations from Aldhelm and Boethius, see below, 'Poetic sources'.

HR iii. 23. The destruction of the 'port of King Ecgfrith' in 794 is recorded in some detail in *ASE* D(E) s.a. 794 (trans. Whitelock, pp. 36–7). The death of Pope Hadrian is recorded both in *ASC* and in the 'Royal Frankish Annals'; but the detailed specification of the length of his papacy (26 years, 10 months, 12 days) was apparently derived from a copy of the *Liber pontificalis*. Charlemagne's destruction of the Avars (called *Huni* here and in Carolingian sources) is described in the 'Royal Frankish Annals', s.a. 796; but the account given there differs in significant respects from what is reported by Byrhtferth, which suggests once again that the version of these annals which he had before him (derived from York, presumably) was not precisely the same as that preserved in Continental manuscripts.

HR iii. 24. Most of the annal-entries for the year 796 in this chapter have parallels in the 'northern recension' (D(E)) of *ASC*, s.a. 796: the

THE SOURCES OF THE *HISTORIA REGVM*   lxv

lunar eclipse, the murder of King Æthelred of Northumbria, the succession of Eardwulf, the death of King Offa of Mercia, the succession of Ecgfrith and then Coenwulf, the death of Archbishop Eanbald, etc. (trans. Whitelock, pp. 37–8). For the two verses quoted from the 'Metrical Calendar of Ramsey', see below, 'Poetic sources'.

HR iii. 25. The events of 798 are recorded in the 'northern recension' of *ASC*, s.a. 798 (trans. Whitelock, pp. 37–8).

HR iii. 26. The proceedings (*acta*) of the synod of Hatfield are quoted verbatim by Byrhtferth from Bede, *HE* iiii. 15. On the verse quotations from Prosper of Aquitaine, see below, 'Poetic sources'.

HR iii. 27. The capture and mutilation of Pope Leo III, which is the principal component of this chapter, is recorded in the 'Royal Frankish Annals'; the pope's miraculous recovery from his mutilations is recorded in the *Liber pontificalis*.

HR iii. 28. The coronation of Charlemagne on Christmas Day 800 is described in the 'Royal Frankish Annals', s.a. 801; the embassy to Charlemagne from Empress Irene is recorded in the same source, s.a. 802, as is the embassy from Jerusalem, s.a. 800.

HR iii. 29. Neither Abbot Eadwine, nor his monastery at Gainford, nor Eardwulf's expedition against Mercia, nor the death of Bishop Heathoberht is known from any other source.

Part IV

Part IV, which concerns the kingdom of Wessex, treats the years from 802 to 887, and—with the exception of a few details derived from a West Saxon regnal list, and some wording from Aldhelm, prose *De uirginitate*—is derived from a single source: Asser's *Vita Ælfredi*. But Byrhtferth's reliance on this single source raises a host of problems, not least because Asser's work is not preserved in any surviving medieval manuscript; it is known from transcripts, often interpolated, of a single lost manuscript once in the library of Sir Robert Cotton, which was destroyed by fire in 1731. Transcriptions and editions of the manuscript were made before its destruction by several early modern scholars, notably Archbishop Matthew Parker (1504–75). That Byrhtferth had access to a manuscript of Asser is seen from his own extensive use of the *Vita Ælfredi* in the present Part IV of his *Historia regum*;[153] indeed,

---

[153] The only reliable edition of Asser's *Vita Ælfredi* is *Asser's Life of King Alfred*, ed. Stevenson. Stevenson knew Byrhtferth's *Historia regum* indirectly through the medium of Symeon of Durham's *Historia de regibus,* as preserved in CCCC 139; in his *apparatus criticus* of Asser he cited the early parts of Symeon's work—what in the present edition constitutes

lxvi INTRODUCTION

he is an important witness to the original state of Asser's text. In order to evaluate the text of Asser as reproduced by Byrhtferth, it is necessary briefly to survey the history of its preservation.[154]

As stated above, the only medieval copy of Asser's *Vita Ælfredi* known to have survived into modern times was a manuscript in the library of Sir Robert Cotton (1571–1631), where it bore his shelfmark Otho A. xii; but this manuscript was completely destroyed in the disastrous fire of the Cottonian library, then housed at Ashburnham House (Westminster), on 23 October 1731. We are therefore dependent on descriptions and transcriptions of the manuscript made before 1731. From these descriptions, it is evident that—like many manuscripts in Cotton's collection—Otho A. xii was a composite manuscript, made up of several originally separate booklets which had been combined by Cotton and his librarians. Asser's *Vita Ælfredi* was the first item in this composite manuscript, occupying fos. 1–55.[155] Before Otho A. xii came into Cotton's possession, however, it had belonged to Matthew Parker, who in 1574 produced an edition of Asser based on it.[156] Unfortunately, this edition cannot be treated as a reliable witness to Asser's original text, because Parker interpolated into it a number of passages from extraneous texts such as the 'Annals of St Neots' (which included the famous story of King Alfred burning the cakes). The first serious scholarly attempt to edit Asser was made over a century later by Francis Wise in 1722, who tried to eliminate Parker's interpolations from the text, and to compose an *apparatus criticus* recording variant readings from Otho A. xii itself, which had been collated for him by James Hill of the Middle Temple.[157] Among the merits of Wise's edition is the fact that he also collated the most important indirect witness to Asser's text, namely the *Chronica* of John of Worcester (which Wise referred to as 'Florence' of Worcester). However, perhaps even more important is

---

HR Parts III–IV, i.e. annal-entries from 732 to 887—as 'SD1' (p. lviii), reserving the sigil 'SD2' for those parts of Asser's work which had been incorporated independently by John of Worcester into his *Chronica* and were subsequently copied from John's *Chronica* by Symeon into his *Historia de regibus* (p. lix). For Symeon's wholesale use of John's *Chronica*, see above, p. xx and n. 28.

[154] A full account of this transmission is given in Lapidge, 'Asser Menevensis ep.'.

[155] The contents of Otho A. xii are known from a catalogue of the Cottonian library published in 1696: Smith, *Catalogus librorum manuscriptorum Bibliothecae Cottonianae*, p. 67. Otho A. xii also once contained the only known copy of the Old English poem 'The Battle of Maldon'. On the manuscript and its contents, see Gneuss, 'Die Handschrift Cotton Otho A. xii'.

[156] *Ælfredi Regis Res Gestae*, ed. Parker.

[157] *Annales Rerum Gestarum Ælfredi Magni*, ed. Wise.

THE SOURCES OF THE *HISTORIA REGVM* lxvii

the fact that he included in his edition a facsimile of the first page of Asser's text in Otho A. xii, which was carefully drawn for him by James Hill. This facsimile shows that the script of Otho A. xii was Anglo-Caroline minuscule of *c.*1000 (s. x/xi), and this dating was confirmed by the pioneering palaeographer Humphrey Wanley (1672–1726), who in a letter of 1721 noted that Asser's text in Otho A. xii was 'not written by one hand but by several', and that its script was very similar to that in a charter of King Æthelred (978–1016), dated 1001, and now preserved as London, BL, Cotton Augustus ii. 22.[158] In other words, the sole manuscript of Asser's *Vita Ælfredi* known to have survived into modern times was written during the lifetime of Byrhtferth, and could therefore hypothetically have been seen and used by him.

But there must have been other manuscripts of Asser in circulation by no later than the early twelfth century, as the evidence of indirect witnesses suggests. John of Worcester, whose *Chronica* extend to AD 1140, clearly had a text of Asser before him.[159] So too did the anonymous compiler of the 'Annals of St Neots', writing at Bury St Edmunds at some point during the third and fourth decades of the twelfth century.[160] Part IV of Byrhtferth's *Historia regum* is itself a third indirect witness to the text of Asser's *Vita Ælfredi*. The interesting but ultimately unanswerable questions are whether Byrhtferth had access to Otho A. xii itself (and, indeed, whether the manuscript of Asser used by Byrhtferth at Ramsey was the same as that used over a century later at not too distant Bury St Edmunds by the compiler of the 'Annals of St Neots') and whether the manuscript used by Byrhtferth was the same as that used by John of Worcester on the other side of the country.

Some sort of answer to these questions can be extrapolated from the *apparatus critici* compiled by Francis Wise in 1722 (based on collation of Cotton Otho A. xii before it had been destroyed) and by W. H Stevenson to accompany his edition of Asser (1904). In particular, it is possible to observe discrepancies between the text of Otho A. xii as reported by Wise and that of the three indirect witnesses as reported

---

[158] Wanley's letter is quoted by Kenneth Sisam, *Studies in the History of Old English Literature*, pp. 148–9, n. 3, as follows: 'My authority for adjusting the age of that exemplar is an original charter of King Æthelred, dated A.D. 1001, which, as to the hand, agreeth very well with the first part of the Asser, Otho A. 12.'

[159] The material derived from Asser, for the years 849 to 887, in John's *Chronica* is printed in *The Chronicle of John of Worcester*, ed. Darlington and McGurk, pp. 260–334.

[160] The annals in question are printed in *The Annals of St Neots*, ed. Dumville and Lapidge, pp. 42–104, with a conspectus of the debts to Asser listed ibid. pp. xlii and lxix–lxii.

lxviii INTRODUCTION

by Stevenson: *Flor.* (= John of Worcester, *Chronica*), *SN* (= the 'Annals of St Neots'), and *SD1* (= Byrhtferth, *HR*, Part IV). Analysis of these variants suggests that the text of Asser's work which was available to John at Worcester was not identical to that available to Byrhtferth at Ramsey (and, possibly, that subsequently available at Bury St Edmunds to the compiler of the 'Annals of St Neots'). But whether either of these two arguably distinct exemplars—let us call them the 'Worcester' and 'East Anglian' exemplars—was the lost manuscript Cotton A. xii cannot be determined decisively. I provide a few examples to illustrate the difficulties involved in assessing the evidence of variant readings.

Let us begin with the first chapter of Asser's *Vita Ælfredi*, in which he provides the genealogy of the West Saxon royal house. This chapter was printed by Parker and Wise, and hence may be presumed to have been present in Otho A. xii. The chapter was copied *in extenso* by Byrhtferth (*HR* iv. 3) and by John of Worcester (ed. Darlington and McGurk, pp. 260–2, s.a. 849) (the 'Annals of St Neots' omit this chapter entirely). At three points John of Worcester supplied entries in the genealogy not found in the Cottonian manuscript: after *Elesa* John added *qui fuit Esla*; after *Geuuis* he added *qui fuit Wig, qui fuit Freawine, qui fuit Freothegar*; and after *Enoch* he added *qui fuit Iared*.[161] None of these additional entries is found in Byrhtferth. This may indicate that John of Worcester's text of Asser preserved a more accurate copy of the West Saxon genealogy than the text laid under contribution by Byrhtferth;[162] but it is also hypothetically possible (if highly unlikely) that the three clauses were simply omitted by Byrhtferth—or by Symeon, or by the later twelfth-century scribe of CCCC 139—through carelessness. But against this latter supposition is the fact that, on the evidence of Wise's (*scil.* James Hill's) collation of the lost Cottonian manuscript, the three clauses in question were already missing from Otho A. xii. On balance, the omission of these three clauses suggests a link between Byrhtferth and Cotton Otho A. xii, and indicates that, by comparison with the exemplar available to John of Worcester, Byrhtferth's exemplar was defective.

In c. 4 Asser describes the great army of Vikings which in 851 came with 350 ships up the Thames to Canterbury and then to London:

---

[161] For the omissions from the Cottonian manuscript, see *Annales Rerum Gestarum Ælfredi Magni*, ed. Wise, p. 4 *ad app. crit.*; and see *Asser's Life*, ed. Stevenson, pp. 2–3.

[162] Darlington and McGurk comment (p. 261, n. 9): 'These are apparent additions to the defective genealogy in As[ser], possibly derived from *ASC*, or just possibly from JW's [*scil.* John of Worcester's] copy of Asser.'

THE SOURCES OF THE *HISTORIA REGVM*   lxix

Eodem quoque anno magnus paganorum exercitus cum trecentis et quin-
quaginta navibus in ostium Tamesis fluminis venit et Doruberniam, id est
Cantwariorum civitatem, <et Lundoniam> (quae est sita in aquilonari ripa
Tamesis fluminis)... depopulati sunt. (ed. Stevenson, *Asser's Life*, p. 5)

The words *et Lundoniam*, which are necessary to the sense (London,
but not Canterbury, is on the north bank of the Thames) and are
undoubtedly original, are preserved in both John of Worcester and the
'Annals of St Neots'.[163] But these essential words were omitted from
Cotton Otho A. xii, as we learn from the *apparatus criticus* of Francis
Wise,[164] and they are likewise omitted by Byrhtferth: 'Eodem anno
magnus exercitus paganorum uenit cum trecentis quinquaginta
nauibus in ostium Tamensis fluminis. Qui Doroberniam, id est,
Cantuariorum ciuitatem, depopulati sunt' (*HR* iv. 3). This suggests
once again the Byrhtferth was drawing on a different exemplar from
that used by John of Worcester, and that—though the evidence is
slender—this exemplar may have been Cotton Otho A. xii itself.

In c. 17 Asser describes the death of King Æthelwulf (in 858) and his
burial at Winchester: 'Defuncto autem Æthelwulfo rege <sepultoque
apud Wintoniam>.'[165] The words *sepultoque apud Wintoniam* were
omitted from the Cottonian manuscript Otho A. xii, but were supplied
by Stevenson from John of Worcester's *Chronica*.[166] They were also
omitted by Byrhtferth, whose account of Æthelwulf's death reads simply: 'Defuncto igitur Æthelwulfo rege glorioso, filius eius... rexit' (*HR*
iv. 5). This omission is another indication (albeit slight) that Byrhtferth's
exemplar of Asser was the lost Cottonian manuscript itself. It was in
any case distinct from the exemplar of Asser used by John of Worcester.

Unfortunately, however, the assessment of variants such as these is
bedevilled by the fact that both Byrhtferth and John of Worcester were
capable of altering the wording of the text of Asser which they were
copying. The kind of alteration introduced by Byrhtferth may be seen
in a minor way in the passage from Asser c. 4 quoted above, where he
moved the main verb *uenit* to an earlier position in the sentence, and

---

[163] *The Chronicle of John of Worcester*, ed. Darlington and McGurk, p. 264; *The Annals of
St Neots*, ed. Dumville, p. 43.
[164] *Annales Rerum Gestarum Ælfredi Magni*, ed. Wise, p. 5 *ad app. crit.*: 'Desunt MS. Cott.'
[165] *Asser's Life*, ed. Stevenson, p. 16.
[166] *The Chronicle*, ed. Darlington and McGurk: 'Defuncto autem illo idibus Ianuarii et
apud Wintoniam sepulto' (p. 274). The 'Annals of St Neots' locate this burial at Steyning:
'Anno .dccclvii. Adheluulfus sepe memoratus rex Occidentalium Saxonum uiam uniuersitatis adiit; quieuit in pace sepultusque est apud Steningam' (ed. Dumville, p. 51). On the basis
of this entry, Francis Wise (p. 13) restored 'Steyning' to the text of Asser, though he mis-
spelled it grotesquely: 'Defuncto autem Æthelwulfo rege sepultoque apud Stemrugam [*sic*]'.

lxx INTRODUCTION

turned Asser's coordinated clause *et Doruberniam...depopulati sunt* into a separate new sentence: *Qui Doroberniam...depopulati sunt.* Changes such as these are perhaps mere tinkering on Byrhtferth's part; but they affect one's impression of the fidelity of his text to Asser's original. Sometimes Byrhtferth's intervention goes far beyond mere tinkering. In c. 33 Asser described the defeat and death of Eadmund, king of East Anglia, in 870. Asser's account is solely concerned with Eadmund's final battle against the Vikings and their subsequent conquest of East Anglia:

Asser c. 33 (s.a. 870)	Byrhtferth, *HR* iv. 8	John of Worcester, p. 286
Eodem anno Eadmund, Orientalium Anglorum rex, contra ipsum exercitum atrociter pugnauit. Sed, proh dolor! paganis nimium gloriantibus, ipso cum magna suorum parte ibidem occiso, inimici loco funeris dominati sunt, et totam illam regionem suo dominio subdiderunt.	Rex autem Eadmundus ipsis temporibus regnauit super omnia regna Orientalium Anglorum, uir sanctus et iustus, sicut finis eius sanctissimae uitae probauit euentus. Eodem uero anno rex praedictus contra ipsum exercitum atrociter et uiriliter cum suis pugnauit.	Eodem anno sanctissimus et gloriosissimus Orientalium rex Eadmundus, ut in sua legitur passione, ab Inguaro rege paganissimo, indictione .ii., .xii. kalend. Decembris die dominico martyrizatus est.

During the course of the tenth century, the cult of Eadmund king and martyr spread beyond East Anglia, largely as the result of the *Passio S. Eadmundi* by Abbo of Fleury (*BHL* 2392), who described Eadmund's death as martyrdom. Byrhtferth—the student of Abbo— could accordingly describe Eadmund as *sanctus et iustus*, and allude to Eadmund's martyrdom in wording which he used frequently elsewhere in his writing (*sicut finis...probauit euentus*: see above, p. xxxi). Only in the final sentence of the quoted example does he revert to Asser's wording (*contra ipsum exercitum...pugnauit*), amplifying it by adding another polysyllabic adverb (*uiriliter*) to Asser's *atrociter*, and stating that he died *cum suis*. A century later, the glory of St Eadmund's martyrdom had become so widely known that John of Worcester could describe him as *sanctissimus et gloriosissimus*, and refer explicitly to Abbo's *Passio S. Eadmundi*, supplying from Abbo (c. 10) the date of Eadmund's martyrdom, *.xii. kalendas Decembris* (20 November). The point is simply that, although both Byrhtferth and John were basing their accounts of Eadmund's death on Asser, they recast Asser's wording

THE SOURCES OF THE *HISTORIA REGVM*   lxxi

according to their own preoccupations—in other words, they cannot be treated as unfailingly reliable witnesses to Asser's original text.

A final example: in the very next chapter (c. 34) Asser records the death of Ceolnoth, archbishop of Canterbury:

Asser c. 34 (s.a. 870)	Byrhtferth, *HR* iv. 8	John of Worcester, p. 286
Eodem anno Ceolnoth archiepiscopus Doroberniae, viam universitatis adiens, in eadem civitate in pace sepultus est.	Eodem anno... Ceolnoth archiepiscopus Doroberniae ciuitatis uiam ueritatis adiit; qui in eadem ciuitate est sepultus a clericis.	Quo etiam anno Ceolnothus Dorobernensis archiepiscopus defunctus, in eadem ciuitate in pace sepultus est.

Here it is clear that both Byrhtferth and John had Asser's text in front of them; they each repeat Asser's final clause—*in eadem civitate in pace sepultus est*—verbatim, though Byrhtferth slightly alters the word order and adds to Asser the minor detail that Ceolnoth was buried by his own clergy (*a clericis*). At first glance it might seem that Byrhtferth's reading *uiam ueritatis* ('the way of truth') for Asser's *viam universitatis* ('the way of all flesh') presents a genuine variant which might be original to Asser; but on balance it seems more likely that *ueritatis* represents a simple scribal error for *uniuersitatis* on the part of Byrhtferth, Symeon, or the scribe of CCCC 139. This example illustrates in a nutshell the problem facing any editor who would attempt to reconstruct the text of Asser on the basis of indirect witnesses.

In addition to Asser, Byrhtferth in Part IV drew briefly on various prose sources (for the poetic sources of the *HR*, see below): a West Saxon regnal list (*HR* iv. 2, with n. 9); Aldhelm, prose *De uirginitate* (*HR* iv. 6, with n. 37, from *De uirginitate*, c. 1; *HR* iv. 13, with n. 94, from *De uirginitate*, c. 4; and *HR* iv. 16, with n. 123, from *De uirginitate*, c. 20); and—possibly—the anonymous *Historia de sancto Cuthberto* (*HR* iv. 12, 13, and 15, with nn. 85–6, 91, and 109). The possible use of the last-named source is problematic, because the author, date, and origin of this work are uncertain: it was apparently composed by a member of the community of St Cuthbert (resident at Durham after 995) in order to provide a record of all the community's dependencies; but whether it was composed in the tenth century or the eleventh is uncertain.[167] In some respects, the wording of this

---

[167] The various evidence is surveyed by Johnson South in *Historia de sancto Cuthberto*, ed. Johnson South, pp. 25–36, who inclines to think, on balance, that 'the *Historia* is a product of

lxxii INTRODUCTION

work closely resembles that of Byrhtferth's *HR* (identical wording is underlined):

Historia de sancto Cuthberto, c. 20: Eodem quoque tempore bonus <u>episcopus Eardulfus et abbas Eadred</u> tulerunt <u>corpus sancti Cuthberti de Lindisfarnensi insula</u> et cum eo errauerunt in terra, portantes illud <u>de loco in locum</u> per septem annos. (ed. Johnson South, p. 58)

Byrhtferth, *HR* iv. 12: <u>Earduulfus episcopus et abbas Eadredus, de Lindisfarnensi insula corpus sancti Cuthberti</u> tollentes, per nouem annos ante faciem barbarorum <u>de loco ad locum</u> fugientes, cum illo thesauro discurrerunt.

These close verbal parallels could perhaps best be explained on the assumption that Byrhtferth was drawing here on the *Historia de sancto Cuthberto*. But (as always) the problem is that we do not have an early manuscript of Byrhtferth's *HR*, but only a transcription of his work by Symeon of Durham, which raises the possibilty that the passages concerning St Cuthbert in Byrhtferth were interpolated into the *HR* by Symeon; and this suspicion receives some support from the fact that all the details concerning St Cuthbert which are reported by Byrhtferth—the years of wandering with the saint's remains (*HR* iv. 12), King Alfred's dream-vision of St Cuthbert (*HR* iv. 13), and the dream-vision of St Cuthbert by Eadred, abbot of Carlisle (*HR* iv. 15)—are to be found in Symeon's *Libellus de exordio atque procursu istius, hoc est Dunhelmensis, ecclesie* (*LDE*), often in wording strikingly similar to what is found in Byrhtferth's text.[168] Considerations such as these led the editor of the *Historia de sancto Cuthberto* to conclude that this text was composed no earlier than the (late) eleventh century, a dating which implies that the *Historia de sancto Cuthberto* could not have been available to Byrhtferth at the end of the tenth century.

But there is a further complication. Ælfric of Winchester, later abbot of Eynsham (d. *c*.1010), who was an exact contemporary of Byrhtferth, compiled for his own use a 'hagiographical commonplace-book', containing saints' Lives (including his own *Vita S. Æthelwoldi*) and excerpts from saints' Lives on which he subsequently drew in composing his vernacular *Lives of Saints*.[169] This 'hagiographical

---

the mid to late eleventh century' (p. 36)—that is to say, that it probably postdates the lifetime of Byrhtferth.

[168] See *LDE*, ed. Rollason, ii. 5, ii. 10, and ii. 13 (pp. 94–5, 110–11, and 124–5, respectively).

[169] The arguments for identifying this 'hagiographical commonplace-book' as a compilation by Ælfric were first made in *Wulfstan of Winchester: Life of St Æthelwold*, ed. Lapidge and Winterbottom, pp. cxlvii–cxlix, and are presented more fully in Lapidge, *The Cult of St Swithun*, pp. 553–7. The attribution of this compilation to Ælfric is accepted by modern

THE SOURCES OF THE *HISTORIA REGVM*   lxxiii

commonplace-book' is preserved in a single manuscript, written either in England or in Normandy in the late eleventh century, now BnF, lat. 5362, fos. 1–84 (England [or Normandy?], s. xi[ex]).[170] Interestingly, among the contents of this commonplace-book is c. 33 of the *Historia de sancto Cuthberto* (on fos. 53[v]–54[r]).[171] There were close intellectual contacts between Winchester and Ramsey, and a text known to Ælfric at Winchester could arguably also have been known to Byrhtferth at Ramsey: Byrhtferth, for example, had acquired a copy of Wulfstan of Winchester's *Vita S. Æthelwoldi* very soon after its composition in 996, and quotes verbatim from it in his *VSO*. Possibly too he had acquired from Winchester a copy of the *Historia de sancto Cuthberto*. Unfortunately, it is not possible to state categorically that the *Historia de sancto Cuthberto* was a source laid under contribution by Byrhtferth in his *Historia regum*, though, as we have seen, it could possibly have been; but equally possibly, the materials concerning St Cuthbert could have been interpolated into Byrhtferth's original text at Durham.

Poetic sources (Parts I–IV)

One of the characteristic features of Byrhtferth's Latin prose is that it is frequently adorned with quotations from earlier Latin verse.

Aldhelm, *Enigmata*: in *HR* iii. 22, Byrhtferth quotes *Enigma* no. vi; the variant reading *cumulato* (in lieu of the word *redundans* in line 4) suggests that he was quoting from a copy of Aldhelm's second, corrected recension of the *Enigmata*.[172] Byrhtferth frequently quotes or paraphrases lines from Aldhelm's *Enigmata* in his other writings: *VSO* iii. 1 (*Enigm.* xlvi. 1–5), iii. 4 (*Enigm.* lxxiii. 6), iv. 4 (*Enigm.* li. 2, lii. 4), v. 1 (*Enigm.* xxxix. 1), *VSE* ii. 12 (*Enigm.* xc. 1), iv. 10 (*Enigm., praef.*).

Arator, *Historia apostolica*: Byrhtferth frequently quotes two lines of Arator's poem (i. 226–7) as a sort of personal prayer, as he calls it: here in *HR* ii. 20, and several times in the *Enchiridion* as well as in *VSE Epil.*; for discussion of his use of these two lines, see above, pp. xlii–xliii.

---

students of Ælfric: see Jones, '*meatim sed et rustica*', pp. 3, n. 12, and 18; and Kleist, *The Chronology and Canon of Ælfric of Eynsham*, pp. 146–8 and 257.

[170] See Gneuss and Lapidge, *Anglo-Saxon Manuscripts*, no. 885. 3, and Lapidge, *The Cult of St Swithun*, pp. 555–6 (which provides a detailed list of the contents of BnF lat. 5362).

[171] The existence of the copy of c. 33 in BnF lat. 5362 was known to Johnson South (*Historia de sancto Cuthberto*, p. 117), but he was unaware of the association of this manuscript with Ælfric, and therefore with arguments for dating the *Historia de sancto Cuthberto* to the late tenth century.

[172] See the *apparatus criticus* to Ehwald's edition (MGH, *AA* xv. 101), with discussion by Lapidge, 'Aldhelmus Malmesberiensis abb.', pp. 19–26.

lxxiv   INTRODUCTION

Bede, *Versus de die iudicii*. Byrhtferth quotes the entirety of Bede's poem, which he (or the scribe of CCCC 139) entitles *Lamentatio Bedae presbyteri*, in *HR* ii. 16. Variant readings indicate clearly that Byrhtferth was quoting from a copy of what I have called the α-recension of the *Versus* (that is, the recension preserved principally in English manuscripts of the work, as against those which underwent substantial revision at the hands of Continental scribes). Byrhtferth knew this poem well, for he quoted from it again in *VSE* i. 11 (but from a different exemplar); see discussion above, p. liv and n. 135.[173]

Boethius, *metra* from *De consolatione Philosophiae*. To judge solely from Byrhtferth's numerous quotations of these *metra*—there are fifteen separate quotations in the *HR* alone—Boethius must have been Byrhtferth's favourite poet. The quotations are as follows: *HR* ii. 2 (i met. ii, lines 3, 25, 27; and ii, met. vii, lines 12–14), iii. 20 (ii, met. ii. 1–2), iii. 22 (i, met. v, lines 29–36), iii. 27 (iv, met. v, lines 21–2), iii. 29 (iii, met. i, lines 7–10; and iii, met. ix, lines 10–12), iv. 1 (iv, met. vi, lines 27–9; and iv, met. v, lines 21–2), iv. 7 (ii, met. ii, lines 19–20; and i, met. v, lines 46–8), iv. 9 (iii, met. iv, lines 1–3, 7–8), and iv. 16 (iii, met. iv, lines 1–4 and 17–22).[174] *Metra* from *De consolatione Philosophiae* are also quoted frequently in Byrhtferth's other writings: *VSO* i. 1 (ii, met. iv, lines 4–7, 22), i. 4 (ii, met. iii, line 5), iv. 1 (i, met. iii, lines 7–8), v. 11 (iii, met. x, line 13); *VSE* iv. 10 (i, met. iii, lines 1–3). This represents a substantial number of quoted lines, many of which offer variants from the standard printed text (CCSL xciv, ed. L. Bieler); but, unfortunately, the *apparatus criticus* in this standard edition is not sufficiently detailed (that is, reporting collation of a sufficient number of manuscripts) to allow the possibility of identifying what type of text Byrhtferth was using. The quotation of Boethian *metra* in *VSO* iv. 1 is accompanied by what appear to be glosses taken by Byrhtferth from the manuscript of Boethius he was using, and some of these glosses apparently derive from the (unprinted) commentary on Boethius by Remigius of Auxerre; significantly, perhaps, these same Remigian glosses have been copied to accompany the text of Boethius in two Anglo-Saxon manuscripts of *De consolatione Philosophiae* contemporary with the lifetime of Byrhtferth: Cambridge, Trinity College, O. 3. 7 (St Augustine's, Canterbury, s. x²), and Cambridge, UL, Kk. 3. 21

---

[173] Byrhtferth also quoted from a computistical poem (inc. 'Me legat annales') which he attributed to Bede at *HR* ii. 15; see discussion above, p. liii.

[174] In addition to these quotations from the *metra*, Byrhtferth twice quotes a famous sentence from the prose portions of *De consolatione* concerning philosopher kings (i, pr. 5) at *HR* iii. 28 and iv. 11.

THE SOURCES OF THE *HISTORIA REGVM* lxxv

(?Abingdon, s. xi[1]).[175] This implies that the manuscript of Boethius quoted by Byrhtferth carried the commentary of Remigius of Auxerre alongside the *De consolatione Philosophiae*; but the manuscript in question cannot be identified among surviving copies of that text.

Caelius Sedulius, *Carmen paschale*. Byrhtferth quotes three lines from this widelyread poem of Sedulius at *HR* iv. 3; however, the quotation is not taken directly from the *Carmen paschale*, but indirectly by way of Asser's *Vita Ælfredi*, who quotes ten lines of the poem in order to elucidate the name *Geta* (which Asser mistakenly identified with *Geat* in the West Saxon royal genealogy); Byrhtferth reproduced the first three of the ten lines quoted by Asser.

'Metrical Calendar of Ramsey'. This metrical calendar (*MCR*), consisting of 128 hexameters, was composed at Ramsey shortly after the death of Bishop Oswald in 992, possibly by Byrhtferth himself. In *HR* iii. 24 Byrhtferth quotes two lines of the poem concerning the Nativity of the Virgin (8 September). The 'Metrical Calendar of Ramsey' is preserved solely as part of Byrhtferth's *Computus*;[176] it is quoted on three occasions by Byrhtferth in *VSO*: *VSO* iii. 17 (*MCR* line 91), v. 11 (*MCR* line 112), and v. 17 (*MCR*, lines 32–3).

Prosper of Aquitaine, *Epigrammata*. In *HR* iii. 26, Byrhtferth includes four quotations from the *Epigrammata* of Prosper (*CPL* 526) in order to illustrate Christian belief in the indivisible Trinity. These quotations correspond to *Epigr.* ciiiA–D in the recent edition of Prosper's *Epigrammata* by A. G. A. Horsting: CSEL vol. c (Berlin and Boston, 2016), pp. 154–6. One variant in the text of *Epigr.* ciiiB quoted by Byrhtferth makes it possible to determine that he was quoting from a manuscript belonging to Horsting's δ-group, which consists of four English manuscripts, three of them contemporary with the lifetime of Byrhtferth.[177]

untraced. In *HR* ii. 12 Byrhtferth quotes a single line in an unknown metre: 'Nox ruit hibernis algida flatibus'. According to the electronic databases, this line does not occur elsewhere, but is modelled on two lines of Vergil—*Aen.* viii. 369 ('*Nox ruit*') and ii. 339 ('orbis, et <u>hibernis</u> parcebant <u>flatibus</u> Euri'—and has a structure unattested elsewhere, consisting of the first part of a hexameter (as far

---

[175] See Byrhtferth, *The Lives*, ed. Lapidge, p. 97, n. 8; these two manuscripts are listed Gneuss and Lapidge, *Anglo-Saxon Manuscripts*, nos. 193 and 23, respectively.

[176] *Byrhtferth's Enchiridion*, ed. Baker and Lapidge, pp. 391–415; ed. in Lapidge, 'A tenth-century metrical calendar from Ramsey', pp. 348–58 [= *ALL* ii. 365–75].

[177] See below, pp. 108–10, nn. 170–3.

lxxvi INTRODUCTION

as the penthemimeral caesura) followed by two dactyls ('algida flatibus').

THE TRANSMISSION OF THE *HISTORIA REGVM*

It might seem odd to attempt to discuss the transmission of a work which is preserved in a single manuscript; but the fact that the work was composed at Ramsey, probably during the last decade of the tenth century, and is preserved in a manuscript from Durham dated *c.*1170 (CCCC 139) raises the question of how and when the work was transmitted from Ramsey to Durham.

The earliest witness to the availability of Byrhtferth's *Historia regum* at Ramsey is the anonymous *Passio SS. Ethelredi et Ethelbricti*, which is preserved uniquely in Oxford, BodL, Bodley 285, fos. 116[r]–120[v].[178] The origin of this manuscript is unknown, but the fact that it contains copies both of the anonymous *passio* of SS. Æthelred and Æthelberht and on fos. 99[v]–108[r] of Goscelin's *Vita, miracula et translatio S. Ivonis*, concerning a Persian bishop whose remains were discovered at *Slepe* (modern St Ives, Hunts.) and translated to Ramsey in AD 1002,[179] suggests that the manuscript was written at Ramsey. The date of Bodley 285 cannot be precisely established: as David Rollason has pointed out, the latest datable text which it contains is a letter by Pope Celestine III (1191–8) concerning the canonization of Peter of Tarentaise in 1191;[180] so perhaps a date of *c.*1200 for the manuscript is appropriate, as Neil Ker suggested.[181] The implication is that the anonymous *Passio SS. Ethelredi et Ethelbricti* was composed sometime before that date. The essential point, however, is that the anonymous author based his *passio* on the earlier *passio* of these royal martyrs by Byrhtferth, as incorporated in Part I of his *Historia regum*: the anonymous author's Latin style

---

[178] See Hardy, *Descriptive Catalogue*, i. 263–4 (no. 685), and *BHL* 2641–2. The text is ed. from Bodley 285 by Rollason, *The Mildrith Legend*, pp. 90–104.

[179] See Hardy, *Descriptive Catalogue*, i. 184–5 (no. 515); and *BHL* 4621–3. Goscelin's account of the Life and Translation of St Ivo was dedicated to Herbert Losinga, abbot of Ramsey (1087–1090/1); it thus provides a rare fixed point in Goscelin's hagiographical activity before he took up permanent residence at St Augustine's, Canterbury, in 1089. On the hagiography relating to St Ivo, see Edgington, *The Life and Miracles of St Ivo*, pp. 79–86. There is no satisfactory edition of Goscelin's Life of St Ivo based on all four surviving manuscripts (see Love, 'Goscelinus sancti Bertini mon.', pp. 239–42, esp. 242: 'An extremely interesting text awaits its editor.'). For now, see *Acta SS.*, *Iun.* ii [1698], pp. 288–92 (repr. PL clv. 81–9) + *Chronicon Abbatiae Rameseiensis*, ed. Macray, pp. lix–lxxv; a later set of miracles, printed ibid. pp. lxxvi–lxxxiv, are probably not by Goscelin. See also above, p. xlv, n. 100.

[180] Rollason, *The Mildrith Legend*, p. 89.

[181] *Medieval Manuscripts in British Libraries*, i. 89; see also Madan, Craster, Hunt, and Record, *A Summary Catalogue of Manuscripts*, pp. 359–60 (no. 2470).

THE TRANSMISSION OF THE *HISTORIA REGVM* lxxvii

has evidently been influenced by Byrhtferth's flamboyant verbosity (especially in the use of superlative adjectives); and in describing the miracles which accompanied the translation of the royal martyrs from Wakering to Ramsey, he reproduced nearly verbatim Byrhtferth's chapter (*HR* i. 7) concerning the miracle of the stolen sheep.[182] But whereas in Byrhtferth's account the miracle is reported to have taken place while the martyrs' remains were still at Wakering, in the anonymous *passio* the same miracle is reported to have taken place *after* the remains had been translated to Ramsey.

A copy of Byrhtferth's *Historia regum* was still available at Ramsey in the mid-fourteenth century, for a catalogue of Ramsey's library, compiled at that time and preserved in London, BL, Cotton Rolls II. 16,[183] contains the following entry: 'Passio sanctorum Ethelredi et Ethelbricti et Beda de die'.[184] Richard Sharpe identified this item as a copy of the anonymous *Passio SS. Ethelredi et Ethelbricti*, as edited by Rollason (see above). But the fact that the *passio* was followed by 'Beda de die' (that is, a copy of Bede's *Versus de die iudicii*) suggests instead that the book in question contained (at least) Parts I and II of Byrhtferth's *Historia regum*, in which Part I contains the *passio* of SS. Æthelred and Æthelbert and Part II a complete copy of Bede's *Versus de die iudicii*.

The next question is how a copy of Byrhtferth's *Historia regum* got from Ramsey and into the hands of Symeon at Durham.[185] The question is unfortunately unanswerable, but there is independent evidence which helps to illuminate Symeon's links with Ramsey, namely the configuration of Ramsey saints' and feast days which were commemorated in Symeon's aforementioned Cantor's Book, now Durham, Cathedral Library, B. IV. 24 (see above, p. xix). The second item in this

---

[182] Rollason, *The Mildrith Legend*, p. 103 ('Accidit ut quidam ... multas gratias agens').

[183] The catalogue is ed. by Macray, *Chronicon Abbatiae Rameseiensis*, pp. 356–67, and by Richard Sharpe in R. Sharpe, J. P. Carley, R. M. Thomson, and A. G. Watson, *English Benedictine Libraries: The Shorter Catalogues* (Corpus of British Medieval Library Catalogues, iv; London, 1996), pp. 350–415, where it is printed as no. B68. The catalogue lists 609 books, indicating that Ramsey at that point had one of the largest monastic libraries in England.

[184] *Chronicon Abbatiae Rameseiensis*, ed. Macray, p. 360; Sharpe *et al.*, *English Benedictine Libraries*, p. 377 [item no. 243].

[185] Cf. the comments of David Rollason ('Symeon of Durham's *Historia de regibus*', p. 110): 'Symeon of Durham was evidently in touch with a range of centres of learning. The fact that he had Byrhtferth's *Historia regum* suggests that at once. How had he obtained it? Had it come north with the two Peterborough monks Æthelric and Æthelwine, who became successively bishops of Durham from 1041 to 1071? Or had it been unearthed by the busy researches in the Ramsey archives of Symeon or one of his "historical workshop"?'

lxxviii INTRODUCTION

book is a copy of the *Martyrologium* of Usuard of Saint-Germain-des-Prés on fos. 12^r–39^v,[186] which has undergone substantial augmentation since it was compiled by Usuard, probably in the years 858 × 860.[187] The first phase in the process of augmentation evidently took place at Fleury, where commemorations were added to record the acquisition by Fleury of the relics of the Holy Cross (24 February) and of the relics of St Benedict (11 July).[188] The next phase in this process of augmentation took place at Ramsey, and it is not difficult to think that a copy of Usuard's *Martyrologium*, suitably augmented with entries relevant to Fleury, was brought to Ramsey by Abbo of Fleury when he came to teach there during the years 985–7. By whatever means the Fleury-augmented copy of Usuard got to Ramsey, it was further augmented by a sequence of entries pertaining to saints culted specifically at Ramsey:[189]

[8 March] Ipso die sancti Felicis qui fuit predicator et episcopus Orientalium Anglorum quique nunc cum magna gloria honoratur in monasterio Hramesyge ubi et conditus iacet.[190]

[15 April] Eodem die translatio sancti Oswaldi archiepiscopi.[191]

[10 June] Ipso die translatio sancti Yuonis episcopi et confessoris.

[17 October] In Ramesiensi coenobio sanctorum Ethelredi et Ethelbyrti martyrum.

Symeon copied these entries into his Cantor's Book from a now lost manuscript of Usuard's *Martyrologium* which had come to Durham by way of Ramsey. This documented acquisition of a Ramsey book by Durham's precentor could reasonably have been accompanied by the acquisition of a copy of Byrhtferth's *Historia regum* from the same

---

[186] The augmented text of Usuard's *Martyrologium* in Durham B. IV. 24 was copied by Gullick's Scribe A, whom Gullick convincingly identifies as Symeon himself: 'The scribes of the Durham Cantor's Book', p. 94.

[187] On Usuard's *Martyrologium*, see Dubois and Lemaitre, *Sources et méthodes de l'hagiographie*, pp. 114–17; the text is ed. in *Le Martyrologe d'Usuard*, ed. Dubois.

[188] See discussion by Piper, 'The Durham Cantor's book', p. 82.

[189] Concerning these additions Piper notes: 'These [additions] have at least one clear local focus: the Fenland monastery of Ramsey' (ibid.); and he goes on to note that 'the transmission of a text from Fleury to Ramsey would not be surprising' (p. 83). The entries which are additional to Usuard's original *Martyrologium* and are preserved in Durham B. IV. 24 are printed by Piper, ibid. pp. 92–4.

[190] Felix, bishop of the East Angles, is treated by Bede, *HE* iii. 18 and 20. His remains were discovered at Soham (Cambs.) and translated to Ramsey during the abbacy of Æthelstan (1020–43) and the reign of King Cnut (1016–35), hence between 1020 and 1035. There is an account of the translation in *Chronicon Abbatiae Rameseiensis*, ed. Macray, pp. 127–8.

[191] Archbishop Oswald was the founder of Ramsey Abbey; he died and was buried at Worcester on 29 February 992; his remains were translated at Worcester on 15 April 1002, as we learn from *John of Worcester: Chronicle*, ed. Darlington and McGurk, p. 452 (s.a. 1002).

THE TRANSMISSION OF THE *HISTORIA REGVM* lxxix

source, which would have had particular interest for Symeon because it described the martyrdom of two saints whose feast day he copied into his Cantor's Book against 17 October.

There is reason to think that Symeon reproduced the text of Byrhtferth's *Historia regum* very accurately, and that he did not attempt to rewrite it according to his own sense of Latin prose style (which, to judge from his *LDE*, was significantly different from that of Byrhtferth). Some index of Symeon's accuracy may be gleaned from the spelling of Old English names in the Byrhtferthian portions of his *Historia de regibus*, as preserved in CCCC 139, in particular in the ways in which he carefully reproduced the Old English letters ð (eth), þ (thorn), and ƿ (wynn). None of these letters was used by Anglo-Norman scribes, and they disappeared from Anglo-Saxon script very soon after the Norman Conquest. The fact that Symeon apparently took care to reproduce them suggests that he was closely following his exemplar of Byrhtferth's *Historia regum*. It is even possible that we can see something of the appearance of this exemplar in the interlinear glosses added to the text of Byrhtferth by the correcting scribe whom I designate C^1: as I shall suggest below, the interlinear corrections added by C^1, who was apparently a contemporary of the main scribe (C) of CCCC 139, may have been alternative readings (possibly by Byrhtferth himself) recorded in the copy of Byrhtferth's text which had been used some forty years earlier by Symeon himself; whereas Symeon had omitted these alternative readings, the contemporary corrector thought they should be included. They are valuable for the light which they *may* throw on Byrhtferth's original.

This is not to say, however, that Symeon made no changes of any kind to the text of Byrhtferth. There are various passages, particularly in Part IV of the *HR*, where materials relating to the church of Lindisfarne and the congregation of St Cuthbert may well have been interpolated into Byrhtferth's original text. These passages occur in *HR* iv. 12, 13, and 15 (see below, with nn. 86, 91, 109). Since their content is very closely paralleled both in the anonymous *Historia de sancto Cuthberto* (a text which was well known to Symeon, inasmuch as he laid it under contribution in his *LDE*)[192] and in Symeon's *LDE* itself, it is arguable, to say the least, that these passages represent interpolations in the original text of Byrhtferth's *Historia regum*. There may be more such passages. Only on stylistic grounds could such-and-such a passage in the *HR* be confidently ascribed to Byrhtferth.

---

[192] *Symeon of Durham: Libellus de exordio*, ed. Rollason, pp. lxxii–lxxiii.

lxxx INTRODUCTION

There are also numerous later redactions of Symeon's *Historia de regibus*. One such redaction is the so-called *Historia post Bedam*, a Durham compilation of the mid-twelfth century,[193] preserved complete in two manuscripts written at Durham *c.*1150: London, BL, Royal 13. A. VI, and Oxford, St John's College 97. The *Historia post Bedam* itself has never been printed (its entire contents are derivative of other sources, and it presents no historical information not found elsewhere, so it is of little interest to editors and historians); but it was reproduced with very little alteration by a somewhat later historian who had access to Durham materials, Roger of Howden (d. 1201). Roger carefully reproduced in the early part of his *Chronica* the *Historia post Bedam*, up to the year 1148,[194] and this work in turn reproduced much of the content of Symeon's *Historia de regibus*, including portions of text which had been copied by Symeon from Parts II, III, and the beginning of IV of Byrhtferth's work.[195] However, it is clear from variant readings in Roger's *Chronica* that his text simply reproduces— via the *Historia post Bedam*—that part of Symeon's work as it is preserved in CCCC 139, and not Symeon's Durham exemplar of Byrhtferth's original work, as may be seen from variant readings in Roger's text (I cite just a few of these, by way of example; many more could be cited; page numbers refer to vol. i of Stubbs's edition, and references to Byrhtferth's *HR* refer to alphabetical exponents in the *apparatus criticus* of the *HR*, printed below):

p. 4 (= *HR* iii. 1, n. *b*): scripturarum (addition by C^2)
p. 4 (= *HR* iii. 3, n. *a*): gallicinium (with C^2)
p. 5 (= *HR* iii. 3, n. *b*): Christiane fidei et religionis (addition by C^2)
p. 5 (= *HR* iii. 3, n. *c*): doctissimus (with C^2)
p. 5 (= *HR* iii. 5, n. *a*): diem (as in C)

---

[193] Gransden, *Historical Writing*, pp. 225–6.

[194] See *Chronica Magistri Rogeri de Houeden*, ed. Stubbs, i, pp. xxvi–xl, esp. pp. xxviii–xxix (on the parts of the *Historia post Bedam* deriving ultimately, via Symeon of Durham, from Byrhtferth's *Historia regum*, Part III), and p. xxx (on the parts of the *Historia post Bedam* deriving ultimately, again via Symeon, from the early chapters of Byrhtferth, *Historia regum*, Part IV). As Stubbs observed, the first part of Roger's *Chronica* 'is an exact copy from an older original [i.e. the *Historia post Bedam*] ... which almost to a certainty was originally made at Durham' (p. xxvii).

[195] *Chronica Magistri Rogeri de Houeden*, ed. Stubbs, i. 3–4 (= *HR* ii. 1–2, 20), i. 4–18 (= *HR* iii. 1–29), and i. 18–19 (= *HR* iv. 1–2). After describing the death of Brihtric (material ultimately from Byrhtferth, *HR* iv. 2), Roger abandons Symeon (as purveyed by the *Historia post Bedam*) and turns to Henry of Huntingdon as a source for the remainder of the ninth century.

PREVIOUS EDITIONS   lxxxi

In a word, Roger of Howden's *Chronica* and *ipso facto* the *Historia post Bedam* are not independent witnesses to the original text of Byrhtferth's *Historia regum*, but are merely transcriptions—direct and indirect—of CCCC 139.

PREVIOUS EDITIONS

The *editio princeps* of Symeon's *Historia de regibus Anglorum et Dacorum* (and with it the text we now know as Byrhtferth's *Historia regum*) was published in 1652 by Sir Roger Twysden, as part of his *Historiae Anglicanae Scriptores X*, with the text of Symeon's *Historia de regibus* occupying cols. 85–256, of which cols. 85–132 reproduce Byrhtferth's *Historia regum*.[196] Twysden's edition of the Byrhtferthian parts of Symeon's work is a careful transcription of the text of CCCC 139. Twysden did not compose an *apparatus criticus*, so it is not always possible to see where he has silently corrected the transmitted text (e.g. by correcting *nulla* at *HR* i. 3, n. *g*, to *nullo*), and where he has simply reproduced what is obviously scribal error (e.g. *agmentatis* at *HR* i. 2, n. *b*). Unlike Symeon (and the original scribe of CCCC 139), Twysden makes no attempt to reproduce Anglo-Saxon letter forms such as þ and ð, which are printed as **th**, or ƿ (wynn), which is printed as **w**. In terms of layout, in what corresponds to Part III of Byrhtferth's *HR*, each annal is printed separately (rather than in paragraphs combining several annal entries), beginning with an enlarged capital *A* (for *Anno*), and the relevant years (in arabic numerals) marked in the margin. With the annals for 740 and 781, concerning Bishops Acca and Alchmund respectively, Twysden included the 'Hexham interpolations', which in the present edition have been relegated to Appendix II, below, insofar as they manifestly did not form part of Byrhtferth's original text. In spite of these reservations, Twysden's edition, at least as far as the text of Byrhtferth is concerned, is a largely accurate and reliable transcription of CCCC 139.

It was nearly two hundred years before the next edition of Symeon was published, this time by Henry Petrie (posthumously) as part of his huge *Monumenta Historica Britannica*, in 1848.[197] Petrie did not

---

[196] *Historiae Anglicanae Scriptores X*, ed. Twysden and Selden (2 vols.; London, 1652).

[197] *Monumenta Historica Britannica*, ed. Petrie with Sharpe. Petrie's edition formed the basis for an English translation by Joseph Stevenson, as part of his huge collected edition of translations of medieval English historians, *The Church Historians of England*, iii/2: *The Historical Works of Simeon of Durham* (1855); that part of Symeon's work which reproduced Byrhtferth's original *Historia regum* is on pp. 425–81 of this volume of Stevenson's translation.

lxxxii INTRODUCTION

attempt to publish the entirety of Symeon's *Historia de regibus*, but printed only the early parts of that work, for the years up to 957, that is to say, that portion of Symeon's text which incorporated the four Parts of Byrhtferth's *Historia regum*, plus the annals for 888–957 subsequently attached (by Symeon?) to Byrhtferth's work and printed here as Appendix I.[198] Petrie's edition is, like Twysden's before him, a very careful transcription of CCCC 139. He provides a skeletal *apparatus criticus*, which sometimes indicates that readings incorporated in his text were marginal additions in the manuscript (e.g. at *HR* ii. 3, n. *a*, Petrie incorporates in his text the erroneous words *et anno septimo regni eiusdem natus est Beda magnus*, which are words added by C^2 to the original text, but he notes in his *apparatus criticus*: 'In margine MS.'); but on other occasions, however, he fails to note that words taken into his text were marginal additions by the correcting scribes of C (as when, at *HR* i. 8, n. *b*, he incorporates the words *ad calorem nimium*, which had been omitted by the original scribe of C, but were supplied in the margin by C^2), which is simply to say that Petrie's recording of variant readings is somewhat inconsistent. Sometimes he corrects a transmitted spelling silently (e.g. at *HR* i. 2, n. *b*, he prints *augmentatis* where C reads *agmentatis*, and silently corrects the erroneous *nulla* to *nullo* at *HR* i. 3, n. *g*), but elsewhere fails to correct erroneous readings such as *stabili* (*HR* i. 3, n. *d*). He does not attempt to reproduce the Anglo-Saxon letter forms, but reproduces þ and ð as th, and ƿ as w. As Twysden had done before him, Petrie prints the annal entries in Part III as individual items, and includes in Part III the 'Hexham interpolations' concerning Bishops Acca (s.a. 740) and Alchmund (s.a. 781), but indicates in marginal notes that these entries concerning the two Hexham bishops date from centuries later than their deaths (e.g. against the mention of Thomas of York in the notice of Acca he notes in the margin 'A.D. 1113', and with the mention of Malcolm, king of Scots in the notice of Alchmund, he adds the note 'A.D. 1054–93'). His *apparatus criticus* frequently contains references to related texts which supply variant readings, such as the 'Chronicle of Melrose' (which he refers to as *Chr.Mail.*) and the *Chronica* of Roger of Howden (which he refers to as *Hoved.*). Petrie's text is clearly laid out and accurately printed, and, as far as its reproduction of Byrhtferth is concerned, is accurate and largely reliable.

---

[198] The portion corresponding to Byrhtferth's *Historia regum* is printed in *Monumenta Historica Britannica*, ed. Petrie with Sharpe, pp. 645–88.

PREVIOUS EDITIONS   lxxxiii

Twenty years after the publication of Petrie's *Monumenta Historica Britannica*, John Hodgson-Hinde published an edition of Symeon of Durham's *Historia de regibus* in a volume for the Surtees Society. In some respects, Hodgson-Hinde's edition marks an important step forward in recognizing (what we can now call) the Byrhtferthian parts of Symeon's work as being a work composed earlier than Symeon's compilation and subsequently incorporated by him, and in realizing that the accounts of the cults of Bishops Acca and Alchmund were later interpolations in the original text.[199] In other respects, however, his edition was retrograde. Hodgson-Hinde wished to foreground the annalistic nature of Symeon's text, and to this end he introduced centred headings which supplied the year of each separate annal in roman numerals. Such a procedure was not appropriate for Part I of Byrhtferth's *HR*, namely the *passio* of the royal martyrs Æthelred and Æthelberht; so Hodgson-Hinde separated the *passio* from the remainder of Symeon's (Byrhtferth's) text, and moved the rubric describing the entirety of Symeon's work (quoted above, p. xviii), which in CCCC 139 occurs immediately before the beginning of the *passio*, to a position immediately before the beginning of what corresponds to Part II of Byrhtferth's work (the genealogy of Northumbrian kings), in effect segregating the *Passio SS. Æthelredi et Æthelberhti* from the remainder of the work. By the same token, since the greater portion of Byrhtferth's Part II (the account of the abbots of Monkwearmouth–Jarrow, the quotations from Bede's verse, especially the complete *Versus de die iudicii*) is not in annalistic form and could not be adapted to Hodgson-Hinde's annalistic schema, he simply eliminated from his text the entirety of (what corresponds to) Byrhtferth's *HR* ii. 3–20.[200] In terms of the Latin text itself, Hodgson-Hinde made no attempt to reproduce

[199] *Symeonis Dunelmensis Opera et Collectanea*, ed. Hodgson-Hinde. The portions of Symeon's *Historia de regibus* incorporating Byrhtferth's much earlier *Historia regum* are printed on pp. 1–61 of Hodgson-Hinde's edition. For his recognition that the Byrhtferthian portions of Symeon's work were earlier than Symeon himself, see his Introduction, pp. xiv–xvi; and for his recognition that the 'Hexham interpolations' are later than the (Byrhtferthian) context in which they occur, see p. xxiv.

[200] Ibid. p. xii: 'Besides the two pieces which precede the *History of the Kings* in the present volume [*scil.* the *Passio SS. Æthelredi et Æthelberhti* and the genealogy of Northumbrian kings], there are in the MS., interposed between the rubric and the body of the work, many pages of extracts from the writings of Bede, including a large portion of the *Lives of the Abbots of Jarrow and Wearmouth*, with several Latin poems, one of them of considerable length [*scil.* the *Versus de die iudicii*]. As all these are accessible in the collected editions of Bede's works, it has not been thought necessary to reproduce them here, especially as they exhibit no marks of that manipulation to which the Northumbrian chronicle and the version of Asser have been subjected.'

lxxxiv INTRODUCTION

the Anglo-Saxon letter forms which Symeon (and the later scribe of CCCC 139) had faithfully reproduced, representing ð as **d**, þ as **th**, and ƿ as **w**. Sometimes he silently corrected corrupt spellings in CCCC 139 (e.g. at *HR* i. 2, n. *b*, the transmitted *agmentatis* is silently corrected to *augmentatis*, *pulcherrimo* at i. 3, n. *f*, to *pulcherrime*, and *nulla* at i. 3, n. *g*, to *nullo*). His handling of interlinear additions to the text by the corrector whom I designate as C² (see below) is inconsistent: some-times he silently incorporates an interlinear addition by C² into his text (e.g. at *HR* iii. 3, n. *c*, he prints the word *doctissimus* without noting that it is an interlinear addition), but in the same chapter he omits the words *uel Christiane fidei et religionis* (an addition by C²) from his text, but notes in his *apparatus criticus* (p. 12): 'Interlined are the words, which Twysden prints unnecessarily'. In what corresponds to Byrhtferth, *HR* i. 8 (at n. *b*), Hodgson-Hinde incorporates the words *ad calorem nimium* into his text, without noting that they are an addition by a later scribe (my C²). In short, Hodgson-Hinde's edition of Symeon's *Historia de regibus* will have some value for modern historians who pre-fer to have their historical sources presented in the form of annals; but his text is far from being a faithful representation of Symeon's (and Byrhtferth's) text as transmitted in CCCC 139.

Seventeen years after Hodgson-Hinde's edition, in 1885, Thomas Arnold produced a new edition of Symeon's *Historia de regibus* as the second volume of his two-volume edition of *Symeonis monachi Opera omnia* for the Rolls Series. In terms of accuracy and fidelity to Symeon (and incidentally to Byrhtferth), Arnold's edition represents an important advance on those of his predecessors. He presents Symeon's text as a sequence of prose paragraphs, not a sequence of annal-entries, so that a paragraph may on occasion enclose five or six separate annal-entries. In terms of the Latin text itself, Arnold fol-lowed the practice of his predecessors and represented the Anglo-Saxon letter forms used by Byrhtferth and copied by Symeon as Roman letters, so that ð and þ were reproduced as **th**, and ƿ as **w**. He silently corrected erroneous spellings in CCCC 139, so that, for example, at *HR* i. 2, n. *b*, the transmitted *agmentatis* is silently corrected to *augmentatis*, *pulcherrimo* at i. 3, n. *f*, to *pulcherrimae*, *nulla* at i. 3, n. *g*, to *nullo*, and *aumento* at i. 3, n. *j* to *augmento*. Like Hodgson-Hinde before him, Arnold's treatment of later additions and corrections to CCCC 139 is inconsistent: thus, at *HR* i. 8 n. *b*, he silently incorporates the words *ad calorem nimium* without indicating that they are a marginal addition by a later scribe (my C²), and similarly at *HR* iii. 3 n. *c*, he incorporates the word *doctissimus*, again without noting that it is an addition by a later

PREVIOUS EDITIONS   lxxxv

scribe; yet in the same chapter (iii. 3), he notes that the words *uel Christiane fidei et religionis* (*HR* iii. 3, n. *b*) have been added to *Christianitatis* by a later scribe: 'Interlined, in a hand considerably later, are the words "vel Christianae fidei et religionis" ' (p. 31, n. *a*). And although Arnold did not compose a separate register of *apparatus criticus*, at various points where he suspected that the transmitted text was corrupt he recorded his doubts in the accompanying notes, often supplying a conjectural correction (e.g. at *HR* i. 8 n. *e*, where the transmitted text reads *formauit*, Arnold sensibly suggested the reading *firmauit* (p. 12 n. *a*), or at *HR* iii. 15, where the transmitted text has the nonce form *coenulentis*, Arnold notes, rightly, *coenulentae?* (p. 46, n. 1)). He rightly recognized that the lengthy treatments of the later cults of Bishops Acca and Alchmund of Hexham (s.aa. 740 and 781) were twelfth-century interpolations into an earlier source, which he correctly deduced had been composed in the tenth century (see above, p. xxii). In short, if Byrhtferth's *Historia regum* is to be read within the larger framework of Symeon's *Historia de regibus Anglorum et Dacorum*, Arnold's presentation is both serviceable and accurate.

Finally, an attempt to present Byrhtferth's text separately from that of Symeon was made in 2006 by C. R. Hart.[201] Hart's Latin text is crawling with error, and it is clear that he simply did not know Latin well enough to undertake an edition of this sort. To illustrate this assertion I list a few egregious errors from Part I (page references are to Hart's 'edition'; references to the present edition are given in parentheses): p. 8 (i. 3) *nominae* (for *nomine*), *vinere feliciter* (for *uiuere feliciter*); p. 10 (i. 3) *successuorum* (for *successurorum*), *celcitudinis* (for *celsitudinis*); p. 12 (i. 5) *frangorem* (for *fragorem*), *recentus* (for *recentis*), *cogitantionibus* (for *cogitationibus*); p. 18 (i. 8) *funerat* (for *fuerat*), *coniugum* (for *coniugium*), *descernens* (for *decernens*); p. 20 (i. 8) *Dietatis*

---

[201] *Byrhtferth's Northumbrian Chronicle*, ed. Hart. The late C. R. Hart was a country doctor who developed an amateur interest in Anglo-Saxon history and became obsessed with Byrhtferth, whom he came to regard as the author of a huge corpus of historical works dating from the late tenth and early eleventh centuries: not only the *Historia regum* (which he persisted in referring to as 'Byrhtferth's Northumbrian Chronicle', even though the first part is wholly concerned with Kent, and the last part with Wessex), but also the B-text of the *Anglo-Saxon Chronicle*, the 'lost precursor' (as he calls it) of the C- and DE-texts of the *Anglo-Saxon Chronicle*; the Old English version of Bede's *Versus de die iudicii* which passes under the name *Be domes dæge*; an 'East Anglian Chronicle' which underlies the *Annals of St Neots*; another Latin Chronicle which underlies the *Chronica* of John of Worcester; and—most absurdly of all—the *Vita Ælfredi* of Asser. Unfortunately, his knowledge of Latin (let alone of Old English) was simply inadequate for the historical task which he set himself. His edition of Byrhtferth's 'Northumbrian Chronicle', as he calls it, was published by a vanity press at his own expense.

lxxxvi INTRODUCTION

(for *Deitatis*), *perculsis* (for *perculsus*), and *corpuis* (for *corpus*). He is frequently unable to tell where one Latin word ends and another begins (so the text is full of constructions such as *ad inventionum* and *cuius libet*). He refers throughout to Bede's verses on Judgement Day as 'de Dei iudicii' (pp. 50–63 *et passim*)—it would be interesting to know how he would construe this title—and to Prosper's *Epigrammatica* (pp. lxxix, n. 2, and 154). The English translation has been lifted, without acknowledgement of any kind, and with very little modification, from that of Stevenson. In short, Hart's 'edition' is simply worthless for scholarly purposes.

EDITORIAL PROCEDURES

The aim of the present edition is to present, through a strategy of editorial reconstruction, Byrhtferth's *Historia regum* in the form in which it was transmitted to Durham and then largely reproduced by Symeon as the first part of his *Historia de regibus Anglorum et Dacorum*. The first and easiest step was to remove the two 'Hexham interpolations' concerning Bishops Acca and Alchmund, since—on internal evidence—they were composed long after Byrhtferth's death (the two interpolations are printed below as Appendix II, but do not form part of Byrhtferth's *HR*), and then to remove the annals for the years 888–957, since these are so distinct from Byrhtferth's usual flamboyant Latin style that they must represent an appendage and can have formed no part of his original design (the annals are printed below as Appendix I). The residue falls naturally into four separate parts: the *passio* of the Kentish martyrs Æthelred and Æthelberht; early Northumbrian history focused on Monkwearmouth–Jarrow and the writings of Bede; eighth-century northern history, largely in annalistic form, from the death of Bede to the beginning of the ninth century, concerned principally with the kingdoms of Mercia and Northumbria; and the history of Wessex, largely based on Asser's *Vita Ælfredi*, up to 887. I take it that this fourfold division, with each part being concerned with a separate English kingdom, was Byrhtferth's original design, since other writings of his—the *Enchiridion* and *Vita S. Ecgwini*—are likewise divided into four parts (the *Vita S. Oswaldi*, which is much longer, is divided into five); within the *Historia regum* the divisions are clearly marked, as for example, when the end of Part II is signalled by the quotation of two lines of Arator which Byrhtferth elsewhere named his personal prayer (*oratio patris Byrhtferði*), and which in the *Historia regum* serve to mark the end of a part, exactly as they were used in the *Enchiridion*

EDITORIAL PROCEDURES   lxxxvii

to mark the end of Part II of that work, and in the *Vita S. Ecgwini* to mark the end of the *Epilogus*.

Within each of the four parts, clearly demarcated, I have followed the example of Thomas Arnold and arranged the material in paragraphs of varying length,[202] rather than as separate annal-entries, as was the practice of editors before Arnold. It will be clear that Symeon simply disregarded Byrhtferth's fourfold division, and that the paragraphing and sporadic rubrication which are found in CCCC 139 are the contribution of the late twelfth-century Durham scribe.

In many ways, however, Symeon appears to have reproduced Byrhtferth's text faithfully. This is particularly noticeable in the use of Anglo-Saxon letter forms—eth (ð), thorn (þ), and wynn (ƿ)—in the spelling of Old English names. These letter forms had been discontinued by Norman scribes, who typically substituted **th** for eth and thorn, and **w** for wynn. It is inconceivable, therefore, that a Durham scribe writing *c.*1170 will have been familiar enough with Anglo-Saxon scribal practice to impose these letter forms on the text as transmitted to him: that is to say, the Anglo-Saxon letter forms in the spelling of names must have been faithfully preserved and reproduced by Symeon from the (lost) Ramsey exemplar of Byrhtferth's *Historia regum* which he had before him. He seems even to have taken care to reproduce one of Byrhtferth's idiosyncratic spelling habits, namely the use of **-y-** in the second theme **-byrht** of Old English personal names, whereas other Late West Saxon scribes typically used **-e-** (hence his spelling *Æthelbyrht* rather than *Æthelberht*, and so on).

The use of the Anglo-Saxon letter forms eth (ð), thorn (þ), and wynn (ƿ), then, very probably goes back to Byrhtferth's exemplar. But even in Byrhtferth's day the letter wynn was falling out of use, and was increasingly being replaced by **uu** (lower case) and **V** or **Vu** (upper case). Norman scribes introduced **w** and **W** to replace them. Accordingly, when the scribe of CCCC 139 writes **w** or **W**, we may be quite sure that he is not reproducing a letter form from Byrhtferth's original (as mediated by Symeon); I have accordingly replaced C's **w** or **W** with **uu** and **Vu**, as being the more likely scribal practice of Byrhtferth himself. Likewise with the letter **k**: Anglo-Saxon scribes did not use this letter, except in calendrical reckonings (.iii. Kal. Maii, for example), whereas

---

[202] I have adopted Arnold's paragraphing, but my numbering of the individual paragraphs is, of course, different, since I begin the number sequence at the beginning of each of the four parts. Arnold did not attempt to impose Byrhtferth's fourfold division into parts, and hence numbered all paragraphs consecutively from beginning to end (§§1–80).

lxxxviii INTRODUCTION

Anglo-Norman scribes tended to use **K** in lieu of **C** in English names beginning with the theme **Cyne-**. I have accordingly restored **C** in places where the scribe of CCCC 139 wrote **K**.

When we turn from orthography to the wording of the text itself, matters become more complicated: it is simply not possible—given that Byrhtferth's text was reproduced by Symeon, and then Symeon's text was copied by the scribe(s) of CCCC 139—to be certain that each and every word in CCCC 139 derives ultimately from Byrhtferth. Byrhtferth's authorship can be ascertained over extended passages of text, because of his tendency to reuse favourite phrases and quotations, and his idiosyncratic and flamboyant manner of expressing himself. Such passages declare themselves overall to be the work of Byrhtferth; but whether every single word in such a passage was his cannot be confidently ascertained: we must always reckon with the possibility of interpolation by Symeon or a later scribe. Nevertheless, on the whole, Byrhtferth's Latin style is so instantly recognizable that we can be confident of his authorship of the text as a whole.

We know from his other writings that Byrhtferth had various orthographical tics. Thus he spells compound words derived from Latin *fari* with *-ph-* rather than *-f-*. The spelling with *-ph-* is used only in medial positions within words, never at the beginning; but so consistently is this idiosyncratic practice found in his other writings that I have thought it appropriate to impose it on spellings in the *Historia regum*: thus I print *prephatus* rather than *prefatus*, *multipharius* rather than *multifarius* (on the assumption that the spellings with *-f-* in the text of CCCC 139 represent corrections by either Symeon or a later scribe). By the same token, but for obscure reasons, Byrhtferth characteristically spells *nempe* as *nemphe*, and I have imposed this idiosyncratic practice on the text of the *Historia regum*.

There is finally the question of the marginal and interlinear additions and corrections in CCCC 139. As we have seen, earlier editors treated these additions in a very inconsistent manner, sometimes incorporating them silently into the text, sometimes omitting them. I have attempted to adopt a more consistent approach, by distinguishing text copied by the main scribe from alterations made by subsequent scribes. Thus I distinguish:

C = the main Durham scribe of CCCC 139, fos. 52ra–74vb

C^1 = a correcting scribe, apparently contemporary with C or nearly so, who may possibly have been working from the same exemplar of Byrhtferth's text as Symeon had used. It is possible that some of the

EDITORIAL PROCEDURES lxxxix

additions by C^1—particularly those introduced by the conjunction *uel*—reproduce interlinear additions from the exemplar used by Symeon, which conceivably were added by Byrhtferth himself (e.g. at *HR* ii. 9, n. *a*, where C^1 added the gloss *uel communem* over *singularem*; or, in the same chapter, at n. *c*, where C^1 added *uel inquietudinis* over *iniquitatis*). It is possible that additions such as these represent Byrhtferth's own further thoughts; but certainty is impossible when we are reading a text through so many layers of copying and recopying.

C^2 = a later scribe, whose script is crude and ungainly, who at times attempted to correct the content of Byrhtferth's text (see, e.g. his alterations to Byrhtferth's account of Bishop Wilfrid II of York, at *HR* iii. 7), and frequently added supplementary information that was extraneous to Byrhtferth's original (e.g. the observation that King Ecgfrith had unjustly destroyed Ireland at *HR* ii. 2, n. *d*, or the (erroneous) addition to Byrhtferth's statement concerning the construction of the monastery at Monkwearmouth, to the effect that Bede was born in the seventh year of Ecgfrith's reign, at *HR* ii. 3, n. *a*).

The additions by both C^1 and C^2 must have been made before the end of the twelfth century, for they were incorporated wholesale by the anonymous Durham compiler of the (unprinted) *Historia post Bedam*, which was subsequently reproduced *in extenso* by Roger of Howden in his *Chronica*, which was completed before Roger's death in 1201. The date of Roger's death thus provides a *terminus ante quem* for the contributions of the two annotating scribes of CCCC 139. In any case, the additions made by C^2 did not form part of Byrhtferth's original *Historia regum*, and have therefore been omitted from the present text, and relegated to notes in the accompanying *apparatus criticus*. The additions by C^1 have likewise been removed from the text; whether some or all of them go back to Byrhtferth himself, must remain an open question.

HISTORIA REGVM

ᵃ\<PARS PRIMA\>ᵃ

fo. 52ʳᵃ **1.**[1] Anno ab incarnatione Dominica .dcxvi., qui est uicesimus primus ex quo sanctissimus Augustinus cum sociis ad praedicandum missus est, Æþelberht rex Cantuariorum, post regnum temporale quod .l. et .vi. annis gloriosissime tenuerat, aeterna caelestis regni subiit gaudia.[2] Erat autem idem rex filius Irmirici, cuius pater Octa, cuius pater Oiric ᵇ\<cognomento Oisc\>,ᵇ cuius pater Hengest, qui cum filio suo Oisc a Þirtigerno rege inuitatus Britanniam primus intrauit,[3] ut Beda luculento describit sermone. Eadbaldus uero filius Æþelbyrhti regni gubernacula suscepit; qui genuit duos filios, Eormenredum atque Earconbyrhtum.[4] Eadbaldus rex, transiens ex hac uita, Earconberhto sceptra dereliquit imperii. Hic primus regum Anglorum in toto regno suo idola relinqui ac destrui praecepit; simul et ieiunium quadraginta dierum obseruari principali auctoritate iussit.[5] Cui natus est filius nomine Ecgberhtus.[6] Natique sunt Eormenredo Æþelberhtus atque Æðelredus; quorum

---

i.1 ᵃ⁻ᵃ *suppl. ed.*; C *supplies the rubric*: Incipit passio sanctorum Ethelberti et Ethelredi regie stirpis puerorum ᵇ⁻ᵇ *suppl. ed. (from Bede)*

---

[1] The first part of Byrhtferth's *Historia regum* is taken up with an account of the murder of two innocent Kentish princes, Æthelred and Æthelberht, an event which is to be placed sometime during the reign of King Ecgberht of Kent (664–73). The princes' bodies were first buried secretly on the royal estate at Eastry (Kent), but their remains were subsequently translated to a minster church at Wakering in Essex (see below, *HR* i. 6), where they remained for several centuries. From Wakering they were translated to Ramsey by that abbey's lay patron, Ealdorman Æthelwine of East Anglia, *c*.990 (978×992). Wakering was an estate belonging to Æthelwine, according to the later Ramsey *Passio SS. Ethelredi et Ethelbricti* [*BHL* 2641–2] preserved uniquely in Oxford, BodL, Bodley 285 (ed. Rollason, *The Mildrith Legend*, pp. 89–104, at 102: 'inclito duce Ethelwino, in cuius uilla reperti sunt tumulati'). The translation to Ramsey occasioned the composition of the *Passio SS. Æthelredi et Æthelberhti* [*BHL* 2643], perhaps on commission by Æthelwine. Stylistic evidence indicates clearly that the *passio* was composed by Byrhtferth of Ramsey, probably in the early 990s; it was subsequently incorporated by him into the *Historia regum* by way of illustrating early Kentish politics. On Byrhtferth's source-text for his *Passio SS. Æthelredi et Æthelberhti*, a lost version of the 'Mildrith legend', see Introduction, pp. xlv–xlix; on surviving sources for these two Kentish martyrs, see Blair, 'A handlist of Anglo-Saxon saints', p. 507.

[2] The words 'Anno ab incarnatione Dominica .dcxvi...subiit gaudia' are from Bede, *HE* ii. 5, quoted verbatim (except that the words *subiit* and *gaudia* have been transposed). Bede's statement poses various difficulties: first, if Æthelberht died in 616, in the twenty-first year after Augustine's arrival in England, the implication is that Augustine arrived in 595, whereas in all other sources, and in Bede's own narrative (*HE* i. 23–4), the date of Augustine's arrival is given as 597. Secondly, the length of Æthelberht's reign—fifty-six years—seems extraordinarily long, and is possibly an error (see Brooks, 'The creation and early structure of the kingdom of Kent', pp. 65–7, who suggests that Æthelberht may have

PART I

1.[1] In the year of the Lord's Incarnation 616, which is the twenty-first from the year in which the very holy St Augustine was sent out with his colleagues to preach [the gospel], Æthelberht, king of the people of Kent, after a temporal reign which he had held gloriously for fifty-six years, entered the eternal joys of the celestial realm.[2] This same king was the son of Irminric, whose father was Octa, whose father was Oiric also known as Oisc, whose father was Hengest, who having been invited by King Wirtigern first entered Britain[3] with his son Oisc, as Bede describes in limpid prose. Then Eadbald, the son of Æthelberht, took up the reins of government; he fathered two sons, Eormenred and Earconberht.[4] King Eadbald, passing from this life, left the sceptres of rule to Earconberht. Earconberht was the first of English kings to order that the idols in his entire kingdom be abandoned and destroyed; at the same time he ordered with princely authority that a fast of forty days be observed.[5] A son by the name of Ecgberht was born to him.[6] To Eormenred were born Æthelberht and Æthelred; it is appropriate to insert an account of their life and the triumph of their martyrdom at

---

become king of Kent between 580 and 593, not in 560, which is more plausibly to be taken as the date of his birth). Byrhtferth is unlikely to have been much concerned with chronological problems of this sort.

[3] The words 'Erat autem ... primus intrauit' are quoted from a later point in the same chapter of Bede's *HE* (ii. 5. 2): '<u>Erat autem idem</u> Aedilberct <u>filius Irminrici, cuius pater Octa, cuius pater Oeric</u> cognomento Oisc, a quo reges Cantuariorum solent Oiscingas cognominare, <u>cuius pater Hengist, qui cum filio suo Oisc inuitatus a Vurtigerno Brittaniam primus intrauit</u>.' I have supplied Bede's words *cognomento Oisc* to Byrhtferth's text, to make it clear that Oeric and Oisc are the same person. The account of Vortigern's invitation to Hengest is in Bede, *HE* i. 14. 2; on Vortigern, see H. M. Chadwick, 'Vortigern'.

[4] Eadbald, the son of King Æthelberht, was king of Kent from 616 until his death on 20 January 640. The statement that Eadbald 'regni gubernacula suscepit' is from Bede (*HE* ii. 5. 3), but the statement that he fathered two sons—Eormenred and Earconberht—is not in Bede, who mentions only that Eadbald was the father of Earconberht (see following note), and makes no mention of Eormenred anywhere in the *HE*.

[5] Earconberht, the son of King Eadbald, was king of Kent from 640 until his death on 14 July 664. The words 'Eadbaldus rex ... principali auctoritate iussit' are from Bede, *HE* iii. 8. 1 (with minor verbal adjustments). At the beginning of the same chapter Bede states that Eadbald died in 640; but Byrhtferth, having given a single date at the beginning of the present chapter, declined to give any more.

[6] Bede (*HE* iiii. 1. 1) says only that when Earconberht died in 664, he left the throne of his kingdom to Ecgberht his son ('Earconberctus rex Cantuariorum ... defunctus, Ecgberct filio sedem regni reliquit'). Ecgberht (I) was king of Kent from 664 until his death on 4 July 673.

HISTORIA REGVM

uitam et passionis triumphum in exordio nostrae historiae placet inserere,[7] et gloriam sanctitatis eorum demonstrare.

2. Erat namque rex Æþelbyrhtus perfectus in imperio gloriosae potestatis; qui delectatus summopere uerbis diuinae agnitionis, tinctus est baptismate salutis. Cuius studio uel sagaci auxilio ubique ecclesiarum Dei diffusus est status, et rerum suarum collatione fidelium roboratus extitit conuentus. Vnde regni monarchia sollertissime pro sibi illato posse disposita, uocante (sequi enim inter omnia fecerat) iusti remuneratoris clementia, carnalibus priuatur, et ad ardua aetheris cum sanctis regnaturus sustollitur. Huic uero in regiminis sumministratione | succedit filius Eadbaldus, sicut superius praephati sumus; de quo procreantur bini regalis stirpis filii, Eormenredus et Earconbyrhtus, quorum iunior imperialis principatum regni patre disponente suscepit. Post autem Earconbyrhti decessum, filius ipsius nomine Ecgbyrhtus illud potenter gubernauit.[8] Eormenredus uero maior absque imperii dominio in huius caducalis uitae permansit uolubili stadio: cui iusto ex iustissima coniuge nati sunt filii duo. Qui, nutriti in herili caelestis regis palatio, multimodis sunt ditati aeternae gloriae munere regio. Quorum unus onomate nituit Æðelredus, alter uero uocabulo fulsit Æþelbyrhtus. Namque in eorum natali sanctissimo, cuncti, ut remur, laetati sunt beatorum spirituum ordines in caelo, quia quos in terris destinari conspiciebant, ipsos fortiores post huius uitae grauia certamina ad se redituros uidebant. Gauisa est telluris sublimitas, se ornari sentiens duplicis doni gratia; et quia ex nimio multatur contrariorum infortunio, se semper sperat immeliorari tali subsidio. Gratulatur insuper et mater sancta ecclesia dum sui tanto sponsi illustratur dotalitio, quo et meritorum luce melius resplendeat et semper in sanctioris rectissimum aequitatis culmen crescat. Huius nemphe praecellentis doctrinae utero traditi—ut sine accuratis disciplinae magistralis loquamur eloquentiis—primo omnium in serenissimo sanctae meditationis illius

---

[7] Byrhtferth now abandons Bede's *HE* in order to develop the narrative of Eormenred's two sons, Æthelberht and Æthelred; the language becomes correspondingly less Bedan and more Byrhtferthian: with the present wording ('in exordio nostrae historiae placet inserere'), cf. *VSO* i. 3 ('placuit hic inserere'), iii. 19 ('in fine huius modici operis placet inserere'), etc., with discussion by Lapidge, 'The early sections', p. 106 = *ALL* ii. 326; and, for similar formulations, see *HR* ii. 3, iv. 8 (below, pp. 24, 140), and Introduction, above, p. xxx.

[8] Byrhtferth repeats—but in his own florid wording—the substance of the previous chapter concerning the Kentish royal succession drawn from Bede (Kings Æthelberht, Eadbald, Earconberht, and Ecgberht); only with the mention of Eormenred does he move on to non-Bedan material.

PARS PRIMA

5

the beginning of our History,[7] and to demonstrate the distinction of their sanctity.

2. Now Æthelberht was a king who was perfect in the exercise of his glorious might; because he greatly loved the words of divine knowledge, he was anointed in the baptism of salvation. Through his energy and wise support, the condition of God's churches was everywhere advanced, and through the acquisition of properties the assembly of the faithful was strengthened. Accordingly, having wisely arranged the governance of the realm to the best of the ability granted to him, at the call of the mercy of the Just Redeemer (for He had made him follow Him in all respects), he is deprived of fleshly existence and is raised up to the heights of heaven, there to reign with the saints. His son Eadbald succeeded him in the administration of his office, as we said above; from him were sprung two sons of royal stock, Eormenred and Earconberht, of whom the younger [Earconberht], in accordance with his father's plan, took on the governance of the imperial realm. And after the death of Earconberht, his son named Ecgberht ruled that [realm] mightily.[8] The elder son, Eormenred, remained without having the authority of rule in the volatile racecourse of this transitory life. To this just man, by his exceedingly just wife, were born two sons. They, having been raised in the Lordly palace of the celestial King, were manifoldly endowed with the royal gift of eternal glory. One of them shone by the appellation Æthelred, the other gleamed with the name Æthelberht. For on the holy day of their birth, as it seems to me, all the orders of blessed spirits rejoiced in heaven, because those whom they noticed being placed on earth, they saw would return to them greatly strengthened after the serious struggles of this life. The higher nobility on earth rejoiced, feeling itself to be adorned by the bounty of a double gift; and because it is assailed by the extreme misfortune of contrary events, always hopes that it will be improved by assistance of this sort. Moreover, holy mother Church rejoices when it is enlightened by so great a dowry by its Bridegroom, through which it may both shine more brightly with the light of its achievements, and the righteous summit of its holy justice may always increase. Delivered first of all to the womb of this excellent teaching in the peaceful shrine of that holy contemplation—if I may speak without the elaborate rhetoric of classroom instruction—they were baptized in the gleaming baptistery of the salvation-bringing water, in the seven grades of whose pure liquid they were granted the seven gifts

6 HISTORIA REGVM

sacrario, nitido salutaris aquae sunt abluti baptisterio, in cuius puri septem gradibus liquoris, septem sunt sortiti dona spiritus sancti,[9] episcopali benedictione perfusi et sancto chrismate delibuti. Quibus undique decentissime fulti, uiuere studuerunt | uirgines*[a]* corpore sancto tenerrimi septenis dierum curriculis, ut septem septies augmentatis*[b]* et monade supposito, singularis in praesenti uita acquirerent fructum iubelei, hoc est annum aeternae felicitatis;[10] hoc deinde insignium illustri cura uirtutum duplicato—<scilicet>*[c]* corpore et anima—post peractum uitae cursum, fructum caperent centesimum sacratissimis uirginibus consecratum.[11] Egregia namque insignes forma sanctitatis, aptissimis deuincti caritatis nodis,*[d]*[12] cernuae locupletes humilitatis officiis, ineuincibilis[13] ter beati patientiae titulis, largis pro posse fungentes eleemosinarum studiis, indeficientis praecordialibus orationis compti priuilegiis, et plurimis patris spirituum debriantur bonitatum speculis. Quia ergo plantaria uirtutum naturaliter eis insita pro nostra capacitate praelibauimus, nunc breui notationis serie aggredi temptamus, qualiter ad gaudia caelestis patriae per coronam martyrii uocantur.

3. Igitur utriusque eorum parentibus ab huius uitae miseria decedentibus cum adhuc iuuenilis potirentur imbecillitate aetatis, Ecgberhto regi,*[a]*[14] consobrino suo, sunt traditi, qualiter et sollertis prudentiae educarentur exercitiis, et humanae infirmitatis sustentarentur solaciis. Talibus uero piorum conaminibus non defuere iniquae uenena iaculationis, quae semper aduersus filios Dei per filios diffidentiae telis inuidiae armatur. In regali namque palatio 'homo quidam peccati' et 'filius'

---

i.2   *[a] after* uirgines *C adds* et   *[b]* agmentatis *C*   *[c] suppl. ed.*   *[d]* radiis *C*
i.3   *[a] after* regi *C adds* germano

---

[9] Reference to the Seven Gifts of the Holy Spirit (Isa. 11: 2) is frequently made in the writings of Byrhtferth, notably in the *Enchiridion* iv. 1, lines 161–73 (ed. Baker and Lapidge, p. 208, with notes at pp. 350–1).

[10] The 'fruit of the Jubilee' is mentioned in Lev. 25: 10 as meaning the 'fruit of the fiftieth year'. Here and elsewhere Byrhtferth treats the number 50 (characteristically given by him in numerological form as seven times seven plus one) as signifying the Day of Judgement (see *Enchiridion* iv. 1, lines 385–90); hence *annus iubeleus* means for Byrhtferth the passage beyond the Day of Judgement into heaven, as here and below (*HR* ii. 12: 'iubeleique anni remissionem percipere' and iv. 11: 'ignorans annum iubilei habere remissionem') and at *VSO* i. 6 ('sumere ab eo iubelei anni remissionem'). See discussion by Lapidge, 'The early sections', pp. 110–11 = *ALL* ii. 330–1, and Introduction, above, p. xxviii.

[11] The ultimate source of this reference is the Parable of the Sower (Matt. 13: 8), whereby some seed is said to yield thirtyfold fruit, some sixtyfold, and some hundredfold; but this parable was much elaborated by patristic exegetes, such that the thirtyfold fruit was taken to represent the contribution of married couples, the sixtyfold that of virgins, and the hundredfold that of martyrs; but authors such as Augustine (*De ciuitate Dei* xv. 26) and Aldhelm (prose *De uirginitate*, c. 19) subsequently modified this scheme so that the three categories

PARS PRIMA

of the Holy Spirit,[9] being moistened with episcopal blessing and anointed with holy unction. Sustained beautifully by these gifts in every way, they sought to live as tender virgins in their holy bodies through the sevenfold cycle of days, so that, with the seven increased sevenfold and with one added, they would acquire the fruit of the distinctive Jubilee in this present life, that is, the year of eternal bliss;[10] and then, with this bright cultivation of outstanding virtues doubled— namely in body and soul—they would receive the hundredfold fruit which is reserved for the most holy virgins after completion of the course of this life.[11] For, being outstanding in the excellent manner of their sanctity, bound by the fitting ties[12] of love, filled with the obligations of subservient humility, thrice blessed through the renown of their unconquerable[13] patience, administering the generous disbursal of alms to the best of their abilities, adorned with the heartfelt endowment of unceasing prayer, they are inspired by the many reflections of goodness of the Father of spirits. Accordingly, because I have described to the best of my ability the seedlings of the virtues sown naturally in them, I now attempt to set out, in a brief sequence of annotation, how they are called to the joys of the celestial homeland through the crown of martyrdom.

3. Therefore, with the parents of each of them departing from the misery of this life when they were still experiencing the weakness of youthful age, they were entrusted to King Ecgberht,[14] their cousin, so that they could be educated in the exercise of subtle wisdom and be sustained by the consolations allowed to human weakness. But the poisons of a wicked attack were not far away from these undertakings of the holy youths, [an attack] which is always furnished with weapons of envy by the sons of unbelief against the sons of God. For in the royal

---

corresponded respectively to marriage, widowhood, and virginity (as here). The numerological significance of the numbers 30, 60, and 100 is explained at length by Byrhtferth, *Enchiridion*, iv. 1, lines 310–32 (ed. Baker and Lapidge, p. 222, with notes at p. 361), and alluded to in *VSO* i. 5 and 6, and *VSE* i. 10.

[12] The transmitted *radiis* is incomprehensible when construed with *deuincti*; hence I have emended it to *nodis*.

[13] No example of this word earlier than Byrhtferth is recorded in *DMLBS* p. 1345, s.v. 'ineuincibilis'; on Byrhtferth's penchant for polysyllabic adjectives in *-bilis*, see *Byrhtferth: The Lives*, ed. Lapidge, p. xlvii, and Introduction, above, p. xxv.

[14] Ecgberht, king of Kent (664–73), was the son of King Earconberht, the younger brother of Eormenred, the father of SS. Æthelberht and Æthelred (and Domneua). Hence Ecgberht was the saints' cousin. Either Byrhtferth or a later scribe has badly misunderstood these family relations, by making Ecgberht both the brother *and* cousin of Eormenred (*Ecgberhto regi germano consobrino suo* C). I have emended the text by removing *germano*, so as to clarify these family relationships.

8   HISTORIA REGVM

inuentus est 'perditionis',[15] membrum diaboli necnon domus zabuli, qui saeculi uanis tumidus pompis munificentiaque regali redimitus, fo. 52vb nec Deum timebat nec hominem | reuerebatur. Hic cum principe, cum pro nimia ambitione honoris super omnes consiliis frueretur, tum pro fetido humanae leuitatis fauore in uanum tollebatur: <sic>[b] Aman super Mardocheum ignicomis mortiferae uexationis[c] furcis stimulabatur, quibus ipse postmodum insperate uinctus suspenderetur.[16] Vocabatur porro conuenienti sibi nomine Đunur, quod Latina interpretatione sonat 'tonitrus'. Furiis namque teterrimorum spirituum morbidis indesinenter uexabatur, quorum horridis fragoribus in inferni tartarum demergeretur. Videns ergo felices (quos supra taxauimus) uiuere feliciter, sordidarum scabenti deturpatus meditationum prurigine, in coenoso mentis impiae uolutabro coepit cogitare, quibus adinuentionum ruderibus eos neci posset tradere. Vnde canino dente apud plurimos aulicorum eorum praeconia praesumebat rodere, uecordique in calumnia ipsorum duci talia proferre:

Cum, rex serenissime, strenua mente, sollerti opere, perspicacis sensus ualetudine ac uigorabili tui potentatus lance, largissima regnorum tuae maiestati subiacentium sinuamina prudentissimo aequitatis disponantur libramine, est quam preciosum, ut non tantum stabilis[d] nunc uirga regni recte moderetur sceptrumque orbis status <iuste>[e] gubernetur, quam pulcherrime[f] tuae propagini prospiciat incolume pacis decus. Non enim tantum tui cura sollicitationum nebulis agitareris, nisi clarissimorum tuae dignitatis successurorum spebus natorum optimis delectareris.[17] Quapropter operae pretium ducimus, fo. 53ra ut semita tranquillitatis eis prospera redimatur, quo et res publica ipsis | successura nullo[g] turbinum fluctu quatiatur, nullis discordiarum angoribus uacilletur. Cuncta eis bonis omnibus exuberans arrideat felicitas, laetitiae pleniter inditis perseuerabilis affluat iocunditas! Videre autem uideor, ut magna huius salubritatis oriatur penes te iniuria, quia nutris cum diligentia <eos>[h][18] qui aliquando sibi usurpare praesument tui regni fastigia; mutabunt quae diligenter

---

[b] *suppl. ed.*   [c] uexationum *C*   [d] stabili *C*   [e] *suppl. ed.*   [f] pulcherrimo *C*   [g] nulla *C*   [h] *suppl. ed.*

---

[15] 2 Thess. 2: 3 ('homo peccati, filius perditionis').

[16] The story of Haman and Mordecai is told in the biblical book of Esther, esp. chs. 2–13. Haman was a counsellor of the Babylonian king Ahasuerus during the period of the Babylonian Captivity. Because of his jealousy of Mordecai and the Jews, Haman attempted to promulgate an edict by which all Jews were to be killed; but through the intervention of Esther, the king was apprised of this plan, and the result was that he sentenced Haman to hang on the gallows which Haman had constructed for Mordecai (Esther 7: 9–10).

[17] Ecgberht had two sons who in due course succeeded to the Kentish throne: Eadric (685–6), and Wihtred (690–725).

PARS PRIMA

9

household was to be found a certain 'man of sin, a son of perdition',[15] an instrument of the devil and of the house of Satan, who, puffed up with the empty displays of this world and crowned with royal support, did not fear God or respect man. This man, as a result of his excessive striving for distinction, because he enjoyed the confidence of his lord more than all the others, was at that time elevated into vainglory for the stinking approbation of human triviality: thus was Haman aroused concerning Mordecai by fiery prongs of deadly annoyance, by which he himself unexpectedly was later hanged.[16] Moreover, he was called by the appropriate name Thunur, which in Latin translation means 'thunder'. For he was ceaselessly tormented by deadly furies of hideous spirits, through whose savage din he would be submerged in the depths of Hell. Observing, therefore, the blessed ones (whom I described above) living blessedly, and being defiled by the grating itch of vile plans, he began to contemplate in the dirty swine-pit of his wicked mind by what rubbish of designs he could consign them to death. Accordingly he started to gnaw away with canine tooth at the praises of the youths in the presence of a number of the courtiers, and with disgusting misrepresentation of them to report to his lord such [sentiments] as these:

'Since, O serene majesty, with your vigorous mind, attentive management, with the vital measure of your shrewd intelligence and the lively balance of your power, the extensive affairs of kingdoms subject to your majesty are handled with the wise counsel of fairness, it is extremely important not only that the rod of your stable kingdom be rightly ruled and the sceptre of the state of your world be governed justly, as that the unimpaired glory of peace should brilliantly favour your descendants. For, [as concerns your own position], you would not be troubled so much by clouds of anxieties if you did not delight in the excellent prospects of your sons, who are to be the glorious successors of your authority.[17] Therefore I consider it important that the prosperous path of peace be secured for them, so that the state to which they will succeed will not be shaken by any tidal wave of storms, will not totter with any anxieties of discord. May all happiness, abounding in all good things, shine on them, may the enduring joy of delight flow over them, so abundantly endowed! But I seem to see that a great threat to this healthy situation might arise with you, because you nourish with care those[18] who one day might presume to seize for themselves the high authority of your kingdom; they will alter the things

---

[18] It is possible that Byrhtferth was here using a rare classical Latin construction, in which the antecedent of *qui* is not stated but implied (see *OLD* s.v. 'qui', 20b); but because of the rarity of this construction I have supplied *eos*, perhaps unnecessarily.

HISTORIA REGVM

eis exhibes, talia in <possessione>[i] tui tuorumque posterorum inutilia. Ex assistentibus tuae celsitudinis loquor Æþelredo et Æþelbyrhto tyrunculis, qui magis in augmento[j] tuae liberorumque crescunt damnationis quam cuiuslibet tuae prouectionis. Ergo perquisita directi ominis scientiola, [k]qua aequa promoueatur in eos rationis sententiola,[k] consultum communis crederem esse utilitatis tuae, ut aut eos in longinquum dirigi exilium iubeas regionis, aut citissime tradi mihi sinas iugulandos.[l]

Rege haec dissimulante, utraque se nolle denegante, illo tamen obnixe ut fieri permitteret stimulante, et hoc saepius repetente, dum tepide et non argute prohibuit, audaciae temeritatem ut perderentur intulit. O quam subdola semper in insontes perfidorum calliditas! O quam immitis fraudulentorum in innocentes saeuitia! Nulla [m]in eis[m] gratissima pietatis cura, non <in>[n] eis ulla mansuetudinis intersunt uiscera, sola quae meditantur acerba, quae portant uenenis similia. Quid plura? Mortifera idem in seipsum armatur pestifer turbo nequitia, qua absente regis praesentia, manus nisus est extendere in Deo cernua innocentium colla.

fo. 53[rb]   4. Hac igitur inuidi persecutoris insectatione martyres Christi coronati sunt palma uictoriae, et a Christo suscepti in praedio perennis uitae, laetantur cum angelis caelestis patriae. Pretiosa uero tantorum membra agonistarum iussit inhonestis subselliorum locis humo contegi regalium, credens latere diu cunctis quod peregerat stupidae commentum peruersitatis nequitia scelesti interemptoris. Porro nullo eis indulto fletus suspirio,[a] nullo decem cordarum reboante officio, non hymnorum pulcherrimo Ambrosiano titulo, nec Gregoriano potitis dulcis armoniae organo, non defuere summae deitatis cum multiplicis <munere>[b] uirtutis exenia.[19]

  5. Et in[a] intempesta noctis quiete uisa est diuinitus corusca super aulam palatii regis fulsisse luminis columna, quae illustratione insolita

---

[i] *suppl. ed.*   [j] aumento *C*   [k-k] *these words were omitted by the original scribe of C, but supplied by C¹ (at the foot of col. 53ʳᵃ, linked by a* signe de renvoi)   [l] iugulis *C* [m-m] lenis *C*   [n] *suppl. ed.*

i.4 [a] suspiro *C*   [b] *suppl. ed.*

i.5 [a] enim *C*

[19] This sentence of Byrhtferth was very likely prompted by a sentence in B., *Vita S. Eadburgae*, c. 2, which similarly describes the lack of liturgical commemoration which attended the murder of SS. Æthelberht and Æthelred: 'Non laudum condigna cantica, non Dauitica decem cordarum psalmodia, non clara lampadum lumina, non Gregoriana pro interemptorum requie commendamina sed illicita ibi perstrepebant carnificum conuiuia'

PARS PRIMA

which you carefully reveal to them, such things being useless in the possession of yourself and your successors. I refer to those young attendants on your lofty power, the youngsters Æthelred and Æthelberht, who grow more in the increased threat to the destruction of you and your children than in the promotion of any cause of yours. Therefore, having examined the hint of this unambiguous forewarning, through which a just sentence of reason may be advanced against them, I would think it advisable to your common advantage, that you either order them to be sent into distant exile in (another) province, or else you allow them to be handed over to me to be killed.'

With the king dissembling his view of these matters, and refusing to accede to either [plan], and with him [Thunor] obstinately insisting that he allow him to proceed, and repeating it frequently, while he [the king] forbade it weakly and not incisively, he contributed rashness to [Thunor's] bold plan that they be killed. O how deceitful is the trickery of the wicked against the guiltless! O how cruel is the savagery of the fraudulent against the innocent! There is no pleasing concern with mercy in them, in them there are no inner feelings of mildness, only the calamities which they contemplate, which bring results similar to poison. Why say more? The pestilent storm is armed with deadly wickedness against itself, where, with the king's presence being absent, it strives to reach out its hands to the necks of the innocent bowed to God.

4. And so through this plot of the envious persecutor the martyrs of Christ were crowned with the palm of victory, and, taken up by Christ into the estate of perpetual life, they rejoice with the angels of the heavenly homeland. Thunor ordered the precious limbs of these great combatants to be covered by soil in inconspicuous parts of the royal courtyards, believing that the plot of stupid wickedness which he had enacted could long lie hidden from everyone by the vileness of the evil murderer. Yet with no sighs of lamentation accorded to them, with no ceremony ringing out on ten-stringed instruments, with no exquisite Ambrosian tribute of hymns, nor sustained by the Gregorian chant of sweet harmony, [nevertheless] the gifts of the highest deity, with an abundance of manifold virtue, were not lacking.[19]

5. And in the dead quiet of night a gleaming column of light was seen shining from on high over the hall of the king's palace, which

---

(ed. Love, 'St Eadburh of Lyminge', p. 374). I am grateful to Rosalind Love for drawing my attention to this striking parallel.

12 HISTORIA REGVM

plures turbauit ex regis familia; dantesque fragorem clamoris in admiratione nimia, expergefactus est rex, et hoc minime cognoscens surrexit a stratus sui cubiculo, et iter parauit ad nocturnales matutinorum hymnos. Cum digressus a domo, uidet orbem noui splendoris incanduisse albedine, cuius procreatio diffluebat a praephato lucis mirabili solio, enimuero tam recenti[b] stupefactus intuitu, mentis agitari coepit sollicitus rex cogitationibus—et ubi essent <pueri>[c] quos[d] pridie praeuiderat, et de confabulatione perdendorum martyrum quam minister iniquitatis cum eo iamdudum habuerat—mouebatur | siquidem meditatione acerrima. Tunc celerrime ascito tanti criminis auctore, sciscitatur qua forent propinqui sui positi regionis longinquitate, quorum non fruebatur praesentiae inclita pulchritudine. Iniquissimo sane surdas his punctionibus aures praebente carnifice, atque Cain uoce superbo mentis supercilio se nescire turpiore grunniente, <rex>,[e] minaci uultu quippe ut perterritus diuinae lucis claritate, ei fertur talia inculcauisse: 'Tu mihi plurima de eis semper sermocinatus es bonis contraria, tu de eorum exilio mala, tu de internecione nefaria, tu aduersus eos multa mordebaris insania. Tibi pleniter enarrare nostrae sollertiae oportet, nequissime, qualiter inueniantur quos graui insectabaris odii zelo, corrupta mente.' Ad haec ille furcifer, sentina malitiae fetidus: 'Sub tuae,' inquit, 'mortua eorum iacent cadauera loco sedis domus.' Princeps quid ageret? Perculsus namque timoris ingenti turbine, quia in parte torquebatur mordaci macula regalis[f] conscientiae, dum fortiter non restitit bonitatis hosti, et quia uindicare nequibat quod peractum iniuste fuerat; stupens inhaerebat, in quantumque poterat poenitebat. Aurora itaque diei terris illucescente, conuocatis quibus ad praesens innitebatur comitibus regnique sui principibus, cum episcopis, in quibus supereminebat archipraesul Dorouernensis, multae beatitatis uir, uocabulo Deusdedit,[20] ad locum praephatorum innocentum concitus pergit, terram suffossorio auellit, corporaque

---

[b] recentis C   [c] suppl. ed.   [d] quas on an erasure in C   [e] suppl. ed.
[f] corr. ed., alis C

---

[20] There is a chronological difficulty in the author's choice of Deusdedit as the archbishop of Canterbury who presided over the translation: Deusdedit died on 14 July 664, and Ecgberht did not accede to the Kentish throne until later that year. It is worth noting that the author of the later Ramsey *Passio SS. Ethelredi et Ethelbricti* in Oxford, BodL, Bodley 285 [*BHL* 2641–2], recognized this discrepancy and attempted to remove it by identifying the archbishop in question as Theodore (668–90): 'concite cogi imperat concilium <principum> et episcoporum suorum, inter quos primus erat uenerabilis Theodorus archiepiscopus' (ed.

PARS PRIMA

aroused several members of the king's family with its unusual brightness. And as they let out a tumult of noise in their extreme astonishment, the king was awakened, and, not understanding any of this, he got up from the sleeping-chamber of his bed and made his way to the nightly hymn-singing of Matins. When he set out from the house, he saw a globe gleaming with the brightness of novel splendour, whose source flowed out from the aformentioned amazing throne of light, for, stunned by so fresh a perception, the king began anxiously to be aroused by mental reflections—as to where were the boys whom he had seen the day before, and about the conversation concerning the murder of the martyrs which the agent of wickedness had had with him only recently—he was moved as it were by the most bitter thoughts. Then, the agent of this great crime having swiftly been summoned, the king enquires as to where in terms of remote exile might be found his kinsmen, the outstanding beauty of whose presence he was not able to enjoy. With the wicked executioner naturally offering deaf ears to these irritations and grunting in the foul voice of Cain with proud mental arrogance that he knew nothing about it, the king, with threatening mien, particularly as he was terrified by the brilliance of the divine light, is said to have obtruded on him the following: 'You said many things to me concerning them [which were] contrary to good faith, you [said] wicked things concerning their exile, you [spoke] of their unspeakable execution, you were consumed by extreme madness against them. It is appropriate for you, you wicked man, to explain fully to my understanding how those [boys] whom you pursued with the zeal of hatred, with corrupted mind, are to be found.' To this that gallows-bait, stinking from the sump of wickedness, said: 'Their dead bodies lie beneath a place in the residence of your house.' What was the king to do? He was struck by a mighty blast of fear, because he was tortured by the stinging stain of his royal conscience, since he did not resist this enemy of goodness, and because he could not defend what had been done unjustly; he stood stupefied, and repented insofar as he could. And so when the dawn of day was shining on the earth, summoning those ealdormen and leading men of his kingdom on whom he relied at that time, together with the bishops, among whom the archbishop of Canterbury stood out, a man of great blessedness named Deusdedit,[20] he goes in an agitated state to the place of the aforesaid innocents, he turns over the earth with a spade, and uncovers the holy

Rollason, *The Mildrith Legend*, p. 96). The same adjustment had earlier been made by B., *Vita S. Eadburgae*, c. 10 (see below, n. 35).

HISTORIA REGVM

sanctissima indecenter iugulata ac inhoneste condita detegit. Heu quam surda aure tunc mentis constitit, si non fleuit, cum filios auunculi sui innocentes perditos conspexit! Heu quam ferreo usus est pectore, si, dum propinquos carnis suae felici | sanguinis uidit tinctos rubore, non tangitur cordis dolore! Heu quam graui lacrimarum potuit suffundi imbre, dum tantae nobilitatis flores inclitos tam futili uidit traditos sepulturae!

fo. 53vb

6. Igitur cum hominum exequiis etiam non defuerunt magnalia perpetuae deitatis, coronatos namque in regni aeternitatis solio, etiam hic uisitare dignatur miro potentiae suae miraculo. Talia gerebantur in uilla regali quae uulgari dicitur Easterige[21] pronuntiatione. Cum ergo sanctorum pretiosissima innocentum corpora, terrae secreto <condita>,[a] forent superstatuta feretro, propositum est ut, delata in urbem Cantiae, Christi sepelirentur in monasterio. Sed[b] moueri non quiuerunt ab illo in quo statuta fuerant loco. Propositum est ut ad sancti Augustini ferrentur ecclesiam, siquidem leuari nequiuerunt. Ad plurima quoque et honorabilia portare decreuerunt loca, et tumbis appositarum manuum deficiebant brachia. Tandem salubri reperto consilio, ut ad famosissimum gestarentur monasterium Wacrinense[22] uocitatum, tam citissimae agilitatis insperato leuantur officio, ut nihil oneris uideretur in gestamine diu desiderato. Quo cum peruentum fuisset, cum pulcherrimis hymnorum cantilenis lenibusque psalmorum melodiis, multis resonantibus choris et iubilationum cymbalis suscipiuntur, tradunturque principalem retro aram sepulturae decenti. Hic multis annorum curriculis eis positis, excelsus Dominus, qui 'humilia respicit et alta a longe cognoscit',[23] eos creberrimis ditare miraculis uoluit, de quibus duo posterorum notitiae nunc propalare praesenti sermone <decreuimus>.[c][24]

---

i.6 [a] *suppl. ed.*   [b] *et C*   [c] *suppl. ed.*

[21] Eastry is near Deal in Kent, some 9 miles east of Canterbury. The name derives from OE *eastr* + *ge*. The second element *-gē* is an archaic element meaning 'region' or 'district', related to Modern German *Gau* (see *DEPN*, p. 158, and Wallenberg, *Kentish Place-Names*, p. 73). In early charters of Christ Church, Canterbury, Eastry is referred to as a 'region': see *Charters of Christ Church, Canterbury*, ed. Brooks and Kelly, nos. 24 (dated 788) [*in regione Eastrgena*], 43 (dated 811) [*in eadem regione Eosterege*], 55A (dated 824) [*in regione Eastrege*]. From these and other charters, it is clear that Eastry was indeed a royal estate.

[22] The place referred to by Byrhtferth as 'Wakering' is now two adjacent communities known as Little Wakering and Great Wakering, which lie directly across the Thames estuary from the Isle of Sheppey in Kent. On the minster at Wakering, see Blair, *The Church in Anglo-Saxon Society*, p. 215 with ill. 28.

PARS PRIMA

bodies disgracefully murdered and buried deceitfully. Alas, how deaf in the ear of his mind was someone who did not weep when he saw the innocent sons of his uncle murdered thus! Alas, how ironclad a heart he had if, when he sees the kinsmen of his own flesh smeared with the blessed redness of blood, he is not touched with pain at heart! Alas, with what a serious flood of tears he could be overwhelmed, when he sees the outstanding flowers of such great nobility consigned to a pointless burial!

6. Accordingly, even with human funerals the mighty works of the eternal godhead were not lacking, for it deigns even here to visit the [two martyrs] crowned on the throne of the eternal kingdom with a wondrous miracle of its own power. The following events took place on the royal estate which in the common tongue is called Eastry [Kent].[21] When, therefore, the precious bodies of the saintly innocents, [which had] secretly been committed to the earth, had been placed on a bier, it was decided that, having been taken into the city of Canterbury, they could be buried in the minster of Christ Church. But they could not be moved from the place in which they had been laid. It was then proposed that they should be carried to the church of St Augustine, since they could not be lifted up. They also decided to carry them to several other important places, but the arms of the hands laid on to the tomb were lacking in strength. At length, when the satisfactory plan was devised that they be taken to the famous minster called Wakering [Essex],[22] the bodies were raised up with the unsuspected assistance of swift speed, so that there seemed to be no burden on the long-anticipated conveyance. When it had arrived there, the bodies are received with the exquisite chanting of hymns and the gentle melodies of psalms, with many choirs and cymbals of jubilation ringing out, and they are commited to decent burial behind the principal altar. While they were lying here during the passage of many years, the heavenly Lord, 'Who observes the humble and recognizes the mighty from afar',[23] wished to enrich them with frequent miracles, from among which I have decided[24] to record two in my present narrative for the benefit of posterity.

---

[23] Ps. 137 (138): 6 ('quoniam excelsus Dominus et humilia respicit et alta a longe cognoscit').

[24] The scribe of C obviously omitted a first-person verb here. Arnold conjectured *statuo*, plausibly enough; but I have preferred to supply *decreuimus*, since *decerno* is a verb used frequently by Aldhelm, and hence by Byrhtferth, whose style is deeply indebted to Aldhelm; cf. *VSO* ii. 2, iii. 9, v. 12, v. 14, and below, *HR* i. 8 ('Decernens itaque eam honorare', etc.), and since Byrhtferth always refers to himself in the first person plural.

HISTORIA REGVM

fo. 54ra

7. Accidit ut quidam, alterius bonis caecatus, | ouem cuiusdam pauperis tolleret secretius; quam gestans in humeris, ligatis pedibus, deferre gliscebat secus arcisterium sanctorum martyrum, sed non potuit. Portari ibidem potuit, sed dehinc uehi non ualuit.[25] Reus itaque huius sceleris continuo frustratur flatu uitali prosterniturque mortuus humi, ouem uiuentem habens in manibus, eo insequente cui furtum fuerat illatum. Recepit innocens proprium, dimittit reum morte praeuentum subitanea sanctorum ultione innocentum. Continuo currens ad aedituum sciscitatur si peremerit latronem illum: a nullo mortali didicit iugulatum. Acceptaque licentia reportandi quod suum fuerat, laetus et hilaris reuertitur in sua, Deo ac sanctis eius multas gratias agens.[26]

8. Igitur quoniam passiones sanctorum martyrum prout potuimus strictim praelibauimus, restat quomodo diuina ultio super iniquissimum iudicem, piissimae necis eorum auctorem, peruenerit, breuiter tangamus.[27] Fuerat eis ex paterno maternoque soror procreata semine, Eormenburga uel Domneua nomine,[28] quam habebat in coniugium copulationis legitimae rex Merciorum, Mearuualh[a29] nomine; quam Ecgberhtus rex ad se, misso legationis suae gerulo, disposuit uocare. Quae ueniens, suscipitur ab omnibus primatibus illius regionis, uti dignum erat, honorabili perspicuae ambitionis dignitate. Decernens itaque eam honorare, ut quodcumque uellet honestatis sibi competentis in potestatis suae ditione rogaret, et sine mora acciperet. Sancta mulier

fo. 54rb

humili responsione | subinfert, ut tantum terrae illi concederet quantum cerua, quam sibi nutrierat, in una die diuino instinctu pede

---

1.8 ᵃ Mearwoldus C

[25] The Latin would most naturally mean that 'the sheep could be carried there, but could not be moved from there'. However, given Byrhtferth's persistent confusion about when to use the passive infinitive form of the verb, I suspect it is more likely here that the thief is the subject of both *potuit* and *ualuit* (thus translated), not the sheep.

[26] This entire chapter was reproduced, nearly verbatim, by the author of the later Ramsey *Passio SS. Ethelredi et Ethelbricti* in Oxford, BodL, Bodley 285 [*BHL* 2641–2], ed. Rollason, *The Mildrith Legend*, p. 103.

[27] Having got the martyrs' remains to Wakering, Byrhtferth returns to his (lost) source-text of the 'Mildrith legend' in order to narrate the foundation of Minster-in-Thanet (and—what presumably most concerned him—the divine vengeance enacted upon Thunor). Since many of the surviving texts which preserve the 'Mildrith legend' have associations with Canterbury (Mildrith's remains were translated to St Augustine's in 1035), it is possible that Byrhtferth came upon a version of the foundation legend in Canterbury itself, which he seems to have visited *c*.1000, since in his *Vita S. Oswaldi* he was able to quote verbatim from a surviving manuscript of the *Vita S. Dunstani* which was written there at about that time, and which is not known to have left Canterbury during the Anglo-Saxon period; see *The Early Lives of St Dunstan*, ed. Winterbottom and Lapidge, p. lxxix, and Introduction, above, p. xlvii.

PARS PRIMA

7. It happened that a certain man, blinded by [covetousness for] another's property, secretly stole a sheep belonging to a certain poor man; carrying it on his shoulders, with its feet bound, he intended to carry it near to the minster of the two martyrs, but he could not. He was able to carry it there, but was unable to move it from there.[25] The man, guilty of this sin, is immediately deprived of life's breath and collapses dead on the ground, having the living sheep in his hands, pursued by the man on whom the theft had been perpetrated. The innocent man took back his own property; he abandons the guilty man, overtaken by sudden death through the vengeance of the holy innocents [SS. Æthelred and Æthelberht]. Running at once to the sacristan, he asks if *he* had killed that robber: he learns that he was killed by no mortal man. Having received permission of carrying away that which had been his, he returns to his own home joyous and happy, giving many thanks to God and His saints.[26]

8. Accordingly, because I have cursorily narrated the deaths of the holy martyrs as best I could, it remains for me briefly to relate how divine vengeance came to the wicked councillor, the author of their most blessed deaths.[27] They had a sister, who was sprung from both paternal and maternal stock, named Eormenburg or Domneua,[28] whom the king of the Mercians, named Merewalh,[29] had taken as wife in legitimate union; King Ecgberht decided to summon her to him, having sent a messenger with his message. Arriving there, she is received by all the leading men of that region with the honourable distinction of this evident favour, as was only fitting. Deciding, therefore, to honour her, such that whatsoever she might wish, she might ask for within the jurisdiction of his authority, provided it was suitable to his reputation, and she would receive it without delay. The saintly woman says in humble reply, that he grant to her only so much land as the hind, which she had raised, could traverse on foot by divine guidance in the course of one day. The king at once gratefully orders that a retinue of ealdormen be made ready on the morrow; accompanied by

---

[28] On the name Domneua, see Introduction, p. xlviii.

[29] Merewalh (fl. 650) was ruler of the *Magonsæte* (the English peoples inhabiting a territory roughly equivalent to modern Herefordshire); see Keynes, 'Rulers', p. 529. According to the later Ramsey *Passio SS. Ethelredi et Ethelbricti* in Oxford, BodL, Bodley 285 [*BHL* 2641–2], Merewalh was a son of King Penda of Mercia (?626–55): 'porro tradita est Domneua Meruueale, filio Pendan Merciorum regis' (ed. Rollason, *The Mildrith Legend*, p. 93); but it is difficult to know how much reliance, if any, can be placed on this report. The scribe of C reproduced this name (known from other sources) in mutilated form as *Mearwoldus*.

18 HISTORIA REGVM

peragraret. Rex uero gratanter continuo iubet in crastinum praeparari comitum agmen; quo fretus, nauibus ad insulam Tenet dictam faceret callem. Quo positi, ipsaque cum cerua insulam nauigio ingressa, uiam cerua lustrandi arripit, a principeque et Christi famula cum plebe militari insequitur equis. Iam ex parte quam plurima circumita, nefandus carnifex turbatur inuidia, et quasi pro fidelitate regis, cui nichil remanere uidebatur ex ipsius uastitate amoena, coepit quasi in uiis eius compatiens garrire talia: 'Cum cuncta peragas perspicacis prudentiae gubernaculo, quare hoc brutum animal, sicut aliquid magni gerat, sequeris incessu deuotissimo?' His dictis, deitatis summis perculsus iaculis, ex sonipede ruit. Continuo suscipitur cum armis equoque nimis nimiumque infelix Þunor nouo terrae hiatu, ac nimio terrore rex cum omnibus suis commilitonibus correptus, operiri concite iubet horrendo lapidum aceruo ipsius corpus, anima perenni seruata incendio, baratri cenosis ignibus, de quibus dictum est poenis, 'Transibunt animae de poenis niuium.'[*b*][30] Qui locus a transeuntibus Þunreshleaþ notatur,[31] talique uocabulo potitur. Talibus stupidae mortis officiis insano lanista utente ac pro delictis[*c*] tormentorum poenas luente, praedicta fera, quantum diuina uoluntas concessit,[*d*] eis immutantibus, iter fecit; et sic gradum fixit mirantibus cunctis. Rex quod spoponderat, uiso territus miraculo fecit, manu propria firmauit,[*e*] sicque domum rediit.[32]

fo. 54ᵛᵃ 9. Mulier uero, sanctae uirtutis amica ac Deo ualde electa, in hac insula ecclesiam almae Dei genitricis Mariae perpetuae uirginis in memoria innocentum Christi martyrum fratrum suorum constituit,[33] filiamque suam, bonae indolis uirginem, Mildryðam appellatam, ecclesiasticis in transmarinis partibus disciplinis eruditam,[34] postmodum ibi constituit, cum septuaginta sanctimonialibus a sancto archiepiscopo

---

[*b*] *after* niuium C² *adds* ad calorem nimium (*from Job 24: 19*) *in marg.*   [*c*] deliciis C
[*d*] cocessit C   [*e*] *corr. Arnold,* formauit C

---

[30] Cf. Job 24: 19 ('ad nimium calorem transeat ab aquis niuium'). Byrhtferth has his own distinctive and characteristic way of quoting this verse of Job: see *VSO* iv. 20: 'Transibunt anime de aquis niuium ad aquas nimium' (ed. Lapidge, p. 142), and *VSE* i. 12: 'Transibunt anime de aquis niuium ad aquas nimium' (ibid. p. 228). The form of the present quotation is clearly a version of this same Byrhtferthian (mis)quotation; see Lapidge, 'The early sections', pp. 117–18 = *ALL* ii. 337–8, and Introduction, p. xl.

[31] There is apparently no place in present-day Thanet which bears a modern equivalent of the OE place-name *Thunreshleauu*, such as (for example) Thunderley; cf. *DEPN*, p. 471.

[32] The charter recording the endowment of Minster-in-Thanet does not survive among the early charters of that house (*The Charters... of Minster-in-Thanet*, ed. Kelly).

[33] There is no record of any commemoration of SS. Æthelred and Æthelberht at Minster-in-Thanet among the early documents pertaining to that house.

PARS PRIMA   19

them, he would make his way by ship to the island called Thanet. Once stationed there, and with the lady together with her hind making her way by ship to the island, the hind sets off travelling the path, and is followed by the king and the handmaid of Christ together with the military retinue on horseback. When a very substantial part of the journey had been traversed, the wicked executioner [Thunor] is assailed by envy, and, as if out of loyalty to the king, to whom nothing from that vast amenity seemed likely to remain, began, as though suffering from the journey, to babble as follows: 'Since you transact all [your business] with guidance of shrewd wisdom, why do you follow this brute animal with devoted fidelity, as if it were doing something of great [importance]?' Having said this, he fell from his horse, struck down by the mighty bolts of the deity. The exceptionally and exceedingly wretched Thunor is straightway received, with his weapons and horse, by a new chasm in the earth, and the king, with all his retinue, seized with extreme terror, hastily orders his body to be covered over by a rough heap of stones, with the soul being kept for the everlasting fire, the foul flames of Hell, concerning whose punishments it is said, 'Their souls shall pass from the punishment of snows.'[30] This place is called *Thunreshleaw* by passers-by,[31] and rejoices in such a name. With the insane executioner enjoying the benefits of so senseless a death and paying the penalty for the crimes of his murders, the aforementioned beast made its way as the divine will permitted, with the retinue altering its route; and thus it completed its progress, with everyone expressing astonishment. What the king had promised, he granted, having been terrified by the miracle he witnessed, [and] confirmed [the grant] with his own hand, and thus returned home.[32]

9. The woman [Domneua], the friend of saintly virtue and the chosen instrument of God, established on this island [Thanet] a church to Mary, the perpetual Virgin and Holy Mother of God, in memory of the innocent martyrs of Christ,[33] her brothers; she later established there her daughter, a virgin of good upbringing called Mildrith, who had been trained in ecclesiastical learning in overseas territories;[34] and she assembled there seventy nuns consecrated by Archbishop Deusdedit,

---

[34] Byrhtferth's vague statement that Mildthryth learned ecclesiastical discipline overseas (*in transmarinis partibus*) is formulated more precisely by B. in his *Vita S. Eadburgae*, c. 7, who specifies that Domneua sent Mildthryth to Gaul for religious instruction: 'Quam gloriosa genitrix ad Gallias usque destinauit' (ed. Love, 'St Eadburh of Lyminge', p. 378).

20   HISTORIA REGVM

Deusdedit consecratis, inibique congregauit.[35] Ibi ergo beata*a* genitrix Mildriðae post excursum plurimorum annorum, post exhibitionem bonarum uirtutum, post aedificationem plurimarum mentium uirorum et uirginum quas in Christo confortauit, cum lampade iustitiae a Christo meruit audire: 'Surge, propera, amica mea; ueni de Libano, ueni, coronaberis.'[36] Cuius anima, ad caeli deducta palatium, a Christo percipit immarcescibilia uictoriae dona, cum eo sanctisque eius regnatura in perenni gloria. Sane in monasterii regimine succedit inclita eius soboles, quam educauerat decentissime, nobilis et in Christi seruitio non deficiens Mildryða praedicta, sanctissima uirgo, multa fulgens miraculorum gratia.

10. Vnde unum narramus miraculum[37] quod sine dubio confirmat quia fecerat ei Dominus plurima quae sunt mortalibus inedicibilia. Quadam namque temporis serie, lassescentibus membris pro nimia laboris diuturnitate, quiescebat in lectulo, modico grauata sopore. Cui astitit angelus Domini in columbae specie residens in eius capite, ut eam tueretur a malignorum spirituum illusione. Haec beata uirgo, sicut eius felix genitrix, bona relinquens sequacibus uestigia, | omnipotente spirituum patre eius animam sumente, terra plorante, caelo gaudente, uiuit in aeterna beatitudine, sacratissimo ipsius corpore in templo beatae Dei genitricis Mariae perpetuae uirginis digniter in condigno loco tradito sepulturae. Praeterea dum spurcissimi persecutoris piorum martyrum subitum mortis interitum statuimus describere, postmodum infleximus oculos ad ueneranda sororis neptisque eorum gesta, quibus insimul Christus fuit uiuere et mori lucrum, cuius gratia ad alia narranda eo succurrente est properandum, retinentes ordinem narrationum.

fo. 54vb

---

i.9   *a* beatę *C (followed by an erasure)*

---

[35] Byrhtferth's syntax is often confusing, and has succeeded in confusing previous commentators. Essentially he has constructed a sentence made up of three cola, the subject of all three verbs being Domneua: (*ecclesiam*) *constituit*, (*filiamque suam*) *constituit*, (*filiam cum septuaginta sanctimonialibus*) *congregauit*. The point is that it was Domneua who established the seventy saintly women at Minster-in-Thanet, not Mildrith (though Byrhtferth's unclear construction could create the impression that Mildrith was the subject of *congregauit*; thus it was understood by Rollason, *The Mildrith Legend*, p. 74). In his *Vita S. Eadburge*, c. 10, B. specifies that Mildthryth, in the company of seventy virgins, took the veil from the hand of Archbishop Theodore: 'accepit [*scil.* Mildthryth] a beato Theodoro, sancte Dorobernensis ecclesie archiepiscopo, sacri ordinis uelamen una cum aliis septuaginta uirginibus' (ed. Love, 'St Eadburh of Lyminge', p. 380); see Introduction, p. l.

[36] Cf. S. of S. 2: 10 ('surge propera amica mea formosa mea et veni; iam enim hiemps transiit').

PARS PRIMA

together with her daughter.[35] And there the blessed mother of Mildrith, after the passage of several years, after the demonstration of good behaviour, after the instruction of many minds of men and virgins whom she comforted in Christ, was found worthy to hear from Christ with the torch of justice the words, 'Arise, hasten, my love; come from Lebanon, come, you shall be crowned.'[36] Her soul, led to the palace of heaven, receives from Christ the imperishable bounties of victory, to reign with Him and His saints in perpetual glory. Of course her distinguished daughter succeeded her in the government of the minster, [her daughter] whom she had educated most appropriately, the noble and aforementioned Mildrith, unremitting in her service of Christ, a most holy virgin, resplendent with a great abundance of miracles.

10. Let us accordingly narrate a miracle[37] which without doubt confirms that the Lord had done for her many things which are indescribable by mortals. At a certain point of time, with her limbs drooping because of excessive expenditure of labour, she was lying on her bed, overcome by light sleep. An angel of the Lord stood before her, sitting on her head in the likeness of a dove, so that he could protect her from the deceptions of evil spirits. This blessed virgin, just like her blessed mother, leaving behind valuable traces for her followers, with the omnipotent Father of the spirits taking her soul as the earth was weeping and heaven rejoicing, lives now in eternal bliss, while her most holy body was worthily consigned for burial in an appropriate place in the church of Mary the perpetual Virgin and Mother of God. Moreover, when I decided to describe the sudden death of the foul persecutor of the holy martyrs, I afterwards turned my eyes to the venerable deeds of their sister and niece, for both of whom to live was Christ, and to die an advantage, for Whose sake, with Him assisting, I must now hasten onwards, keeping to the sequence of the narrative.

---

[37] This miracle story was probably inherited by Byrhtferth from the lost source-text of the 'Mildrith legend', but note that it is also related by B., *Vita S. Eadburgae*, c. 14: 'Alio quoque tempore, cum uirgo Dei casta mente oracioni incumbebat, subito de celo ueniens angelus domini in specie columbe, candidior niue, in beate uirginis consedit capite, alisque suis candidis diu familiari dilecione caput illius collumque complexus est' (ed. Love, 'St Eadburh of Lyminge', p. 382). The same story is subsequently narrated by Goscelin, *Vita S. Mildrethae*, c. 26 (ed. Rollason, *The Mildreth Legend*, p. 140). In Goscelin's account, as in B. and Byrhtferth, the angel appears in the form of a dove ('in specie columbe'), a detail probably influenced by the biblical account of the dove which was seen descending during Christ's baptism (Matt. 3: 16: 'et vidit spiritum Dei descendentem sicut columbam').

a<PARS SECVNDA>*a*

fo. 54ᵛᵇ **1.** In exordio huius operis genealogiam regum Cantuariorum strictim praelibauimus; nunc Northanhymbrorum libet demonstrare, ut ad eorum tempora ualeamus peruenire, de quibus non est narratum post obitum reuerentissimi sacerdotis Bedae.

2. Ida rex annis regnauit undecim, quo abstracto Glappa uno regnauit anno, quem secutus Adda, octo annis tenuit regni fastigia. Illo uero penetrante ima pro meritis, Æðelric regnum inde adeptus est terrenum, quod tenuit .vii. annis. Is secreta inferni uisitans Theoderico imperia dereliquit, qui bis binis annis regnum tenens, regnum simul perdidit et uitam,[1]

> Tendens in externas ire tenebras
> quo, pressus grauidis colla catenis,
> cogitur nunc miserum cernere regnum.[2]

Post hunc Friþupold adeptus est sceptrum regni .vii. annis; qui subtractus a saeculo monarchiam regni dereliquit regi Husso. Ipse uero .vii. annis iura imperii tenens, didicit per se uerum esse quod sequitur:[3]

> Mors spernit altam gloriam;
> inuoluit humile pariter et celsum caput,

fo. 55ʳᵃ aequatque summis infima.[4]

Octauus in regno refulsit Æðelfryþ fortissimus regum, qui uiginti et octo annis regno potitus uita et regno est priuatus. Huic successit Edþinus rex; qui fidem Christianitatis percipiens, rex et martyr caelos

---

ii.1 *ᵃ⁻ᵃ suppl. ed.*

---

[1] Byrhtferth derives his information on early Northumbrian kings from a Northumbrian regnal list, similar (but not identical) to that preserved as the 'Moore Memoranda', in Cambridge, University Library, Kk. 5. 16, the famous 'Moore manuscript' of Bede's *Historia ecclesiastica* (Gneuss and Lapidge, *Anglo-Saxon Manuscripts*, no. 25). The so-called 'Moore Memoranda' are on fo. 128ᵛ, and are ed. in Hunter Blair, 'The *Moore Memoranda*', p. 246. The relevant passage reads: 'Anno .dxlvii. Ida regnare coepit, a quo regalis Nordanhumbrorum prosapia originem tenet, et .xii. annos in regno permansit. Post hunc Glappa .i. annum, Adda .viii., Aedilric .iiii., Theodric .vii.' These regnal years differ from those given by Byrhtferth, who assigns to Æthelric seven years and Theodric eight years. The reigns in question are dated as follows by modern historians: Ida (acc. 547, d. 559 or 560), Glappa (acc. 559, d. 560), Adda (acc. 560, d. 568), Æthelric (acc. 568, d. 572), Theodric (acc. 572, d. 579); see Keynes, 'Rulers', p. 524. Note that the 'Moore manuscript' itself could not have been Byrhtferth's source, because the manuscript had travelled to the Continent by the late eighth century.

PART II

1. At the beginning of this work I set out briefly the genealogy of the kings of Kent; now it is appropriate to reveal that of the Northumbrians, so that we may arrive at the era of those concerning whom nothing has been written after the death of Bede, the most reverent priest.

2. King Ida ruled eleven years; when he had been removed, Glappa ruled for one year; Adda followed him, and held the authority of the kingdom for eight years. With him penetrating to the lower depths for his just deserts, Æthelric then succeeded to the earthly kingdom, which he held for seven years. Visiting the inner recesses of hell he relinquished the sovereignty to Theodric, who, holding the kingdom for four years, lost the kingdom and his life at the same time,[1]

> Setting out to travel to the remote darkness
> where, burdened with heavy chains about the neck,
> he is now forced to view a wretched kingdom.[2]

After him Frithuwald succeeded to control of the kingdom for seven years; being removed from this world he left the authority of the kingdom to King Hussa. He, holding the control of the realm for seven years, learned for himself the truth of what follows:[3]

> Death spurns lofty glory;
> it envelops the lowly as well as the lofty head
> and equates the lowest with the highest.[4]

The eighth in the kingdom was the resplendent Æthelfrith, the most powerful of kings, who, after holding the kingdom for twenty-eight years, was deprived of life and kingdom. King Edwin succeeded him;

---

[2] Boethius, *De consolatione Philosophiae*, i, met. ii, lines 3, 25, and 27; the transmitted text of Boethius in fact reads 'Tendit in externas ire tenebras.../ et pressus grauibus colla catenis.../ cogitur, heu, stolidam cernere terram' (CCSL xciv. 3–4).

[3] After the quotation from Boethius, Byrhtferth returns to his Northumbrian regnal list for the next two kings; in the version of the 'Moore Memoranda', the text reads as follows: 'Friduuald .vi., Hussa .vii.' (ed. Hunter Blair in 'The *Moore Memoranda*', p. 246). Byrhtferth assigns seven years (not six) to Frithuuald. Their regnal years are to be dated as follows: Frithwald (acc. 579, d. 585) and Hussa (acc. 585, d. 592) (Keynes, 'Rulers', p. 524).

[4] Boethius, *De consolatione Philosophiae*, ii, met. vii, lines 12–14 (CCSL xciv. 34).

24 HISTORIA REGVM

penetrauit pro meritis, .xvii. annis regnum conseruans cum honore summae potestatis. Osuualdus uero post hunc regnum Northanhymbrorum*a* Christianissimus suscepit, quod et octo annis tenuit; qui supernae ciuitatis gaudia petens *b*et caeli secreta scandens,*b* regnum post ipsum Ospius rex suscepit ad tuendum uiginti et octo annis. Quo ablato*c* ab imis ad supera, Ecgfrido commisit terrena imperia, qui regnum quindecim annis tenuit. Quo a Pictis interfecto,*d* regnauit pro eo Aldfriðus frater eius .xix. annis. Aldfriðo uero successit filius eius Osredus .xi. annis. Quo occiso, Coenredus regni gubernacula suscepit .ii. annis. Cui in regnum successit Osricus undecim annis. Osrico uero successit Ceoluulfus frater Coenredi octo annis.[5] Huic Beda historiographus Anglorum historiam destinauit.[6]

3. In regni statu regis praedicti Ecgfridi anno quarto, constructum est quoddam nobile monasterium[7] In Viuremuthe.*a*[8] Sed qualiter id factum sit, ueriloquus Beda testatur in uita beatissimi abbatis sui Benedicti, atque Ceolfridi, quam ipse lenibus exarauit uerbis, quae in plerisque habetur descripta locis.[9] Aedificatus est idem locus et in honore principis apostolorum Petri consecratus.[10] Sed et aliud est coenobium constructum in ueneratione 'doctoris gentium' Pauli,[11] in loco qui dicitur Æt Gyruum.[12] His dictis, libet huic nostro operi inserere

---

ii.2 *a* porthanhymbrorum *C*   *b–b* added *C¹*   *c* uel sub- *added over* ablato *by C¹*   *d after* interfecto *C² adds* quia iniuste uastauerat Hiberniam

ii.3 *a* *at the foot of col. 55ra C² adds the words* et anno septimo regni eiusdem natus est Beda magnus, *linked by a* signe de renvoi

---

[5] Still following his Northumbrian regnal list, Byrhtferth brings the record up to the reign of Ceolwulf (729–37; d. 764), to whom Bede dedicated his *Historia ecclesiastica*. The regnal years for these kings are specified as follows in the 'Moore Memoranda': 'Aedilfrid .xxiiii., Æduini .xvii., Osuald .viiii., Osuiu .xxviii., Ecgfrid .xv., Aldfrid .xx., Osred .xi., Coinred .ii., Osric. .xi., Ceoluulf .viii.' Byrhtferth assigns twenty-eight (not twenty-four) years to Æthelfrith, eight (not nine) to Oswald, nineteen (not twenty) to Aldfrith, and eleven (not ten) to Osred. These regnal years are interpreted as follows by modern historians: Æthelfrith (acc. 592, d. 616), Edwin (acc. 616, d. 633), Oswald (acc. 634, d. 642), Oswiu (acc. 642, d. 670), Ecgfrith (acc. 670, d. 685), Aldfrith (acc. 686, d. 705), Osred (acc. 706, d. 716), Coenred (acc. 716, d. 718), Osric (acc. 718, d. 729), and Ceolwulf (acc. 729, resigned 737); see Keynes, 'Rulers', pp. 524–5. Byrhtferth supplements this bare chronological framework with details drawn from his reading of Bede's *Historia ecclesiastica*: the might of King Æthelfrith is described at *HE* i. 34 and ii. 2; the baptism of Edwin, the first Northumbrian king to be baptized, at *HE* ii. 9; Oswald is described as *rex Christianissimus* ibid. ii. 5. 1. The description of Ecgfrith's devastation of Ireland, added to Byrhtferth's text by C² but not originally part of Byrhtferth's text, is found at *HE* iiii. 24. 1, and his death in Pictland ibid.

[6] Bede, *HE*, praef. 1: 'Gloriosissimo regi Ceoluulfo Baeda famulus Christi et presbyter'.

[7] The date of the construction of Monkwearmouth was known from Bede, *Historia abbatum*, i. 4: 'Quod factum est [*scil.* construction of Monkwearmouth]...ad ostium fluminis

PARS SECVNDA 25

adopting the Christian faith, he entered the heavens as king and martyr for his merits, preserving the kingdom for seventeen years with the distinction of the highest authority. After him, the very Christian Oswald succeeded to the kingdom of the Northumbrians, which he held for eight years; seeking the joys of the heavenly city and ascending to the recesses of heaven, King Oswiu took on the kingdom after him, so as to protect it for twenty-eight years. When he was removed from the lower world to the upper, he entrusted his earthly authority to Ecgfrith, who held the kingdom for fifteen years. When he was killed by the Picts, Aldfrith his brother reigned in his place for nineteen years. For eleven years his son Osred was successor to Aldfrith. When he was killed, Coenred took up the governance of the kingdom for two years. Osric succeeded him in the kingdom for eleven years. Ceolwulf, the brother of Coenred, succeeded Osric for eight years.[5] The historian Bede dedicated his history of the English to him.[6]

3. Within the state of the realm, in the fourth year of the aforementioned King Ecgfrith, a noble monastery[7] was built at Monkwearmouth [674].[8] But as to how that came about, the reliable Bede demonstrates in his Life of his most blessed abbot Benedict, and of Ceolfrith, which he composed in modest words; it [the Life] is found copied in numerous places.[9] This same place was dedicated in honour of Peter, the prince of the apostles.[10] But another monastery was constructed in veneration of Paul, the 'teacher of peoples',[11] in the place which is called *Æt Gyruum* [Jarrow].[12] Having said all this, it is appropriate to

---

Viuri ad aquilonem anno ab incarnatione Domini sexcentesimo septuagesimo quarto, indictione secunda, anno autem quarto imperii Ecgfridi regis' (Bede, *VBOH* i. 368; *Abbots*, ed. Grocock and Wood, pp. 30–2).

[8] It is unclear where the later scribe (C²) derived the notion that Bede was born in 'the seventh year' of Ecgfrith's reign (see *app. crit.*: 'anno septimo regni eiusdem natus est Beda magnus'), i.e. in 677. In the final chapter of his *HE* (v. 24. 2) Bede tells us that he had been devoted to learning up to the fifty-ninth year of his life ('usque ad annum aetatis meae .lviiii.'); since the *Historia ecclesiastica* was completed and dedicated to King Ceolwulf in 731, the implication is that Bede was born in 672 or 673, not in 677.

[9] Bede's *Historia abbatum* (*CPL* 1378; *BHL* 8968): Bede, *VBOH* i. 364–87; *Abbots*, ed. Grocock and Wood, pp. 21–75.

[10] The dedication of Monkwearmouth to St Peter is stated by Bede at the very beginning of his *Historia abbatum* i. 1: 'monasterium construxit in honore beatissimi apostolorum principis Petri, iuxta ostium fluminis Viuri ad aquilonem' (Bede, *VBOH* i. 364; *Abbots*, ed. Grocock and Wood, p. 22).

[11] St Paul describes himself as *doctor gentium* in 1 Tim. 2: 7.

[12] The foundation of the monastery of St Paul at Jarrow is described by Bede, *Historia abbatum* i. 7 (Bede, *VBOH* i. 370; *Abbots*, ed. Grocock and Wood, p. 38).

HISTORIA REGVM

quaedam quae gesta sunt in diebus istorum abbatum, ut hi qui uitam illorum non legerunt, audiant quanta Christianitatis flamma refulsit

fo. 55ʳᵇ illis diebus in his ipsis regionibus, ut | ait Beda in suis dictionibus.

4. 'Fuit uir uitae uenerabilis, gratia Benedictus et nomine, ab ipso pueritiae suae tempore cor gerens senile, aetatem quippe moribus transiens nulli animum uoluptati dedit. Nobili quidem stirpe gentis Anglorum progenitus, sed non minori nobilitate mentis ad promerenda semper angelorum consortia suspensus. Denique cum esset minister Osuuii regis, et possessionem terrae suo gradui competentem illo donante perciperet, annos natus circiter uiginti et quinque fastidiuit possessionem caducam ut acquirere posset aeternam. Despexit militiam cum corruptibili donatiuo terrestrem, ut uero regi militans regnum in superna felicitate mereretur habere perpetuum. Reliquit domum, cognatos et patriam propter Christum et propter euangelium, ut centuplum acciperet et uitam aeternam possideret. Respuit nuptiis seruire carnalibus, ut sequi ualeret agnum uirginitatis gloria candidum in regnis caelestibus. Abnuit liberos carne procreare mortales, praedestinatus a Christo ad educandos ei spirituali doctrina filios caelesti in uita perennes.'[13]

5. 'Dimissa ergo patria Romam adiit, beatorum apostolorum, quorum desiderio semper ardere consueuerat, ᵃ<etiam loca corporum corporaliter uisere atque>ᵃ adorare curauit; ac patriam mox reuersus, studiosius ea quae uiderat ecclesiasticae uitae instituta diligere, uenerari, et quibus potuit praedicare non desiit.'[14] Profectus est dehinc ad limina sanctorum apostolorum tempore Vitaliani papae; qui inde egrediens ad Lirinensem insulam, se monachorum coetui tradidit, tonsuram

---

ii.5 ᵃ⁻ᵃ *suppl. ed. (from Bede)*

---

[13] 'Fuit uir uitae uenerabilis...in uita perennes': quoted *in extenso* and nearly verbatim from Bede, *Historia abbatum* i. 1 (Bede, *VBOH* i. 364–5; *Abbots*, ed. Grocock and Wood, pp. 22–4). The first sentence of the quotation ('Fuit uir uitae uenerabilis...animum uoluptati dedit') was quoted verbatim by Bede from Gregory, *Dialogi* ii. 1 (SChr cclx. 128). The reading *militans* (in the phrase *ut uero regi militans*) is found in only one surviving manuscript of the *Historia abbatum*, namely London, BL, Harley 3020 (s. x/xi), which is the earliest witness of the work and happens to be contemporary with the lifetime of Byrhtferth; the remaining manuscripts read *militare*. No manuscript of the work reads *felicitate* (in the phrase *regnum in superna felicitate mereretur habere perpetuum*); all manuscripts here read *ciuitate*.

[14] Bede, *Historia abbatum* i. 2 (Bede, *VBOH* i. 365; *Abbots*, ed. Grocock and Wood, p. 24). Byrhtferth's sentence is awkward because he has omitted a significant part of Bede's sentence: 'Dimissa ergo patria Romam adiit, beatorum apostolorum, quorum desiderio semper

PARS SECVNDA   27

insert in our work various things which happened in the days of these abbots, so that those who have not read their Life may hear how great a flame of Christianity shone out in those days in these same regions, as Bede [reports] in his own writings.

4. 'He was a man of venerable life, Benedictus ["blessed"] in distinction and name, having a mature outlook from the very period of his childhood; passing his time in good behaviour, he did not turn his mind to any pleasure. He was born of noble English stock, but was elevated by no lesser mental nobility in always earning the companionship of angels. And so when he was a thegn of King Oswiu, and was to receive from his [Oswiu's] gift the ownership of land consonant with his status, at the age of about 25 he scorned this transient ownership in order that he might obtain an eternal one. He spurned earthly military service with its corrupting rewards, so that, fighting on behalf of the true King, he might be found worthy to gain the perpetual kingdom in heavenly bliss. He left his home, kinsmen, and country for the sake of Christ and the gospel, so that he could receive the hundredfold reward and possess eternal life. He rejected subservience to carnal marriage, so that he would be able to follow the Lamb, gleaming with the glory of virginity, in the celestial realms. He refused to procreate mortal children in the flesh, being predestined by Christ to educate for Him sons in spiritual teachings so they would be everlasting in heavenly life.'[13]

5. 'Having renounced his homeland he went to Rome; he was concerned to venerate that [homeland] of the blessed apostles, and also to see in person the places [preserving] their bodies, for whom he had always had a burning desire; and returning anon to his homeland, he did not desist from eagerly loving [and] venerating the institutions of ecclesiastical life which he had seen, and from preaching to those whom he could.'[14] He had set out from here [England] for the shrines of the apostles in the time of Pope Vitalian; departing from there [Rome] for the island of Lerins, he entrusted himself to the throng of monks [and]

---

ardere consueuerat, <u>etiam loca corporum corporaliter uisere atque</u> adorare curauit.' Some coherence could be imparted to Byrhtferth's sentence by supplying (from Bede) the words *loca corporum* after *adiit* and before *beatorum apostolorum*. The remainder of the sentence (*ac patriam... non desiit*) was taken verbatim from Bede.

28 HISTORIA REGVM

accepit; ubi per biennium institutus, rursus beati Petri amore deuictus sacra eius limina repedare statuit.[15]

6. His diebus apostolicus papa Theodorum episcopum atque

fo. 55ᵛᵃ Hadrianum abbatem cum uiro Dei Benedicto ad Anglicam | direxit gentem. Quot uero Benedictus diuina uolumina, quantas beatorum apostolorum siue martyrum Christi reliquias attulit, quis annunciet?[16] Rex uero Ecgfrid his diebus regnum Northanhymbrorum pio moderamine tenuit. In cuius conspectu tantam inuenit gratiam summae clementiae, ut confestim ei terram septuaginta familiarum de suis largiretur praediis, et monasterium inibi primo pastori ecclesiae facere praeciperet, ad ostium fluminis Viuri ad laeuam, anno ab incarnatione Domini .dclxxiiii., indictione secunda, anno autem quarto imperii eiusdem regis.[17] Deinde cementarios adquisiuit, uitrique factores inuitauit, et omnia quae necessaria erant copiose est adeptus.[18] Qui quinquies, ut liber uitae eius demonstrat, est profectus ultra maris salsi gurgites; qui tanta munera et tanta attulit dona in omnibus speciebus, ut prae multitudine nequeant referri.[19]

7. 'Igitur uenerabilis Benedicti uirtute, industria ac religione rex Ecgfridus non minimum delectatus, terram quam ad construendum monasterium ei donauerat, quia bene ac fructuose ordinatam conspexit, quadraginta adhuc familiarum data possessione[a] augmentare regali munere curauit.'[20] O benigna clementia Christi, O clemens pietas regis, quae non solum libens contulit sua bona bonis, uerum etiam data possessione augmentare curauit, ut illud impleretur quod legitur,

---

ii.7 *a* possione C

---

[15] Byrhtferth's sentence ('Profectus est dehinc…limina repedare statuit') is loosely paraphrased from Bede, *Historia abbatum* i. 2 (wording retained by Byrhtferth is underlined): 'Romam rediit tempore…Vitaliani papae…post menses aliquot inde egrediens ad insulam Lirinensem, ibidem se monachorum coetui tradidit, tonsuram accepit…ubi per biennium…institutus, rursus beati Petri apostolorum principis amore deuictus, sacratam eius corpore ciuitatem repedare statuit' (Bede, *VBOH* i. 365–6; *Abbots*, ed. Grocock and Wood, p. 26). Vitalian was pope from 657 to 672.

[16] Bede, *Historia abbatum* i. 4: 'quot diuina uolumina, quantas beatorum apostolorum siue martyrum Christi reliquias adtulisset, patefecit' (Bede, *VBOH* i. 367; *Abbots*, ed. Grocock and Wood, p. 30). Byrhtferth has recast Bede's statement into a characteristic Byrhtferthian rhetorical question ('Who shall say…?'); on his fondness for such rhetorical questions, see Lapidge, 'The early sections', pp. 107–8 = *ALL* ii. 327–8, and Introduction, p. xxxix.

[17] Paraphrased from Bede, *Historia abbatum* i. 4: 'tantamque apud eum [*scil.* Ecgfridum] gratiam familiaritatis inuenit, ut confestim ei terram septuaginta familiarum de suo largitus, monasterium inibi primo pastori ecclesiae facere praeciperet. Quod factum est…ad ostium fluminis Viuri ad laeuam anno ab incarnatione Domini sexcentesimo septuagesimo quarto, indictione secunda, anno autem quarto imperii Ecgfridi regis' (Bede, *VBOH* i. 367–8;

PARS SECVNDA   29

accepted tonsure; being taught there for a period of two years, he was again overcome by love of St Peter and decided to return to his [Peter's] holy shrines.[15]

6. In these days the apostolic father [Vitalian] sent Bishop Theodore and Abbot Hadrian, in the company of Benedict the man of God, to the English people. Who shall say how many sacred volumes, how many relics of the blessed apostles or of the martyrs of Christ he brought with him?[16] At this time Ecgfrith held the kingdom of the Northumbrians with dutiful governance. Benedict found such welcome of favour in his [Ecgfrith's] sight that he immediately wished to grant him land of seventy hides from his own estates, and would command him to build there a monastery [dedicated] to the first Shepherd of the Church [i.e. St Peter] at the mouth of the river Wear, on its left bank, in the year of our Lord 674, the second indiction, and the fourth year of the reign of the same king [Ecgfrith].[17] Thereafter he acquired stone masons and invited glass-makers, and obtained in abundance all things which were necessary for the task.[18] Benedict travelled overseas, across the waves of the salty sea, five times, as the book of his life demonstrates; he brought back so many treasures and gifts of every kind that they cannot be reported here because of their great number.[19]

7. 'King Ecgfrith, therefore, pleased in no small measure by the probity, energy, and piety of the venerable Benedict, concerned himself to enlarge by royal endowment the lands which he had given him [Benedict] for constructing the monastery—40 hides had thus far been granted—because he saw that the original endowment was well and productively managed.'[20] O the benign mercy of Christ, O the merciful devotion of the king, which not only willingly granted its bounties to good causes, but also took care to increase what had already been granted, so that that [saying] would be fulfilled which reads, 'Is not our heart burning within

---

Abbots, ed. Grocock and Wood, pp. 30–2). The reading *ad l(a)euam* is found in the two earliest manuscripts of the *Historia abbatum*, the aforementioned Harley 3020, and Durham, CL, B. II. 35; the remaining eight manuscripts all read *ad aquilonem*.

[18] Byrhtferth summarizes a chapter of Bede, *Historia abbatum* i. 5 (Bede, *VBOH* i. 368; *Abbots*, ed. Grocock and Wood, p. 32).

[19] Once again Byrhtferth simply summarizes a long chapter of Bede (*Historia abbatum* i. 6), in which Bede describes all the treasures which Benedict Biscop brought back from Rome on his fourth trip to the eternal city (Bede, *VBOH* i. 368–70; *Abbots*, ed. Grocock and Wood, pp. 34–6).

[20] This sentence ('Igitur uenerabilis...regali munere curauit') is quoted verbatim from Bede, *Historia abbatum* i. 7 (Bede, *VBOH* i. 370; *Abbots*, ed. Grocock and Wood, pp. 36–8); note, however, that the transmitted text of Bede adds the word *se* between *bene* and *ac*, and reads *donasse* in lieu of Byrhtferth's *ordinatam*; the words *regali munere* are an addition by Byrhtferth.

HISTORIA REGVM

'Nonne cor nostrum ardens erat in eo?'[21] Vae inimicis Christi, uae qui destruunt, qui comburunt templa Dei![22] Comburentur[b] et ipsi, ubi uermes eorum non moriuntur et ignis non extinguitur.[23] De his nunc taceamus, et quid gestum sit laeti dicamus.

fo. 55[vb] **8.** 'Peractis | bis senis mensibus, coadunati sunt monachi numero ferme decem et septem, praeposito ac presbytero eis constituto Ceolfrido. Benedictus uero Iesu Christi famulus, consultu immo etiam iussu praephati regis Ecgfridi, aliud construxit monasterium in honore sanctissimi Pauli apostoli, non procul ab altero constitutum: ea dumtaxat ratione, ut una utriusque loci pax et concordia, eadem perpetuo familiaritas conseruaretur et gratia; ut sicut, uerbi gratia, corpus a capite per quod spirat non potest auelli, caput corporis sine quo non uiuit nequit obliuisci: ita nullus haec monasteria primorum apostolorum fraterna societate coniuncta, aliquo ab inuicem temptaret disturbare conatu.'[24] Constituit denique religiosus uir Domini Benedictus reuerentissimum Ceolfridum monasterio sancti Pauli apostoli, et Eosteruuinum praefecit abbatem in coenobio sancti Petri apostoli. Ipse uero Benedictus idcirco hoc gessit, ut regularis custodia semper seruaretur, ne propter illius laboris profectionem minus custodiretur sanctae disciplinae monarchia. 'Et ipse magnus abbas Benedictus, sicut de illo beatus papa Gregorius scribit, duodecim abbates sub se praefecit, sine caritatis detrimento, immo pro augmento.'[25]

9. 'Suscepit igitur Eosteruuinus curam monasterii regendi nono ex quo fundatum est anno, permansitque in ea usque ad obitum suum, annis quatuor. Vir ad saeculum nobilis, sed insigne nobilitatis non ad iactantiae materiem, ut quidam, despectumque aliorum, sed ad maiorem, ut Dei seruum decet, animi nobilitatem conuertens. Patruelis fo. 56[ra] quippe erat abbatis sui Benedicti; sed amborum tanta | ingenuitas, talis mundanae ingenuitatis fuit pro nihilo contemptus, ut neque iste monasterium ingressus aliquem sibi prae ceteris ob intuitum

---

[b] comburuntur *C*

[21] Cf. Luke 24: 32 ('nonne cor nostrum ardens erat in nobis dum loqueretur in via et aperiret nobis scripturas').

[22] This is apparently a reference to a (contemporary) Viking destruction of churches.

[23] Cf. Mark 9: 43 ('ubi vermis eorum non moritur et ignis non extinguitur').

[24] The sentence ('Peractis bis senis mensibus... disturbare conatu') is quoted with only minor alteration from Bede, *Historia abbatum* i. 7 (Bede, *VBOH* i. 370; *Abbots*, ed. Grocock and Wood, p. 38); Byrhtferth has substituted the phrase *peractis bis senis mensibus* (with his characteristic penchant for distributive numerals) for Bede's plain *post annum*.

PARS SECVNDA

him?'[21] Woe to the enemies of Christ, who destroy and burn the temples of God![22] They themselves will be burned, where the worms do not die and the fire is not extinguished.[23] Let us now be silent concerning these matters, and let us happily report what took place.

8. 'When twelve months had passed, the number of monks had reached nearly seventeen, with Ceolfrith appointed as their prior and priest. But Benedict, the servant of Jesus Christ, at the advice—indeed at the command—of the aforementioned King Ecgfrith, constructed another monastery in honour of St Paul the apostle, not far distant from the other one: on this principle, that the one peace and harmony, the same intimacy and love would be maintained in each place in perpetuity, such that, in a word, just as the body cannot be torn from the head through which it breathes, so the head cannot forget the body without which it ceases to live, so that no one would attempt by any undertaking to disturb these monasteries joined together in the fraternal fellowship of the two principal apostles.'[24] The devout man of God Benedict appointed the most reverend Ceolfrith as abbot of the monastery of St Paul [Jarrow], and made Eosterwine abbot in the monastery of St Peter [Monkwearmouth]. Benedict himself did this for the reason that regular discipline should always be preserved, so that the authority of holy discipline not be undermined through the advancement of that enterprise. 'And the great St Benedict himself, as the blessed Pope Gregory writes concerning him, appointed twelve abbots, without any diminution, indeed with an increase, of his love.'[25]

9. 'Eosterwine undertook charge of ruling the monastery in the ninth year after its foundation, and remained in charge for four years, up until his death. He was a nobleman in the world; but the mark of his nobility was not grounds for pomposity and scorn for others, as in some persons, directing it to a greater nobility of spirit, as is fitting in a servant of God. He was a cousin on his father's side of his abbot, Benedict; but there was such great inborn nobility in both of them, and such contempt for worldly nobility as being worth nothing, that neither would the one [Eosterwine], on entering the monastery, seek for himself any advancement over others in respect of his

---

[25] The sentence ('Et ipse magnus abbas...pro augmento') is quoted verbatim from Bede, *Historia abbatum* i. 7 (Bede, *VBOH* i. 371; *Abbots*, ed. Grocock and Wood, p. 40); the previous sentences are paraphrased from the same chapter. Ceolfrith became abbot of Jarrow on its foundation in 685; Eosterwine was appointed abbot of Monkwearmouth in 682/3, to serve in this capacity during the absences of Benedict Biscop in Rome. Bede's reference to Gregory the Great is to the latter's *Dialogi* ii. 3 (SChr cclx. 130).

HISTORIA REGVM

consanguinitatis aut nobilitatis honorem quaerendum, neque ille putaret offerendum, sed aequali cum fratribus lance boni propositi iuuenis gloriabatur se singularem*a* per omnia seruare disciplinam. Et quidem cum fuisset minister Ecgfridi regis, relictis semel negotiis saecularibus, depositis armis, assumpta militia spirituali, tantum mansit humilis fratrumque simillimus aliorum, ut uentilare cum eis et triturare, oues uitulasque mulgere, in pistrino, in horto, in coquina, in cunctis monasterii operibus iocundus et obediens gauderet exerceri. Sed et abbatis nomine assumpto, idem animo qui prius manebat ad omnes, iuxta id quod quidam sapiens admonet, dicens: "Rectorem te constituerunt, noli extolli; sed esto in illis quasi unus ex illis."[26] Erat enim mitis, affabilis et benignus omnibus, et quidem, ubi opportunum competebat, peccantes regulari disciplina coercens, sed magis tamen ingenita diligendi*b* consuetudine sedulus admonens, ne quis peccare uellet et limpidissimam uultus eius lucem nubilo sibi suae iniquitatis*c* abscondere. Saepe pro curandis monasterii negotiis alicubi digrediens, ubi operantes inuenit fratres, solebat eis confestim in opere coniungi, uel aratri gressum stiua regendo, uel ferrum malleo domando, uel uentilabrum manu concutiendo, uel aliud quid gerendo. Erat enim et uiribus fortis iuuenis, et lingua suauis; sed animo hilaris, et beneficio largus, et honestus aspectu. Eodem quo fratres ceteri cibo, semper eadem uescebatur in domo. Ipso quo priusquam abbas esset, communi dormiebat in loco, adeo ut etiam morbo correptus, et obitus sui certis ex signis iam praescius, duos adhuc dies in dormitorio fratrum quiesceret. Nam quinque reliquos usque ad exitus horam | dies, in secretiore se aede locabat. Qua die quadam egrediens et sub diuo residens, accitis ad se fratribus cunctis, more naturae misericordis osculum pacis eis flentibus ac de abscessu tanti patris et pastoris merentibus dedit. Obiit autem per nonas Martias noctu, fratribus matutinae psalmodiae laude uacantibus. Viginti quatuor annorum erat cum monasterium peteret, duodecim in eo uixit annis, septem presbyteratu functus est annis, quatuor ex eis monasterii regimen agebat; ac sic "terrenos artus

fo. 56*rb*

---

ii.9 *a* uel communem *added above line C¹*   *b* diligenti C (diligendi *Bede*)   *c* uel inquietudinis *added above line C¹*

[26] Ecclus. 32: 1.

PARS SECVNDA

33

blood-relationship or nobility, nor would the other [Benedict] think it should be granted, but the younger man rejoiced to be able to maintain, with the brothers, through the equipoise of a worthy undertaking, a strict discipline in every respect. And indeed, although he had been a thegn of King Ecgfrith, having abandoned worldly affairs once and for all, having laid down his weapons and taken up spiritual weaponry, he remained so humble and so similar to the other brothers, that he would rejoice to cooperate, happily and obediently, in all the works of the monastery—to winnow and thresh [grain] with them, to milk sheep and calves, [to work] in the bakery, the garden, the kitchen. But having assumed the title of abbot, he remained in his attitude to everyone what he had previously been, in accordance with what a wise man urges: "They appointed you ruler: do not vaunt yourself, but be among them as one of them."[26] For he was gentle, friendly and kind to everyone and, indeed, when the situation required, he restrained sinners through the discipline of the Rule, but more by carefully urging them, through his inborn inclination for loving, that no one should wish to sin, and should not hide from him the clear light of his face behind the cloud of his wickedness. Often, when setting out somewhere to attend to the affairs of the monastery, when he met brothers at work, he was in the habit of joining quickly in their work, either by guiding the progress of the plough with the plough-handle, or by shaping the iron with a hammer, or beating the winnowing-fork with his hand, or doing something else. He was a strong young man, and gentle of speech; but he was happy at heart, and generous in his favours, and honest in appearance. He always ate the same food as the other brothers, in the same room. He used to sleep in the same common dormitory as he slept before he became abbot, to the point that, when he was overcome with illness, and was aware of his impending death from certain signs, he still rested for two days in the brothers' dormitory. For the five days remaining before the hour of his death, he removed himself to a more private location. Coming out of there one day and sitting in the open air, having summoned all the brothers to him, he gave to them the kiss of peace as they were weeping in the natural manner of compassion and lamenting over the departure of so great a father and shepherd. He died at night on the nones of March [7 Mar. 686], when the brothers were engaged in the celebration of the psalmody of Matins. He was 24 years old when he sought out the monastery; he lived there twelve years, enjoying the rank of the presbyterate for seven years, and spent four of those years in governing the monastery; and thus, "leaving his

34 HISTORIA REGVM

moribundaque membra relinquens", caelestia regna petiuit',[27] ut duo diademata capiti imponeret <Christus>[d] secundum nominis sui palmam, hoc est *Eoster-* et *-uuine*, uerum Pascha ipse inclitus percipiendo, quod est uerum epinicion.[28] Verum his de uita uenerabilis Eosteruuini breuiter praelibatis, redeamus ad ordinem narrationis.[29]

10. 'Constituto illo abbate[a] monasterio beati Petri apostoli, constituto et domino Ceolfrido monasterio beati Pauli, non multo post temporis spatio Benedictus impiger miles Domini, quinta uice de Britannia Romam accurrens, innumeris sicut semper ecclesiasticorum donis commodorum locupletatus rediit.'[30] 'Nec multo post etiam felix Benedictus morbo coepit ingruente fatigari, quo per triennium languore paulatim accrescente, paralysi dissolutus est infirmitate, ut ab omni prorsus factus sit parte praemortuus inferiorum membrorum, superioribus solum, sine quorum uita uiuere nequit homo, ad officium patientiae uirtutemque reseruatis. Studebant in dolore semper auctori gratias referre utrique abbates, Benedictus scilicet atque Sigfridus, semper Dei laudibus fraternisue hortatibus uacare.'[31] Multa quidem fratribus colloquebatur, sed et hoc sedulus eisdem solebat iterare mandatum, ne quis | in electione abbatis generis prosapiam, et non magis uiuendi docendique probitatem putaret esse quaerendam.[32]

fo. 56[va]

11. 'At ubi uterque abbas lassatus infirmitate diutina iam se morti uicinum nec regendo monasterio idoneum fore conspexisset, tanta eos namque affecit infirmitas carnis ut perficeretur uirtus Christi in eis; cum uero quadam die desideratus[33] eis, se inuicem, priusquam de hoc

---

[d] *suppl. ed.*

ii.10 [a] *after* abbate *C adds* Benedictus   [b] uitat *C* (uita *Bede*)

---

[27] The entire chapter ('Suscepit igitur Eosteruuinus...caelestia regna petiuit') is taken with very little alteration from Bede, *Historia abbatum* i. 8 (Bede, *VBOH* i. 371–2; *Abbots*, ed. Grocock and Wood, pp. 40–2); but note that Byrhtferth's text reads *singularem* (*per omnia seruare disciplinam*) where Bede has *regularem*, and that in the phrase *ubi opportunum competebat* Byrhtferth has apparently substituted *competebat* for Bede's *comperiebat*. The words 'terrenos artus moribundaque membra relinquens' constitute a hexameter modelled on Vergil, *Aen.* vi. 732 ('terrenique hebetant artus moribundaque membra'). It seems likely that Bede himself composed this hexameter, and I have included it as an 'unlocated line' from (my reconstruction of) his lost *Liber epigrammatum: Bede's Latin Poetry*, ed. Lapidge, p. 348 (*Epigr.* xix). The following words, *caelestia regna petiuit*, are a hexameter cadence from Alcimus Avitus, *Carm.* vi. 302.

[28] Cf. Byrhtferth, *Enchiridion* iv. 1, line 395: 'epinicion, quod nomen palmam siue triumphum possumus appellare' (ed. Baker and Lapidge, p. 226); see also *DMLBS*, p. 785 (s.v. 'epinicion'). Byrhtferth uses the word again at *HR* iii. 14 (below, p. 76). See discussion by Lapidge, 'The early sections', p. 100 = *ALL* ii. 320, and Introduction, p. xxvi.

[29] The final words of this chapter (*ut duo diademata...redeamus ad ordinem narrationis*) are Byrhtferth's.

PARS SECVNDA

earthly frame and moribund limbs", he sought the celestial realms',[27] so that Christ might place two diadems on his head in accordance with the victory of his name, that is, *Eoster* ['Easter'] and *wine* ['friend'], but in his distinction receiving thereby the true Passover, which is the true song of victory.[28] But having made these remarks concerning the life of the venerable Eosterwine, let us return to the sequence of the narrative.[29]

10. 'With Eosterwine having been appointed abbot of the monastery of St Peter the apostle, and Ceolfrith appointed to the monastery of St Paul, after no great passage of time Benedict, the Lord's tireless soldier, travelling a fifth time from Britain to Rome, returned enriched with countless gifts, always of ecclesiastical utility.'[30] 'Not long afterwards the blessed Benedict began to be weakened by an aggressive illness, which, growing slowly in intensity for a period of three years, left him shattered in diseased paralysis, so that he was virtually already dead in respect of his lower limbs, with his upper parts, without the vitality of which man cannot live, alone preserved for the exercise of patience and strength. Both abbots, Benedict and Sigfrith, sought always in their illness to give thanks to their Creator, and always to be active in praise of God and exhortations to the brothers.'[31] Indeed he said many things to the brothers, but this commandment he was careful to repeat to them, that in electing an abbot no one was to think that the nobility of kin and not rather the probity of living and teaching were to be considered.[32]

11. 'And when each of these abbots, exhausted by lengthy illness, had realized that they were near to death and that it was not appropriate for them to be ruling a monastery, such great bodily illness afflicted them that the power of Christ was accomplished in them; for when on a certain day there was a desire[33] in each of them, before they should

---

[30] The sentence ('Constituto illo abbate...locupletatus rediit') is from Bede, *Historia abbatum* i. 9 (Bede, *VBOH* i. 373; *Abbots*, ed. Grocock and Wood, ed. Grocock and Wood, pp. 42–4).

[31] These words ('Nec multo post...hortatibus uacare') are from Bede, *Historia abbatum* i. 11 (Bede, *VBOH* i. 374; *Abbots*, ed. Grocock and Wood, p. 46).

[32] The final sentence of ch. 10 is Byrhtferth's brief summary of an extensive discussion by Benedict Biscop on monastic governance which Bede reports in *Historia abbatum* i. 11 (Bede, *VBOH* i. 374–6; *Abbots*, ed. Grocock and Wood, pp. 46–50).

[33] Most manuscripts of the *Historia abbatum* here read *desiderantibus*; only one, the aforementioned BL Harley 3020, reads *desideratus*, 'desire' (hence 'there was a desire in each of them'), rather than the meaning conveyed by the majority of manuscripts ('with each of them desiring'). The unattested form **desideratus* is apparently a fourth-declension masculine noun; but no such noun is attested in *DMLBS* or *TLL*. In any case, the occurrence of the form in Byrhtferth indicates once again that he was using either Harley 3020 itself, or a very closely related manuscript now lost.

HISTORIA REGVM

saeculo migrarent, uidere et alloqui, Sigfridus in feretro deportaretur ad cubiculum ubi Benedictus et ipse suo iacebat in grabato, eisque uno in loco ministrorum manu compositis, caput utriusque in eodem ceruicali locaretur lacrimabili spectaculo, nec tantum habuere uirium ut propius posita ora ad osculandum se alterutrum coniungere possent. Inito Benedictus cum eo cumque uniuersis fratribus salubri consilio, acciit abbatem Ceolfridum, quem monasterio beati Pauli apostoli praefecerat, uirum uidelicet sibi non tam carnis necessitudine quam uirtutum societate propinquum, et eum utrique monasterio, cunctis fauentibus atque hoc utilissimum iudicantibus, praeposuit patrem, salubre ratus per omnia ad conseruandum pacis unitatem concordiamque locorum, si unum perpetuo patrem rectoremque tenerent; commemorans saepius Israelitici regni exemplum, quod inexterminabile semper exteris nationibus inuiolatumque perdurauit, quamdiu unis eisdemque suae gentis regebatur a ducibus. At postquam praecedentium causa peccatorum inimico ab inuicem est certamine direptum, periit paulisper, et a sua concussum soliditate defecit.'[34]

fo. 56ᵛᵇ 12. 'Igitur, postquam cuncta complessent "quae Dei erant",[35] reuolutis mensibus duobus, primo uenerabilis ac Deo dilectus abbas Sigfridus, pertransito igne et aqua tribulationum temporalium, inductus est in sempiternae quietis refrigerium, introiuit in domum regni caelestis in holocaustis perpetuae iubilationis.'[36] Benedictus uero, uictor uitiorum, deinde adiunctis aliis mensibus quatuor, uictus infirmitate carnis ad extrema peruenit. Tunc uirtutum patrator egregius, ut purpuraret terminum sui exitus, cateruas contempsit inimicorum funditus. Qui sacrae fidei militiam proferens, qui dispensationis suae talenta sustollens, qui egregiae castitatis fructus in manibus retinens, qui oleum recondidit in thalamo cordis, ut dignus existeret sancta sanctorum intrare, iubeleique anni remissionem percipere.[37] 'Nox ruit

---

[34] This entire chapter ('At ubi uterque abbas . . . soliditate defecit') is taken nearly verbatim from Bede, *Historia abbatum* i. 13 (Bede, *VBOH* i. 376–7; *Abbots*, ed. Grocock and Wood, pp. 50–2).

[35] Cf. Matt. 16: 23, Mark 8: 33, and Luke 20: 25 ('quae Dei sunt').

[36] The wording of this first sentence ('Igitur . . . iubilationis') is taken from Bede, *Historia abbatum* ii. 14 (Bede, *VBOH* i. 377; *Abbots*, ed. Grocock and Wood, p. 52), save that Byrhtferth has substituted the words *postquam cuncta complessent quae Dei erant* for Bede's simpler *post haec*, and has replaced Bede's word *laudationis* with *iubilationis*.

[37] The beginning of this passage is based, with substantial modification, on Bede, *Historia abbatum* ii. 14: 'ac deinde adiunctis aliis mensibus quattuor, uitiorum uictor Benedictus et uirtutum patrator egregius uictus infirmitate carnis ad extrema peruenit' (Bede, *VBOH* i. 377; *Abbots*, ed. Grocock and Wood, pp. 52–4). The remainder of the passage ('ut purpuraret

PARS SECVNDA

37

depart from this life, to see and converse with each other, Sigfrith was carried in a litter to the bedroom where Benedict himself was lying on a camp-bed; and with each of them positioned in the one place by a contingent of attendants, their heads were placed together on the one pillow in a tear-jerking spectacle, nor did they have sufficient strength that they could reach each other so that their adjacent mouths could kiss each other. Benedict, having initiated a productive plan with him [Sigfrith] and all the brothers, summoned Abbot Ceolfrith, whom he had appointed to the monastery of St Paul the apostle [i.e. Jarrow], a man close to him not only by ties of kinship as by shared virtues, and proposed him as the father of each monastery, with everyone approving and judging this a most useful plan, thinking it beneficial in every way for maintaining the unity of peace and harmony of the two places, if they had the one father and leader in perpetuity, recalling often the example of the Israelite kingdom, which endured inviolable and always unconquerable to external nations so long as it was ruled by the one leader, and he being of this same people. But subsequently, as a result of its previous sins, being torn apart by hostile strife, it perished slowly, and passed away, shaken from its [former] solidarity.'[34]

12. 'Accordingly, after they had concluded "all God's business",[35] when two months had passed, first the venerable Abbot Sigfrith, beloved of God, having passed through the fire and water of temporal tribulations, being led into the consolation of eternal peace, entered into the home of the celestial kingdom in an offering of perpetual rejoicing.'[36] But Benedict, the conqueror of sins, after four further months were added, arrived at his final days, overcome by weakness of the flesh. At that point the excellent agent of virtue, so that he could adorn the conclusion of his departure, entirely scorned the throngs of his enemies. Advancing the campaign of the sacred faith, taking up the talents of his superintendence, retaining the fruits of his outstanding chastity in his own hands, he laid down the oil in the recesses of his heart so that he would be worthy to enter the holy of holies and to receive the remission of the year of jubilee.[37] 'Night fell, chilly with its

---

terminum...anni remissionem percipere') is Byrhtferth's own wording. The receipt of the year of Jubilee as a metaphor for entry into the eternal life is a characteristic Byrhtferthian conceit; cf. above, *HR* i. 2 (with n. 10) and below, iv. 11 (with n. 73), as well as *VSO* i. 6: 'sumere ab eo iubelei anni remissionem' (ed. Lapidge, *Byrhtferth of Ramsey*, p. 26), and discussion by Lapidge, 'The early sections', p. 111 = *ALL* ii. 331. For the unusual verb *purpurare*, literally 'to make dark red or crimson', used figuratively here to mean 'to give rich colouring', hence 'to adorn', see *DMLBS*, p. 2585, s.v. 'purpurare', sense 2b.

38 HISTORIA REGVM

hibernis algida flatibus',[38] diem*a* mox sancto nascitura aeternae felicitatis, serenitatis et lucis. Suscepit sanctus Domini seruus 'Dominici corporis et sanguinis sacramentum, hora exitus sui instante, pro uiatico; et sic anima illa sancta, longis flagellorum felicium excocta atque examinata flammis, luteam carnis fornacem deserit, et supernae beatitudinis libera peruolat ad gloriam. Sextodecimo postquam monasterium fundauit anno quieuit in Domino pius confessor, pridie Iduum Ianuariarum.'[39]

13. 'Ceolfridus uero abbas, illustris per omnia uir, acutus ingenio, actu impiger, maturus animo, religionis feruens zelo, prius,*a* sicut et supra meminimus, iubente pariter et iuuante Benedicto, monasterium beati Pauli apostoli .vii. annis fundauit, perfecit, rexit; ac deinde

fo. 57ʳᵃ utrique monasterio, uel, sicut rectius dicere | possumus, in duobus locis posito uni monasterio beatorum apostolorum Petri et Pauli, uiginti et octo annis sollerti regimine praefuit, et cuncta quae suus praedecessor egregia uirtutum opera incepit, ipse non segnius perficere curauit.'[40] Statuit igitur plurima altaria, fecit et oratoria, et uestimenta omnis generis ampliauit, tresque bibliothecas adquisiuit, duas utrique monasterio reliquit. Priuilegium monasterio a papa Sergio accepit, quod perlatum et coram synodo patefactum, magnifici regis Aldfridi subscriptione est confirmatum.[41] At ubi post multam regularis obseruantiae disciplinam, post incomparabilem orandi psallendique sollertiam, post mirabilem et coercendi improbos feruorem et modestiam consolandi infirmos, post insolitam rectoribus escae potusque parcitatem et habitus uilitatem, uidit se iam senior et 'plenus dierum'[42] non ultra posse subditis spiritualis exercitii uel docendo, uel uiuendo praefigere formam; multa diu secum mente uersans, utilius decreuit, dato

---

ii.12 *a* die *C* (diem *Bede*)
ii.13 *a* pius *C* (prius *Bede*)

---

[38] Byrhtferth has repeated this line of verse from Bede, *Historia abbatum* ii. 14 (Bede, *VBOH* i. 377; *Abbots*, ed. Grocock and Wood, p. 54). According to electronic databases, including *Poetria Nova 2*, the line is not found in earlier verse; but it is evidently based on two lines of Vergil: *Aen.* viii. 369 ('Nox ruit'), and *Georg.* ii. 339 ('orbis, et hibernis parcebant flatibus Euri'). The first part of the line ('Nox ruit hibernis') consitutes the first part of a hexameter (as far as the strong caesura); the remaining words are two dactyls ('algida flatibus'). No classical Latin verse form has such a structure.

[39] Adapted from Bede, *Historia abbatum* ii. 14: 'dominici corporis et sanguinis sacramentum hora exitus instante pro uiatico datur; et sic anima illa sancta longis flagellorum felicium excocta atque examinata flammis luteum carnis fornacem deserit, et supernae beatitudinis libera peruolat ad gloriam... Sexto decimo postquam monasterium fundauit anno quieuit in Domino confessor, pridie iduum Ianuarium' (Bede, *VBOH* i. 378; *Abbots*, ed. Grocock and

PARS SECVNDA

39

wintery blasts',[38] soon to give birth to the day of eternal bliss, serenity and light for the saint. The Lord's holy saint received the sacrament of 'the Lord's body and blood as a viaticum, when the hour of his death was imminent; and thus that holy soul, melted and purified by the enduring flames of propitious punishments, abandons the gold-coloured furnace of the flesh and flies free to the glory of heavenly bliss. In the sixteenth year after he founded the monastery, the holy confessor rested peacefully in the Lord, on 12 January.'[39]

13. 'Abbot Ceolfrith, a distinguished man in every respect, sharp in intelligence, vigorous in activity, mature in spirit, burning with religious zeal, at the command and with the support of Benedict, as I recorded above, had previously founded, completed, and ruled the monastery of St Paul the apostle for seven years; and thence for twenty-eight years he ruled each monastery with wise guidance, or, as we can more accurately say, of the one monastery of SS. Peter and Paul located in two places; and all the excellent works of virtue which his predecessor began, he himself undertook energetically to bring to completion.'[40] He therefore established several altars, constructed oratories, increased the ecclesiastical vestments of every kind, and commissioned three pandects and left two to either monastery. He received a [papal] privilege for his monastery from Pope Sergius, which was brought and revealed in the presence of a synod, and confirmed by the subscription of the magnificent King Aldfrith.[41] But when, after much instruction in the regular observance, after incomparable attention to prayer and psalmody, after amazing ardor in restraining reprobates and modesty in consoling the weak, after abstinence in food and drink unusual in rulers and simplicity in dress, he saw himself, as an old man 'full of days',[42] no longer able to determine a model spiritual discipline either by teaching or living, for those under him; and turning over at length many [of these concerns] in his mind, he decided it would be more useful,

---

Wood, p. 54). Note that Bede mistakenly construed *fornax* as masculine (*luteum ... fornacem*); Byrhtferth silently corrected to *luteam ... fornacem*.

[40] The sentence ('Ceolfridus uero abbas ... perficere curauit') is quoted nearly verbatim from Bede, *Historia abbatum* ii. 15 (Bede, *VBOH* i. 379; *Abbots*, ed. Grocock and Wood, p. 56), save that Byrhtferth substituted *illustris* for Bede's *industrius*, and *praedecessor* for Bede's *prodecessor*. Throughout his writings Bede himself vacillated between the forms *prodecessor* and *praedecessor*; cf. discussion by Lapidge in *Beda: Storia degli inglesi*, i. 367–8.

[41] The passage from *Statuit igitur* to *subscriptione est confirmatum* is summarized by Byrhtferth from a longer, more detailed passage in Bede, *Historia abbatum* ii. 15 (Bede, *VBOH* i. 380; *Abbots*, ed. Grocock and Wood, pp. 56–60).

[42] Gen. 25: 8, and 35: 29; 1 Chr. 23: 1, and 29: 28.

40   HISTORIA REGVM

fratribus praecepto, ut iuxta sui statuta priuilegii, iuxtaque regulam sancti abbatis Benedicti, de suis sibi ipsi patrem qui aptior esset eligerent.[43] 'Obnitentibus licet primo omnibus et in lacrimas singultusque genua cum obsecratione crebra flectentibus, factum est quod pius pater desiderauit.'[44]

14. 'Eligitur igitur Hpætbyrhtus, uir bonus et iustus, qui erat discipulus abbatis Sigfridi, ad cuius consecrationem Acca episcopus inuitatus est, qui illum solita in abbatis officium benedictione confirmauit.'[45] Profectus est beatus uir Ceolfridus ad limina sanctissimi principis apostolorum, sed priusquam ibidem peruenire potuisset, tactus est infirmitate, qua et mortuus est. Peruenit autem Lingonas miles emeritus circa horam diei tertiam .vii. kalendas Octobris ut diximus, fo. 57ʳᵇ applicauitque in pratis | eiusdem ciuitatis. Contigit autem Dei dispositione, ut ipso die circa horam decimam migraret ad Dominum. Cuius beatum corpus sepultum est in ecclesia sanctorum martyrum Speusippi, Eleusippi, et Meleusippi, ubi multa signa et sanitates patratae dinoscuntur, donante eo qui sanctos suos et in praesenti certantes iuuare, et in futuro consueuit uictores coronare.[46]

15. Haec autem quae scripta sunt ex dictis beatissimi Bedae excerpsimus. Iam ratum uidetur ut de eo quid loquamur, reminiscentes memoriam sanctitatis eius, et gratias ei referentes pro suis laboribus. Ait enim de annalibus, hoc est, de rebus singulorum annorum:

> Me legat, annales cupiat qui noscere menses,
> tempora dinumerans aeui uitaeque caducae.
> Omnia tempus agit, cum tempore cuncta trahuntur;
> alternant elementa uices et tempora mutant.
> Accipiunt augmenta dies noctesque uicissim.   [5]
> Tempora sunt florum, retinet sua tempora messis:
> sic iterum spisso uestitur gramine campus.
> Tempora gaudendi, sunt tempora certa dolendi;

---

[43] The passage from *At ubi post multam* to *qui aptior esset eligerent* is taken from Bede, *Historia abbatum* ii. 16 (Bede, *VBOH* i. 380–1; *Abbots*, ed. Grocock and Wood, pp. 60–2), with substantial abbreviation.

[44] This sentence ('Obnitentibus licet...pater desiderauit') is from Bede, *Historia abbatum* ii. 17 (Bede, *VBOH* i. 381; *Abbots*, ed. Grocock and Wood, p. 62), save that at the end of the sentence Byrhtferth replaced Bede's words *factum est quod uoluit* with the words *factum est quod pius pater desiderauit*.

[45] This sentence ('Eligitur igitur Hpætberhtus...benedictione confirmauit') has been cobbled together from disparate passages in Bede's *Historia abbatum*: ii. 18 ('Eligitur itaque abbas Huetberctus'), ii. 20 ('ossa Sigfridi abbatis ac magistri quondam sui' [*scil.* Huætberhti]),

PARS SECVNDA 41

once he had given the mandate to the brothers, that, in accordance with the provisions of his [papal] privilege and in accordance with the Rule of St Benedict, they could elect an abbot from among their number who would be more appropriate [for the task].[43] 'Although all of them objected at first and, in tears and sobs bending their knees in intense supplication, what the holy father desired came to pass.'[44]

14. 'And so Hwætberht is elected, a good man and true, who was the disciple of Abbot Sigfrith; Bishop Acca was invited to his [Hwætberht's] consecration, and confirmed him in the office of abbot with the usual blessings.'[45] The holy man Ceolfrith set out for the shrines of the most holy prince of the apostles [St Peter's in Rome], but before he could get there he was struck down with the illness from which he died. The retired soldier arrived at Langres at the third hour of the day [9:00 a.m.] on 25 September, as I said, and set up camp in the fields surrounding that city. It happened through God's dispensation that, at the tenth hour [4:00 p.m.] of the same day, he passed to the Lord. His sacred body was buried in the church of the holy martyrs Speusippus, Eleusippus, and Meleusippus, where many miracles and cures are known to have taken place at the bequest of Him Who is accustomed to assist those saints struggling in the present and to crown the victors in the future.[46]

15. I have excerpted these passages from the writings of the blessed Bede. It now seems right that I should say something about Bede himself, recalling the reputation of his holiness and giving thanks to him for his labours. For he said this concerning annals, that is, the events of individual years:

Let anyone who might wish to know the months of the year, reckoning the times of the age and of transient life, read me. Time drives on all things; all things are dragged along with time. The elements change places and times change. Day and night receive increments in turn [5]. There are times of flowers, the harvest keeps to its time: thus the field is covered once again with thick grass. There are certain times for rejoicing and certain times for griev-

---

and an earlier passage in ii. 20: 'aduocatur episcopus Acca, et solita illum in abbatis officium benedictione confirmat' (Bede, *VBOH* i. 383, 385, and 384 respectively; *Abbots*, ed. Grocock and Wood, pp. 66, 70, and 68 respectively).

[46] The remainder of c. 14 (*Profectus est...uictores coronare*) is summarized by Byrhtferth from three chapters of Bede's *Historia abbatum* ii. 21–3, though he tries, where possible, to retain Bede's wording (Bede, *VBOH* i. 385–7; *Abbots*, ed. Grocock and Wood, pp. 70–4). Thereafter, Byrhtferth ceases to draw on Bede's *Historia abbatum*.

42 HISTORIA REGVM

> tempora sunt uitae, sunt tristia tempora mortis.
> Tempus et hora uolat. Momentis labitur aetas. [10]
> Omnia dat, tollit, minuitque uolatile tempus.
> Ver, aestas, autumnus, hiems: redit annus in annum.[47]

> Hos claros uersus uenerabilis edidit auctor
> Beda sacer, multum nitido sermone coruscans.[48]

16. LAMENTATIO BEDAE PRESBYTERI. Versus quoque quos de die iudicii composuit ad episcopum Accam, hoc in loco libet caraxare.[49] De quorum positione strictim nescientes instruere, obsecro scientibus oneri non sit.

> Inter florigeras fecundi caespitis herbas,
> flamine uentorum resonantibus undique ramis,
> arboris umbriferae maestus sub tegmine solus
> dum sedi, subito planctu turbatus amaro,
> carmina praetristi cecini haec lugubria mente, [5]
> utpote commemorans scelerum commissa meorum,
> et maculas uitae, mortisque inamabile tempus,
> iudiciique diem horrendo examine magnum,
> perpetuamque reis districti iudicis iram,
> et genus humanum discretis sedibus omne, [10]
> gaudia sanctorum necnon poenasque malorum.
> Haec memorans, mecum tacito sub murmure dixi:
> Nunc, rogo, nunc uenae, fontes aperite calentes,
> dumque ego percutiam pugnis*a* rea pectora, uel dum
> membra solo sternam, meritosque ciebo dolores, [15]
> uos, precor, effusis lacrimis non parcite statim,
> sed maestam salsis faciem perfundite guttis
> et reserate nefas Christo cum uoce gementi;
> nec lateat quicquam culparum cordis in antro.

fo. 57ᵛᵃ

---

ii.16 *a* pungnis *C*

---

[47] These hexameters on the transience of time are listed in *ICL* no. 9480, and have been edited by Emil Baehrens in *Poetae Latini Minores*, v. 349–50 [no. LVIII], and by Alexander Riese in *Anthologia Latina*, no. 676. They are preserved in a substantial number of early medieval manuscripts, where they frequently, but not invariably, are attributed to Bede. However, it is very unlikely that they are a genuine work of Bede; they are, in fact, simply a cento of verses lifted from earlier poets, esp. Dracontius, so that line 3 ('Omnia tempus...cuncta trahuntur') = Dracontius, *Satisfactio* 219; line 4 ('alternant...mutant') = Dracontius, *Satisfactio* 247; line 5 ('accipiunt...uicissim') = Dracontius, *Satisfactio* 249; line 6 ('tempora...messis') = Dracontius, *Satisfactio* 251; and line 11 ('omnia dat...tempus') =

PARS SECVNDA 43

ing; there are times for living, and sad times of dying. Time and the hour fly by. Life slips away moment by moment [10]. Fleeting time grants all things, takes them away, and reduces them [to nothing]. Spring, summer, autumn, winter: the year comes back annually.[47]

The venerable author, the holy Bede, greatly shining through his gleaming speech, composed these outstanding verses.[48]

16. *The Lamentation of Bede the Priest.* It is also fitting to transcribe here the verses which he composed for Bishop Acca concerning the Day of Judgement.[49] I pray that it not be a burden to those who know them already briefly to instruct those who don't know them concerning their theme.

Among the flowering plants of the fertile meadow, with branches soughing on all sides in the breath of the winds, while I sat alone in sadness under the covering of a shady tree, disturbed suddenly by a bitter plangency, I sang these doleful songs in my sad heart [5], remembering, as it were, the sins of my evil deeds and the stains of my life, the unlovely hour of death and the mighty Day of Judgement with its terrifying inquisition, and the eternal rage of the severe Judge towards the guilty, and the entire human race in its distinct locations [10] and the joys of the saints as well as the punishments of malefactors. Reflecting on these things, I said to myself in a quiet murmur, now, I pray, now my tear-ducts, open your warm streams, and while I shall strike my guilty breast with my fists, or shall prostrate my limbs on the ground, and produce my well-deserved laments [15], you, I pray, do not spare unyieldingly the floods of tears, but inundate my sad visage with salty drops and open up the sin to Christ in a mournful voice, nor let any trace of guilt remain in my heart's cavern.

Dracontius, *De laudibus Dei* iii. 539. For an edition, translation and discussion, see *Bede's Latin Poetry*, ed. Lapidge, pp. 515–17 (Appendix III).

[48] It is probable that these two hexameters were composed by Byrhtferth himself; they are also found prefixed to this poem ('Me legat annales') in Oxford, St John's College 17 (Thorney, AD 1110–11), fo. 14ʳ, a 12th-c. copy of Byrhtferth's *Computus*; see *Byrhtferth's Enchiridion*, ed. Baker and Lapidge, pp. lii–lv and 384.

[49] Byrhtferth here inserts the entire text of Bede's *Versus de die iudicii* [*CPL* 1370]. This poem, an early composition by Bede, is preserved in more than forty manuscripts (see *Bede's Latin Poetry*, ed. Lapidge, pp. 34–70 (introduction) and 155–79 (text)). These manuscripts group themselves into three major recensions, of which the two principal recensions are what I describe as the α-recension, consisting largely of manuscripts written in England, and the β-recension, consisting of manuscripts written on the Continent. The manuscript from which Byrhtferth copied the poem clearly belonged to the α, (or English) recension, as is clear from the characteristic reading *animos* in line 25 (see below, n. 50). The title which Byrhtferth assigned to the poem—'Lamentatio Bedae presbyteri'—is possibly of his own devising, since it occurs in none of the remaining forty-three witnesses, but could equally well be the contribution of the scribe of C.

HISTORIA REGVM

44

Omnia quin luci uerbis reddantur apertis— [20]
pectoris et linguae, carnis uel crimina saeua.
Haec est sola salus animae[b] et spes certa dolendi:
uulnera cum lacrimis medico reserare superno,
qui solet allisos sanare et soluere uinctos;
quassatos nec uult animos[c50] infringere dextra, [25]
nec lini tepidos undis extinguere fumos.[d]
Nonne exempla tibi pendens dabat in cruce latro,
peccati quantum ualeat confessio uera?
Qui fuit usque crucem sceleratis impius actis,
mortis in articulo sed uerba precantia clamat, [30]
et solo meruit fidei sermone salutem,
cum Christo et portas paradisi intrauit apertas.
Cur, rogo, mens, tardas medico te pandere totam?
Vel cur, lingua, taces, ueniae dum tempus habebis?
Auribus omnipotens te nunc exaudit apertis. [35]
Ille dies ueniet, iudex dum uenerit orbis,
debebis qua tu rationem reddere de te.
Suadeo praeuenias lacrimis modo iudicis iram.
Quid tu in sorde iaces, scelerum caro plena piaclis?
Cur tua non purgas lacrimis peccata profusis, [40]
et tibi non oras placidae fomenta medelae?

fo. 57[vb] Fletibus assiduis est dum data gratia flendi
poenituisse iuuat tibi nunc et flere salubre est.
Aeternus fuerit placidus te uindice[e] iudex
nec Deus aethereus bis crimina uindicat ulli; [45]
spernere tu noli ueniae tibi tempora certa.
Quanta malis maneant etiam tormenta memento
uel quod[f] celsithronus metuendus ab arce polorum:
adueniet iudex rationem reddere cunctis.
Praecurrent illum uel qualia signa: repente [50]
terra tremet montesque ruent collesque liquescent,
et mare terribili confundet[g] murmure mentes,
tristius et caelum tenebris obducitur atris.
Astra cadunt, rutilo et Titan tenebrescit in ortu,

---

[b] uel -i *written above* animae *by* C[2]   [c] uel calamos *written above* animos *by* C[2]
[d] *corr. ed.*, fungos C   [e] uel iudice *written above* uindice *by* C[2]   [f] uel quam *written
above* quod *by* C[2]   [g] uel -dit *written above* confundet *by* C[2]

PARS SECVNDA 45

Rather let all things be brought to light in unambiguous words [20]—the cruel sins of the heart and the tongue and the flesh. This is the only salvation of the soul and the certain outcome of grieving: tearfully to open up the wounds before the heavenly Physician Who is accustomed to cure those in danger and to release those in bonds; nor does He wish to snap off shaken minds[50] with His right hand [25], or to extinguish the languid smoke of the lamp wick with water. Did not the thief hanging on the cross give you an example of how much avails the true confession of sin? That thief was sinful in his heinous deeds until he mounted the cross itself, but in the moment of death he shouted out words of entreaty [30] and merited salvation through his words of faith alone, and entered the open gates of Paradise with Christ. Why, I ask, O my soul, are you slow to reveal your entire self to the Physician? Or why, tongue, are you silent, while you still have time for repentance? The Omnipotent God is now listening to you with open ears [35]. That day shall come, when the Judge of the world will arrive, on which you shall have to account for yourself. I urge you now to anticipate the Judge's wrath with your tears. Why do you lie in filth, your flesh steeped in the evil of sins? Why do you not cleanse your sins with profuse tears [40] and why do you not pray for poultices of soothing medication? As long as forgiveness is given for weeping with insistent tears, it is appropriate for you to have repented even now, and it is healthy to weep. The eternal Judge will be benign with you as defendant, nor does God in heaven twice take vengeance on someone for his sins [45]; do not spurn the times appointed to you for repentance. Remember what great torments remain for malefactors, or how terrifying is the high-throned One at the citadels of heaven: He shall come as Judge to settle accounts with everyone. These signs shall precede Him: suddenly [50] the earth will tremble, and mountains collapse and hills dissolve, and the sea will confound understanding with a terrifying roar and the sky will sadly be obscured with black clouds. Stars fall and the sun darkens in its reddish rising, nor does the pale

---

[50] The reading *animos* in line 25 is characteristic of what I call the α, (or English) recension of the *Versus de die iudicii*; manuscripts belonging to other recensions of the work here read *calamos*, where the reference is to Isa. 42: 3 ('calamum quassatum non conteret et linum fumigans non extinguet'). The scribe of the archetype of the α-recension, or possibly even Bede himself, in substituting *animos* for *calamos*, was evidently attempting to draw out the tropological sense of the allusion: 'nor does He wish to snap off shaken minds with His right hand'. See *Bede's Latin Poetry*, ed. Lapidge, pp. 57–8, and Introduction, p. lv, n. 136.

HISTORIA REGVM

pallida nocturnam nec praestat[h] luna lucernam.　　　[55]
De caelo uenient et signa minantia mortem:
tum superum subito ueniet commota potestas,
coetibus angelicis regem stipata supernum.
Ille sedens solio fulget sublimis in alto;
ante illum rapimur, collectis undique turmis,　　　[60]
iudicium ut capiat gestorum quisque suorum.
Sis memor illius, quia tum pauor ante tribunal
percutiet stupidis cunctorum corda querelis,
dum simul innumeris regem comitata polorum
angelica aduenient caelestibus agmina turmis,　　　[65]
atque omnes pariter homines cogentur adesse:
qui sunt, qui fuerant, fuerint uel quique futuri.
Cunctaque cunctorum cunctis arcana patebunt:
quod cor, lingua, manus, tenebrosis gessit in antris,
et quod nunc aliquem uerecundans scire uerebar,　　　[70]
omnibus in patulo pariter tunc scire licebit.
Insuper impletur flammis ultricibus aer,
ignis ubique suis ruptis regnabit habenis;
et quo nunc aer gremium diffundit inane,
ignea tunc sonitus perfundet flamma feroces,　　　[75]
festinans scelerum saeuas ulciscere causas.[i]
Nec uindex ardor cuiquam tunc parcere curat,
sordibus ablutus ueniat nisi ab omnibus illuc.
Tunc tribus et populi ferient rea pectora pugnis.[j]
Stabit uterque simul timidus—pauperque potensque,　　　[80]
et miser et diues, simili ditione timebunt:
fluuius igniuomus miseros torquebit amare,
et uermes scelerum mordebunt intima cordis.
Nullus ibi meritis confidit iudice praesens,
singula sed nimius percurrit pectora terror　　　[85]
et stupet adtonito simul impia turma[51] timore.[k]
Quid, caro, quid facies, illa, quid, flebilis, hora,
quae modo (uae!) misera seruire libidine gaudes?
Luxuriaeque tuae stimulis te[l] agitabis[m] acutis—
ignea tu tibimet cur non tormenta timebis,　　　[90]
daemonibus dudum fuerant [n]quae parta[n] malignis,

fo. 58[ra]

---

[h] uel -e- [*i.e.* praestet] *written above* praestat *by* C^2　　　[i] uel flammas *written above* causas *by* C^2　　　[j] pungnis *C*　　　[k] uel tre- [*i.e.* tremore] *written above* timore *by* C^2　　　[l] uel nunc *written above* te *by* C^2　　　[m] uel -bat [*i.e.* agitabat] *written above* agitabis *by* C^2　　　[n-n] praeparata *written above* quae parta *by* C^2

PARS SECVNDA 47

moon offer its nocturnal light [55]. And signs threatening death shall come from the sky: then suddenly the mighty power of the heavenly throngs will come, surrounding the heavenly King with their angelic hosts. He, sitting aloft on His heavenly throne, is resplendent; in collected hordes we are all carried before Him [60] so that each person may receive judgement for his deeds. Be mindful of that person, because fear before the tribunal shall then strike the hearts of everyone with senseless lamentation while, at the same time, angelic hosts accompanying the King in countless celestial throngs shall come [65], and all men shall be compelled to be present: those who exist now, who have existed, or who shall do so in the future. And all the hidden secrets of all men shall be revealed to all—what the heart, the tongue, the hand did in shady corners, and that which I now shamefully fear anyone to know [70], it will at that time be appropriate for everyone to know openly. What is more, the air is filled with avenging flames and fire shall rule everywhere, having broken its reins; and where now the atmosphere extends its empty bosom, the fiery flame shall then pour forth ferocious sounds [75], hastening to avenge the savage sources of sin. Nor does this avenging fire take trouble then to spare anyone, unless he comes there washed clean of all filth. Then the tribes and the peoples shall strike their guilty breasts with their fists. Everyone will stand together in fear—the poor man and the powerful man [80], both the wretch and the rich man, and they shall tremble at the same authority: the fire-belching river will torture the wretches cruelly, and the worms of their sins will gnaw their inwards. No one there present before the Judge will rest on his laurels, but an extreme terror races through their hearts [85] and the evil throng[51] is thunderstruck by stupefied terror. What, flesh, what will you do, as you weep at that hour, which you now (shame on you!) rejoice to behave with pitiable wantonness? And will you rouse yourself with the sharp goads of your self-indulgence?— why will you not fear for your own sake the fiery torments [90] which were prepared long ago by evil demons, and which exceed the comprehension and

---

[51] The manuscript of Bede's *Versus de die iudicii* which Byrhtferth was copying evidently read *turma* at this point (with other manuscripts of the α-recension); Continental manuscripts of the β-recension here read *turba* (*Bede's Latin Poetry*, ed. Lapidge, p. 168 *ad app. crit.*).

HISTORIA REGVM

quae superant sensus cunctorum et dicta uiuorum?[o]
Nec uox ulla ualet miseras edicere poenas:
ignibus aeternae nigris loca plena gehennae,
frigora mixta simul feruentibus algida flammis;   [95]
nunc oculos nimio flentes ardore camini,
nunc iterum nimio stridentes frigore dentes.
His miseris uicibus miseri uoluuntur in aeuum,
obscuras inter picea caligine noctes.
Vox ibi nulla sonat, durus nisi fletus ubique;   [100]
non nisi tortorum facies ibi cernitur ulla.
Non sentitur ibi quicquam nisi frigora, flammae.
Fetor et ingenti complet putredine nares;
os quoque flammiuomo lugens implebitur igne,
et uermes lacerant ignitis dentibus ossa.   [105]
Insuper et pectus curis torquetur amaris,
cur caro luxurians sibimet sub tempore paruo
atro perpetuas meruisset carcere poenas,
lucis ubi miseris nulla scintilla relucet,
nec pax nec[p] pietas, immo spes nulla quietis   [110]
flentibus arridet. Fugiunt solacia cuncta.
Auxilium nullus rebus praestabit amaris;
laetitiae facies iam nulla uidebitur illic.
fo. 58[rb] Sed dolor et gemitus, stridor, pauor et timor horrens,
taedia, tristitae, trux indignatio, languor,   [115]
errantesque animae flammis in carcere caeco.
Noxia tunc huius cessabunt gaudia saecli:
ebrietas, epulae, risus, petulantia, iocus,
dira cupido, tenax luxus, scelerata libido,
somnus iners, torporque grauis, desidia pigra.   [120]
Illicit at quicquid modo delectatio carnis
et caeca scelerum uertit uertigine mentem,
tunc caecis merget flammis sine fine misellos.
Felix o nimium,[q] semperque in saecula felix
qui illas effugiet poenarum prospere clades,   [125]
cum sanctisque simul laetatur in omnia saecla!
Coniunctus Christo caelestia regna tenebit,
nox ubi nulla rapit splendorem lucis amoenae,
non dolor aut gemitus ueniet, nec fessa senectus,
non sitis, esuries, non somnus,[r52] non labor ullus,   [130]

---

[o] uirorum *written above* uiuorum *by* C[2] [p] uel aut *written above* nec *by* C[2] [q] uel
hominum *written above* nimium *by* C[2] [r] *corr. ed.*, sonus C

PARS SECVNDA   49

description of living men? Nor can any voice describe those wretched punishments: places filled with the black fires of eternal hell, freezing cold mixed together with searing flames [95]; at one moment eyes weeping from the excessive heat of the furnace, now again teeth chattering with excessive cold. The wretches are tossed forever between these miserable alterations, in the night black with its pitch-like darkness. No voice sounds there, except for the relentless moaning on all sides [100]; no face but that of torturers is seen there. Nothing is felt there but cold, flames. A stench fills the nostrils with a mighty foulness; the wailing mouth shall be filled with fire-spewing flame, and worms tear the bones with fiery teeth [105]. What is more, the conscience is tormented with bitter remorse as to why the flesh, luxuriating in itself for so short a time, should have deserved eternal punishments in a black prison where no spark of light shines on the wretches, where no peace nor mercy—indeed no hope of rest [110]—smiles on those weeping. All comforts flee. No one shall provide help in this bitter situation; no joyful face shall be seen there. But sadness and moaning, screaming, fear and awesome terror, loathing, bitterness, savage indignation, weariness [115], and souls wandering amidst the flames in the black prison. Then shall the foul joys of this world cease: drunkenness, feasting, laughter, wantonness, joking, abominable desire, clinging debauchery, sinful sexual appetite, inert dozing, heavy torpor, sluggish laziness [120]. Whatsoever fleshly delight now seduces, and thus overturns the mind in a blind whirlpool of sins, shall then swamp the poor wretches in blind flames forever. O blessed is he, always and forever blessed, who luckily shall escape those disastrous punishments [125] and with the saints rejoices for all time! United with Christ he will possess the heavenly realms, where no night snatches away the splendour of kindly light, where misery and moaning come not, nor exhausted old age, not thirst, hunger, not sleep,[52] not any travail [130],

---

[52] In lieu of *non somnus* all remaining manuscripts of the *Versus de die iudicii* read *somnus et* (*Bede's Latin Poetry*, ed. Lapidge, p. 174 *ad app. crit.*).

HISTORIA REGVM

non febres, morbi, clades, non frigora, flammae,
taedia, tristitiae, curae, tormenta, ruinae,
fulmina, nimbus, hiems, tonitrus, nix, grando, procella,[s]
angor, paupertas, moeror, mors, casus, egestas:
sed pax et pietas, bonitas, opulentia regnant,[53]   [135]
gaudia, laetitia,[t] uirtus, lux, uita perennis,
gloria, laus, requies, honor et concordia dulcis.
Insuper omne bonum cunctis Deus ipse ministrat.
Semper adest praesens, cunctos fouet, implet, honorat,
glorificat, seruat, ueneratur, diligit, ornat,   [140]
collocat altithrona laetosque in sede polorum,
praemia perpetuis tradens caelestia donis,
angelicas inter turmas sanctasque cohortes,
uatidicis iunctos patriarchis atque prophetis,
inter apostolicas animis laetantibus arces,   [145]
atque inter roseis splendentia castra triumphis,
candida uirgineo simul inter et agmina flore,
quae trahit alma Dei genitrix, pia uirgo Maria,
per benedicta patris fulgenti regna paratu,
inter et ecclesiae sanctos natosque patresque   [150]
inter et aethereum caelesti pace senatum.
[u]Quid, rogo,[u] quid durum saeclo censetur in isto,
utque illas inter liceat habitare cohortes,
sedibus et superum semper gaudere beatis?[v54]

Incolumem mihi te Christus, carissime frater,   [156]
protegat, et faciat semper sine sine beatum!
En, tua iussa sequens cecini tibi carmina flendi;
tu tua fac promissa, precor, sermone fideli
commendans precibus Christo modo meque canentem.   [160]
Viue Deo felix et dic uale fratribus almis,
Acca pater, trepidi et pauidi reminiscere serui[w]
meque tuis Christo precibus commenda benignis.

fo. 58[va]

---

[s] uel -e [*i.e.* procellae] *written above* procella *by* C[2]   [t] uel -e [*i.e.* laetitiae] *written above* laetitia *by* C[2] *(correctly)*   [u–u] uel ergo *written above* Quid, rogo *by* C[2]   [v] Ac dominum benedicere saecla per omnia Christum *interlined by* C[2]   [w] uel uerne *written above* serui *by* C[2]

---

[53] The reading *regnant* is characteristic of manuscripts of the α-recension of the *Versus de die iudicii*; manuscripts of other recensions read either *rerum* or *regnum* (*Bede's Latin Poetry*, ed. Lapidge, p. 174 *ad app. crit.*).

PARS SECVNDA 51

not fevers, diseases, disasters, not cold, flames, loathing, bitterness, cares, torments, catastrophes, lightning, storm clouds, winter, thunder, snow, hail, storm, anxiety, poverty, sadness, death, misfortune, need: but rather peace and mercy, goodness, abundance reign[53] [135], joy, happiness, virtue, light, life eternal, honour, praise, peace, glory, and sweet harmony. Moreover, God Himself administers all good things to everyone. He is always present, He nourishes all, fills them, respects them, honours, protects, venerates, loves, adorns [140], and assembles the blessed on the high-throned seat of heaven, granting heavenly rewards in the form of perpetual gifts, amidst the angelic throngs and holy assemblies, joined to the patriarchs and prescient prophets, within the apostolic citadels, with rejoicing hearts [145], and amidst the shining palaces with their rosy triumphs, and likewise amidst the bright throngs with their virginal bloom, whom the gentle mother of God, the holy Virgin Mary, leads through the blessed realms of the Father, in shining array, and among the saints and sons and fathers of the Church [150] and among the eternal senate in heavenly peace. What, I ask, what could be thought a hardship in this world, considering that it were possible to live among those legions and rejoice always on the blessed seats of heavenly citizens?[54]

Dear brother, let Christ protect you safely for me and may He always make you blessed without end! Look: following your requests I have sung these songs of weeping for you; you keep your promises, I beseech you, made in trustworthy speech, commending me the poet in your prayers to Christ [160]. Live blessedly in God, and give my regards to the good brothers, Father Acca, and remember your fearful and trembling servant, and commend me to Christ in your kindly prayers.

---

[54] At this point an extra line (155) was inserted into the text by C[2] ('ac Dominum benedicere saecla per omnia Christum'); it did not form part of the text which Byrhtferth originally transcribed into his *Historia regum*, which, as the variant *animos* (for *calamos*) in line 25 clearly shows, belonged to what I call the α-recension of the *Versus de die iudicii*, whereas the line (155) interpolated by C[2] is characteristic of manuscripts belonging to the Continental γ-recension. The metrical form of the interpolated verse—having no strong (penthemimeral) caesura, and a single triemimeral caesura—marks it as spurious, since whenever in his genuine verse Bede employs a triemimeral caesura, he invariably balances it by a hephthemimeral caesura: see Lapidge, 'Beda Venerabilis', pp. 135–6, and *Bede's Latin Poetry*, ed. Lapidge, pp. 60–1.

52   HISTORIA REGVM

17. His peractis gaudiis ex sanctissimi doctoris Anglorum riuulis, libet ex ipsius historia*a* fundamentum assumere huius operis, incipientes ab ultima ipsius praedicti uiri sententia, et sic annos Domini consignantes et regum tempora cauta ratione disponentes, ceterorumque fidelium uitam et miracula*b* pro posse describentes,*c* optamus summopere cum ipsis aeternae retributionis palmam a Christo percipere. Sic enimuero in calce suae historiae ait beatus et ueriloquus Beda, ut in exordio huius libri constat conscriptum.

18. 'Anno Dominicae incarnationis .dccxxxii., Byrhtpaldus archiepiscopus longa consumptus aetate, defunctus est die .v. Iduum Ianuariarum; qui sedit annos .xxxvii., menses .vi., dies .xiiii.*a* Pro quo anno eodem factus est archiepiscopus uocabulo Tatpine de prouincia Merciorum, cum fuisset presbyter in monasterio quod uocatur Briodun. Consecratus est autem in Dorouerni ciuitate a uiris uenerabilibus Daniele Ventano, et Ingualdo Lundoniensi, et Alduuino Licetfeldensi, | et Aldulfo Hrofensi antistitibus, die .x. Iunii mensis, dominica; uir religione et prudentia insignis.'[55]

fo. 58ᵛᵇ

19. 'Itaque in praesenti ecclesiis Cantuariorum Tatuine et Hrofensi Ældulfus episcopi praesunt. Porro prouinciae Orientalium Anglorum Eadbertus[56] et Headdolac episcopi. Prouinciae Occidentalium Saxonum, Danihel et Forðere episcopi. Prouinciae Merciorum, Ealduine episcopus; et eis populis qui ultra amnem Sabrinam ad occidentem habitant, Vualchstod episcopus. Prouinciae Huicciorum, Vuilfridus episcopus. Prouinciae Lindisfarorum uel Lindisse, Cyniberhtus episcopus praeest. Episcopatus Vectae insulae ad Danielem pertinet, episcopum Ventae ciuitatis. Prouincia Australium Saxonum iam aliquot annis absque episcopo manens, ministerium sibi episcopale ab Occidentalium Saxonum antistite quaerit. Et hae omnes prouinciae ceteraeque australes ad confinium usque Humbre fluminis, cum suis quaeque regibus Merciorum regi Æthilbaldo subiectae sunt. At uero prouinciae Northanhymbrorum, cui rex Ceoluulfus praeest, quatuor nunc episcopi

---

ii.17 *a* hystorie C   *b* *after* miracula C² *adds* breuiter   *c* uel notantes *added above* describentes *by* C²

ii.18 *a* *after* .xiiii. C² *adds* et in ecclesia sancti Petri sepultus

[55] This paragraph was taken verbatim from Bede, *Historia ecclesiastica* v. 23. 3 (ed. Lapidge, ii. 468; ed. Colgrave and Mynors, p. 558). But note that the text of Bede, in all manuscripts thus far collated, reads (for the year in which Archbishop Berhtwald died) '.dccxxxi.' (i.e. 731), not .dccxxxii. (i.e. 732). Possibly this represents a simple copying error

PARS SECVNDA
53

17. With these delights from the streams of the most holy teacher of the English completed, it is appropriate to lay the foundations of this present work from his [Bede's] *History*, beginning with the final chapters of this same man, and, assigning the dates *anno Domini* and setting out the reigns of kings with circumspect attention, and describing the life and miracles of other devout men to the best of my ability, let us hope finally to receive with them the palm of eternal reward. At the end of his *History* the blessed and eloquent Bede restated what was written in the beginning of this book [i.e. Book V of Bede's *Historia ecclesiastica*].

18. 'In the year of the Lord's incarnation 732, Archbishop Berhtwald, exhausted by old age, died on the fifth Ides of January [9 Jan.]; he occupied the archbishopric for thirty-seven years, six months, and fourteen days. In place of him, in the same year, Tatwine from the province of the Mercians was made archbishop, since he had been a priest in the monastery called Breedon. He was consecrated in Canterbury by the venerable churchmen Daniel [bishop of] Winchester, Ingwald [bishop of London], Ealdwine bishop of Lichfield, and Aldwulf bishop of Rochester, on 10 June, a Sunday. He was outstanding for his holiness and wisdom.'[55]

19. 'And so in the present state of affairs Tatwine and Aldwulf are bishops [respectively] of Canterbury and Rochester. Then Bishops Eadberht[56] and Headolac are bishops of the East Angles. Daniel and Forthere are bishops of the West Saxons. Ealdwine is bishop of the province of the Mercians; and for those peoples who live west of the river Severn, Walhstod is bishop. Wilfrid is bishop of the Hwicce. Cyniberht is bishop of the Lindis-dwellers, or Lindsey. The bishopric of the Isle of Wight pertains to Daniel, bishop of Winchester. The province of the South Saxons, remaining without a bishop for several years, seeks ecclesiastical governance from the bishop of the West Saxons. And all the southern provinces, up to the border of the river Humber, together with their kings, are subject to Æthelbald, king of the Mercians. But in the province of the Northumbrians, over which King Ceolwulf rules, four bishops exercise authority: Wilfrid in York,

---

on Byrhtferth's part. What is more significant, however, is that the date of Berhtwald's death is given as 9 January ('die .v. Iduum Ianuariarum'). For the importance of this variant, see Introduction, pp. lv–lvi.

[56] The text of Bede's *HE* reads *Aldberct* here, not *Eadbertus*.

54   HISTORIA REGVM

praesulatum tenent: Vilfrid in Eboracensi ciuitate, Ætheluualdus in Lindisfarnensi ecclesia, Acca in Hagustaldensi, Pecthelmus[a] in ea quae Candida Casa uocatur; quae nuper multiplicatis fidelium plebibus, in sedem pontificatus addita ipsum habet primum antistitem.'[57] 'Pictorum quoque natio hoc foedus habet pacis cum gente Anglorum, et catholicae pacis ac ueritatis cum uniuersali ecclesia particeps existere gaudet. Scotti qui Britanniam incolunt suis contenti finibus, nil contra gentem Anglorum insidiarum moliuntur aut fraudium. Brittones, quamuis[58]

fo. 60ra | et maxima ex parte domestico sibi odio gentem Anglorum—et totius catholicae ecclesiae statum—Pascha minus recte <obseruando>[b] moribusque improbis impugnent, tamen, et diuina sibi et humana prorsus resistente uirtute, in neutro cupitum possunt obtinere propositum, quippe qui, quamuis ex parte sui sint iuris, nonnulla tamen ex parte Anglorum sunt seruitio mancipati.'[59] 'Qua arridente pace ac serenitate temporum, plures in gente Northanhymbrorum, tam nobiles quam priuati, se suosque liberos, depositis armis, satagunt magis accepta tonsura monasterialibus ascribere uotis quam bellicis exercere studiis.'[60]

20. Haec quae diximus ex dictis beatissimi Bedae sacerdotis et historiae huius gentis scriptoris strictim assumpsimus. Is denique, cum esset .vii. annorum, cura propinquorum datus est educandus reuerentissimi abbati Benedicto ac deinde Ceolfrido, quorum uitam ipse adultus postmodum glorioso explicuit titulo. Cunctum uero uitae suae tempus in eiusdem monasterii, hoc est In Gyruum, habitatione peragens, omnem meditandis scripturis operam dedit, atque inter obseruantiam disciplinae regularis et cotidianam cantandi in ecclesia curam, semper ipse ter beatus aut discere, aut docere, aut scribere, dulce habuit.[61] Si cuilibet eius gesta peramplius et perfectius[62] cognoscere uoluerit,[a] legat capitulum .xxv. historiae Anglorum gentis, quo

---

ii.19   [a] Wecthelmus *C*   [b] *suppl. Arnold*

ii.20   [a] *added by C² (rightly)*

---

[57] This long passage ('Itaque in praesenti...primum antistitem') is taken verbatim from Bede, *Historia ecclesiastica* v. 23. 4 (ed. Lapidge, ii. 468–70; ed. Colgrave and Mynors, pp. 558–60).

[58] It will be noticed that the foliation in C of this part of Byrhtferth's *Historia regum* skips from fo. 58 to fo. 60; this is because fo. 59 is an inserted leaf (on which the recto is blank, and the verso contains part of a text by Roger of Howden) which has nothing to do with the text of Byrhtferth.

[59] This passage ('Pictorum quoque natio...seruitio mancipati') was taken verbatim from Bede, *Historia ecclesiastica* v. 23. 5 (ed. Lapidge, ii. 470; ed. Colgrave and Mynors, p. 560).

PARS SECVNDA 55

Æthelwald in Lindisfarne, Acca in Hexham, and Pecthelm in the place
called Candida Casa [Whithorn], which, with the number of the faithful having been increased, is elevated to an episcopal see and has its
own first bishop.[57] The race of the Picts has at this time a peace treaty
with the English people and rejoices to be a participant with the universal church in catholic peace and truth. The Irish who inhabit
Britain, being content within their borders, attempt nothing in the way
of deceit or fraud against the English. The Britons, although[58] to a
large extent they treat the English people—and the entire catholic
church—with personal contempt, and wrongly oppose [the Roman
method of observing] Easter, nevertheless, with divine and even human
forces resisting them, they are unable to achieve their desired goal on
either count, particularly since they are subject to the English in
respect of the law, although only to a certain degree.'[59] 'With this
peaceful and calm situation obtaining, many people among the
Northumbrians, both noblemen and ordinary citizens, having laid
down their weapons and been tonsured, are concerned to enlist in
monastic undertakings rather than in military engagements.'[60]

20. I have summarily taken all this discussion from the writings of
Bede, the priest and author of the history of this people. This man,
when he was seven years old, was given through the concern of his
relatives to be educated by the most reverend Abbot Benedict, and
thereafter by Ceolfrith, whose lives he later as an adult recorded in a
literary work. Spending the entirety of his life in residence in this same
monastery, that is, Jarrow, he gave his entire attention to reflection on
the Scriptures, and amidst the practice of regular monastic discipline
and the daily chore of chanting in church, thrice happy, he always took
pleasure either in learning or teaching or writing.[61] If anyone should
wish to know his accomplishments more thoroughly and completely,[62]
let him read chapter 25 [of Book V] of his *Historia* [*ecclesiastica*]
gentis Anglorum, wherein he will be able attentively to determine how

---

[60] The final sentence of this chapter ('Qua arridente... exercere studiis') was taken verbatim from Bede, *Historia ecclesiastica* v. 23. 6 (ed. Lapidge, ii. 470; ed. Colgrave and Mynors,
p. 560).

[61] This description of Bede's life was adapted from Bede's own words in the final
chapter of his *Historia ecclesiastica*, v. 24. 2 (ed. Lapidge, ii. 480; ed. Colgrave and Mynors,
p. 566). Byrhtferth has put Bede's first-person verbs into the third person (*cum esset* for *cum
essem*, etc.).

[62] The distinctive phrase *perfectius et peramplius* is used again by Byrhtferth in the
Enchiridion i. 2, line 144 (ed. Baker and Lapidge, p. 32); see Introduction, p. xxx.

56   HISTORIA REGVM

quibit diligenter inuestigare quam sollers, quam prudenter erat eruditus. Nos uero opus ac negotium sollerti cura, Christi clementia succurrente, peragemus, sic exorando:

> Spiritus alme ueni, sine te non diceris unquam;
> munera da linguae qui das in munere linguas.[63]

---

[63] These two hexameters are from the Late Latin poet Arator, *Historia apostolica* i. 226–7. The lines are used by Byrhtferth as a sort of personal prayer to ask the Holy Ghost's continuing support of his writing; thus, they are quoted at the transition between parts ii and iii of the *Enchiridion* (ii. 3, lines 265–6, ed. Baker and Lapidge, p. 120), and again at the beginning of *Enchiridion* iii. 2, where they are quoted and described as *Oratio patris Byrhtferði* (ed.

PARS SECVNDA

skilfully and wisely he had been trained. But let me, with Christ's mercy assisting me, continue this work and undertaking with attentive care, praying thus:

> Come, Holy Spirit: without you, you are never expressed;
> grant the gift of tongues, you who give tongues as your gift.[63]

Baker and Lapidge, p. 136). At the beginning of his *VSE*, in his so-called *Epilogus*, Byrhtferth quotes the two lines again as the *exordium meae orationis* (ed. Lapidge, p. 208). The quotation of the same two lines at the transition between parts ii and iii of the *Historia regum* is one of the strongest indications that Byrhtferth is the author of the (early sections of) the *Historia regum*. See discussion by Lapidge, 'The early sections', p. 118 = *ALL* ii. 338, and Introduction, pp. xlii–xliii.

^a<PARS TERTIA>^a

1. Anno ab incarnatione Domini .dccxxxii., ut praephati sumus,
fo. 60rb Berhtpaldus | archiepiscopus est defunctus. Eodem anno Tatuuine est consecratus archiepiscopus nonus Dorouernensis ecclesiae, Æðilbaldo rege Merciorum quintum decimum agente annum imperii.[1] Ipso quoque anno Ceoluulfus rex captus, attonsus, et remissus est in regnum.[2] Erat uero miro^b studio imbutus, ut Beda testatur in exordio sui prohemii ueridicus.[3] Acca episcopus eodem anno de sua sede est fugatus,[4] et Cyneberht Lindisfarorum .i. Lindisse ecclesiae antistes obiit.[5] Ipso autem anno Alric et Esc cum aliis plurimis occisi sunt die .x. kalendas Septembris, .v. feria.[6]

2. Anno .dccxxxiii. Tatuuine archiepiscopus, accepto ab apostolica auctoritate pallio, ordinauit Aluuig et Sigfrid episcopos.[7] Eclipsis facta est solis .xix. kalendas Septembris circa horam diei tertiam, ita ut paene totus orbis solis quasi nigerrimo et horrendo scuto uideretur esse coopertus.[8]

3. Anno .dccxxxiiii. luna sanguineo rubore est perfusa, quasi hora integra, .ii. kalendas Februarii circa gallicantum,^a dehinc nigredine subsequente ad lucem propriam est reuersa.[9] Eodem anno Tatuuine archiepiscopus nonus Dorouernensis ciuitatis in Cantia obiit die .iii.

---

iii.1   ^{a–a} *suppl. ed.*   ^b *after* miro C² *adds* scripturarum

iii.3   ^a *over* gallicantum C² *adds* uel -cinium (*i.e.* gallicinium)

---

[1] The first two sentences of *HR* iii. 1 are taken, with minor alteration, from Bede, *HE* v. 24. 1: 'Anno .dccxxxi. Berctuald archiepiscopus obiit. Anno eodem Tatuini consecratus archiepiscopus nonus Doruuernensis ecclesiae, Aedilbaldo rege Merciorum .xv. agente annum imperii' (Bede, *HE*, ed. Lapidge, ii. 478; ed. Colgrave and Mynors, p. 566). It is not clear why Byrhtferth should have altered Bede's date 731 (.dccxxxi.) to 732 (.dccxxxii.); perhaps the alteration is simply an error by the scribe of C.

[2] From *HE Continuatio* (I): 'Anno .dccxxxi. Ceoluulf rex captus et adtonsus et remissus in regnum' (ed. Colgrave and Mynors, p. 572; ed. Story, 'After Bede', p. 183).

[3] Bede's *HE* was dedicated to King Ceolwulf; in the *praefatio* Bede refers explicitly to Ceolwulf's love of the Scriptures: 'satisque studium tuae sinceritatis amplector, quo non solum audiendis scripturae sanctae uerbis aurem sedulus accommodes...' (Bede, *HE*, ed. Lapidge, i. 6; ed. Colgrave and Mynors, p. 2). It was possibly this statement which prompted the later annotator (C²) to add the word *scripturarum* to the text after *miro*.

[4] From *HE Continuatio* (I), s.a. 731: 'Acca episcopus de sua sede fugatus' (ed. Colgrave and Mynors, p. 572; ed. Story, 'After Bede', p. 183).

[5] From *HE Continuatio* (II), s.a. 731: 'Cynibertus episcopus Lindisfarorum obiit' (ed. Colgrave and Mynors, p. 572).

PART III

1. In the year of our Lord 732, as we said earlier, Archbishop Berhtwald died. In the same year Tatwine was consecrated as the ninth archbishop of Canterbury, as Æthelbald was living through the fifteenth year of his reign as king of the Mercians.[1] In that same year King Ceolwulf was captured, tonsured, and restored to his kingdom.[2] He was a man imbued with marvellous learning, as the truthful Bede testifies at the beginning of his Preface [of the *Historia ecclesiastica*].[3] In the same year Bishop Acca was driven from his see,[4] and Cyneberht, bishop of the church of the Lindis-dwellers, that is, Lindsey, died.[5] In that very same year Alric and Esc were killed with many others on Thursday 23 August.[6]

2. In 733 Archbishop Tatwine, having received the pallium from the papal authority, ordained Alwig and Sigeferth as bishops.[7] An eclipse of the sun took place on 14 August at about the third hour of the day [9:00 a.m.], so that the entire disc of the sun seemed to be nearly covered with a black and terrible shield.[8]

3. In 734, on 31 January, at about cockcrow, the moon was stained with bloody redness for almost an entire hour; thereafter, in the ensuing darkness, it returned to its normal light.[9] In the same year Tatwine,

---

[6] The identity of Alric and Esc is unknown, and this event is not recorded in any other source.

[7] From *HE Continuatio* (II), s.a. 733: 'Anno ab incarnatione Domini .dccxxxiii. Tatuuini archiepiscopus, accepto ab apostolica auctoritate pallio, ordinauit Aluuich et Sigfridum episcopos' (ed. Colgrave and Mynors, p. 572). Alwig was bishop of Lindsey (Keynes, 'Rulers', p. 558), Sigeferth of Selsey (ibid. p. 547).

[8] From *HE Continuatio* (I), s.a. 733: 'Anno .dccxxxiii. eclipsis facta est solis .xviii. kal. Sept. circa horam diei tertiam, ita ut pene totus orbis quasi nigerrimo et horrendo scuto uideretur esse coopertus' (ed. Colgrave and Mynors, p. 572; ed. Story, 'After Bede', p. 183; cf. 'Ramsey Annals', s.a. 733: 'Eclypsis facta est' (p. 41)). (Note that Byrhtferth—or the scribe of C—has changed the date of the eclipse from .xviii. kal. Sept. (15 Aug.) to .xix. kal. Sept. (14 Aug.).) For the correct date of the eclipse, see Schove and Fletcher, *The Chronology of Eclipses*, pp. 150–1, who describe the eclipse on 14 August as 'total solar', and note that, 'modern computations...make the band of annularity run through Southern Ireland, Central and South Wales, Central England short of London, East Anglia, Holland, Berlin, the Sea of Azov and the Caspian' (p. 150).

[9] From *HE Continuatio* (I), s.a. 734: 'Anno .dccxxxiiii. luna sanguineo rubore perfusa quasi hora integra .ii. kal. Febr. circa galli cantum, dehinc nigredine subsequente ad lucem propriam reuersa' (ed. Colgrave and Mynors, p. 572; ed. Story, 'After Bede', p. 183). For the dating of the eclipse (and the confusion over whether it occurred on 24 or 31 January), see Schove and Fletcher, *The Chronology of Eclipses*, p. 152.

60   HISTORIA REGVM

kalendas Augusti.[10] Primus ipsius ciuitatis episcopus erat Augustinus, gloriosus doctor totius regni ac egregius fundator Christianitatis.[b] Qui ad supernae ciuitatis gaudia subleuatus, sceptra tanti fastigii dereliquit Laurentio. Is pro meritis supernis allectus ciuibus, dispensationem catholicae ecclesiae commendauit Mellito episcopo. Mellitus denique post laborum suorum certamina tamquam miles emeritus caelestium donorum consecutus est praemia. Post eum quarto in loco Iustus suc-

fo. 60ᵛᵃ cedit, qui in Domino Deo confisus, | ad montem uirtutum secundum nominis sui palmam transmigrauit uictoriosus. Secutus est ipsum Honorius, hoc est 'honore plenus', qui officium sibi commissum bene ministrans, poli culmina conscendit pro meritis. Deusdedit cathedram ascendit sexto in loco, qui patrum secutus uestigia, heres factus est in caelesti curia. Deinde Theodorus[c] exsurgens, septimum locum gloriose exornauit. Berhtuualdus octauo succedit loco, quem secutus est Tatuuine episcopus, sicut prephati sumus.[11] Eodem anno ordinatus est Frioðuberht Haugustaldensis ecclesiae episcopus sub die .vi. idus Septembris.[12]

4. Anno .dccxxxv. Nothelmus archiepiscopus ordinatus est, et Ecgberhtus Eboraci antistes primus post Paulinum, accepto ab apostolica sede pallio, genti Northanhymbrorum in archiepiscopatum[a] confirmatus est. Beda doctor obiit in Gyruum.[13]

Anno .dccxxxvi. Nothhelm, pallio a Romano pontifice suscepto, ordinauit tres episcopos: Cuthberhtum uidelicet, Hereuualdum,[b] et Æthelfridum.[14]

Anno .dccxxxvii. Alduuine, qui et Vuor, episcopus defunctus est;[15] et pro eo Huuita et Totta Mercis et Midil-Anglis sunt consecrati

---

[b] *over* Christianitatis *C²* adds uel Christiane fidei et religionis   [c] *after* Theodorus *C²* adds doctissimus

iii.4   [a] *C² here adds* uel ordinatum est   [b] Heordwaldum *C*

---

[10] On Tatwine, see *ODNB* liii. 831–2 [M. Lapidge], and *WB Encyc.* p. 457 [M. Lapidge]. The year of Tatwine's death is recorded in *HE Continuatio* (I) and (II). The day of his death (30 July) is not given in any Anglo-Saxon liturgical calendar, and is only found in post-Conquest Benedictine calendars from Canterbury (see *Early Monastic Litanies*, ed. Morgan, p. 188). Possibly, therefore, the statement ('die .iii. kalendas Augusti') is a post-Byrhtferthian addition in C.

[11] Byrhtferth was evidently consulting an episcopal list in which the archbishops of Canterbury were given in a numbered sequence. Four such lists have been printed by Page, 'Anglo-Saxon episcopal lists': pp. 4 (BL, Cotton Vespasian B. vi), 8 (CCCC 183), 18 (CCCC 140), and 22 (CCCC 173).

[12] From *HE Continuatio* (II), s.a. 735: 'Ecgberht episcopus…ordinauitque Fridubertum…' (ed. Colgrave and Mynors, p. 572), which does not, however, specify Frithuberht's see. He was bishop of Hexham (734–66): see Keynes, 'Bishops', p. 564, and cf. *ASC* D(E), s.a. 766: 'Frithuberht of Hexham, who had been bishop 34 years, died' (trans. Whitelock, p. 33).

PARS TERTIA 61

the ninth archbishop of Canterbury, died in Canterbury on 30 July.[10] The first bishop of this same city was Augustine, the glorious teacher of the entire realm and the excellent founder of Christianity [in England]. When he was raised up to the joys of the heavenly city, he entrusted the governance of so lofty a summit to Laurence. This man, associated with the heavenly citizens by reason of his accomplishments, entrusted the management of the catholic church to Bishop Mellitus. And so Mellitus, after the difficulties of his struggles, achieved the rewards of heavenly gifts as a retired soldier. After him Iustus succeeded as the fourth [archbishop], who, trusting in the Lord God, passed victorious to the summit of virtues according to the reward embodied in his name. Honorius followed him, that is [a man] 'replete with honour', who, managing well the duty entrusted to him, ascended the summits of heaven because of his achievements. Deusdedit ascended the bishop's cathedra in sixth place; following the footsteps of the fathers, he was made an heir in the heavenly court. Then Theodore, on arrival, adorned the seventh position gloriously. Berhtwald succeeded in eighth place; Archbishop Tatwine followed him, as we said.[11] In the same year Frithuberht was ordained bishop of the church of Hexham on 8 September.[12]

4. In 735, Nothhelm was ordained as archbishop [of Canterbury], and Ecgberht was confirmed in the archbishopric of the Northumbrians, the first bishop after Paulinus to have received the pallium from the papal see. Bede the teacher died in Jarrow.[13]

In 736, Nothhelm, having received the pallium from the Roman pope, ordained three bishops: namely Cuthberht, Herewald, and Æthelfrith.[14]

In 737, Bishop Ealdwine, also known as Wor, died;[15] and in his place Hwita and Totta were consecrated bishops of the Mercians and Middle

---

[13] From *HE Continuatio* (II), s.a. 735: 'Anno ab incarnatione Domini .dccxxxv. Nothelm archiepiscopus ordinatur, et Ecgberht episcopus, accepto ab apostolica sede pallio, primus post Paulinum in archiepiscopatum confirmatus et Baeda presbyter obiit' (ed. Colgrave and Mynors, p. 572); cf. 'Ramsey Annals', s.a. 734: 'Obiit BEDA monachus et ystoriographus' (p. 41).

[14] This information does not derive from either of the *HE* Continuations, which have no entry for 736. Cuthbert was bishop of Hereford from 736 until 740, when he was translated to Canterbury (Keynes, 'Bishops', p. 560), Herewald bishop of Sherborne from 736 until 766×774 (ibid. p. 550), and Æthelfrith bishop of Elmham (ibid. p. 554).

[15] Aldwine (Wor) was in office in 731 (Bede, *HE* v. 23. 3) and died in 737 (Keynes, 'Bishops', p. 556).

62 HISTORIA REGVM

antistites.[16] Eodem anno regnum Northanhymbrorum[c] Eadberht filius patrui eius successit.[17]

Anno .dccxxxviii. Suuefbriht[d] Orientalium Saxonum rex obiit.[18]

5. Anno .dccxxxix. Æthelheard rex Occidentalium Saxonum defunctus est, et pro eo Cuthred frater eius rex constituitur. Ipso quoque anno Nothhelm archiepiscopus post annos quatuor accepti episcopatus[a] obiit in pace, et Aldulf Hrofensis ecclesiae episcopus diem clausit ultimum.[19]

fo. 60vb Anno .dccxl. Ætheluuald Lindisfarnensis ecclesiae antistes migrauit ad Dominum, et Cyneuulf in episcopatum subrogatus est.[20]

6. Eodem uero anno reuerendae memoriae Acca episcopus subleuatus est in regionem uiuentium. Erat ipse beatus strenuissimus actu, et coram Deo et hominibus magnificus. In ecclesiasticae quoque institutionis regulis sollertissimus extiterat, et usque dum praemia piae deuotionis capiat, existere non desistit, utpote qui a pueritia in clero sanctissimi atque Deo dilecti Bosae Eboracensis episcopi nutritus atque eruditus est. Deinde ad Vilfridum episcopum spe melioris propositi adueniens, omnem in eius obsequio usque ad obitum eius expleuit aetatem. Cum quo etiam Romam ueniens, multa illic quae in patria nequiuerat ecclesiae sanctae instituta utilia didicit, et suis subiectis tradidit.[21] Sustollitur[a] sanctus de praesenti saeculo .xiii. kalendas Nouembris, cuius perducitur spiritus ab angelis ad brauium supernae

---

[c] *C² here adds* Celwlfus [regnum, *erased*] dimisit et monachus apud Lindisfarnensem insulam factus est, et pro eo *at foot of col. 60[va], linked by a* signe de renvoi   [d] Swebriht *C*

iii.5 [a] *after* episcopatus *C adds* diem

iii.6 [a] substollitur *C*

---

[16] The see of the Middle Angles was divided at this time between Lichfield and Leicester, each of which had its own bishop. Hwita became bishop of Lichfield (Keynes, 'Bishops', p. 556), and Torhthelm, the hypocoristic form of whose name was Totta, of Leicester (ibid. p. 557).

[17] Cf. *HE Continuatio* (II), s.a. 737: 'Ceoluulfus sua uoluntate attonsus regnum Eadbercto reliquit' (ed. Colgrave and Mynors, p. 572), and *ASC* D(E), s.a. 737: 'King Ceolwulf received St Peter's tonsure and gave his kingdom to Eadberht, the son of his paternal uncle, and Eadberht reigned 21 years' (trans. Whitelock, p. 29).

[18] The death of Swæfberht is not known from any other source; see discussion by Yorke, 'The kingdom of the East Saxons', p. 23, and Keynes, 'Rulers', p. 533.

[19] Cf. *HE Continuatio* (II), s.a. 739: 'Anno ab incarnatione Christi .dccxxxix. Edilhard Occidentalum Saxonum rex obiit, et Nothelm archiepiscopus' (ed. Colgrave and Mynors, p. 572), and *ASC* s.a. 740: 'In this year King Æthelheard died and Cuthred succeeded to the kingdom of the West Saxons' (trans. Whitelock, p. 29; cf. Keynes, 'Rulers', p. 534). The

PARS TERTIA

Angles [respectively].[16] In the same year Eadberht, the son of his uncle, succeeded.[17]

In 738, Swæfberht, king of the East Saxons, died.[18]

5. In 739, Æthelheard, king of the West Saxons, died, and in his place Cuthred his brother is established as king. In the same year Archbishop Nothhelm, four years after having accepted the archbishopric, died in peace, and Ealdwulf, bishop of the church of Rochester, finished his last day.[19]

In 740 Æthelwald, bishop of the church of Lindisfarne, passed to the Lord, and Cynewulf was chosen for the episcopacy.[20]

6. In that same year Bishop Acca of reverend memory was elevated to the realm of the living. This blessed man was most energetic in his activities, and eminent before God and men. He had been most attentive to the rules of ecclesiastical discipline, and, up to the time when he would receive the rewards for his holy devotion, did not cease to be so, inasmuch as he was raised and educated from childhood among the clergy of Bosa, the bishop of York beloved by God. Then, proceeding to Bishop Wilfrid with the hope of advancement, he spent all his career in his service up until the time of his [Wilfrid's] death. Travelling to Rome with him [Wilfrid], he learned there many useful teachings of the holy church which he had been unable to learn in his homeland, and passed them on to those subject to him.[21] The holy man was raised up from the present world on 20 October; his soul is conducted by the

---

death of Aldwulf, bishop of Rochester, is not recorded in either of these sources; see Keynes, 'Bishops', p. 545.

[20] Cf. *HE Continuatio* (II), s.a. 740: 'Aediluuald quoque episcopus obiit, et pro eo Cyniuulf ordinatur antistes' (ed. Colgrave and Mynors, p. 574), and *ASC* D(E), s.a. 737: 'And Bishop Æthelwold and Acca died, and Cynewulf was consecrated bishop' (trans. Whitelock, p. 29).

[21] This material on Bishop Acca is mostly taken verbatim from Bede, *HE* v. 20. 2: 'uir et ipse strenuissimus et coram Deo et hominibus magnificus . . . in ecclesiasticae quoque institutionis regulis sollertissimus extiterat; et usque dum praemia piae deuotionis accipiat, existere non desistit, utpote qui a pueritia in clero sanctissimi ac Deo dilecti Bosa Eboracensis episcopi nutritus atque eruditus est; deinde ad Vilfridum episcopum spe melioris propositi adueniens, omnem in eius obsequio usque ad obitum illius expleuit aetatem; cum quo etaim Romam ueniens multa illic, quae in patria nequiuerat, ecclesiae sanctae institutis utilia didicit' (*Beda: Storia*, ed. Lapidge, ii. 430; ed. Colgrave and Mynors, pp. 530–2). Acca was originally buried outside the wall of the church, but was subsequently translated inside, where his tomb was marked by two distinctive crosses, on which, see Taylor and Taylor, *Anglo-Saxon Architecture*, i. 304–5, and Cramp, *County Durham and Northumberland*, pp. 174–93.

64 HISTORIA REGVM

felicitatis, corpus uero eius ad orientalem plagam extra parietem ecclesiae Haugustaldensis, quam .xxiv. annis pontificali rexit dignitate, sepultum est.[22]

fo. 62[rb]   7. Ipso uero anno quo sanctus Acca episcopus ad caelestia migrauit, Arnuuine filius Eaduulfi occisus est, die .x. kalendas Ianuarii, feria .vii.[23] Refert historia uel cronica huius patriae, quod eodem anno Cuthberht undecimus Dorouernensis ecclesiae archiepiscopatum susceperit.[24] At uero post Alduulfum Hrofensis ecclesiae Dun sacerdotium assumpsit.

Anno .dccxli. monasterium in Eboraca ciuitate succensum est .ix. kalendas Maii, feria .i.[25]

Anno .dccxliv. factum est proelium inter Pictos et Brittones.[26]

[a]Anno .dccxlv.[a] uisi sunt in aere ictus ignei quales numquam ante mortales illius aeui uiderunt; et ipsi paene per totam noctem uisi sunt, kalendis scilicet Ianuarii.[27] Eodem quoque anno, ut quidam referunt, dominus Vilfridus[b][28] Eboracae ciuitatis[c][29] migrauit ad Dominum .iii. kalendas Maii;[30] nos uero dicimus quod priusquam Beda suam historiam explicuisset, translatus sit[d][31] ex hoc mundo ad celsitudinem aeternae uisionis. Ipsis quoque diebus Lundoniae ciuitatis episcopus, nomine Inguuald, de Ægypto huius saeculi translatus est.[32] Eadem

---

iii.7   [a-a] *written over an erasure by* C^2 [b] secundus *added above line by* C^2 [c] episcopus *added above line by* C^2 [d] ille primus Wilfridus *added by* C^2

[22] At this point in the text there is a lengthy interpolation (of 12th-c. date) concerning miracles which took place at the tomb of Bishop Acca. Because it could not have been composed by Byrhtferth, I have removed it from the present text (it is printed in *Symeonis Monachi Opera Omnia*, ed. Arnold, ii. 33–8, and below, Appendix II (a)). As Hunter Blair pointed out, 'a *terminus post quem* for the composition of the Acca interpolation is supplied by the reference to the gift of Hexham to the canons regular by Thomas II, archbishop of York, an event which occurred in 1113' ('Some observations', p. 88).

[23] Cf. *HE Continuatio* (II), s.a. 740: 'Arnuini et Eadbertus interempti' (ed. Colgrave and Mynors, p. 574); cf. 'Ramsey Annals', s.a. 740: 'Obiit Acca' (p. 41). The identity of Arnwine is unknown. Was he the son of the Eadwulf who briefly held the Northumbrian throne in 705–6? Note that Byrhtferth (or Symeon, or the scribe of C) has written *Eaduulfi* for *Eadbertus* in the *HE Continuatio* (II). Cf. also the entry in the *Annals of Ulster*, s.a. 741: 'The killing of Ernón, descendant of Eculp' (*The Chronicle of Ireland*, trans. Charles-Edwards, i. 213), where it is possible that *Ernón* and *Eculp* represent mutilations by Irish scribes of the English names *Arnwine* and *Eadwulf*.

[24] One would very much like to know what Byrhtferth meant by 'the history or chronicle of this country'. Was he referring to some redaction of the *Anglo-Saxon Chronicle*, for example? In fact, the *Anglo-Saxon Chronicle* has the following entry s.a. 740: 'And Cuthbert was consecrated archbishop and Dunn bishop of Rochester' (trans. Whitelock, p. 29). If such an entry were in Byrhtferth's source, he has added the details that Cuthbert was the eleventh archbishop of Canterbury, presumably from an episcopal list, and also that Dun succeeded Ealdwulf as bishop of Rochester (which could also have been deduced from an episcopal list): see above, n. 11.

PARS TERTIA 65

angels to the reward of eternal bliss, but his body was buried in the eastern area, beyond the wall, of the church of Hexham which he had ruled with episcopal distinction for twenty-four years.[22]

7. In the same year [740] in which the saintly Bishop Acca passed to heaven, Arnwine the son of Eadwulf was killed on Saturday, 23 December.[23] The history or chronicle of this country states that in the same year Cuthberht accepted the archbishopric of the church of Canterbury, the eleventh [archbishop] in succession.[24] And, after Ealdwulf, Dun assumed the episcopacy of the church of Rochester.

In 741, the minster in the city of York was burned on Sunday, 23 April.[25]

In 744, a battle was fought between the Picts and the Britons.[26]

In 745, bolts of fire were seen in the sky such as mortals of that time had never seen; and these were seen almost all night, namely on 1 January.[27] In the same year, as some people say, Wilfrid,[28] [bishop][29] of the city of York, passed to the Lord on 29 April.[30] But I say that, before Bede had finished his *Historia*, he [Wilfrid] was translated from this world to the lofty reaches of the eternal vision.[31] In these same days the bishop of the city of London, named Ingwald, was translated from the Egypt of this world.[32]

---

[25] Cf. *ASC* D(E) s.a. 741: 'In this year York was burnt down' (trans. Whitelock, p. 29).

[26] See Anderson, *Early Sources of Scottish History*, i. 238, who records a battle between the Picts and Britons in this year, taken from the 'Chronicle of Melrose', s.a.; it is clear, however, that the entry in the 'Chronicle of Melrose' is ultimately derived from the present entry in Byrhtferth. The possible background to such a battle is explored by Fraser, *From Caledonia to Pictland*, pp. 312–19, who suggests that the Pictish king Onuist (on whom, see below, n. 58) was the moving force behind this battle, and that the aggression initiated in this year ultimately led to the treaty of Clyde Rock (on which, see below, *HR* iii. 9, s.a. 756).

[27] Cf. *ASC* D(E) s.a. 744: 'And shooting stars were frequent' (trans. Whitelock, p. 30).

[28] Byrhtferth has evidently confused Wilfrid (II), who died in 745, with his predecessor, the great Wilfrid (d. 710); cf. 'Ramsey Annals', s.a. 748: 'Obiit Wilfridus' (p. 41). C² attempted to repair this error by adding *secundus* after *Vilfridus*.

[29] C² continues to emend Byrhtferth's text by adding *episcopus* after *ciuitatis*.

[30] The death of Bishop Wilfrid (II) is recorded against 745 in *HE Continuatio* (II) (ed. Colgrave and Mynors, p. 574), with no detail given, and again in *ASC* D(E) s.a. 744: 'And Wilfrid the Younger, who had been bishop of York, died on 29 April. He had been bishop for 30 years' (trans. Whitelock, p. 30); in fact Wilfrid (II) was bishop of York from only 714 until 732, when he resigned in favour of Ecgberht; and see next note.

[31] C² adds above the line: *ille primus Wilfridus*, in the attempt to correct the error made by Byrhtferth, who has confused the first Bishop Wilfrid of York (d. 710)—who did indeed die before Bede finished his *Historia ecclesiastica*—with the second (d. 745), who was bishop of York from 714 until 732 (when he resigned in favour of Ecgberht) and who is the subject of the present annal-entry.

[32] Cf. *HE Continuatio* (II), s.a. 745: '[Vilfridus]...et Ingualdus Londoniae episcopus migrauerunt ad Dominum' (ed. Colgrave and Mynors, p. 574). The phrase *Ægyptum huius saeculi* is used by Byrhtferth to mean 'departure', the metaphor being that of the exodus of the Israelites from Egypt.

66 HISTORIA REGVM

tempestate antistes in Huiccum defunctus est.[33] Etiam anno eodem
Herebald abbas obiit.[e][34]

8. Anno .dccxlix. Ælfuuald rex Orientalium Anglorum defunctus
fo. 62va est,[35] | regnumque [a]Hun, Beonna[a] et Alberht sibi diuiserunt.[36]
[b]Anno .dccl.[b] Eadberht rex Cyniuulfum episcopum in urbem
Bebban captiuum adduxerat, basilicamque beati Petri obsidere fecit in
Lindisfarnea.[37] Offa[c] filius Aldfridi quoque reliquias sancti Cuthberhti
pontificis innocens coactiue accurrebat; paene defunctus fame de
ecclesia sine armis abstractus est.[38] Eodem anno Aluuih episcopus
translatus est ad alterius uitae contemplationem, et Alduulf diaconus
eius ordinatur in episcopum.[39] Cuthred autem rex Occidentalium
Saxonum surrexit contra Æthilbaldum regem Merciorum.[40]

Anno ab incarnatione Dominica .dcclii. eclipsis lunae facta est pridie kalendas Augusti.[41] Quia mentio facta est de hac re, libet ignorantibus pandere quid sit eclipsis, id est deliquium uel defectus[d] lunae.
'Eclipsis lunae est, quotiens in umbram terrae luna incurrit; non enim

---

[e] his temporibus floruit sanctus anachorita Guthlacus *add. C*[2]

iii.8 [a-a] Hunbeanna *C* [b-b] *added C*[2] [c] Offo *C* [d] defectum *C*

---

[33] Either the scribe or possibly Byrhtferth himself has omitted the name of the bishop of
the Hwicce who died in 745. In fact, this bishop was none other than Wilfrid (II), bishop of
York, whose death has been recorded two sentences earlier: the implication is that, like a
number of archbishops in the tenth and eleventh centuries, Wilfrid (II) held the sees of York
and Worcester in plurality, and that, although he resigned York in favour of Ecgberht in 732,
he retained the bishopric of Worcester until his death in 745.

[34] In describing a miracle performed by Bishop John of Beverley, Bede (*HE* v. 6) relates
that a young man named Herebald had been injured in a fall from a horse and had been cured
overnight by the prayers of Bishop John; Bede goes on to report that, at the time, Herebald
was a member of John's clergy, but when Bede was writing the *HE* in 731, Herebald was
abbot of the monastery at the mouth of the Tyne: 'qui tunc quidem in clero illius conuersa-
tus, nunc monasterio quod est iuxta ostium Tini fluminis abbatis iure praeest' (*Beda: Storia*,
ed. Lapidge, ii. 344; ed. Colgrave and Mynors, p. 464). This Herebald is presumably the
abbot in question here. Note also that at this point in the manuscript C[2] adds above the line:
His temporibus floruit sanctus anachorita Guthlacus. It is unclear where C[2] derived this information: according the the *Anglo-Saxon Chronicle*, Guthlac died in 715 (*ASC*, trans.
Whitelock, p. 26). Guthlac is not mentioned anywhere by Bede, *HE*.

[35] Ælfwald was king of the East Angles from 713 to 749 (Keynes, 'Rulers', p. 530); his obit,
however, is not recorded in either the *HE Continuatio* (II) or the *ASC*; but cf. 'Ramsey
Annals', s.a. 749: 'Obiit Ælfwald rex' (p. 41).

[36] Although C gives the name of one of the kings who divided the kingdom of the East
Saxons as *Hunbeanna*, Anglo-Saxon coinage of the period verifies the existence of a king
named Beonna (presumably a hypocoristic form of a name in *Beorn*-); the implication is that
Ælfwald's kingdom was divided among three successors: see *EHD* i. 265, and Keynes,
'Rulers', p. 530.

PARS TERTIA 67

At the same time, the bishop of the Hwicce died.[33] In that same year Abbot Herebald died.[34]

8. In 749, Ælfwald, king of the East Angles, died,[35] and Hun, Beonna, and Æthelberht divided the kingdom between them.[36]

In 750, King Eadberht had taken Bishop Cyniwulf as prisoner to the city of Bamburgh, and had the church of St Peter at Lindisfarne besieged.[37] Under compulsion Offa, the innocent son of Aldfrith, also sought refuge with the relics of St Cuthbert; nearly dead with hunger, he was dragged unarmed from the church.[38] In the same year Bishop Alwig was translated to the contemplation of the next life, and Aldwulf, his deacon, is ordained to the bishopric.[39] Cuthred, king of the West Saxons, rose up against Æthelbald, king of the Mercians.[40]

In the year of the Lord's incarnation 752, an eclipse of the moon occurred on 31 July.[41] Because this event has been mentioned, it is appropriate to explain to the ignorant what an eclipse is, namely a 'defect' or 'deficiency' of the moon. 'An eclipse of the moon occurs whenever the moon runs into the shadow of the earth; for it is said not

---

[37] Cf. 'Ramsey Annals', s.a. 750: 'Æadbyrht rex' (p. 41). Neither *HE Continuatio* (II) nor *ASC* records the capture of Bishop Cynewulf. Cynewulf was bishop of Lindisfarne from 737×740 until he resigned the see in 779 or 780; he died in 782 or 783 (Keynes, 'Bishops', p. 565). Note that (characteristically) Byrhtferth has confused the active and passive forms of the infinitive.

[38] On the sanctuary afforded by the relics of St Cuthbert, see Hall, 'The sanctuary of St Cuthbert', with discussion of this episode at p. 432. Offa son of Aldfrith is otherwise unknown.

[39] Alwig was bishop of Lindsey from 733 to 750; he was succeeded by Aldwulf in 750 (Keynes, 'Bishops', p. 558).

[40] Cuthred's rebellion against Æthelbald of Mercia is recorded in the *HE Continuatio* (II), s.a. 750: 'Cuthredus rex Occidentalium Saxonum surrexit contra Aedilbaldum regem' (ed. Colgrave and Mynors, p. 574); relevant too is the entry in *ASC* s.a. 750: 'In this year King Cuthred fought against the arrogant ealdorman Æthelhun' (trans. Whitelock, p. 30), and s.a. 752: 'Cuthred fought at *Beorhford* against Æthelbald' (ibid.). The implication is that the Æthelhun mentioned in the *HE Continuatio* (II) was a thegn of King Æthelbald.

[41] No eclipse of the moon is recorded in contemporary sources against 31 July 752; but cf. perhaps *HE Continuatio* (II), s.a. 753: 'postea eodem anno et mense, hoc est nona kalendarum Februarium, luna eclipsim pertulit, horrendo et nigerrimo scuto, ita ut sol paulo ante, cooperta' (ed. Colgrave and Mynors, p. 574); and cf. 'Ramsey Annals', s.a. 752: 'Eclypsis' (p. 41). But unless there has been a vast error of transmission, the dates imply that the sources are recording two separate eclipses. Cf. Schove and Fletcher, *The Chronology of Eclipses*, p. 153, who note that the 'total' eclipse occurred in 752 (as stated here in Byrhtferth), and they date it to either 30 or 31 July.

68   HISTORIA REGVM

suum lumen habere dicitur, sed a sole illuminari putatur.'[42] Eclipsis lunae non nisi plena, id est .xv., erit. 'Defectus solis numquam nisi ortu lunae fieri solet.'[43] 'Certum est', inquit Plinius, 'defectum solis non nisi nouissima, id est tricesima primaue fieri luna, quod coitum uocant. Omnibus autem annis fieri utriusque sideris defectus statutis diebus horisque[e] sub terra. Nec tamen, cum superne fiunt, ubique cerni possunt, aliquando propter nebulam, saepius globo terrae obstante conuexitatibus mundi.'[44] 'Eclipsis solis est, quotiens luna .xxx. ad eandem lineam qua sol uehitur peruenit, eique se obiiciens solem obscurat. Nam deficere nobis sol uidetur dum illi orbis lunae opponitur.'[/45]

fo. 62[vb] Anno .dccliiii. Bonifacius archiepiscopus, qui et Vinfridus, Francorum martyrio | coronatus est, cum quinquaginta tribus.[46]

9. Anno[a] .dcclv. Cuthred rex Occidentalium Saxonum obiit, cuius regni sceptra Sigberht accepit.[47]

Anno ab incarnatione Dominica .dcclvi. Eadberht rex duodeuicesimo anno regni sui, et Vnust rex Pictorum, duxerunt exercitum ad urbem Alcluith. Ibique Brittones indecoram[b48] condicionem receperunt, prima die mensis Augusti.[49] Decima autem die eiusdem mensis interiit exercitus paene omnis quem duxit de Ouania ad Niuuanbirig, id est ad nouam ciuitatem.[50] Eodem anno Balthere anachorita uiam sanctorum patrum est secutus, migrando ad eum qui se reformauit ad imaginem filii

---

[e] horis *C*   [f] *in the left-hand margin a later hand (s. xiii?) has written* Eata obiit in Craic apud Eboracum

iii.9 [a] *added C²*   [b] *corr. ed.,* inde *C*

---

[42] Isidore, *Etym.* iii. 59: 'Eclipsis lunae est, quotiens in umbram terrae luna incurrit. Non enim suum lumen habere, sed a sole inluminari putatur.'

[43] Bede, *De temporum ratione,* c. 27: 'Cum defectus solis numquam nisi ortu lunae fieri soleat...' (CCSL cxxiiiB. 363), quoted by Bede from Jerome, *Comm. in euangelium Matthaei* (CCSL lxxvii. 273).

[44] Pliny, *Naturalis historia,* ii. 56: 'certum est, solis defectus non nisi novissima primave fieri luna, quod vocant coitum... omnibus autem annis fieri utriusque sideris defectus <u>statis</u> diebus horisque sub terra; nec tamen, cum superne fiant, ubique cerni, aliquando propter <u>nubila</u>, saepius globo terrae obstante convexitatibus mundi'; and note the variant readings in Byrhtferth's quotation: *statutis* for Pliny's *statis* and *nebulam* for Pliny's *nubila*. Now Bede quoted this entire passage from Pliny in *De temporum ratione,* c. 27, as follows: 'Certum est, inquit [*scil.* Plinius], solis defectum non nisi nouissima primaue fieri luna, quod uocant coitum... omnibus autem annis fieri utriusque sideris defectus, <u>statutis</u> diebus horisque sub terra; nec tamen cum superne fiant ubique cerni. Aliquando propter <u>nebula</u>, saepius globo terrae obstante conuexitatibus mundi' (CCSL cxxiiiB. 363). (Bede quotes the same passage, without naming Pliny as his source, in his *De natura rerum,* c. 22.) The variant readings indicate that Byrhtferth was copying this passage from Bede rather than Pliny.

PARS TERTIA 69

to have its own light, but is thought to be illuminated by the sun.'[42] An eclipse of the moon will not take place unless it is 'full', that is, on its fifteenth day. 'An eclipse of the sun happens only at the beginning of the moon's cycle.'[43] 'It is certain', says Pliny, 'that there is no eclipse of the sun unless it is a new moon, that is, the thirtieth or first moon, which they call their "conjunction". In every year a "defect" [eclipse] of either celestial body takes place on certain days and hours, beneath the [shadow of the] earth. But yet, because they take place in the heavens, they cannot always be seen, sometimes because of cloud, most often because the sphere of the earth is blocking the vault of the heavens.'[44] 'A solar eclipse occurs whenever the moon in its thirtieth day arrives at the same line along which the sun travels, and, interposing itself, obscures the sun. For it seems to us that the sun is eclipsed when the orb of the moon is placed against it.'[45]

In 754, Boniface, also known as Winfrith, archbishop of the Franks, was crowned with martyrdom along with fifty-three others.[46]

9. In 755, Cuthred, king of the West Saxons, died; Sigeberht took up the governance of his kingdom.[47]

In the year of the Lord's incarnation 756, King Eadberht, in the eighteenth year of his reign, and Onuist, king of the Picts, led an army to the city of Alcluith [Dumbarton]. And there the Britons accepted an unseemly[48] agreement, on the first day of the month of August.[49] On the tenth day of the same month, nearly the entire army which he [Eadberht] led from Govan to Newburgh, that is, to the 'new city', perished.[50] In the same year Balthere the anchorite followed the path of the holy fathers, passing to Him who recreated him in the likeness of

---

[45] Isidore, *Etym.* iii. 58: 'Eclipsis solis est, quotiens luna trigesima ad eandem lineam, qua sol vehitur pervenit, eique se obiiciens solem obscurat. Nam deficere nobis sol videtur, dum illi orbis lunae opponitur.'

[46] *HE Continuatio* (II), s.a. 754: 'Bonifacius, qui et Vuinfridus, Francorum episcopus cum quinquaginta tribus martyrio coronatur' (ed. Colgrave and Mynors, p. 574). Byrhtferth's entry shows that he was aware that Boniface was archbishop, not simply bishop.

[47] Cf. *ASC* s.a. 756 [754]: 'In this year Cuthred died...And Sigeberht succeeded to the kingdom and held it for one year' (trans. Whitelock, p. 30); cf. 'Ramsey Annals', s.a. 755: 'Obiit Cuthred rex' (p. 41).

[48] The transmitted adverb *inde* here makes for extremely awkward syntax; I suspect, therefore, that *inde* is an uncompleted word by C such as *indecoram* (thus supplied). A very similar copying error by C occurs above, *HR* i. 5, where -*alis* was written for *regalis*.

[49] On the siege of Dumbarton and the terms forced upon the Britons by Onuist and Eadberht, see Fraser, *From Caledonia to Pictland*, pp. 312–17.

[50] Eadberht's role in the siege of Dumbarton and the destruction of the army at Newburgh is not apparently recorded in any other source.

HISTORIA REGVM

sui.[51] Luna autem quindecima sanguineo rubore superducta .viii. kalendas Decembris .xv. aetate, id est, plena luna; sicque paulatim decrescentibus tenebris ad lucem pristinam peruenit. Nam mirabiliter ipsam lunam sequente lucida stella et pertranseunte, tanto spatio eam antecedebat illuminatam,[c] quanto sequebatur antequam esset obscurata.[52]

Anno .dcclvii. Æthelbald rex Merciorum a suis tutoribus fraudulenter interfectus est.[53] Eodem uero anno Merci bellum inter se ciuile inierunt. Beornred in fugam uerso, Offa rex uictor extitit.[54]

Anno .dcclviii. Eadberht rex[d] sponte contulit filio suo regnum sibi a Deo collatum, nomine Osuulfo, qui uno anno regnum tenuit, amisit, perdidit, quia occisus est nequiter a sua familia iuxta Mechil Wongtune .ix. kalendas Augusti.[55]

10. Anno[a] .dcclix. Ætheluuald, qui et Moll dictus erat, regnare incipit nonas Augusti.[56] Cuius tertio anno inchoante, grauissimum
fo. 63ra iuxta | Eldunum[b] gestum est bellum .viii. idus Augusti, in quo cecidit Osuuine post triduum prima feria; Ætheluuald uero rex, qui Moll est nominatus, uictoriam sumpsit in bello.[57] Ipso quoque anno Vnust Pictorum rex defunctus est.[58]

---

   c add. C[1]   *d after rex C[2] adds northymbrorum*

iii.10   *a add. C[2]*   *b after Eldunum C[2] adds secus Melros*

---

[51] Balthere the anchorite is also described in Alcuin's poem on the saints of York (*Carm.* i), lines 1318–86 (MGH, *PLAC*, i. 198–200); and an anchorite named Balthere is listed among the *nomina anchoritarum* in *LVD* (ed. Sweet, p. 155, line 52). The death of Balthere is also recorded by Symeon of Durham, *LDE* ii. 2, where it is stated that he led his eremitical life at Tyninghame in East Lothian, and died on 6 March 756 (ed. Rollason, p. 80, with n. 6).

[52] Cf. the comment of Whitelock, *EHD* i. 266: 'There was no total eclipse of the moon late in 756, but there was one in the evening of 23 November 755'; and see Schove and Fletcher, *The Chronology of Eclipses*, p. 154, who likewise assign the 'total eclipse in N.E. England' to 23 November 755, and go on to explain that the 'bright star' was due to 'Jupiter occultation', since 'Jupiter was retrograding in opposition (about a degree from the Anti-Sun) and was certainly occulted by the moon as seen from at least part of England' (p. 155).

[53] From *HE Continuatio* (II), s.a. 757: 'Anno .dcclvii. Aedilbald rex Merciorum a suis tutoribus nocte morte fraudulenta miserabiliter peremptus occubuit' (ed. Colgrave and Mynors, p. 574); cf. *ASC* s.a. 757: 'And in the same year Æthelbald, king of the Mercians, was slain at Seckington, and his body was buried at Repton' (trans. Whitelock, p. 31); and 'Ramsey Annals', s.a. 757: 'Eadbald rex occiditur' (p. 41).

[54] *HE Continuatio* (II): 'Eodem etiam anno Offa, fugato Beornredo, Merciorum regnum sanguinolento quaesiuit gladio' (ed. Colgrave and Mynors, p. 574).

[55] *HE Continuatio* (II), s.a. 758: 'Eadberhtus rex Nordanhymbrorum Dei amoris causa et caelestis patria [*sic*] uiolentia [*sic*], accepta sancti Petri tonsura, filio suo Osuulfo regnum reliquit. Anno .dcclix. Osuulf a suis ministris facinore occisus est' (ed. Colgrave and Mynors, p. 574; the text printed by Colgrave and Mynors is nonsense: for *patria* read *patriae*, and for *uiolentia* read *uolentia*); cf. *ASC* D(E), s.a. 758 [757]: 'In this year Eadberht, king of the Northumbrians, received the tonsure, and his son Oswulf succeeded to the kingdom, and ruled for one year, and the men of his household slew him on 24 July' (trans. Whitelock,

PARS TERTIA 71

His Son.[51] The fifteen [day] moon was covered with blood-red colouring on 24 November, at the age of fifteen [days], that is, at full moon; and thence, with the shadows slowly diminishing, it returned to its original bright light. For, remarkably, with a bright star following the moon itself and bypassing it, it preceded the moon's brightness by as great a distance as it followed before it had been obscured.[52]

In 756, Æthelbald, king of the Mercians, was treacherously killed by his bodyguard.[53] In the same year the Mercians engaged in civil war among themselves. When Beornred turned to flight, Offa emerged as victor.[54]

In 757, King Eadberht willingly entrusted to his son, named Oswulf, the kingdom bestowed on him by God; Oswulf held the kingdom for one year, then relinquished and lost it, because he was wickedly killed by his kinsmen near *Mechil Wongtune* [unidentified] on 24 July.[55]

10. In 759, Æthelwald, also called Moll, began to reign on 5 August.[56] As the third year of his reign was beginning [i.e. in 761], a ferocious battle was fought on 6 August, near Eldon, in which Oswine fell after three days' [fighting], on Sunday [9 August]. But King Æthelwald, also called Moll, obtained the victory in this battle.[57] In the same year also Onuist, king of the Picts, died.[58]

---

p. 32); and 'Ramsey Annals', s.a. 758: 'Eadbyrht rex occiditur, et Oswulf regnat' (p. 41). The identity of *Mechil Wongtune* is uncertain. The same place is apparently mentioned in the anonymous *Vita S. Cuthberti* (iv. 6), where the form given is *Medilwong* (*Two Lives*, ed. Colgrave, p. 118). Whitelock comments: 'It has been suggested that it is one of the Middletons in Ilderton or Middleton in Belford, Northumberland' (*EHD* i. 266, n. 5).

[56] *HE Continuatio* (II), s.a. 759: 'Ediluald anno eodem a sua plebe electus intrauit in regnum' (ed. Colgrave and Mynors, p. 574); cf. *ASC* D(E), s.a. 759: 'And Moll Æthelwold succeeded to the kingdom of the Northumbrians, and reigned six years and then lost it' (trans. Whitelock, p. 32), and 'Ramsey Annals', s.a. 759: 'Æthelwald regnum suscepit' (p. 41).

[57] *ASC* D(E), s.a. 761: 'And Moll, king of the Northumbrians, killed Oswine at "Edwin's Cliff" on 6 August' (trans. Whitelock, p. 32); cf. *HE Continuatio* (II), s.a. 761: 'et Osuuini occisus est' (ed. Colgrave and Mynors, p. 576). Byrhtferth's *Eldunum* is possibly to be identified as Eldon (Co. Durham).

[58] Cf. *HE Continuatio* (II), s.a. 761: 'Oengus Pictorum rex obiit, qui regni sui principium usque ad finem facinore cruentum tyrannus carnifex perduxit' (ed. Colgrave and Mynors, p. 576); the year 761 is confirmed by entries recording his death in the Annals of Ulster and Annals of Tigernach (*The Chronicle of Ireland*, ed. Charles-Edwards, i. 230), which suggests that the present entry has been misplaced by two years. Onuist son of Vurguist, king of the Picts (whose name is given in Irish annals as Oengus) was one of the most powerful war leaders of his time. His career has been traced by Fraser, *From Caledonia to Pictland*, pp. 287–319, who shows that Onuist first came to prominence in 728, when he expelled the Pictish king Elphin in a battle at Moncrieffe, and assumed the high kingship of the Picts on the death of Naiton in 732, a position which he held by means of ferocious aggression until his death in 761, when he must have been 70 or more years old. He was the first and only Pictish king known to have invaded Northumbria; and, in alliance with the Northumbrian king Eadberht, he forced the Britons of Strathclyde to accept the terms of a treaty in 756 (see above, iii. 9 with n. 26). Interestingly, he is recorded as *Unust* among the 'Nomina regum vel ducum' in *LVD* (ed. Sweet, p. 154, line 8).

HISTORIA REGVM

Anno .dcclxii. Ætheluuald rex praephatus accepit reginam Ætheldrytham kalendas ⸢Nouembris⸣ in Cateracta.[c][59]

[d]Anno .dcclxiv.[d] nix ingens gelu ligata, omnibus retro saeculis incomparabilis, a principio hiemis paene usque ad medium ueris terram oppressit. Cuius ui arbores holeraque magna ex parte aruerunt, ac marina animalia multa inuenta sunt mortua.[60]

11. Eodem quoque anno Ceoluulf, quondam rex, tunc Domini nostri Iesu Christi seruus monachusque, obiit. Huic uero regi Beda historiographus ueridicus direxit epistolam, sic inchoando: 'Gloriosissimo regi Ceoluulfo Beda famulus Christi et presbyter. Historiam gentis Anglorum quam nuper edideram, libentissime tibi desideranti, rex, et prius ad legendum et nunc ad scribendum ac plenius ex tempore meditaturum transmitto.'[61]

Anno eodem multae urbes monasteriaque atque uillae per diuersa loca, necnon et regna, repentino igne uastatae sunt, uerbi gratia Stretburg, Venta ciuitas, Homuuic, Londonia ciuitas, Eboraca ciuitas, Donaceaster, aliaque multa loca illa plaga concussit,[62] ut illud impleretur quod scriptum est, 'Erit terrae motus'.[63] Eodem anno Freohelm presbyter et abbas obiit;[64] et episcopus Merciorum gentis nomine Totta defunctus est, et Eadberht pro eo ordinatus est episcopus.[65] His quoque temporibus Frithuuald episcopus Candidae Casae ex hoc saeculo migrauit,[a] pro quo Pechtuuine loco illius episcopus subrogatur.[66]

12. Anno .dcclxv. ignei ictus in aere uisi sunt, quales quondam apparuerunt tempore nocturno kalendas Ianuarii, ut superius

---

[c-c] *add.* C^2 [d-d] *add.* C^2

iii.11   [a] Nonis Maii *add.* C^2

---

[59] The marriage of Æthilwald Moll and Æthelthryth is not recorded in any other source.

[60] The 'great winter' is recorded in *ASC*, but there is confusion about what year it took place; cf. *ASC* 763 [762C, 761 ADEF]: 'In this year occurred the great winter' (trans. Whitelock, p. 32).

[61] Byrhtferth quotes, with some omissions, the very beginning of Bede, *HE praef.* 1: 'Gloriosissimo regi Ceoluulfo Baeda famulus Christi et presbyter. Historiam gentis Anglorum ecclesiasticam, quam nuper edideram, libentissime tibi desideranti, rex, et prius ad legendum ac probandum transmisi, et nunc ad transscribendum ac plenius ex tempore meditandum retransmitto' (Bede, *HE*, ed. Lapidge, i. 6; ed. Colgrave and Mynors, p. 2). Byrhtferth's variant reading (*meditaturum* for *meditandum*) is found only in MS C (= BL, Cotton Tiberius C. ii), a manuscript of the Southumbrian recension (κ); cf. also Hunter Blair, 'Some observations', pp. 90–1, and Introduction, p. lxii.

[62] These fires are not recorded in any other source. Of the cities mentioned, only *Stretburg* cannot be identified, although judging from its name, it was a fortified town on a Roman road (OE *stræt*).

PARS TERTIA

In 762, the aforesaid King Æthelwald took Æthelthryth as queen on 1 November, at Catterick.[59]

In 764, massive snowfall mixed with ice, unlike any that had occurred in all previous times, oppressed the land almost from the beginning of winter up until the midst of spring. Because of its severity, trees and plants largely withered, and many marine animals were found dead.[60]

11. In the very same year [764], Ceolwulf, sometime king, but at that time servant and monk of our Lord Jesus Christ, died. To this king Bede the truthful historian sent a letter, beginning thus: 'To the most glorious king Ceolwulf, Bede, priest and servant of Christ [sends greetings]. The *History of the English People* which I recently produced I send to you at your eager wish, O king, both for reading as previously and now for copying and thoroughly considering in the fullness of time.'[61]

In the same year many cities and monasteries and towns in various locations and different kingdoms, were destroyed by sudden fire, that is to say, that disaster struck *Stretburg* [unidentified], the city of Winchester, *Hamwic* [Southampton], the city of London, the city of York, Doncaster, and many other places,[62] so that what is written would be fulfilled: 'There shall be earthquakes.'[63] In the same year Freohelm the priest and abbot died, and the bishop of the people of Mercia, named Totta, passed away,[64] and Eadberht was ordained bishop in his place.[65] At this time, too, Frithuwald, bishop of Whithorn, departed from this world, in place of whom Pechtwine was appointed bishop.[66]

12. In 765, fiery bolts were seen in the sky, such as once had appeared at night time on the kalends of January [1 January], as we

---

[63] Matt. 24: 7 ('et erunt pestilentiae et fames et terraemotus per loca').

[64] Freohelm is not mentioned in any other source, and the monastery of which he was abbot is uncertain; *PASE* (s.v. 'Freohelm') suggests Lindisfarne. A person named 'Frehelm' is listed among the 'Nomina abbatum gradus presbyteratus' in *LVD* (ed. Sweet, p. 155, line 62).

[65] Torhthelm or Totta was mentioned previously (*HR* iii. 4, s.a. 737) as bishop of the Mercians, with his see at Leicester (Keynes, 'Bishops', p. 557); he was succeeded by Eadberht (764–81×785), about whom nothing further is known. He is listed by Keynes, 'Bishops', p. 557, and by *PASE* s.v. 'Eadberht 16'.

[66] Cf. *ASC* D(E), s.a. 763: 'And Frithuwald, bishop of Whithorn, died on 7 May. He had been consecrated in the city [York] on 15 August in the sixth year of Ceolwulf's reign, and was bishop 29 years. Then Pehtwine was consecrated bishop of Whithorn at Elvet [Durham] on 17 July' (trans. Whitelock, p. 32); see Keynes, 'Bishops', p. 566.

74   HISTORIA REGVM

fo. 63ʳᵇ praenotauimus.[67] Eodem anno Ætheluuald regnum Northanhymbrorum |
amisit in Vuincanheale .iii. kalendas Nouembris.[68] Cui Alchred prosapia Idae regis exortus, ut quidam dicunt, successit in regnum.[69] Quo
anno Hemeli Merciorum episcopus obiit, cuius uice Cuthfrid ordinatus est episcopus in Liccetfeldan.[70] Eademque tempestate Breguuine
archiepiscopus Cantiae ciuitatis ex hac uita subtractus est, cui
Iaenberht successit uice regiminis.[71] Alduulf quoque antistes in
Lindisse eodem anno hanc uitam dereliquit, aliamque petiuit; post
quem Ceoluulf electus et consecratus est.[72]

Anno .dcclxvi. Ecgberht archiepiscopus Eboracae ciuitatis in pace
Christi requieuit .xiii. kalendas Decembris, tricesimo quarto anno
episcopatus sui; et Frithuberht Haugustaldensis ecclesiae antistes
eodem anno de hac mortali carne migrauit ad uerae lucis perennitatem
.x. kalendas Ianuarii, episcopatus sui anno tricesimo secundo.[73]

13. Anno .dcclxvii. Ælberht Eboracae ciuitatis et Alchmund
Haugustaldensis ecclesiae ordinati sunt episcopi .viii. kalendas Maii.
Eodem tempore Aluberht ad Ealdseaxos ordinatus est episcopus,[74] et
Ceoluulf in Lindissi antistes consecratus est.[75] Ipso quoque anno Echa

---

[67] *HR* iii. 7, s.a. 745 (see above, p. 64, with n. 27).

[68] Æthelwald Moll's loss of kingdom was foretold by *ASC* s.a. 759 (quoted above, n. 56). The identification of *Vuincanheal* is unknown, save to say that the earlier identification with Finchale is now rejected (see Whitelock in *EHD* i. 267, n. 6). Part of the problem is uncertainty about whether the initial letter represents an attempt to reproduce the OE letter wynn (Ƿ), or is simply P. On this occasion (iii. 12) the name is spelled with W- (reproducing OE wynn); on two subsequent occcasions (iii. 20, iii. 25), it is spelled with the initial letter P.

[69] *HE Continuatio* (II), s.a. 765: 'Alchred rex susceptus est in regnum' (ed. Colgrave and Mynors, p. 576); cf. *ASC* D(E), s.a. 765: 'In this year Alhred succeeded to the kingdom of the Northumbrians, and ruled nine years' (trans. Whitelock, p. 33); see Keynes, 'Rulers', p. 525. Alhred's descent from King Ida is recorded in the Northumbrian 'Regnal Lists'; see Dumville, 'The Anglian collection', pp. 30, 32.

[70] Hemele was bishop of the Mercians, in succession to Hwita (see above, *HR* iii. 4, s.a. 737) with his bishopric at Lichfield; he was succeeded by Cuthfrith (765–?769): see Keynes, 'Bishops', p. 556.

[71] Bregowine, archbishop of Canterbury from 760 to 764, was succeeded by Jænberht (765–92): Keynes, 'Bishops', p. 543. On Jænberht, see *ODNB* xxix. 580 [M. Costambeys] and *WB Encyc.*, pp. 262–3 [S. D. Keynes]. Before his election to the archbishopric, Jænberht had been abbot of St Augustine's in Canterbury, and was buried there after his death on 12 August 792. *ASC* records his consecration s.a. 765 [763 AC, 762 DEF] (trans. Whitelock, p. 32), and his receipt of the pallium s.a. 766 [764] (ibid. p. 33).

[72] Aldwulf, bishop of Lindsey (750–65), was succeeded by Ceolwulf (767–96); see Keynes, 'Bishops', p. 558.

PARS TERTIA

75

noted above.[67] In the same year Æthelwald relinquished the kingdom of the Northumbrians at *Vuincanheal* [unidentified] on 30 October.[68] Alchred, sprung from the kin of King Ida, as some people say, succeeded to the kingdom.[69] In this year Hemel, bishop of the Mercians, died, in whose place Cuthfrith was ordained bishop in Lichfield.[70] At the same time Bregowine, archbishop of Canterbury, was taken from this life; Jænberht succeeded him in the role of governor.[71] Also in the same year Aldwulf, bishop in Lindsey, relinquished this life and sought another. Ceolwulf was elected and ordained after him.[72]

In 766, Ecgberht, archbishop of York, passed away in the peace of Christ on 19 November, in the thirty-fourth year of his bishopric; and in the same year Frithuberht, the bishop of the church of Hexham, passed from this mortal flesh to the eternity of true light on 23 December, in the thirty-second year of his bishopric.[73]

13. In 767, Ælberht and Alchmund were ordained bishop of the city of York and the church of Hexham [respectively], on 24 April. At the same time Aluberht was ordained bishop of the Old Saxons,[74] and Ceolwulf was consecrated bishop in Lindsey.[75] In the same year Echha

---

[73] *HE Continuatio* (II), s.a. 766: 'Ecgbertus archiepiscopus, prosapia regali ditatus ac diuina scientia inbutus, et Frithubertus, uere fideles episcopi, ad Dominum migrauerunt' (ed. Colgrave and Mynors, p. 576). This is the final entry in *HE Continuatio* (II), and it has been plausibly suggested by Joanna Story that the annals in this text were kept at York through the patronage of Archbishop Ecgberht: 'After Bede', p. 180; see also the Introduction, p. lvii. Cf. the entry in *ASC* D(E), s.a. 766: 'In this year Egbert, archbishop of York, who had been bishop 37 years, died on 19 November; and Frithuberht, of Hexham, who had been bishop 34 years, died. And Ethelbert was consecrated for York and Alhmund for Hexham' (trans. Whitelock, p. 33); see Keynes, 'Bishops', pp. 562 (Ecgberht), 564 (Frithuberht).

[74] This entry is problematical, for various reasons. If the transmitted text—*ad Ealdseaxos ordinatus*—is retained, the meaning is that Aluberht was consecrated as a missionary bishop for the Old Saxons (in the Netherlands and N. Germany). This is the interpretation of the passage favoured by Dorothy Whitelock (*EHD* i. 268), and is endorsed by Story, *Carolingian Connections*, p. 53, who points out that Aluberht's Continental mission is described in Altfrid's *Vita S. Liudgeri* [*BHL* 4937], cc. 10–12; cf. also ibid. pp. 94 and 96, as well as Rollason, *Sources for York*, pp. 131–2. It is less likely that the Aluberht in question was the shadowy bishop of Selsey (747×765–772×780, on whom, see Kelly, *Charters of Selsey*, pp. lxxxix and 32, and Keynes, 'Bishops', p. 547), as was suggested by Arnold (*Symeonis Monachi Opera Omnia*, ii. 43, n. *a*). Such an identification would carry the implication that the transmitted reading *ad Ealdseaxos* would have to be emended to *ad Suðseaxos*, 'to the South Saxons'. A person named *Alubercht* is recorded under the 'Nomina abbatum' in *LVD* (ed. Sweet, p. 156, line 90).

[75] On Ceolwulf, bishop of Lindsey (767–96), see Keynes, 'Bishops', p. 558.

76   HISTORIA REGVM

anachorita feliciter in Cric obiit, qui locus distat ab Eboraca ciuitate .x. miliariis.[76] Anno .dcclxviii. Eadberht,[a] decimo anno amissionis regni sui in clericatu Deique omnipotentis seruitio,[b] feliciter spiritum emisit ad superos .xiii. kalendas Septembris.[77] Eodem anno Pippin rex Francorum mortuus est;[78] et Haduuine ordinatus est episcopus ad Machni.[79] Atque Alchred rex eodem tempore accepit reginam Osgeofu.[c80] Anno .dcclxix. Cateracte succensa est ab Earnredo tyranno, et ipse fo. 63ᵛᵃ infelix | eodem anno incendio periit Dei iudicio.[81]

14. Anno .dcclxxi. Sigbald abbas obiit,[82] et Ecgric, <presbyter>[a] et lector de hoc instabilis uitae cursu migrauit ad consortium electorum,[83] quo percipit epinicion[b] perpetuum.[84] His diebus Offa rex Merciorum Haestingorum gentem armis subegerat.[85] Eodem quoque anno Carloman[c] rex Francorum subita praeuentus infirmitate defunctus est. Sed et frater eius Carolus,[d] cum dimidium prius patris obtinuit[e]

---

iii.13   [a] *after* Eadberht *C² adds* quondam rex, tunc autem clericus   [b] *after* seruitio *C²* *adds* apud Eboracum   [c] *corr. ed.,* Osgearn *C*

iii.14   [a] *suppl. ed.*   [b] *over* epinicion *C¹ adds* .i. triumphum   [c] *after* Carloman *C²* *adds* famosissimus   [d] Karl *C*   [e] uel -isset *C²*

---

[76] An anchorite name Echha is recorded among the 'Nomina anchoritarum' in *LVD* (ed. Sweet, p. 155, line 53); he is described briefly by Alcuin in his poem on the saints of York (*Carm.* i), lines 1387–92 (MGH, *PLAC* i. 200). Alcuin does not mention Crayke, which is known to have had close connections with York, and is very possibly the site of the unnamed cell of Lindisfarne described in Aediluulf's poem *De abbatibus*; see Lapidge, 'Aediluulf and the school of York', pp. 174–8 = *ALL* i. 394–8.

[77] King Eadberht's death is recorded in *ASC* D(E), s.a. 768: 'In this year Eadberht, son of Eata, died on 20 August' (trans. Whitelock, p. 33); cf. 'Ramsey Annals', s.a. 768: 'Æadbryht rex obiit' (p. 41). It is odd that the *ASC* annalist does not mention here that Eadberht had formerly been king of Northumbria (737–58). Note that among the list of 'Nomina abbatum' in *LVD* is found the entry *Eadberct rex* (ed. Sweet, p. 156, line 85).

[78] The death of Pippin (III) is recorded against the year 768 in various Continental annal collections, notably the *Annales regni Francorum* or 'Royal Frankish Annals' (ed. Kurze, pp. 26–7; *Carolingian Chronicles*, trans. Scholz, p. 46). There is no doubt that Byrhtferth had access to a set of Carolingian annals which agreed in many respects with the 'Royal Frankish Annals', even if it was not identical; see the detailed discussion in Story, *Carolingian Connections*, pp. 93–133, esp. 96, 113–14. A copy of these Frankish annals could have been brought to England by Alcuin when he returned to York during the years 790–3.

[79] The church to which Hadwine was consecrated bishop in 768 was in Co. Connaught in Ireland, and was known in Irish as *Mag n-Éo na Saxan* or 'Mayo of the Saxons'. Mayo had first been established for the English monks of Lindisfarne who accompanied Bishop Colmán when he resigned from Lindisfarne after the Synod of Whitby in 664; it continued in existence, under the charge of an English bishop, down to the time of Alcuin and beyond; see N. K. Chadwick, 'Bede, St Colmán, and the Irish abbey of Mayo', with discussion of Hadwine at pp. 194–5. Hadwine's death is recorded below (*HR* iii. 14), against 773; see below, n. 89.

PARS TERTIA 77

the anchorite died blessedly in Crayke, which is some ten miles from the city of York.[76]

In 768, Eadberht released his soul to the heavens on 20 August, in the tenth year after his resignation of the kingdom, in the service and clergy of omnipotent God.[77] In the same year Pippin, king of the Franks, died,[78] and Hadwine was ordained bishop at *Machni* [Mayo].[79] And at the same time King Alchred married Queen Osgeofu.[80]

In 769, Catterick was burned down by the tyrant Earnred, and the wretch himself perished by fire that same year through the judgement of God.[81]

14. In 771, Abbot Sigbald died,[82] and Ecgric, <priest> and lector, passed from the course of this unstable life into the community of the elect,[83] where he received the eternal *epinicion* [triumph].[84] At this time Offa, king of the Mercians, subjected the people of the *Hæstingas* by armed force.[85] In the same year as well, Carloman, king of the Franks, died, having been overtaken by a sudden illness. But his brother Charles, after he had previously acquired one half of the dominion of

---

[80] The marriage of King Alhred and Queen 'Osgearn' (thus the name is given in C) is not recorded elsewhere; and in any case, 'Osgearn' is not a possible form for a woman's name in OE. In the corpus of Bonifatian correspondence there is a letter addressed to Archbishop Lull of Mainz (Boniface's English successor) from King Alhred and his wife, who in the salutation to the letter is named Osgeofu: 'Alhredus rex et Osgeofu regina Lullo venerabili episcopo...salutem' (MGH, *Ep. sel.* i. 257 [*Ep.* cxxi]). For discussion of this letter, see Story, *Carolingian Connections*, p. 53; and note also that a woman named *Osgeofu* is listed last in *LVD* among the 'Nomina reginarum et abbatissarum' (ed. Sweet, p. 155, line 48). The sum of this evidence indicates that the transmitted form *Osgearn* is simply an error of transcription, by Byrhtferth, Symeon, or the scribe of C. For that reason, the transmitted text has been emended to *Osgeofu*.

[81] Neither the 'tyrant' Earnred nor the burning of Catterick is recorded elsewhere.

[82] It is possible that this Abbot Sigbald is identical to the fourth abbot of an unidentified monastic cell dependent on Lindisfarne and described by the Northumbrian poet Aediluulf in his poem *De abbatibus*, lines 431–72 (Æthelwulf, *De abbatibus*, ed. Campbell, pp. 34–9; cf. also MGH, *PLAC* i. 594–5). For arguments that this unidentified cell is to be identified as Crayke, situated some 10 miles north of York, see above, *HR* iii. 13, with n. 76.

[83] This Ecgric is otherwise unknown. A noun describing Ecgric has evidently fallen out of the text here; I have supplied *presbyter* on the analogy of a rubric in Aediluulf's poem *De abbatibus* concerning one Hyglac ('De Hyglaco presbytero atque lectore': ed. Campbell, *De abbatibus*, p. 41; MGH, *PLAC* i. 596), and the obituary notice of Colgu given below (*HR* iii. 23: *presbyter et lector*) without any conviction that such a restoration is certain.

[84] Byrhtferth had previously used the word *epinicion* above, *HR* ii. 9 (see above, p. 34 and n. 28, and Introduction, p. xxvi).

[85] On Offa's subjection of the *Hæstingas* ('people of Hastings') and the kingdom of Kent, see Stenton, *Anglo-Saxon England*, pp. 206–8, as well as *WB Encyc.* pp. 275–6 ('Kent, kingdom of'), 347–8 ('Offa'), and Keynes, 'The control of Kent', pp. 112–13.

78   HISTORIA REGVM

principatum, totius regni monarchiam et Francorum fastigium populorum dehinc est indeptus inuicta fortitudine.[86]

*f*Anno .dcclxxii.*f* Pictel dux et Suuithuulf abbas obierunt in Domino.[87] Carolus*g* quoque Francorum rex, collecta manu ualida et bellicosis suae maiestati*h* uiris coniunctis, Saxonum gentem est ingressus. Multisque ex principibus ac nobilibus*i* suis amissis, in sua se recepit.[88]

Anno ab incarnatione Dominica .dcclxxiii. Haduuinus Migensis ecclesiae antistes sublatus est,[89] et Leutfrith pro eo est subrogatus episcopus.[90] Vulfhaeth quoque hoc anno abbas*j* diem Domini uidere desiderauit, cui et concessum est, quem subsecutus est.[91] Eodem tempore Ælberht, Eboracae antistes ecclesiae, pallii ministerium ab Adriano papa sibi directum accepit.*k*[92]

15. Anno .dcclxxiiii. Eaduulf dux ex huius uitae naufragio subtrahitur,[93] et eodem tempore Alchredus rex, consilio et consensu suorum omnium, regiae familiae ac prinicipum destitutus societate, exilio imperii mutauit maiestatem.[94] Primo in urbem Bebban, postea ad regem Pictorum nomine Cynoth,[95] cum paucis fugae comitibus secessit.*a*

---

f-f added C²   *g Carl C*   *h maiestatis C*   *i after nobilibus C² adds uiris*
j after abbas C² adds Beuerlacensis   *k C² adds Wlfach obiit abbas in left-hand margin*

iii.15 *a over secessit C² adds uel se gessit*

---

[86] The death of Carloman is reported in the 'Royal Frankish Annals' (*Annales regni Francorum*), s.a. 771: 'In the same year King Carloman died at the villa of Samoussy on 4 December' (ed. Kurze, pp. 32–3; trans. Scholz, p. 48). It is not stated specifically here that Charles (Charlemagne) thereupon took over the entire kingdom, but the inference is obvious. See discussion by Story, *Carolingian Connections*, pp. 96–7.

[87] Neither Ealdorman Pihtel nor Abbot Swithwulf is known from another source.

[88] Charlemagne's invasion of the (Old) Saxons is recorded in the 'Royal Frankish Annals' (*Annales regni Francorum*), s.a. 772 (ed. Kurze, pp. 32–5; trans. Scholz, pp. 48–9); see discussion by Story, *Carolingian Connections*, p. 97.

[89] The death of Bishop Hadwine is recorded in the 'Annals of Ulster', s.a. 773: 'The death of Áedán, bishop of Mag nÉo [Mayo]' (*The Chronicle of Ireland*, trans. Charles-Edwards, i. 239). Charles-Edwards notes: 'The use of the name Áedán in place of the English name Haduini may be explained either as simple Hibernicizing by the annalist, or a copyist, of an unfamiliar foreign name or, more interestingly, as Haduini himself using an Irish name not too remote from his own in reverence for Aidan, the saintly bishop of the Northumbrians' (ibid. n. 1).

[90] On Leutfrith, see N. K. Chadwick, 'Bede, St Colmán and the Irish abbey of Mayo', p. 195. In the collection of Alcuin's letters there is one dated 773×786 (no. ii) addressed to this Leutfrith (MGH, *Epist.* iv. 19).

[91] Wulfhæth, abbot of Beverley, is not known from any other source; but a person named *uulfhaeth* is listed among the 'Nomina abbatum' in *LVD* (ed. Sweet, p. 156, line 86).

PARS TERTIA   79

his father, thereafter obtained, through his unconquerable strength, control of the entire kingdom and rule of the Frankish peoples.[86]

In 772, Ealdorman Pihtel and Abbot Swithwulf died in the Lord.[87] And Charles, king of the Franks, having assembled a mighty army and joined their warlike strength to his own majesty, invaded the people of the Saxons. Having lost many of his leading men and nobles, he returned to his own realms.[88]

In 773, Hadwine, bishop of the church of Mayo, was carried off [in death],[89] and Leutfrith was appointed bishop in his place.[90] Also in that year Abbot Wulfhæth desired to see the light of the Lord, which was granted to him, and he followed Him.[91] At the same time Ælberht, bishop of the church of York, received the dignity of the pallium, sent to him by Pope Hadrian.[92]

15. In 774, Ealdorman Eadwulf is removed from the shipwreck of this life,[93] and at the same King Alchred, through the advice and consent of all his [councillors], deprived of the companionship of the royal family and ealdormen, exchanged the majesty of royal command for exile.[94] He withdrew first to Bamburgh, and thereafter to the king of the Picts named Ciniod,[95] with the few companions of his flight.

---

[92] This entry is apparently the only record of Archbishop Ælberht receiving the pallium (see Levison, *England and the Continent*, p. 243, and Story, *Carolingian Connections*, p. 54). From Alcuin's poem on the saints of York (*Carm.* i, lines 1457–8) we know that Ælberht had travelled to Rome and visited the holy places (MGH, *PLAC* i. 201–2), but this trip must have taken place before his election as archbishop in 767, since Alcuin makes no mention of the pope or the pallium (Hadrian I did not become pope until 772). The papacy was in turmoil during the years 767–72, which may be one of the reasons why Ælberht did not seek, or receive, the pallium during those years.

[93] This Ealdorman Eadwulf is otherwise unknown (he is not apparently included among the fifty-eight persons named Eadwulf listed in *PASE* s.v.); he is presumably the same Eadwulf whose death is recorded s.a. 775 later on in the present chapter. If so, it is possible that Byrhtferth has here misunderstood his source, which (hypothetically) explained that in 774 Ealdorman Eadwulf *departed from Northumbria* (not: *from the shipwreck of this life*) and went, in company with King Alchred, to seek the protection of the Pictish king Ciniod. When Ciniod died the following year (775), Eadwulf lost his protector, as a result of which he was 'killed, buried, forgotten' (see below).

[94] Cf. *ASC* D(E), s.a. 774: 'In this year the Northumbrians drove their King Alhred from York at Easter' (trans. Whitelock, p. 33).

[95] Ciniod filius Wredech was king of the Picts from 761, when Onuist died (see above, *HR* iii. 10, with n. 58), until his own death in 775, which is recorded later in the present chapter (see below, n. 99): see Anderson, *Kings and Kingship*, pp. 86, 249, and 263, and Fraser, *From Caledonia to Pictland*, p. 385. As Charles-Edwards points out (*The Chronicle of Ireland*, i. 240, n. 3), the fact that Byrhtferth (or his source) gives the name as *Cynoth* suggests that this source was Pictish rather than Irish, since in Irish sources the same king is named as Cináed (often rendered in modern English as 'Kenneth').

80   HISTORIA REGVM

Bebba uero ciuitas urbs est munitissima, non admodum magna, sed quasi duorum uel trium agrorum spatium, habens unum introitum

fo. 63ᵛᵇ cauatum, et gradibus miro modo | exaltatum. Habet in summitate montis ecclesiam praepulchre factam, in qua est scrinium speciosum ᵇet pretiosum,ᵇ in quo inuoluta pallio iacet dextera manus sancti Osuualdi regis incorrupta, sicut narrat Beda historiographus huius gentis. Est in occidente et in summitate ipsius ciuitatis fons miro cauatus opere, dulcis ad potandum et purissimus ad uidendum.⁹⁶

Æthelredus quoque filius Ætheluualdi pro eo regnum suscepit; qui tanto honore coronatus uix quinque annos tenuit, ueluti declarat subsequens sermo scriptoris.⁹⁷ Eadem tempestate Carolusᶜ Francorum rex inuictissimus nobilissimam Langobardorum urbem Ticinum longa obsidione uexatam, simul cum ipso rege Desiderio ac totius Italiae imperio, cepit.⁹⁸

Anno .dcclxxv. rex Pictorum Cynoth ex uoragine huius coenulentaeᵈ uitae eripitur;⁹⁹ et Eaduulf dux, per insidias fraudulenter captus, post spatium exigui temporis occiditur, sepelitur, obliuiscitur. Ebbi quoque abbas uectigal morti dedit, egrediens et pergens ad eum qui mortuus uitam perpetuam concedit.¹⁰⁰

16. Carolusᵃ deniqueᵇ rex, ut praephati sumus, bellicosissimus Francorum, cum omni exercitus sui uirtute uallatus, confortatus, glorificatus, gentem Saxonum est ingressus, centuriatis atque legionibus stipatus; quam magnis et inedicibilibus regionem proeliisᶜ uastauit, igne ferroque debacchans, quia erat consternatusᵈ animo. Vrbes

---

ᵇ⁻ᵇ *add.* C¹   ᶜ Karl C   ᵈ *corr. Arnold,* coenulentis C

iii.16 ᵃ Karl C   ᵇ uel quoque C¹   ᶜ *after* proeliis C² *adds* grauissimis ᵈ uel efferatus C¹

⁹⁶ The hand of King Oswald was known to be preserved as a relic at Bamburgh from Bede, *HE* iii. 12. 3: 'caput [*scil.* Osuualdi] quidem in cymiterio Lindisfarnensis ecclesiae, in regia uero ciuitate manus cum brachiis condidit' (Bede, *HE*, ed. Lapidge, ii. 60; ed. Colgrave and Mynors, p. 252); see discussion by Thacker, 'Membra disiecta', pp. 100–1. On Bamburgh and the cult of St Oswald in pre-Conquest Northumbria, see Cambridge, 'Archaeology and the cult of St Oswald', esp. pp. 134–40.

⁹⁷ Cf. *ASC* D(E), s.a. 774: 'The Northumbrians took as their lord Ethelred, Moll's son, and he reigned for four years' (trans. Whitelock, p. 33); cf. 'Ramsey Annals', s.a. 774: 'Alhred rex regnum perdit. Æthelred filius Æthelwoldi regnat pro eo. Anno .iiii. regni eius, tres duces occisi sunt' (p. 42); see also Keynes, 'Rulers', p. 525.

⁹⁸ Cf. the entry in the 'Royal Frankish Annals' (*Annales regni Francorum*), s.a. 774: 'On his return from Rome the Lord King Charles came again to Pavia and captured the city and

PARS TERTIA 81

Bamburgh is a strongly fortified city, not all that large, but occupying roughly the space of two or three fields, having only one entrance, hollowed out [of the rock] and made accessible in wondrous fashion only by steps. At the summit of the rock outcrop it has a beautifully built church, in which there is an attractive and precious reliquary shrine, in which, wrapped in a cloth, lies the incorrupt right hand of St Oswald the king, as Bede, the historian of this people, tells us. On the west side, and at the summit of this city, there is a fountain hollowed out by marvellous workmanship, delicious to drink from and crystal-clear to look at.[96]

Æthelred, the son of Æthelwald, took over the kingdom [of the Northumbrians] in his place; crowned with this great distinction, he held it for scarcely five years, as the subsequent account of the [present] writer makes clear [s.a. 779].[97] At the same time Charles, the unconquerable king of the Franks, having harassed Pavia, the noble city of the Lombards, with a lengthy siege, captured it together with the king himself, Desiderius, and the control of all Italy.[98]

In 775, Ciniod, king of the Picts, is snatched from the whirlpool of this filthy life;[99] and Ealdorman Eadwulf, captured treacherously in an ambush, after a short period of time is killed, buried, forgotten. Abbot Ebbi, too, made his tax return to death, departing and travelling to Him Who, when dead, granted us eternal life.[100]

16. And so Charles, the exceedingly warlike king of the Franks, as we said, surrounded, comforted, adorned by the total strength of his army, accompanied by centuries and legions, attacked the Saxon peoples; he laid waste to the region with mighty and indescribable battles, running riot with fire and sword, because he was mentally deranged. In the end he effectively added to his great empire two cities,

---

Desiderius, with his wife and daughter' (ed. Kurze, pp. 38–9; trans. Scholz, p. 50). As Story points out (*Carolingian Connections*, p. 99), the closest equivalent of the present entry is that in the 'Royal Frankish Annals', where, as here, the name of Pavia is given in its Roman form, *Ticinum*.

[99] The *Annals of Ulster* record against 775 'the death of Cináed' (*The Chronicle of Ireland*, trans. Charles-Edwards, i. 240). On the Pictish form of the name—*Cynoth* rather than Cináed—see above, n. 95.

[100] It is not known where Ebbi was abbot (cf. *PASE*, s.v. 'Ebbi 1'). One person named Ebbi is listed among the 'nomina presbyterorum' in *LVD* (ed. Sweet, p. 157, line 131), and another among the 'nomina clericorum' (ibid. p. 160, line 250).

82   HISTORIA REGVM

denique duas, Sigeburg et Aresburg, atque prouinciam Bohuueri olim a Francis oppressam, suo potenter adiecit summo imperio.[101]

Anno .dcclxxvii. Pechtuuine episcopus Candidae Casae .xiii. kalendas Octobris migrauit ex hoc saeculo ad aeternae salutis gaudium, qui eidem ecclesiae quatuor decim annis praefuit; cui Æthelbyrht successit.[102]

Anno quarto Æthelredi regis, *scilicet anno .dcclxxviii., tres duces,*

fo. 64ra Alduulf | uidelicet, Cynuulf et Ecga, eodem rege praecipiente, fraude necati sunt ab Æthelbaldo et Heardberhto principibus .iii. kalendas Octobris.[103] Quid gestum sit anno .dcclxxix., *sequens declarabit sermo.

Anno igitur .dcclxxix. Æthelredo* expulso de regali solio et in exilium fugato, cogitur 'maestos inire modos',[104] 'miserasque habere querelas'.[105] Ælfuuald uero filius Osuulfi, Æthelredo expulso, regnum Northanhymbrorum suscepit, tenuitque .x. annis.[106] Erat enim iste rex pius et iustus, ut sequens demonstrabit articulus.

17. Anno .dcclxxx. Osbald et Æthelheard duces, congregato exercitu, Bearn patricium Ælfuualdi regis in Seletune succenderunt .ix. kalendas Ianuarii.[107] Eodem anno Ælberht archiepiscopus ex hac luce migrauit ad aeternae lucis perennitatem, Eanbaldo, se adhuc uiuente, ad eandem sedem ordinato.[108] Cyniuulf quoque episcopus eodem anno,

– *add. C²*   *f–f add. C²*

---

[101] Charlemagne's campaign against the Saxons is described in the 'Royal Frankish Annals', s.a. 775: 'From here [Düren] he launched a campaign into Saxony and captured the castle of Syburg, restored the castle of Eresburg, and came as far as the Weser and Braunsberg. There the Saxons prepared for battle since they wished to defend the bank of the Weser. With the help of God and by their own vigorous efforts, the Franks put the Saxons to flight' (ed. Kurze, pp. 40–1; trans. Scholz, p. 51). Note, however, that the 'Royal Frankish Annals' make no mention of the *prouincia Bohuueri* (the territory around Bückeburg, some 50 miles north of Eresburg), which suggests that the Carolingian annals which Byrhtferth had before him were not identical in every respect to the 'Royal Frankish Annals' as they have been preserved. See discussion by Story, *Carolingian Connections*, pp. 100–1. Several features of Byrhtferth's vocabulary in this paragraph deserve comment. The superlative adjective *bellicosissimus* is a typical example of Byrhtferth's preference for polysyllabic forms; see Lapidge, 'The early sections', p. 102 = *ALL* ii. 322; Byrhtferth, *The Lives*, ed. Lapidge, pp. xlvi–xlvii; and Introduction, p. xxiv. The word *centuriatus* has no relevant entry in *DMLBS* (cf. p. 315, s.v. 'centuria'); a *centuria* means a 'military force of 100 men', and the correct form required here would have been *centuriis*, not *centuriatis*. The polysyllabic adjective *inedicibilis* is one of Byrhtferth's favourite words: it is used 6× in *VSO* and 4× in *VSE* (and 6× in *HR*). Finally, the expression *consternatus animo* is biblical, from 1 Macc. 3: 31, 4: 27; Byrhtferth uses it again at *HR* iv. 10 (see below, p. 144, n. 65).

[102] On Pechtwine and *Candida Casa* [Whithorn], cf. *ASC* D(E), s.a. 776: 'In this year Bishop Pehtwine died on 19 September; he had been bishop for 14 years' (trans. Whitelock, p. 33); and, in a separate entry, still from MSS. D(E), s.a. 777: 'And in that same year [777]

PARS TERTIA   83

Syburg and Eresburg, and the territory of *Bohuueri* [Bückeburg], which had formerly been subdued by the Franks.[101]

In 777, Pechtwine, bishop of Whithorn, passed from this world to the joy of eternal salvation on 19 September; he was in charge of that church for fourteen years, and Æthelberht succeeded him.[102]

In the fourth year of King Æthelred, namely in 778, three ealdormen— that is, Aldwulf, Cynwulf, and Ecga—at the same king's command were treacherously killed by the thegns Æthelbald and Heardberht, on 29 September.[103] As to what happened in 779, the following narrative will explain.

And so in 779, Æthelred, having been expelled from his royal throne and driven into exile, is compelled to 'begin sad songs'[104] and to 'express wretched laments'.[105] Ælfwald, the son of Oswulf, once Æthelred was driven out, took over the kingdom of the Northumbrians and held it for ten years.[106] This same king was dutiful and just, as the following paragraph will demonstrate.

17. In 780, Ealdormen Osbald and Æthelheard, having assembled an army, burned Beorn, the highborn kinsman of King Ælfwald, in *Seletune* [?Selby], on 24 December.[107] In the same year Archbishop Ælberht passed from this light to the eternity of perpetual light, with Eanbald having been consecrated to the same see while he [Ælberht] was still alive.[108] In the same year, too, Bishop Cyniwulf, having

---

Ethelbert was consecrated bishop of Whithorn at York on 15 June' (ibid.). See also Keynes, 'Bishops', p. 566.

[103] Cf. *ASC* D(E), s.a. 778: 'In this year Æthelbald and Heardberht killed three high-reeves, Ealdwulf, son of Bosa, at Coniscliffe, Cynewulf and Ecga at *Helathirnum*, on 22 March' (trans. Whitelock, p. 34). From this entry it appears that the killings took place in two separate stages, which Byrhtferth (or his source) conflated. The dates given in the two sources do not coincide, which perhaps suggests that Ealdwulf was killed at Coniscliffe on 29 September (as here in the *HR*), but that Cynewulf and Ecga had earlier been killed on 22 March at *Helathirnum* (an unidentified place).

[104] Boethius, *De consolatione Philosophiae* i, met. i, line 2: 'flebilis heu maestos cogor inire modos' (CCSL xciv. 1).

[105] Cf. Boethius, *De consolatione Philosophiae* iii, met. v, lines 8–10: 'tamen atras pellere curas / miserasque fugare querelas / non posse potentia non est' (CCSL xciv. 45).

[106] Cf. *ASC* D(E), s.a. 778: 'And then Ælfwold succeeded to the kingdom and drove Æthelred from the country; and he reigned for ten years' (trans. Whitelock, p. 34); cf. 'Ramsey Annals', s.a. 779: 'Ælfwald filius Oswulfi regnum suscepit' (p. 42).

[107] Cf. *ASC* D(E), s.a. 779: 'And the high-reeves of the Northumbrians burnt Ealdorman Beorn in *Seletun* on 25 December' (trans. Whitelock, p. 34). The identity of *Seletun* is uncertain: it may perhaps be Selby (N. Yorks.), which Ekwall explains as 'a Scandinavianized form of OE *Seletun*' (*DEPN*, p. 411).

[108] Cf. *ASC* D(E), s.a. 779: 'And Archbishop Ethelbert, in whose place Eanbald had previously been consecrated, died in the city [York]' (trans. Whitelock, p. 34).

84 HISTORIA REGVM

relictis saecularibus curis, Hygbaldo gubernacula ecclesiae cum electione totius familiae commisit.[109] Eodem etiam anno Eanbald episcopus pallium ab apostolica sede sibi directum accepit; qui eo suscepto*a* in episcopatum solempniter est confirmatus.*b*[110]

18. Anno .dcclxxxi.[111] Alchmundus Haugustaldensis ecclesiae praesul, eximiae religionis et magnarum uir uirtutum, postquam tredecim annis sublimiter praefatam rexisset ecclesiam, regnante gloriosissimo Northanhymbrorum rege Ælfuualdo, anno tertio regni eius, .vii. idus Septembris huic uitae modum fecit, qui pro meritis aeternae beatitudinis est particeps factus.[112] Sepultus uero est iuxta praedecessorem suum, reuerendae memoriae sanctum Accam episcopum.[113]

fo. 65*ra*   19. Tilberhtus namque*a* pro eo in episcopatum subrogatur, consecratur, eleuaturque in solio episcopalis cathedrae in loco qui appellatur Vulfesuuelle, hoc est fons lupi. Actum est hoc .vi. nonas Octobris.[114]

Anno .dcclxxxiii., qui est annus quintus*b* Ælfuualdi regis, Werburg quondam regina Merciorum, tunc uero abbatissa, defuncta est, semper cum Christo (ut credi fas est) uictura; ipso quoque tempore Cyniuulf episcopus, de quo supra diximus, anno pontificatus sui quadragesimo dereliquit terrestria; qui ad supernam feliciter migrauit patriam.[115]

Anno .dcclxxxvi., qui est annus Ælfuualdi regis octauus, Botuuine, uenerabilis abbas Hrypensis ecclesiae, in conspectu astantium fratrum, ergastulum huius laboriosae uitae deseruit, mercedem iubelei anni

---

iii.17 *a* uel ac- *C¹*   *b* *C² adds* Hibaldus consecratus est episcopus *at foot of col. 64ra* (*linked by a* signe de renvoi)

iii.19 *a* *after* namque *C² adds* sanctus   *b* *add. C¹*

---

[109] Cf. *ASC* D(E), s.a. 779: 'And Bishop Cynewulf resigned' (trans. Whitelock, p. 34); and *ASC* D(E), s.a. 780: 'And Hygbald was consecrated bishop of Lindisfarne at Sockburn' (trans. Whitelock, p. 34); and see Keynes, 'Bishops', p. 565. The village of Sockburn (N. Yorks.) lies a few miles south of Darlington.

[110] According to the *ASC* D(E), s.a. 780, it was King Ælfwald who sent to Rome for the pallium on Eanbald's behalf (trans. Whitelock, p. 34). We know from other sources that it was Alcuin who travelled to Rome in 780 or 781, at Ælfwald's request, to fetch the pallium for his colleague, Archbishop Eanbald: *Vita Alcuini*, c. 9 (MGH, *SS* xv/1. 190).

[111] Byrhtferth assigns the death of Alchmund, bishop of Hexham, to the year 781, whereas in *ASC* D(E) it is assigned to 780 (see below, n. 112). Cf. Keynes, 'Bishops', p. 564, who gives '780 or 781'.

[112] *ASC* D(E), s.a. 780: 'In this year Alhmund, bishop of Hexham, died on 7 September' (trans. Whitelock, p. 34).

[113] At this point in the text there is another lengthy interpolation concerning the later translation of Bishop Alchmund. The interpolation was composed no earlier than 1030 (the

PARS TERTIA

85

relinquished his worldly cares, entrusted the governance of the church, with the acquiescence of the entire household, to Hygbald.[109] Also in that same year Bishop Eanbald received the pallium sent to him from the papal see; having received it, he was solemnly confirmed in his episcopacy.[110]

18. In 781,[111] Alchmund, bishop of the church of Hexham, a man of outstanding piety and great virtues, after he had ruled the aforesaid church righteously for thirteen years, during the reign of the glorious king of the Northumbrians, Ælfwald, in the third year of his reign, made an end to this life on 7 September; because of his achievements he was made a participant of eternal bliss.[112] He was buried next to his predecessor, Bishop Acca of revered memory.[113]

19. Tilberht is appointed to the bishopric in his place; he is consecrated and raised up on the throne of the episcopal cathedra in the place named *Vulfesuuelle*, that is, 'Wolf's Well' [unidentified]. This happened on 2 October.[114]

In 783, which is the fifth year of King Ælfwald, Werburg, once the queen of the Mercians, but then an abbess, died, always to conquer with Christ, as it is appropriate to believe. At the same time Bishop Cyniwulf, of whom we spoke earlier, in the fortieth year of his bishopric, departed from earthly concerns; he passed blessedly to the heavenly homeland.[115]

In 786, which is the eighth year of King Ælfwald, Botwine, the venerable abbot of the church of Ripon, in the sight of his fellow-monks standing by, abandoned the prison-house of this laborious life, receiving

---

translation was said to have taken place *post annos plusquam .ccl.*), and has been omitted here, since it could have formed no part of Byrhtferth's original text (it is printed in *Symeonis Monachi Opera Omnia*, ed. Arnold, ii. 47–50, and below, as Appendix II (b)).

[114] *ASC* D(E), s.a. 780: 'And Tilberht was consecrated in his [Hygbald's] place on 2 October' (trans. Whitelock, p. 34).

[115] *ASC* D(E), s.a. 782: 'In this year Werburh, Ceolred's queen, and Cynewulf, bishop of Lindisfarne, died' (trans. Whitelock, p. 34). There is some confusion here. The only King Ceolred known to Anglo-Saxon history was king of Mercia, 709–16 (Keynes, 'Rulers', p. 527). It seems unlikely that a queen who was widowed in 716 should have lived until 782. Also relevant to the confusion may be the fact that King Ceolred is known to have translated a saint named Werburg (who was the daughter of King Wulfhere, d. 675) at Hanbury: see Blair, 'A handlist of Anglo-Saxon saints', p. 557. In any case, Byrhtferth's description of the Werburg who died in 782 as *quondam regina Merciorum*—if, as the *ASC* entry states, the *rex* in question was Ceolred—requires explanation; alternatively, Werburg may have been the queen of an unidentified but later Mercian king. Note also that the name of Werburg is listed among the 'Nomina reginarum et abbatissarum' in *LVD* (ed. Sweet, p. 154, line 22).

86   HISTORIA REGVM

percipiendo.[116] Ipso quoque obeunte, Alberht pro eo abbas praeelectus et consecratus est.

Eodem anno Alduulf consecratus episcopus ab Eanbaldo archiepiscopo, Tilberhtoque et Hygbaldo praesulibus, in monasterio quod dicitur Æt Corabrige, multisque muneribus ac donis ditatus, honorifice ad suam ecclesiam est remissus.[117]

His diebus Ricthryth regina dudum, iam tunc abbatissa, optata percepit munera alterius uitae, deferens coram sacris obtutibus Domini oleum cum lampadibus.[118]

Ea tempestate Cynuulf Occidentalium Saxonum rex a perfido tyranno Cynheardo lugubri interfectus est morte, et ille crudelis interemptor ab Osredo duce in ultione domini sui inmisericorditer interemptus est, regnumque Occidentalium Saxonum Brihtric accepit.[119]

Tempore illo legati ab apostolica sede a domno Adriano papa ad Britanniam directi sunt, in quibus uenerabilis episcopus Georgius primatum | tenuit; qui antiquam inter nos amicitiam et fidem catholicam quam sanctus Gregorius papa per beatum Augustinum docuit innouantes, honorifice suscepti sunt a regibus et a praesulibus, siue a principibus[c] huius patriae, et in pace domum reuersi sunt cum magnis donis, ut iustum erat.[120]

fo. 65[rb]

---

[c] *after* principibus *C²* adds et primatibus

---

[116] Cf. *ASC* D(E), s.a. 786: 'In this year Abbot Botwine of Ripon died' (trans. Whitelock, p. 35). Abbot Botwine is known to have sent a letter to Archbishop Lull in Mainz, which is preserved in the corpus of Bonifatian correspondence (ed. Tangl, MGH, *Ep. sel.* i. 269–70 [*Ep.* cxxxi]), and a man named Botuini is listed among the 'nomina abbatum gradus presbyteratus' in *LVD* (ed. Sweet, p. 155, line 65; and note that the name of this Botwine is followed by that of Alberht, who was Botwine's successor as abbot of Ripon). At a later time, Archbishop Oswald of York (d. 992) visited Ripon and translated the remains of Bishop Wilfrid, along with those of several abbots, including Botwine, to York: see Byrhtferth, *VSO* v. 9 (Byrhtferth, *Lives*, ed. Lapidge, p. 170). The election and consecration of Botwine's successor, Alberht, is not recorded in *ASC*.

[117] The consecration of Ealdwulf is not recorded in *ASC*. As Whitelock notes (*EHD* i. 270 n. 8), Ealdwulf was consecrated bishop of Mayo in Ireland, on which, see above, nn. 79, 89.

[118] According to *PASE* s.v., Ricthryth was the queen of Oswulf, king of Northumbria, from 758 until he was murdered in 759 (see above, iii. 9, s.a. 757). It is not known what abbey she was abbess of; her name is recorded among the 'nomina reginarum et abbatissarum' in *LVD* (ed. Sweet, p. 154, line 26). The reference to *oleum cum lampadibus* is an allusion to the parable of the Wise and Foolish Virgins (Matt. 25: 1–8, esp. verse 4: *prudentes vero acceperunt oleum... cum lampadibus*).

[119] Cf. *ASC*, s.a. 786 (784 DE): 'In this year Cyneheard killed King Cynewulf, and was himself slain there and 84 men with him' (trans. Whitelock, p. 34). Cynewulf had been king of the West Saxons since 757, and had reigned for thirty-one years. In the first year of his reign he had expelled the reigning monarch, Sigeberht (756–7), from the kingdom (Sigeberht

PARS TERTIA

87

the reward of the jubilee year.[116] With Botwine passing away, Alberht was elected and consecrated abbot in his place.

In the same year Aldwulf was consecrated bishop by Archbishop Eanbald together with Bishops Tilberht and Hygbald, in the monastery which is called Corbridge, and, enriched by many donations and gifts, he was sent off honourably to his own church [Mayo].[117]

In these days Ricthryth, once a queen but then an abbess, received the hoped-for gifts of the other life, carrying oil with her lamps into the holy sight of the Lord.[118]

At this time Cynewulf, king of the West Saxons, was killed by the treacherous tyrant Cyneheard in a mournful death, and that cruel murderer was mercilessly killed by Ealdorman Osred as revenge for the death of his lord, and Brihtric assumed the kingdom of the West Saxons.[119]

At that time legates from the apostolic see were sent by Pope Hadrian to Britain; among them the venerable bishop George held the primacy; renewing among us the ancient friendship and catholic faith which St Gregory the pope established through St Augustine, they were honourably received by kings and bishops, or by the leaders of this country, and they returned home peacefully with great gifts, as was proper.[120]

had subsequently been killed by a swineherd). Thirty-one years later Cynewulf had taken the decision to expel Sigeberht's brother Cyneheard; in revenge for this, Cyneheard had ambushed Cynewulf at *Meretun* and killed him there; the following day Cyneheard had himself been killed at *Meretun* by Cynewulf's loyal ealdorman, Osric (not, as in the present chapter of *HR*, Osred). The story, which is reported at unusual length in *ASC* s.a. 757, is one of the most famous in Anglo-Saxon history, and has been the subject of much scholarly discussion; see, in particular, White, 'Kinship and lordship in early medieval England: The story of Sigeberht, Cynewulf and Cyneheard', and Bremmer, 'The Germanic context of "Cynewulf and Cyneheard"'.

[120] Cf. *ASC* D(E), s.a. 786: 'And at this time messengers were sent by Pope Hadrian from Rome to England to renew the faith and the friendship which St Gregory sent us through Bishop Augustine, and they were received with great honour and sent back in peace' (trans. Whitelock, p. 35). As Story notes, 'The OE annal reads like an epitome of the Latin version as preserved in the *Historia regum*' (*Carolingian Connections*, p. 59). Bishop George was bishop of Ostia (*c*.753–*c*.798) and of Amiens: see Levison, *England and the Continent*, pp. 127–9, and Story, *Carolingian Connections*, pp. 55–6, n. 4. The other *legati* mentioned here included Theophylact, bishop of Todi; but the legation also included *missi* sent by Charlemagne, including Wigbod (Story, ibid. p. 61) and Alcuin himself. Bishop George's own account of the proceedings, in a report dated 786 and sent to Pope Hadrian, has been preserved: MGH, *Epist.* iv. 19–29 [no. iii], partly trans. Whitelock, *EHD* i. 836–40. For discussion of the importance of this Northumbrian council (as well as the two Mercian councils which took place at the same time), and the form of the report which issued from it, see Story, *Carolingian Connections*, pp. 55–92, and Cubitt, *Anglo-Saxon Church Councils*, pp. 153–90.

88   HISTORIA REGVM

20. Anno .dcclxxxvii. synodus congregata est in Pincanhala .iiii. nonas Septembris.[121] In quo tempore Alberht abbas Hrypensis ex 'rapidis flatibus'[122] huius saeculi spiritum emisit ad superos aeternae felicitatis iubilos.[123] Mox uero, ablato ipso, Sigred ordinatur pro eo.

Anno .dcclxxxviii. Ælfuualdus rex, coniuratione facta ab eius patricio Sicgan nomine, miserabili occisus est morte .ix. kalendas Octobris in loco qui dicitur*a* Scythlesceaster iuxta Murum.[124] Corpus uero eximii regis ad Hehstealdesige cum magnis monachorum cuneis et clericorum cantilenis perlatum est, et in ecclesia sanctissimi Andreae apostoli honorifice sepultum est, quam construxit dignissimus pater Vilfridus archiepiscopus ad laudis praeconium supradicti apostoli. Praecellit opus ipsius coenobii cetera aedificia in gente Anglorum, licet multa sint et inedicibilia in plerisque locis; sed in eo loco longitudines latitudinesque atque pulchritudines excellunt. In quo coenobio sunt parietes uariis coloribus exornati, et historiae depictae, sicut supradictus Vilfridus episcopus instituit. Verum etiam dominus Acca, qui post ipsum illum locum gubernauit, glorioso compsit ornatu.[125]

fo. 65*va* Sepulto rege, ut praediximus, regnauit Osred filius | Alchredi regis,*b* pro eo unum annum. In loco uero quo Ælfuualdus rex*c* interfectus est, caelitus lux emissa dicitur uideri a plurimis. Constructa est ibidem

---

iii.20   *a* *add.* *C¹*   *b* *after* regis *C² adds* nepos eius   *c* *after* rex *C² adds* iustus

---

[121] Cf. *ASE* D(E), s.a. 787 (788): 'In this year a synod was assembled in Northumbria at *Pincanheale* on 2 September' (trans. Whitelock, p. 35). It is a pity that Byrhtferth (or his source) did not trouble to record what the synod was convened to discuss. The forms of the name *Pincanhala* given here and above (iii. 12, s.a. 765) and below (iii. 25, s.a. 798) suggest that it derives from a personal, hypocoristic name *Pinca*, construed in the genitive (*Pincan*) and OE *halh*, 'nook' or 'hollow'. The place cannot be identified (see above, n. 68), but it was obviously a place of some importance: King Æthelwald was deposed here in 765, and two synods met here, in 787 and 798, on which, see Cubitt, *Anglo-Saxon Church Councils*, pp. 317–18.

[122] Boethius, *De consolatione Philosophiae* ii, met. ii. 1–2 ('Si quantas rapidis flatibus incitus / pontus uersat harenas...').

[123] Cf. *ASC* D(E), s.a. 787 (788): 'And Abbot Ealdberht of Ripon died' (trans. Whitelock, p. 35). *ASC* does not, however, mention that Alberht was succeeded by Sigred, and the succession is recorded in no other source.

[124] Cf. *ASC* D(E), s.a. 788 (789): 'In this year Ælfwold, king of the Northumbrians, was killed by Sicga on 23 September' (trans. Whitelock, p. 35); cf. also the very similar account of Ælfwald's murder in *LDE* ii. 4 (ed. Rollason, p. 86). Historians accept the identification, first proposed by Plummer and endorsed by Mawer, that *Scythlesceaster iuxta Murum* is to be identified as the fort of Chesters on Hadrian's Wall, located near to where the great north–south Roman road (now the A1) crosses the wall. On this

PARS TERTIA

89

20. In 787, a synod was convened at *Pincanhale* [unidentified] on 2 September.[121] At that time Alberht, abbot of Ripon, released his soul from the 'impetuous blasts'[122] of this world to the heavenly joys of eternal bliss.[123] But soon afterwards, when he had died, Sigred is ordained in his place.

In 788, King Ælfwald was killed in a deplorable murder by a conspiracy formed by his ealdorman named Sicga, on 23 September, at a place called *Scythlesceaster*-near-the-Wall [?Chesters].[124] The body of this outstanding king was conveyed to Hexham accompanied by great throngs of monks and the chanting of clergy, and was honourably buried in the church of the holy apostle St Andrew, which the worthy father Archbishop Wilfrid had constructed in honour and praise of the aforesaid apostle. The workmanship of this monastery excelled all other buildings in the nation of the English, although there are many and indescribable [examples of these] in many places; but in this place [Hexham], the length and width and beauty [of execution] stand out. In this monastery the walls are decorated in various colours, and narratives painted on them, as the aforementioned Wilfrid determined. But Lord Acca, who ruled that place after him, also adorned it with glorious decoration.[125]

When the king had been buried, as I said above, Osred, the son of King Alchred, reigned in his place for one year. And in the place where King Ælfwald was murdered, a light shining down from heaven was said to be seen by many people. A church was built there by the faithful of

identification, see *DEPN*, p. 101, and Whitelock, *EHD* i. 271 n. 8. Even closer to the Roman road, however, is the fort of Haltonchesters on Hadrian's Wall, as suggested by Rollason (*LDE*, p. 86, n. 19).

[125] *ASC* D(E), s.a. 788 (789), also records that Ælfwald was buried at Hexham; on the cult of Ælfwald at Hexham, see Rollason, 'The cults of murdered royal saints', pp. 3–5. The praise lavished on the architectural beauty of Hexham suggests that this entry originated in Hexham itself, and is of a piece with the lengthy interpolations on Bishops Acca and Alhmund noted above (nn. 22, 113). The fact that the name of Hexham as given here—*Hehstealdesige*—is philologically inaccurate (the first element is not derived from OE *heah*, 'high', but from OE *hagosteald*, 'young warrior') and is different from the form normally used by Byrhtferth (*Haugustald*-) may suggest that the interpolation was made by someone other than Byrhtferth. The interpolator may also be responsible for the egregious error of anachronism by which Bishop Wilfrid (d. 710), the founder of Hexham, is made an archbishop (*archiepiscopus*). On the other hand, however, note that the passage shows several of Byrhtferth's stylistic peculiarities: the polysyllabic superlatives *sanctissimus* and *dignissimus*, and especially the adjective *inedicibilis*. Here, as elsewhere in the *HR*, it is not always possible to establish precisely the wording of Byrhtferth's original text.

90   HISTORIA REGVM

ecclesia a fidelibus illius loci, atque in honore Dei et sanctorum Cuthberti episcopi et Osuualdi regis et martyris consecrata.[126]

21. Anno .dccxc. Æthelredus de exilio liberatus est, et iterum per gratiam Christi regni solio est subthronizatus. Osredus autem rex, dolo suorum principum circumuentus*a* ac regno priuatus, attonsus est in Eboraca ciuitate, et postea necessitate coactus exilium petiit.*b*[127] Cuius anno secundo Earduulf dux captus est et ad Hrypum perductus, ibique occidi iussus*c* extra portam monasterii a rege praephato. Cuius corpus fratres cum Gregorianis concentibus ad ecclesiam portantes, et in tentorio foris ponentes, post mediam noctem uiuus est in ecclesia inuentus.[128]

Eodem anno Baduulf ad Candidam Casam ordinatur episcopus in loco qui dicitur Hearrahalch, quod interpretari potest 'locus dominorum'.[129] Anno uero priori Æthelberht episcopus sua sede relicta, sancto*d* Tilberhto episcopo iam obeunte, praedictus praesul episcopatum Haugustaldensis ecclesiae accepit in propriam dominationem.[130]

Anno .dccxci. filii Ælfuualdi regis ab Eboraca ciuitate ui abstracti, et de ecclesia principali per promissa fallacia*e* abducti, miserabiliter sunt perempti ab Æthelredo rege in Vuonuualdremere; quorum nomina Ælf et Ælfuuine fuere.[131] Eo quoque anno Iænberhtus Dorouernensis ecclesiae archiepiscopus ex hac lucis tenebrositate transmigrauit ad

---

iii.21   *a after* circumuentus *C² adds* et captus   *b* petit *C*   *c C² adds* uel occisus   *d add. C¹*   *e* fallaciae *C*

---

[126] The succession of Osred, Alhred's son, is mentioned in *ASC* D(E), s.a. 788 (789), as well as the fact (omitted by Byrhtferth) that Alhred was the nephew of Ælfwald, but omitting the fact, stated here by Byrhtferth, that Osred's reign lasted only a year (*ASC*, trans. Whitelock, p. 35); see also *LDE* ii. 4 (ed. Rollason, p. 86). The entries in *ASC* and *LDE* also mention that a heavenly light was often seen where Ælfwald had been killed. There is apparently no other record of an Anglo-Saxon church dedicated to SS. Cuthbert and Oswald at either Chesters or Haltonchesters.

[127] Cf. *ASC* D(E), s.a. 790: 'And Osred, king of the Northumbrians, was betrayed and driven from the kingdom, and Ethelred, Æthelwold's son, again succeeded to the kingdom' (trans. Whitelock, p. 36); cf. 'Ramsey Annals', s.a. 790: 'Æthelredus de exilio liberatur, et Osredus dolo occiditur' (p. 42), and Keynes, 'Rulers', pp. 525–6. Osred II, after being driven from the kingdom, was tonsured at York. According to *LDE* ii. 4, he went into exile on the Isle of Man (ed. Rollason, p. 86); he died on 14 September 792 and was buried at Tynemouth. Æthelred I, who had been king from 774 and was driven into exile in 778 or 779, ruled for the second time until 18 April 796, when he was killed near the river Cover.

[128] The miraculous recovery of Ealdorman Eardwulf at Ripon is not recorded in any other source. It is assumed (e.g. by Whitelock, *EHD* i. 272 and n. 1) that this Ealdorman

PARS TERTIA 91

that locality, and was dedicated in honour of God and of SS. Cuthbert the bishop and Oswald, king and martyr.[126]

21. In 790, Æthelred was released from exile, and was again established on the throne of the kingdom through Christ's mercy. And King Osred, beset by the deceit of his ealdormen and deprived of his kingdom, was tonsured in the city of York, and thereafter, driven by necessity, sought exile.[127] In the second year of his [Osred's] [reign], Ealdorman Eardwulf was captured and taken to Ripon, and ordered by the aforesaid king to be killed there outside the gate of the monastery. The monks carried his body with Gregorian chants to the church, and set it down outside under a tent; after midnight he was found alive in the church.[128]

In the same year Badwulf is ordained bishop of Whithorn in the place called *Hearrahalch* [unidentified], which can be rendered as 'the place of the lords'.[129] In the previous year Bishop Æthelberht, having relinquished his see [Whithorn], with Bishop Tilberht already having died, this aforesaid bishop [Æthelberht] took the bishopric of the church of Hexham into his own control.[130]

In 791, the sons of King Ælfwald were taken by force from the city of York, and, abducted from the principal church by deceitful promises, were wretchedly murdered by King Æthelred in *Vuonuualdremere* [unidentified]; their names were Ælf and Ælfwine.[131] In that same year Jænberht, archbishop of the church of Canterbury, passed from the darkness of this [earthly] light to the bliss of true light. But Abbot

---

Eardwulf is the same Eardwulf who succeeded to the Northumbrian throne in 796 (see below, iii. 24, s.a. 796); and indeed in discussing his accession to the throne, Byrhtferth (or his source) stated that Eardwulf has been mentioned before; the cross-reference thus confirms the identification of the king with the former ealdorman. See also Keynes, 'Rulers', p. 526.
[129] Cf. *ASC* D(E), s.a. 791: 'In this year Badwulf was consecrated bishop of Whithorn by Archbishop Eanbald and by Bishop Ethelbert on 17 July' (trans. Whitelock, p. 36). Byrhtferth omitted to mention the date of the consecration, or the fact that the consecration was performed by Archbishop Eanbald of York and Bishop Æthelberht of Hexham; the redactor of the 'northern recension' of *ASC* (MSS. DE) omits to mention that the consecration took place at *Hearrahalch* (unidentified).
[130] Bishop Tilberht of Hexham died on 2 October 789, at which time Bishop Æthelberht was translated from the bishopric of Whithorn to that of Hexham, which he held until his death on 16 October 797; see Keynes, 'Bishops', p. 564. The sentence describing the translation is a good example of Byrhtferth's awkward and clumsy expression.
[131] The murder of Ælfwald's two sons (Ælf and Ælfwine) by King Æthelred II is not recorded in any other source.

92   HISTORIA REGVM

uerae lucis beatitudinem. Abbas uero Æthelheardus, Hludensis monasterii, ad eandem sedem est electus et ordinatus episcopus.[132]

Anno .dccxcii. Carolus^f rex Francorum misit synodalem librum ad

fo. 65vb Britanniam, | sibi a Constantinopoli directum; in quo libro (heu pro
dolor!) multa inconuenientia et uerae fidei contraria reperientes, maxime
quod paene omnium orientalium doctorum non minus quam trecento-
rum uel eo amplius episcoporum unanima assertione confirmatum,
imagines adorare debere, quod omnino ecclesia Dei execratur.[133] Contra
quod scripsit Albinus epistolam ex auctoritate diuinarum scripturarum
mirabiliter affirmatam, illamque cum eodem libro, et persona episcoporum et principum nostrorum, regi Francorum attulit.[134]

Ipso denique anno Osredus de exilio sacramentis et fide quorundam
principum clam de Eufania uenit, ibique, deficientibus ab eo suis militibus, captus est a rege praephato,^g atque eo iubente occisus in loco qui
dicitur Aynburg .xviii. kalendas Octobris. Corpus uero eius ad ostium
Tyni fluminis perlatum est, et in basilica eiusdem eximii coenobii sepultum. Eodem anno Æthelred rex accepit reginam Ælffledam filiam
Offae regis Merciorum .iii. kalendas Octobris apud Cataractam.[135]

22. Anno .dccxciii., qui est annus Æthelredi regis quartus, dira
prodigia miseram Anglorum terruere gentem. Siquidem fulmina
abominanda, et dracones per aera, igneique ictus^a saepe uibrare et
uolitare uidebantur; quae scilicet signa famen magnam, et multorum
hominum stragem pessimam atque inedicibilem, quae subsecuta
est, demonstrauere.[136] Ipso quoque anno Sicga dux, qui interemit

---

^f Karolus C   ^g scilicet Ethelredo add. C²

iii.22 ^a crebres aere add. C²

---

[132] Cf. *ASC* s.a. 792 (790): 'In this year Archbishop Jænberht died, and Abbot Æthelheard
was elected archbishop the same year' (trans. Whitelock, p. 35). Jænberht died on 12 August
792; Æthelheard succeeded and was consecrated on 21 July 793, and held the see until his
death on 12 May 805. See Keynes, 'Bishops', p. 543. The place where Æthelheard was abbot
before his elevation—*Hludensis monasterii*—cannot certainly be identified, but Stenton reasonably suggested that Æthelheard had been 'abbot of a monastery at Louth in Lindsey'
(*Anglo-Saxon England*, p. 225), a suggestion which is supported by place-name evidence: the
adjective *Hludensis* is derived from the name of the river Lud (*DEPN*, p. 305), a fact which
Stenton will certainly have known.

[133] The *liber synodalis*: the Acts of the Second Council of Nicaea (787) are ed. Mansi,
Concilia xii. 951–1154; for discussion, see (briefly) *ODB* ii. 1465, as well as Dumeige, *Nicée II*.
The version of the *acta* sent by Charlemagne to Northumbria was presumably an abbreviated
(Latin) version of the original *acta*; but no manuscript of this abbreviated text appears to survive.

[134] Alcuin's letter on the Acts of Nicaea II, and on the question of image-worship, is lost:
see Bullough, 'Alcuin and the kingdom of heaven', p. 35. (In any case it is important to stress

PARS TERTIA 93

Æthelheard of the monastery of *Hludensis* [?Louth], was elected and ordained to that same see.[132]

In 792, Charles, king of the Franks, sent to Britain [a copy of] the canons of an oecumenical council, sent to him from Constantinople; finding in this book (alas!) many things unsuitable and contrary to the true faith, most of all that it was confirmed by the unanimous declaration of nearly all teachers of the Eastern churches, not fewer than three hundred or more, that images ought to be adored: which in general the [Western] church abominates.[133] In confutation of it Alcuin composed a letter, splendidly supported by the authority of holy writings and endorsed by our bishops and leaders, and took it, together with the same book [of canons], to the king of the Franks.[134]

Finally, in that same year, Osred came secretly out of exile in the Isle of Man, [seduced] by the oaths and pledges of certain ealdormen, and there, with his own soldiers deserting him, was captured by the aforementioned king [Æthelred], and at his command was killed in the place called *Aynburg* [unidentified] on 14 September. His body was taken to the mouth of the river Tyne, and buried in the church of that same excellent monastery. In the same year King Æthelred took Queen Ælfflæd, the daughter of Offa, king of the Mercians, in marriage on 29 September, at Catterick.[135]

22. In 793, which is the fourth year of King Æthelred, dire portents terrified the English people, inasmuch as there were horrendous lightning bolts and dragons in the air, and fiery bolts were often seen to tremble and fly about; these portents betokened a great famine, and the terrible and indescribable death of many people, which followed.[136] In

---

that the letter of Alcuin mentioned here is *not* to be identified with the so-called *Libri Carolini*, which treat the same subject of image-worship and are recognized as the composition of Theodulf of Orléans: see Freeman, 'Theodulf of Orléans and the *Libri Carolini*', and Meyvaert, 'The authorship of the *Libri Carolini*'.) On the lost letter of Alcuin, cf. the remarks of Bullough: 'I hazard the guess that the lost letter was not a sustained, properly argued answer to the central points raised by the "image-worshippers" but rather one that dealt discursively with several points that particularly interested or excited Alcuin, along the lines of his *Epp.* cxliii, cxlv, clxiii, etc.' ('Alcuin and the kingdom of heaven', p. 35 n. 73).

[135] Cf. *ASC* D(E), s.a. 792: 'And Osred, who had been king of the Northumbrians, was captured after he had returned home from exile, and killed on 14 September, and his body is buried at Tynemouth. And King Ethelred took a new wife, who was called Ælfflæd, on 29 September' (trans. Whitelock, p. 36); cf. 'Ramsey Annals', s.a. 792: 'Osredus capitur et occiditur' (p. 42). *Aynburg* cannot be identified.

[136] Cf. *ASC* D(E), s.a. 793: 'In this year dire portents appeared over Northumbria and sorely frightened the people. They consisted of immense whirlwinds and flashes of lightning, and fiery dragons were seen flying in the air. A great famine immediately followed those signs' (trans. Whitelock, p. 36).

94 HISTORIA REGVM

Ælfuualdum regem, interiit propria nece; cuius corpus ad insulam Lindisfarnensem perlatum est .ix. kalendas Maii.[137]

Lindisfarnensis insula magna est per ambitum, uerbi gratia octo uel amplius miliariis se extendens. In qua est nobile monasterium, quo eximius Cuthbertus antistes positus erat, | cum aliis praesulibus qui eius successores dignissimi extiterant. De quibus dici congruenter[b] potest quod canitur, 'Corpora sanctorum in pace sepulta sunt'.[138] Lindis dicitur flumen quod excurrit in mare, duorum pedum latitudinem habens, quando ledon fuerit, id est, minor aestus, et uideri potest; quando uero malina fuerit, id est maior aestus maris, tunc nequit Lindis uideri.[139] 'Aestus oceani lunam sequitur, tamquam eius aspiratione retrorsum trahatur in accessum, eiusque impulsu retracto refundatur. Qui cotidie bis affluere et remeare, unius semper horae dodrante et semiuncia, quae est dimidia, transmissa uidetur', ut Beda testatur.[140] 'Sicut enim luna quatuor punctis spatio cotidie tardius oriri, tardius occidere, quod pridie orta est uel occiderat, solet: ita etiam maris uterque aestus, siue diurnus sit et nocturnus, seu matutinus et uespertinus, eiusdem paene temporis interuallo tardius cotidie uenire, tardius redire non desinit. Punctus uero, quinta pars est horae; quinque enim puncti horam faciunt.'[141] De concordia maris et lunae sic quidam cecinit rhetor, id est, Aldhelmus praesul:

> Nunc ego cum pelagi[c] fatis communibus insto,
> tempora reciprocis conuoluens menstrua caelis.
> Vt mihi lucifluae decrescit gloria formae,
> sic augmenta latex cumulato gurgite perdit.[142]

---

[b] uel conuenienter C^2 [c] pelago C

---

[137] The death of Ealdorman Sicga, who had killed King Ælfwald in 788: cf. *ASC* D(E), s.a. 793: 'And Sicga died on 22 February' (trans. Whitelock, p. 36). Byrhtferth's words *interiit propria nece* are usually taken to mean that Sicga committed suicide (thus Whitelock, *EHD* i. 273: 'perished by his own hand'). But given the early medieval attitude to suicide (see Murray, *Suicide in the Middle Ages*, i. 48–58; ii. 183–8, 316–22, 323–34 (on the suicide of Judas), 464–71, *et passim*), it is highly unlikely that someone who had 'perished by his own hand' would be accorded burial in consecrated ground at Lindisfarne; the normal place for disposing of a suicide's body was the local carrion pit (ibid. ii. 45–53). It seems more likely that this is another example of Byrhtferth's clumsy expression, and that the phrase was intended by him to mean that Sicga, who had murdered Ælfwald, later 'died his own death', i.e. was himself murdered. On the use of *proprius* as a possessive pronoun (= *suus*) in Medieval Latin, cf. Stotz, *Handbuch*, iv. 407; for a similar example of Byrhtferth's usage, cf. *VSO* ii. 5: 'uelut Isaac ab immolatione <u>proprie</u> necis liberatus est' (ed. Byrhtferth, *Lives*, ed. Lapidge, p. 42, where *proprie necis* simply means 'his own death').

[138] Cf. Ecclus. 44: 14 ('corpora ipsorum in pace sepulta sunt').

[139] Cf. Bede, *De natura rerum*, c. 39: 'omnis cursus in ledones et malinas, id est in minores aestus diuiditur et maiores' (CCSL cxxiiiA. 224).

PARS TERTIA

95

that same year Ealdorman Sicga, who had killed King Ælfwald, died a death of his own; his body was taken to the island of Lindisfarne on 23 April.[137]

Lindisfarne is an island large in circumference, that is, it extends for 8 or more miles. On this island is a noble monastery, in which the excellent bishop Cuthbert was stationed, together with other bishops who were his very worthy successors. Concerning them it can appropriately be said: 'The bodies of the saints are buried in peace'.[138] 'Lindis' is the name of the river which flows into the sea, and is two feet across when it is at *ledon*, that is, at low tide, and [the river Lindis] may be seen; but when it is at *malina*, that is at high tide, the Lindis cannot then be seen.[139] 'The tide of the ocean follows the moon, as though by its breathing it is drawn backwards at its advent, and pours back when its force is withdrawn. It is daily seen to flood and ebb twice, for three-quarters of an hour and a further half-ounce, which is a half', as Bede says.[140] 'For just as the moon is daily accustomed to rise later by a period of four *puncti*, and to set later, than it had risen and set the previous day, thus each of the sea's flood-tides, whether by day or by night, or morning or evening, so it does not cease from coming later each day by nearly the same interval of time, and returning likewise. A *punctus* is the fifth part of an hour; five *puncti* make up an hour.'[141] Concerning the harmony of sea and moon a certain eloquent writer sang thus, that is, Bishop Aldhelm:

> Now I stand, linked with the common fate of the sea,
> unfolding monthly cycles with the heavens responding.
> As the glory of my light-bearing form decreases,
> so too does the water lose its accumulated swell.[142]

---

[140] Bede, *De natura rerum*, c. 39: 'Aestus oceani lunam sequitur, tamquam eius aspiratione retrorsum trahatur eiusque inpulsu retracto refundatur. Qui cotidie bis adfluere et remeare, unius semper horae dodrante et semiuncia transmissa uidetur' (CCSL cxxiiiA. 224).

[141] Bede, *De temporum ratione*, c. 29: 'Sicut enim luna....iiii. punctorum spatio quotidie tardius oriri tardius occidere quam pridie orta est uel occiderat solet, ita enim maris aestus uterque, siue diurnus sit et nocturnus seu matutinus et uespertinus, eiusdem pene temporis interuallo tardius quotidie uenire tardius redire non desinit. Punctus autem quinta pars horae est, quinque enim puncti horam faciunt' (CCSL cxxiiiB. 366–7).

[142] Aldhelm, *Enigma* no. vi (ed. Ehwald, MGH, *AA* xv. 101); *Aldhelm: The Poetic Works*, trans. Lapidge and Rosier, p. 72. Note that in the fourth line of the *enigma*, Ehwald prints the reading *redundans* attested in two manuscripts of the earliest recension of the *Enigmata* (MSS F¹F²); the variant reading *cumulato* is characteristic of the second, corrected recension, attested in MSS BP³. See Ehwald's *apparatus criticus ad loc.*, and Lapidge, 'Aldhelmus Malmesberiensis Abb.', pp. 19–26. This indicates that Byrhtferth had before him a manuscript of the second, corrected edition of Aldhelm's *Enigmata*.

96 HISTORIA REGVM

Farne autem insula, qua beatissimus Cuthbertus heremiticam duxit uitam, non tanta est ut Lindisfarne; sed est posita in mare, magnis exturbata fluctibus diebus et noctibus.[143]

His strictim dictis, ad ordinem reuertamur narrationis. Eodem sane anno pagani ab aquilonali climate nauali exercitu ut aculeati crabrones[144] Britanniam uenientes, hac illacque ut dirissimi lupi discurfo. 66ʳᵇ rentes, praedantes, | mordentes, interficientes non solum iumenta, oues et boues, uerum etiam sacerdotes leuitasque chorosque monachorum atque sanctimonialium. Veniunt, ut praephati sumus, ad Lindisfarnensem ecclesiam, miserabili praedatione uastant cuncta, calcant sancta pollutis uestigiis, altaria suffodiunt, et omnia thesauraria sanctae ecclesiae rapiunt. Quosdam e fratribus interficiunt, nonnullos secum uinctos assumunt, perplurimos opprobriis uexatos nudos proiiciunt, aliquos in mare demergunt.[145] Apte de illis dicitur quod sequitur:[d]

> Fortuna uices premit insontes,
> debita sceleri noxia poena,
> at peruersi resident celso
> mores[e] solio sanctaque calcant
> iniusta uice colla nocentes;
> latet obscuris condita uirtus
> clara tenebris, iustusque[f] tulit
> crimen iniqui.[146]

Illis uero recedentibus, et de praeda uel malis[g] gratulantibus, quid eis fortuna sequentis anni aduexit, stylus fidelis demonstrabit.

23. Anno .dccxciiii. praedicti pagani portum Ecgfridi regis uastantes, monasterium ad ostium Doni amnis praedarunt. Sed sanctus Cuthbertus non sine punitione eos sinebat abire. Princeps quippe eorum ibidem crudeli nece occisus est ab Anglis, et post exigui temporis

---

[d] uel Quibus recte illud aptari potest *C²*   [e] more *C*   [f] iustosque *C*   [g] et prauis actibus *add. C²*

---

[143] St Cuthbert's retreat on Farne is described by Bede, *HE* iiii. 26. 1–3.

[144] Cf. Pliny, *Naturalis historia* xx. 247 ('aculeata animalia, ut crabrones et similia').

[145] The Viking attack on Lindisfarne was one of the most disturbing and most widely publicized events of the eighth century. It was recorded in *ASC* D(E), s.a. 793: 'in the same year, on 8 June, the ravages of heathen men miserably destroyed God's church on Lindisfarne' (trans. Whitelock, p. 36). Alcuin, who was back in Francia with Charlemagne at the time, commemorated the event in a long poem (*Carm.* ix) on 'The disaster of the church of

PARS TERTIA

97

The island of Farne, where the blessed Cuthbert spent his life as a hermit, is not as large as Lindisfarne; but is is located in the sea, assailed by waves by day and night.[143]

Having discussed these things briefly, let us return to the sequence of our narrative. In the same year [793], the pagans, arriving in Britain from the northern regions in a fleet of ships like stinging hornets,[144] running here and there like savage wolves, robbing, stinging, killing not only flocks of sheep and cattle, but also priests and deacons and choirs of monks and nuns. They come, as I said, to the church of Lindisfarne; they destroy everything in wretched devastation, they tread on holy objects with their polluted feet, they dig up altars, they carry off all the treasure-chests of the holy church. They kill a number of the monks, they take some with them bound up as prisoners, they cast away many left naked by their outrages, and drown others in the sea.[145] What follows appropriately pertains to them:

> Fortune oppresses the guiltless
> with odious punishments due to their sins,
> but wicked behaviour occupies
> a lofty throne, and criminals tread down
> saintly necks in an unfair reversal;
> outstanding virtue lies hidden by dark shadows,
> and the just man bears the sin of the wicked.[146]

But with the pagans withdrawing, and rejoicing in their booty and evil, what the fortune of the following year brought to them, my faithful pen will demonstrate.

23. In 794, the aforesaid pagans, ravaging the port of King Ecgfrith, plundered the monastery at the mouth of the river Don. But St Cuthbert did not allow them to depart without punishment. In fact their leader was killed there by the English in a violent death, and after the passage of a short period of time, the force of a mighty storm shattered,

---

Lindisfarne' (MGH, *PLAC* i. 229–35), and it formed the subject of several of his letters sent to the bishop of Lindisfarne (Hygbald) soon after the event (*Epp.* xx–xxii; MGH, *Epist.* iv. 56–60); the event is also described at length in Symeon, *LDE* ii. 5 (ed. Rollason, p. 88).

[146] Boethius, *De consolatione Philosophiae*, i, met. v, lines 29–36 (CCSL xciv. 12). Byrhtferth's quotation implies that he understood 'Fortuna uices premit insontes' as one clause; in the text of Boethius, however, the previous line concludes with 'Fortuna uices': 'Nam cur tantas lubrica uersat / Fortuna uices?' I have translated the poem as Byrhtferth seems to have understood it.

98　　HISTORIA REGVM

spatium uis tempestatis eorum naues quassauit, perdidit, contriuit, et perplurimos mare operuit. Nonnulli itaque ad litus sunt eiecti, et mox interfecti absque misericordia. Et recte illis haec contigerunt, quoniam se non laedentes grauiter laeserunt.[147]

His diebus Colcu presbyter et lector ex hac luce migrauit ad Dominum, quo percipit laudem felicitatis pro laboribus terrenis.[148]

Ea tempestate Æthelheard quondam dux, tunc autem clericus, in Eboraca ciuitate defunctus est kalendas Augusti.[149] Adrianus papa uenerandus eodem anno subleuatus est ad Dei uisionem | .vii. kalendas Ianuarii, qui sedit annos .xxvi., menses .x., dies .xii. Est quoque in ecclesia sancti principis apostolorum Petri sepultus, et super sepulchrum platoma[a] parieti infixa, gesta bonorum eius aureis litteris et uersibus scripta. Hoc marmor ibi Carolus rex ob amorem et memoriam praedicti patris facere iussit, regali fretus diademate.[150]

Anno .dccxcv. idem rex[b] Carolus cum manu ualida Hunorum gentem armis uastando subegerat, eorum principe fugato, et ipsius exercitu superato uel perempto, sublatis inde .xv. plaustris auro argentoque palliisque olosericis preciosis repletis, quorum quodque quatuor trahebant boues. Quae omnia idem rex propter uictoriam a Domino sibi

fo. 66[va]

---

iii.23　　[a] .i. marmor *add. C[1]*　　[b] fortissimus *add. C[2]*

---

[147] Cf. *ASC* D(E), s.a. 794: 'And the heathens ravaged in Northumbria, and plundered Ecgfrith's monastery at *Donemuthan*; and one of their leaders was killed there, and also some of their ships were broken to bits by stormy weather, and many of the men were drowned there. Some reached the shore alive and were immediately killed at the mouth of the river' (trans. Whitelock, pp. 36–7). Note that whereas Byrhtferth speaks of the 'port of King Ecgfrith', *ASC* refers to the 'monastery of King Ecgfrith'. Symeon, *LDE* ii. 5 (ed. Rollason, pp. 88–90), refers to the same event, and identifies the 'port of King Ecgfrith' as Jarrow (*portum Ecgfridi regis (hoc est Gyruum)*).

[148] The Annals of Ulster record the death of 'Colgu descendant of Duinechaid' against the year 796 (*The Chronicle of Ireland*, trans. Charles-Edwards, i. 258). Colgu was a correspondent of Alcuin, and may at one time have studied with Alcuin at York; see Alcuin, *Ep.* vii (MGH, *Epist.* iv. 31–3), a letter written from the Continent in early 790. There is unfortunately no secure evidence about where Colgu was a 'priest and lector'.

[149] This Ealdorman Æthelheard is otherwise unknown, unless he is the ealdorman of that name who attests Mercian charters between 785 and 792 (see Keynes, *Atlas*, Table X (2)).

[150] The death of Pope Hadrian I (772–95) is briefly recorded against 796 in both the 'Royal Frankish Annals' or *Annales regni Francorum* (ed. Kurze, pp. 98–9; *Carolingian Chronicles*, trans. Scholz, p. 74) and the *ASC* (trans. Whitelock, p. 36); but the detailed specification of

PARS TERTIA 99

destroyed, demolished their ships, and the sea swamped a number of them. Some were cast up on the shore, and killed at once without mercy. And rightly did these things beset them, since they had gravely wounded those who did them no harm.[147]

In these days Colgu, priest and lector, passed from this light to the Lord, where he receives the reward of bliss for his earthly labours.[148]

At this time Æthelheard, once an ealdorman but then a cleric, died in the city of York on 1 August.[149] The venerable Pope Hadrian was taken to the sight of God in the same year, on 26 December; he had been pope for twenty-two years, ten months, and twelve days. He was buried in the church of St Peter, prince of the apostles, and over his tomb a marble slab was set up, with his good deeds written out in verse, in gold lettering. King Charles, invested with the royal diadem, commanded this marble [memorial stone] to made for the love and memory of the aforesaid father.[150]

In 795, the same King Charles had subdued the nation of the Huns with a powerful force, destroying them with weapons, having put to flight their leader and having overcome or destroyed his army, removing thence fifteen wagons, each drawn by four oxen, loaded with gold and silver and precious silk garments. Because of his victory granted to him by the Lord, the same king commanded all these things to be

---

the length of his papacy, given in years, months and days, appears to derive from the *Liber pontificalis* (ed. Duchesne, i. 486: 'Hadrianus... sedit ann. XXIII, mens. X, dies XVII'; trans. Davis, *The Lives of the Eighth-Century Popes*, p. 123). There is, however, a discrepancy: the *Liber pontificalis* specifies 23 years (not 26), 10 months, and 17 days (not 12). The discrepancy can plausibly be explained in terms of confusion of Roman numerals (.xxiii./.xxvi., .xvii./ xii.), as suggested by Joanna Story (*Carolingian Connections*, pp. 104–5). The epitaph of Hadrian commissioned by Charlemagne and inscribed in gold letters on a slab of black marble may still be seen in the portico of St Peter's in the Vatican: see the illustration in Story (ibid. fig. 4.2). The thirty-eight line epitaph, in elegiac couplets, is ed. MGH, *PLAC* i. 113–14; the language of the epitaph suggested to its editor (Ernst Dümmler) that Alcuin was its author; and note that the statement concerning the length of Hadrian's papacy ('Sedit beatae memoriae Hadrianus papa annos XXIII menses X dies XVII') is inscribed following the conclusion of the metrical epitaph. The word *platoma* is a spelling of *platumma* (from Greek πλάτυμμα, 'flat cake'), meaning 'an inscription on a flat plate or tablet' (see *DMLBS*, p. 2312, s.v.). On the epitaph, and the marble slab on which it is inscribed, see the valuable discussion of Story (*Carolingian Connections*, pp. 105–10), as well as her two more detailed studies, 'Charlemagne and the epitaph of Pope Hadrian I', and 'Charlemagne's Black Marble'.

HISTORIA REGVM

concessam Christi ecclesiis atque pauperibus diuidere praecepit, grates Deo referens cum omnibus secum pugnantibus.[151]

24. Anno .dccxcvi., qui est annus septimus Æthelredi regis, Alric quondam dux, tunc clericus, in Eboraca ciuitate defunctus est.[152] Et paulo post, id est .v. kalendas Aprilis, eclipsis lunae facta est inter gallicinium et auroram.[153] Eodem uero anno Æthelredus rex occisus est apud Cobre .xiiii. kalendas Maii.[a][154] Osbald uero patricius a quibusdam ipsius gentis principibus in regnum est constitutus, et post .xxvii. dies omni regiae familiae ac principum est societate destitutus, fugatusque et de regno expulsus, atque ad insulam Lindisfarnensem cum paucis secessit, et inde ad regem Pictorum cum quibusdam e fratribus nauigio peruenit.[155] Earduulf enim, de quo supra diximus, filius Earduulfi, de exilio uocatus, regni infulis est sublimatus, et in Eboraca in ecclesia sancti Petri ad

---

iii.24   *a after* Maii *C*[2] *adds* anno .vii. regni sui

---

[151] Charlemagne's destruction of the Avars (called *Huni*, 'Huns', in Carolingian sources) is recorded in the 'Royal Frankish Annals', s.a. 796 (ed. Kurze, pp. 98–101; *Carolingian Chronicles*, trans. Scholz, p. 74); but the account given there is significantly different from that given here by Byrhtferth. According to the 'Royal Frankish Annals', it was Duke Eric of Friuli who entered the Avar Ring and plundered its treasure, and then sent the treasure to Charlemagne at Aachen; according to the present entry, it was Charlemagne himself who subdued the Huns, and then loaded fifteen carts, each drawn by four oxen, with the Huns' treasure, which he subsequently distributed to the Church and to the poor. No Frankish source specifies the amount of captured treasure in such precise terms; but it is clear that Charlemagne did indeed redistribute the treasure for political purposes. A letter from Charlemagne to King Offa of Mercia dated to 796 refers to the emperor's gift to Offa of 'one sword-belt, one Hunnish sword and two silk robes' (*unum balteum et unum gladium Huniscum et duo pallia sirica*: MGH, *Epist.* iv. 146). See discussion by Story, *Carolingian Connections*, pp. 101–2.

[152] The identity of Ealdorman Alric is unknown. He is listed in *PASE* as 'Alric 5', without further specification, and is not recorded as a witness to late eighth-century charters (see Keynes, *Atlas*, Table X(2)). A person named Alric is listed among the 'Nomina clericorum' in *LVD* (ed. Sweet, p. 160, line 248).

[153] The lunar eclipse is also recorded in *ASC* D(E), s.a. 796: 'In this year there was an eclipse of the moon between cock-crow and dawn on 28 March' (trans. Whitelock, p. 37). See Schove and Fletcher, *The Chronology of Eclipses*, pp. 165–6, who record a 'total eclipse' on 28 March (a.m.) in 796.

[154] The murder of King Æthelred I is recorded briefly in *ASC* D(E), s.a. 796 (794): 'and Ethelred, king of the Northumbrians, was killed by his own people on 19 April' (trans. Whitelock, p. 36); cf. 'Ramsey Annals', s.a. 796: 'Æthelred occiditur, et Eardwulf eligitur in regem. Eodem anno Kenwulf Merciorum regnum possedit' (p. 42). See Stenton,

PARS TERTIA 101

distributed to the churches of Christ and to the poor, giving thanks to God together with all those who fought with him.[151]

24. In 796, which is the seventh year of King Æthelred, Alric, once an ealdorman but then a cleric, died in the city of York.[152] And shortly afterwards, that is on 28 March, there was an eclipse of the moon between cockcrow and dawn.[153] In the same year, King Æthelred was killed near the river Cover on 18 April.[154] But the nobleman Osbald was established in the kingship by some ealdormen of that nation, and after twenty-seven days was deserted by the entire company of the royal family and ealdormen, and he was put to flight and expelled from the kingdom and withdrew to the island of Lindisfarne with a few companions, and went from thence by ship with certain of the monks to the king of the Picts.[155] Eardwulf, of whom I spoke earlier, the son of Eardwulf, was called back from exile and installed with the insignia of the kingdom, and was consecrated in York in the church of St Peter at

---

Anglo-Saxon England, p. 225; Keynes, 'Rulers', p. 526; and Story, *Carolingian Connections*, pp. 162–4. It is probable that he is the *Eðilred* recorded among the 'Nomina regum vel ducum' in *LVD* (ed. Sweet, p. 154, line 2). The murder caused great consternation to Alcuin, who had exchanged many letters with Æthelred (*Epp.* viii–x, xvi, xviii, xxx, lxxix, ci–cii, cv, cxxii, ccxxxi) and who, on learning of the murder, wrote to King Offa of Mercia to express not only his own disgust, but also that of Charlemagne, who was reportedly so enraged that he wished to recall the diplomatic gifts (from the Avar treasure) which he had sent to England: *Ep.* ci (ed. MGH, *Epist.* iv. 147–8). In a letter addressed at the same time to Offa's daughter Æthilburg, abbess of Fladbury, Alcuin suggested that Æthelred's widow Æthelflæd (see above, iii. 21, s.a. 792) should now enter a monastery: *Ep.* cii (ed. MGH, *Epist.* iv. 148–9).

[155] The brief reign (twenty-seven days) of Osbald is not recorded in *ASC*, and not mentioned by Stenton, *Anglo-Saxon England*. After fleeing first to Lindisfarne (where he will have been allowed sanctuary for thirty-seven days), Osbald was offered protection in Pictland by the king of the Picts, where he died three years later (see below, *HR* iii. 27, s.a. 799); see Keynes, 'Rulers', p. 526. At an earlier stage, in 793, Alcuin had written jointly to King Æthelred and to Osbald *patricius*, both of whom he described as *dulcissimi amici* (*Ep.* xviii; ed. MGH, *Epist.* iv. 49–50); three years later, in 796, Alcuin wrote again to Osbald, after he had been expelled from his twenty-seven-day reign, and when he was evidently already in exile in Pictland, expressing the hope that he [Osbald] was not implicated in the murder of King Æthelred, and urging him to abandon the life of a layman and to return to the monastery (*Ep.* cix; ed. MGH, *Epist.* iv. 156; trans. Whitelock, *EHD* i. 852–3). As Whitelock observes (ibid.), Osbald evidently followed Alcuin's advice, because, at the time of his death in 799, Byrhtferth (or his source) recorded that he was 'formerly an ealdorman and nobleman, but at that time an abbot' (below, iii. 27); and indeed the name *Osbald* is recorded among the 'Nomina abbatum' in *LVD* (ed. Sweet, p. 156, line 91).

102   HISTORIA REGVM

altare beati apostoli Pauli, ubi illa gens primum perceperat gratiam baptismi, consecratus est .vii. kalendas Iunii.[156]

Et non multo post, id est, .vii. kalendas Augusti, Offa rex potentis-
fo. 66[vb] simus Merciorum, | postquam .xxxix. annos regnauit, defunctus est; cui successit in regno filius eius Ecgferth, qui eodem anno morte super-ueniente debitum neci inuitus concessit.[157] Coenuulf quoque, pater sancti Coenhelmi martyris, dehinc diadema regni Merciorum suscepit gloriose, tenuitque inuicta uirtute potenti uigore sui potentatus.[158]

Ipso quoque anno Ceoluulf in Lindisse uitae huius tempora con-tempsit, futuri saeculi consolationem exspectans.[159]

Et paulo post, id est .iiii. Idus Augusti, Eanbaldus archiepiscopus obiit in monasterio quod dicitur æt Laete, corpusque eius magno comitante agmine ad Eboracam ciuitatem portantes, in ecclesia beati Petri apostoli sepultum est honorifice. Statim uero alter Eanbaldus, eiusdem ecclesiae presbyter, in episcopatum est electus, conuenientibus ad ordinationem eius Æthelberhto et Hygbaldo atque Baduulfo episcopis, in monasterio quod dicitur Sochasburg, .xviii. kalendas Septembris, die dominca.[160]

Anno .dccxcvii. Eanbaldus ille posterior, accepto ab apostolica sede pallio, in archiepiscopatum genti Northanhymbrorum solempniter

---

[156] Cf. *ASC* D(E), s.a. 796: 'and Eardwulf succeeded to the kingdom of the Northumbrians on 14 May; and he was afterwards consecrated and enthroned on 26 May in York, by Archbishop Eanbald, and Ethelbert, Hygbald and Badwulf' (trans. Whitelock, p. 37); see also Keynes, 'Rulers', p. 526. Eardwulf, when still an ealdorman, had been captured in 790 and taken to Ripon, where he was executed (incompetently, so it seems), and miraculously healed (see *HR* iii. 21, above, p. 90), whereupon he escaped his captors and lived to be installed as king of Northumbria six years later. He was subsequently expelled from the kingdom in 806 (?), restored in 808 (?); he apparently died in 810. When he was elevated to the throne in 796, he received a letter of congratulation and admonition from Alcuin, reminding him of their old friendship (*Ep.* cviii; ed. MGH, *Epist.* iv. 155; trans. Whitelock, *EHD* i. 851–2). In another letter written about the same time to a Mercian nobleman named Osbert, Alcuin expressed his anxiety that Eardwulf would be expelled from the kingdom—as indeed he soon was—because he had put aside his legitimate wife and taken up with a concubine (MGH, *Epist.* iv. 179).

[157] On the death of Offa and the succession of his son Ecgfrith, see *ASC*, s.a. 796 (794): 'In this year … King Offa died … And Ecgfrith succeeded to the kingdom of the Mercians and died the same year', and cf. *ASC* D(E), s.a. 796: 'In this year Offa, king of the Mercians, died on 29 July. He had reigned 40 years' (trans. Whitelock, pp. 36, 37). Ecgfrith had been consecrated as Offa's successor as early as 787; but he survived his father by barely half a year, dying on 17 December 796; see Keynes, 'Rulers', p. 528. On Offa, one of the most powerful and influential of all Anglo-Saxon kings, see Stenton, *Anglo-Saxon England*, pp. 205–24; *ODNB* xli. 545–8 [S. E. Kelly]; and *WB Encyc.* pp. 347–8 [S. D. Keynes].

PARS TERTIA 103

the altar of the blessed apostle St Paul, where that people had first received the gift of baptism, on 26 May.[156]

And not much later, that is, on 26 July, Offa, the most mighty king of the Mercians, died after he had reigned for thirty-nine years; his son Ecgfrith succeeded him on the throne, who in the same year, with death supervening, unwillingly paid his debt to mortality.[157] Thereafter Coenwulf, the father of St Kenelm the martyr, royally assumed the diadem of the Mercian kingdom, and held it with unconquerable power through the mighty strength of his authority.[158]

In the same year, in Lindsey, Ceolwulf scorned the temporalities of this life, awaiting the consolation of the future world.[159]

And shortly thereafter, that is on 10 August, Archbishop Eanbald died in the minster which is called *æt Læte* [unidentified; Otley?], and, with a huge cortege accompanying his body, taking him to the city of York, he was honourably buried in the church of St Peter the apostle. Immediately thereafter another Eanbald, a priest in the same church, was elected to the bishopric, with Æthelberht and Hygbald and Badwulf coming together for his consecration in the minster which is called Sockburn, on 16 August, a Sunday.[160]

In 797, this second Eanbald, having received from the apostolic see the pallium, was solemnly confirmed in the archbishopric for the

---

[158] The succession of Coenwulf (796–821) to the Mercian throne is not recorded as such in *ASC*, which does, however, record Coenwulf's invasion of Kent in 798, an event which is also recorded below, iii. 25 (p. 104). On Coenwulf, see *ODNB* x. 817 [M. K. Lawson], and *WB Encyc.*, pp. 114–15 [S. D. Keynes]; on St Kenelm, see *WB Encyc.*, pp. 274–5 [R. Love]. The fact that Coenwulf was St Kenelm's father is known from hagiographical sources such as the *Vita S. Kenelmi* [*BHL* 4641]; but since this work was probably composed by Goscelin of Saint-Bertin (see Love, *Three Eleventh-Century Anglo-Latin Saints' Lives*, pp. xciii–ci), it is too late to have been known to Byrhtferth. However, liturgical evidence suggests that the cult of St Kenelm was already established at Winchcombe by the late tenth century; and since there were close relationships between Winchcombe and Ramsey in the late tenth century (following the so-called 'anti-monastic reaction' in 975 the monks of Winchcombe were housed at Ramsey), Byrhtferth was probably drawing on local knowledge rather than a written source for this information.

[159] The death of Ceolwulf, bishop of Lindsey, is recorded in *ASC* D(E), s.a. 796: 'And that same year Bishop Ceolwulf died' (trans. Whitelock, p. 37).

[160] Cf. *ASC* D(E), s.a. 796: 'And Archbishop Eanbald died on 10 August of the same year, and his body is buried in York...and Eanbald the second was consecrated in place of the other Eanbald on 14 August' (trans. Whitelock, p. 37); see Keynes, 'Bishops', p. 562. The location of the monastery *æt Læte* is unknown; the OE word *læte* means simply 'a junction of roads'; on the location of Sockburn (N. Yorks.), see above, n. 109.

104 HISTORIA REGVM

confirmatus est .vi. idus Septembris, qua die celebratur solemnitas,[b] de qua poeta ait,

> Splendet honore dies, est in quo uirgo Maria,
> stirpe Dauid regis procedens, edita mundo.[161]

Eodem anno Æthelberhtus episcopus defunctus est .xvii. kalendas Nouembris in loco qui dicitur Bartun; cuius corpus ad Hehstealdesige est perlatum, et uenerabiliter a fratribus ipsius coenobii sepultum. Electus uero est pro eo Heardred in episcopatum, et post excursum paucorum dierum, hoc est, .iii. kalendas Nouembris, ab Eanbaldo archiepiscopo et Hygbaldo episcopo, spirituali honore ordinatus est in loco qui nuncupatur Vuduforda.[162]

25. Anno .dccxcviii. coniuratione facta ab interfectoribus Æthelredi regis, Vuada dux in illa coniuratione cum | eis bellum inierunt contra Earduulfum regem in loco qui appellatur ab Anglis Billingahoth, iuxta Vualalege, et ex utraque parte plurimis interfectis, Vuada dux cum suis in fugam uersus est, et Earduulfus rex uictoriam regaliter sumpsit ex inimicis.[163]

fo. 67ʳᵃ

Eodem anno Lundonia igne repentino cum magna hominum multitudine consumpta est.

His tempestatibus Cenuulf rex Merciorum cum omni exercitus sui uirtute prouinciam Cantuariorum ingressus, miserabili praedatione paene usque ad internitionem potenter uastauit. Captus est eodem tempore Eadberht rex Cantuariorum, cuius oculos praecepit auelli rex Merciorum, et manus immisericorditer praecidi, prae superbia et fraude ipsorum.[164] Deinde Domini suffragio potitus, adiecit imperium ipsius regni suo imperio, imponens sibi coronam in capite, sceptrumque in manu.

---

[b] *after* solemnitas *C²* *adds* id est natiuitas sanctae Mariae   [c] *after* Æthelberhtus *C²* *adds* Augustaldensis

---

[161] This couplet is quoted from the 'Metrical Calendar of Ramsey', a poem of some 128 lines which was composed at Ramsey in the last decade of the tenth century: see Lapidge, 'A tenth-century metrical calendar from Ramsey', pp. 348–58 [repr. *ALL* ii. 365–75]; the lines on the Nativity of the Virgin are lines 93–4 (ibid. p. 365 = *ALL* ii. 382). It is probable that Byrhtferth was himself the author of the 'Metrical Calendar of Ramsey'. In any case the quotation of this Ramsey poem is another solid piece of evidence in favour of Byrhtferth's authorship of the *HR*.

[162] *ASC* D(E), s.a. 797: 'Bishop Ethelbert died on 16 October, and Heardred was consecrated bishop in his place on 30 October' (trans. Whitelock, p. 38). On Bishops Æthelberht

PARS TERTIA 105

Northumbrian nation on 8 September, the day on which is celebrated the solemn occasion, about which the poet says,

> The day gleams with distinction, on which the Virgin Mary, issuing from the stock of King David, is born to the world.[161]

In the same year, Bishop Æthelberht died on 16 October in the place called Barton; his body was brought to Hexham and buried reverently by the monks of that monastery. In place of him Heardred was elected to the bishopric, and after the passage of a few days, that is, on 30 October, he was ordained with spiritual dignity by Archbishop Eanbald and Bishop Hygbald, in the place which is called Woodford.[162]

25. In 798, through a conspiracy formed by the murderers of King Æthelred, Ealdorman Wada, a member of that conspiracy, initiated a war against King Eardwulf in the place which is called Billington Moor by the English, near to Whalley, and a number having been killed on both sides, Ealdorman Wada with his men turned to flight, and King Eardwulf royally accepted the victory over his enemies.[163]

In the same year London was consumed by fire, along with a great number of people.

At this time Coenwulf, king of the Mercians, with all the might of his army, invaded the province of the men of Kent, and through merciless depredation powerfully reduced it nearly to annihilation. At the same time Eadberht, king of Kent, was captured; the king of the Mercians commanded that his eyes be put out and his hands mercilessly cut off, as a result of their pride and deceit.[164] Thereupon, sustained by the Lord's support, he added control of this kingdom to his own empire, placing a crown on his head and a sceptre in his hand.

(789–97) and Heardred (797–800) of Hexham, see Keynes, 'Bishops', p. 564. On the dubious OE form *Hehstealdesige*, see above, n. 125. The name *Vuduforda* is preserved as ModE 'Woodford' (see *DEPN*, p. 531); but although there are numerous places with this name, most of them are in south-west England or Cornwall. Given that Heardred was consecrated by the bishops of York and Lindisfarne, the Woodford in question is probably to be located somewhere in Northumbria.

[163] *ASC* D(E), s.a. 798, has a different account of this important battle, which had as its result the restoration of King Eardwulf: 'In this year there was a great battle in Northumbria in spring, on 2 April, at Whalley, and Alric, Heardberht's son, was killed and many others with him' (trans. Whitelock, p. 38).

[164] Cf. *ASC* 798 (796): 'Cenwulf, king of the Mercians, ravaged the people of Kent and of the Marsh, and they seized Præn their king and brought him in fetters into Mercia' (trans. Whitelock, p. 37).

HISTORIA REGVM

Eodem quoque anno, qui est annus tertius Cenuulfi praedicti regis, synodo congregata in loco qui appellatur Pincanhalh, praesidente Eanbaldo archiepiscopo aliisque quamplurimis[a] uiris; multa de utilitate sanctae Dei ecclesiae gentisque Northanhymbrorum omniumque prouinciarum consiliati sunt, et de obseruatione Paschalis festi, et iudiciorum diuinorum atque saecularium, quae [b]<promulgata erant>[b] in diebus iustorum regum et ducum bonorum atque sanctorum episcoporum aliorumque sapientum, monachorum scilicet [c]atque clericorum,[c] quorum prudentia et iustitia atque diuinis artibus status regni Northanhymbrorum [d]suauiter et[d] inedicibiliter redolebat his temporibus.[165] Rationabili uero consilio prouidebant, ut de honore ecclesiarum Dei seruorumque eius necessitatibus disputarent et seruitium Domini augerent, ut pro his mercedem aeternae retributionis bonam perciperent. Praecepit domnus antistes Eanbaldus recitari | quinque synodorum fidem, de quibus in historia Anglorum sic habetur.[e][166]

fo. 67[b]

26. 'Suscipimus sanctas et uniuersales quinque synodos beatorum et Deo acceptabilium patrum',[167] sicut praesentis libri continet textus. 'Glorificamus sane et adoramus atque ueneramur Dominum nostrum Iesum Christum sicut isti glorificauerunt, nihil addentes uel subtrahentes. Et anathematizamus corde et ore quos anathematizauerunt praedicti patres, glorificantes Deum Patrem omnipotentem sine initio, et Filium eius unigenitum ex Patre generatum ante saecula, et Spiritum Sanctum procedentem ex Patre et Filio inenarrabiliter; sicut praedicauerunt hii quos supra memorauimus—sancti apostoli, et prophetae, et doctores.'[168] Et nos credimus, propter quod et locuti sumus. 'Hos itaque praedictos patres nos pie atque orthodoxe iuxta diuinitus inspiratam doctrinam eorum professi credimus constanter, et confitemur secundum sanctos patres, proprie et ueraciter, Patrem, et Filium, et Spiritum Sanctum, Trinitatem in Vnitate consubstantialem, et

---

iii.25 [a] *after* quamplurimis C^2 *adds* principalibus et ecclesiasticis [b-b] *suppl. ed.* [c-c] *add.* C^1 [d-d] *add.* C^1 [e] uel scribitur *add.* C^2

[165] On the Northumbrian synod of 798, which met under the presidency of Archbishop Eanbald II, see Cubitt, *Anglo-Saxon Church Councils*, p. 292. On *Pincanhalh*, see above, nn. 68, 121.

[166] In *HE* iiii. 15, Bede described the proceedings of a synod convened at Hatfield by Archbishop Theodore in 679 which endorsed the *acta* of the earlier Lateran Council of 649 convened by Pope Martin to issue a defence of dyothelete doctrine; and his description of the synod of Hatfield includes extensive quotations from the *acta* of the Lateran Council of 649. Whether the Northumbrian annalist had in fact included the recycled quotations from the synod of Hatfield or whether these quotations are the contribution of Byrhtferth is unclear.

PARS TERTIA 107

In the very same year, which is the third year of Coenwulf, the afore-mentioned king, a synod was convened at a place called *Pincanhalh* [unidentified], presided over by Archbishop Eanbald, and [attended by] numerous other men; they discussed many things to the advantage of the holy church of God and of the Northumbrians as well as of all provinces, both concerning the celebration of the Easter feast and divine and worldly decrees, which were passed in the days of just kings and good ealdormen and holy bishops and other wise men, namely monks and clerics, through whose wisdom and justice and sublime skills the state of the kingdom of the Northumbrians was sweetly and indescribably redolent at that time.[165] They took care, with reasonable counsel, that they should discuss the reputation of the churches and the servants of God and their needs, and should increase worship of the Lord, so that they would receive the fitting reward of eternal repayment for these things. Lord Bishop Eanbald ordered that the credal statements of the five ecumenical councils be read out, concerning which there is this account in the *Historia Anglorum*:[166]

26. 'We endorse the five holy and Ecumenical Councils of the blessed Fathers approved by God',[167] as preserved in the present text. 'We of course glorify and adore and venerate our Lord Jesus Christ, just as they glorified Him, adding nothing and subtracting nothing. And in our hearts and words we anathematize those whom the afore-mentioned Fathers anathematized, glorifying God the Father without beginning, and his Only-Begotten Son born from the Father before time, and the Holy Spirit proceeding inexpressibly from Father and Son, just as those proclaimed whom we mentioned above—the holy apostles and prophets and doctors.'[168] And we believe, just as we have spoken. 'Following these aforesaid fathers, and in a holy and orthodox way professing their divinely inspired teaching, we similarly believe and confess truly and particularly, in accordance with the holy fathers, the Father and Son and Holy Spirit, the consubstantial Trinity in unity

---

And note that the sequence of quotations given by Byrhtferth (from Bede's quotation of the Lateran Council of 649) is the reverse of the order in which they occur in Bede's *HE*.

[167] *HE* iiii. 15. 3: 'Suscipimus sanctas et uniuersales quinque synodos beatorum et Deo acceptabilium patrum' (Bede, *HE*, ed. Lapidge, ii. 238; ed. Colgrave and Mynors, p. 386).

[168] *HE* iiii. 15. 4: 'Et glorificamus Dominum nostrum Iesum, sicut isti glorificauerunt, nihil addentes uel subtrahentes, et anathematizamus corde et ore quos anathematizarunt, et quos susceperunt suscipimus, glorificantes Deum patrem sine initio, et filium eius unigenitum ex patre generatum ante saecula, et spiritum sanctum procedentem ex patre et filio inenarrabiliter, sicut praedicauerunt hi, quos memorauimus supra, sancti apostoli et prophetae et doctores' (Bede, *HE*, ed. Lapidge, ii. 240; ed. Colgrave and Mynors, p. 386).

108 HISTORIA REGVM

Vnitatem in Trinitate, hoc est, unum Deum in tribus subsistentibus personis consubstantialibus, aequalis gloriae et honoris.'[169] His dictis et confirmatis reuersi sunt ad propria, laudantes Deum pro omnibus beneficiis suis.

Huius fidei integritatem sic alibi esse descriptam legimus, per quam saluari speramus sicut ceteri iusti confidebant:

> Cum pater in uerbo sit semper et in patre uerbum,
>   sitque unus uerbi spiritus atque patris:
> sic de personis tribus est tibi non dubitandum,
>   unum ut tota fide confiteare Deum.[170]

Et infra:

> Corde patris genitum creat et regit omnia uerbum,
>   nec tamen est aliquid quod sine patre gerat.
> Vnus enim amborum motus, ratio una, uoluntas,
>   par uirtus, idem spiritus, unus amor.[171]

Et iuxta:

> Sic magnus Deus est de se, ualet et manet in se,
>   cui summum et proprium est semper id esse quod est.
> Splendet enim uerum uero de lumine lumen,
>   ut genitum agnoscens nouerit ingenitum.[172]
>
> Vna trium deitas, una est essentia ab uno,
>   idem est cum uerbi spiritus atque patris.

fo. 67ᵛᵃ

---

[169] *HE* iiii. 15. 2: 'Hos itaque sequentes nos pie atque orthodoxe iuxta diuinitus inspiratam doctrinam eorum professi credimus consonanter et confitemur secundum sanctos patres proprie et ueraciter patrem et filium et spiritum sanctum trinitatem in unitate consubstantialem et unitatem in trinitate, hoc est unum Deum in tribus subsistentiis uel personis consubstantialibus aequalis gloriae et honoris' (Bede, *HE*, ed. Lapidge, ii. 238; ed. Colgrave and Mynors, p. 386).

[170] Prosper of Aquitaine, *Epigram.* ciiiA (ed. Horsting, CSEL c. 154–5; cf. PL li. 531). The recent edition of Prosper's *Epigrammata* by A. G. A. Horsting is based on collation of forty manuscripts of the twelfth century or earlier. Horsting's detailed *apparatus criticus* makes it possible to determine that Byrhtferth's text of Prosper belonged to Horsting's δ-group, a class of four English manuscripts, three of which are contemporary with the lifetime of Byrhtferth; see following note.

[171] Prosper of Aquitaine, *Epigram.* ciiiB (ed. Horsting, CSEL c. 155; cf. PL li. 531). In line 3, where Byrhtferth's text reads *uoluntas*, the text printed by Horsting reads *uolendi est*. Importantly, the reading *uoluntas* in Byrhtferth's text is attested in four manuscripts of Horsting's δ-group, three of which are Anglo-Saxon manuscripts contemporary with

PARS TERTIA 109

and unity in Trinity, that is, One God in three subsistences or consubstantial persons of equal glory and honour.'[169] When these things had been stated and approved, they returned home, praising God for all His bounties.

We read of the correctness of this creed as it was written down elsewhere, through which we hope to be saved just as other righteous men believed.

> Since the Father exists always in the Word and the Word in the
>   Father,
> and since there is one Spirit of Word and Father:
> thus you must not doubt concerning the three Persons,
> and confess the One God in total trust.[170]

And further on:

> The Word, born in the heart of the Father, creates and rules all
>   things;
> nor is there anything which it produces without the Father.
> There is one motion in both of them, one reason, one will,
> equal power, the same spirit, one love.[171]

And next:

> Thus God is mighty within Himself, He is strong and remains
>   within Himself;
> to Him is always the essence of His might and individual nature.

> He shines as true light from true light,
> such that what is begotten knows what is unbegotten.[172]

> There is one Deity in Three, one essence from One,
> since the spirit of the Word and of the Father are the same thing.

Byrhtferth: Co (Cambridge, Corpus Christi College 448; Gneuss and Lapidge, *Anglo-Saxon Manuscripts*, no. 114); H_1 (London, BL, Harley 110; Gneuss and Lapidge, ibid. no. 415), Tr_1 (Cambridge, Trinity College, O. 2. 31; Gneuss and Lapidge, ibid. no. 190), and Tr_2 (Cambridge, Trinity College, O. 3. 41 (s. xii)). The variant *uoluntas* indicates that Byrhtferth was quoting from an Anglo-Saxon manuscript belonging to Horsting's δ-group, which was possibly identical with either Co, H_1, or Tr_1.

[172] Prosper of Aquitaine, *Epigram.* ciiiC (ed. Horsting, CSEL c. 155; cf. PL li. 532); in the first line, where the text quoted by Byrhtferth reads *Sic*, various Continental manuscripts read either *Se* or *Sed*; *Sic* is the reading of an important early manuscript of the *Epigrammata* (Leiden, Universiteitsbibliotheek, Voss. lat. Q. 86, Horsting's L_1). In line 4, Horsting emends *nouerit* to *noueris*.

110   HISTORIA REGVM

Nullum opus abiunctum, nulla est non aequa potestas:
  in cunctis unum sunt tria principium.[173]

De orthodoxa fide haec pertractantes, ad historiae nostrae narrationem
redeamus.

27. Anno .dccxcix. naues plurimae in mari Britannico ui tempestatis quassatae sunt atque concussae uel collisae, et cum magna multitudine hominum sunt dimersae.[174] Eodem anno Brorda Merciorum
princeps, qui et Hildegils uocabatur, defunctus est. Abbas uero uocitatus More a Tilthegno praefecto suo lugubri morte interemptus est.
Moll quoque dux paulo post, iussione urgente Earduulfi regis, occisus
est. Ipso quoque tempore Osbald quondam dux et patricius et ad tempus rex, tunc uero abbas, diem suscepit ultimum, cuius corpus in
ecclesia Eboracae ciuitatis sepultum est.[175] Aldred uero dux, interfector
Æthelredi regis, a Torhtmundo duce in ultionem domini sui eiusdem
regis interfectus est.[176]

Quid gestum sit eodem anno, referre libet. Romani quoque inter se
dissecabantur, et magnam dissensionem habebant, in qua Leonem
papam sanctissimum apprehenderunt ligaueruntque, cuius lingua
inter maxillas duriter protracta et in gutture crudeliter extensa prae-
cisa est ab ipsis.[177] Eruerunt et oculos praedicti pontificis radicitus,
quae res cunctis cernentibus crudele spectaculum est factum. Dehinc
absque ulla humanitate semiuiuum[a] eum relinquentes, inconsulte
domum reuersi sunt. Sed magnus conditor orbis ex alto cuncta intuens,
quem, quia respicit omnia solus, uerum possumus dicere solem, non
sic suum[b] contempsit fidelem famulum. Omnipotens igitur Dominus
post pauci temporis interstitium sic eum salutifero sanauit antidoto, ut

---

iii.27   [a] semiuiuus C   [b] suam C

[173] Prosper of Aquitaine, *Epigram.* ciiiD (ed. Horsting, CSEL c. 156; PL li. 532).
[174] This event is not recorded elsewhere. The term *mare Britannicum* ('British sea') was
used by classical geographers such as Pomponius Mela to describe what we now call the
English Channel.
[175] On Osbald, see above, n. 155.
[176] In a letter to Charlemagne dated 801 (*Ep.* ccxxxi), Alcuin refers to the forthcoming
visit of Torhtmund, who was King Æthelred's faithful servant, and who showed his fidelity to
his lord by avenging his murder: 'sed et Torchmundum, Hedilredi regis fidelem famulum,
virum in fide probatum, strenuum in armis, qui fortiter sanguinem domini sui vindicavit'
(MGH, *Epist.* iv. 376; trans. Whitelock, *EHD*, p. 863). Torhtmund was perhaps passing
through the Carolingian kingdom on a penitential pilgrimage to Rome in order to expiate the
murder; he seems to have been travelling in the company of Archbishop Æthelheard—

PARS TERTIA 111

No work of theirs is separate, there is no power which is not equal:
the three [essences] are one principle in all things.[173]

After treating these aspects of orthodox belief, let us return to the narrative of our history.

27. In 799, many ships were battered, shaken and shattered by the force of a gale in the English Channel, and sunk with a great number of men.[174] In the same year Brorda, leader of the Mercians, who was also called Hildegils, died. And the abbot named More was killed by Tilthegn his prior in a lamentable murder. Shortly thereafter Ealdorman Moll was killed at the urgent request of King Eardwulf. At the same time Osbald, once ealdorman and nobleman and briefly king, but at that point an abbot, breathed his last; his body was buried in the church in the city of York.[175] But Ealdorman Aldred, the murderer of King Æthelred, was killed in revenge for his lord the king by Ealdorman Torhtmund.[176]

It is fitting to report what else happened in that same year. The Romans were torn apart internally and had a huge disagreement, in which they arrested the most holy Pope Leo [III] and bound him; his tongue was roughly drawn out and cruelly stretched in his throat, and then cut off by them.[177] They wholly plucked out the eyes of the said pope; this event provided a cruel spectacle for all those witnessing it. Then leaving him half dead, without any human feelings they inconsiderately went home. But the mighty Creator of the world, watching all this from on high—because He alone sees all things: He whom we can call the true Sun—did not scorn his true servant in this way. The omnipotent Lord, therefore, after the interval of a brief space of time, healed him with a health-restoring antidote, so that he could afterwards

---

Alcuin's letter to Charlemagne also mentions Æthelheard—and Bishop Cyneberht, both of whom, according to *ASC* (s.a. 801), travelled to Rome in that year (trans. Whitelock, p. 38).

[177] The capture and mutilation of Pope Leo III (795–816) is not mentioned in any other Anglo-Saxon text, and was presumably derived from Continental sources; cf. the entry in the 'Royal Frankish Annals', which record (s.a. 799) that 'The Romans captured the pope at the Major Litanies, blinded him, and tore his tongue out. After being cast into prison, he escaped over the wall at night, went to the envoys of the Lord King [Charlemagne]... and was taken to Spoleto' (ed. Kurze, pp. 106–7; *Carolingian Chronicles*, trans. Scholz, p. 77). A derivative of this entry is in 'Ramsey Annals', s.a. 799: 'Romani Leonis pape oculos eruerunt, et linguam perciderunt [*sic*]; sed dei gratia et visum et loquelam mox adeptus est, et iterum papa urbis fit' (p. 42). The story of the pope's miraculous recovery from his mutilations is told in the *Liber pontificalis* (ed. Duchesne, ii. 5; *Lives of the Eighth-Century Popes*, trans. Davis, pp. 186–7); and see discussion by Story in *Carolingian Connections*, pp. 97, 110, and 123–5.

HISTORIA REGVM

fo. 67vb postmodum uidere clare et loqui | posset, prorsus ab eo expellens caligines oculorum et concedens ei pristinae sanitatis linguam, ut paenitissima[178] *uel profundissima* edere uerba praedicationis ualuisset, et omnia officia honorifice implere.

> Cesset inscitiae* nubilus error,
> cessent profecto mira uideri,[179]

uniuersa opera Domini! Hoc miraculum repente diffusum est per cardines quadrati orbis, ad gloriam et laudem Christi nominis, ut ab omnibus ubique praedicetur et laudetur, quia 'mirabilis est Deus in sanctis suis'.[180]

Anno .dccc. Heardred, Haugustaldensis ecclesiae praesul, anno tertio episcopatus sui regiminis diem uidit ultimum, pro quo Eanbyrht electus est et ordinatus episcopus in loco qui dicitur Æt^e Cettingaham.[181] Eodem anno Alchmund filius Alchredi regis, ut dicunt quidam, a tutoribus Earduulfi regis est apprehensus, eiusque iussione cum suis profugis occisus est.

Tempore quoque eodem ante Natale Domini .ix. kalendas Ianuarii uentus ingens, ab Affrico uel a Fauonio exsurgens, suo inenarrabili flatu urbes multae, domus ac uillae perplurimae per diuersa loca sunt destructae et ad solum dirutae; arbores quoque innumerae radicitus euulsae, et ad terram prostratae sunt. Quo anno inundatio maris ultra terminos suos profluxit, illud secum obliuiscens quod dicit Psalmus: 'Terminum posuisti quem non transgredientur.'[182] Facta est et magna pecorum strages in locis diuersis.

28. Carolus quoque, eximiae uirtutis rex Francorum, paulo ante ipso anno cum magna exercitus sui multitudine Romuleae urbis moenia ingreditur, ibique per aliquot menses demoratus est, locaque sancta frequenti uisitatione adorat, ditat, exornat munere regali. Praecipue uero ecclesiam beati Petri apostoli, necnon et sancti Pauli, donis exornauit regalibus, auro scilicet et argento, gemmisque pretiosis. Leonem quoque uenerabilem papam magnifice munerauit, eiusque aduersarios dispersit,

---

> *c–c* add. C^l　　　*d* uel ignorantiae add. C^l　　　*e* apud C

---

[178] The adjective *paenitissimus*, apparently formed from a positive **paenitus*, is a Byrhtferthian solecism (the verb *paeniteo* does not have a supine); no such form is recorded in *DMLBS*. See Introduction, p. xxvii.

[179] Boethius, *De consolatione Philosophiae*, iv, met. v, lines 21–2 (CCSL xciv. 79); and note that the text of Boethius as edited by Bieler in CCSL reads *cedat* in lieu of *Cesset* in line 21. When Byrhtferth quotes the same two lines of Boethius in *HR* iv. 1 (below, p. 120), his quotation correctly reads *cedat* (not *cesset*).

[180] Ps. 67 (68): 36.

PARS TERTIA
113

see clearly and speak, entirely driving from him the darkness of his vision and granting him the pristine use of his tongue, so that he could produce the repentant[178] or profound words of his preaching, and fulfil all his duties honourably.

> Let the dark error of ignorance depart,
> indeed let cease to seem wondrous[179]

all the works of the Lord! This miracle was rapidly spread to the corners of the fourfold globe, to the glory and praise of the name of Christ, so that He may be proclaimed and praised, since 'God is wonderful in His saints'.[180]

In 800, Heardred, the bishop of the church of Hexham, closed the ultimate day [of his life] in the third year of his episcopal governance; in his place Eanberht was elected and ordained bishop in the place named *Æt Cettingaham* [unidentified].[181] In the same year Alchmund, the son of King Alchred, was captured by the guards of King Eardwulf, as certain people say, and killed on his orders, along with those fleeing with him.

At the very same time, before Christmas, on 24 December, many towns, homes, and numerous estates were destroyed in various locations and levelled to the ground by the indescribable blast from a mighty wind, blowing up from the south-west or from the south; countless trees as well were torn up by the roots and cast to the ground. In this year a surge of the sea flowed beyond its bounds, forgetting what the psalm says: 'You laid down a boundary which they shall not exceed.'[182] A great slaughter of flocks took place in various locations.

28. A little earlier in this same year Charles, too, the exceedingly powerful king of the Franks, entered the walls of the Romulean city with a great multitude of his army, and remained there for several months; he admires, enriches, and adorns the holy places with royal gifts on his frequent visits. He particularly embellished the church of St Peter the apostle, not to mention that of St Paul, with royal gifts—gold, that is, and silver, and precious jewels. He magnificently

---

[181] On these two bishops of Hexham—Heardred (797–800) and Eanberht (800–13)—see Keynes, 'Bishops', p. 564. Eanberht is mentioned in Symeon, *LDE* ii. 5 (ed. Rollason, p. 90). The place-name *Æt Cettingaham* is associated by Ekwall with the modern village of Chettisham in Cambridgeshire (*DEPN*, p. 101); but it is difficult to imagine circumstances in which a bishop of Hexham would be consecrated so far from Northumbria. A Northumbrian *Æt Cettingaham* remains to be identified.

[182] Ps. 103 (104): 9.

HISTORIA REGVM

fo. 68ra quosdam extinxit uel exilio damnauit, nonnullos | interfecit qui contra eum impie coniurationem promouerunt. His atque aliis quamplurimis rebus ordinatis, ipse armipotens imperator, quae ad honorem et correptionem ecclesiarum Christi Christianorumque populorum pertinebant, in die Natalis Domini nostri Iesu Christi ingreditur cum ducibus et magistratibus et militibus in ecclesiam sanctissimi principis apostolorum Petri, in qua a domino Leone papa purpura regaliter induitur, cui corona aurea capiti imponitur et regale sceptrum in manibus datur. Hanc dignitatem ipso die meruit ab omni populo percipere, ut 'imperator totius orbis' appellaretur, et esset.[183] Eo quoque tempore legati Graecorum cum magnis muneribus a Constantinopoli directi ad eum ueniebant, rogantes ut illorum susciperet regnum et imperium.[184] Similiter legati ab Hierosolimis a Christianis populis ibi manentibus missi, Romamque uenientes, uexillum argenteum inter alia munera regi ferentes, clauesque locorum sanctorum Dominicae resurrectionis aliorumque ei optulerunt, obnixe flagitantes ipsorum esse susceptorem et defensorem. Rogabant eum ut Christianae religioni subdita sancta coenobia conseruaret, regeret ac defenderet, et contra insurgentes gentes exsurgeret bellica uirtute et regali maiestate.[185] Annuit benignissimus rex beatis precibus eorum[a] qui ad se confluxerant, et non solum se paratum esse ad deuincendos inimicos in terra, uerum etiam in mari, si necessitas compulisset. Intellexit 'beatas fore res publicas, si eas uel studiosi sapientiae regerent, uel si earum rectores studere sapientiae contigisset'.[186] Is ad urbem Rauennam perueniens, ad Aquas deinde perrexit, de his omnibus cum suis optimatibus tractaturus.

29. Anno .dccci. Eaduuine, qui et Eda dictus est, quondam dux Northanhymbrorum, tunc uero per gratiam saluatoris mundi abbas in

---

iii.28 *a suppl. ed.*

---

[183] The coronation of Charlemagne by Pope Leo III on Christmas Day, 800, is described by Continental annalists, notably the 'Royal Frankish Annals', s.a. 801: 'On the most holy day of Christmas, when the king rose from prayer in front of the shrine of the blessed apostle Peter, to take part in the Mass, Pope Leo placed a crown on his head, and he was hailed by the whole Roman people: to the August Charles, crowned by God, the great and peaceful emperor of the Romans, life and victory! After the acclamations the pope addressed him in the manner of the old emperors. The name of Patricius was now abandoned and he was called Emperor and Augustus' (ed. Kurze, p. 112–13; *Carolingian Chronicles*, trans. Scholz, p. 81). See discussion by Story in *Carolingian Connections*, pp. 112, 114.

[184] The embassy to Charlemagne from the Empress Irene is described in the 'Royal Frankish Annals', s.a. 802: 'Empress Irene sent the spatarius Leo as envoy from Constantinople to ratify a peace between Franks and Greeks' (ed. Kurze, p. 117; *Carolingian Chronicles*, trans. Scholz, p. 82).

[185] The embassy from Jerusalem is described in the 'Royal Frankish Annals', s.a. 800: 'On the same day Zacharias returned from the East to Rome with two monks, one from Mount

PARS TERTIA

115

endowed Leo, the venerable pope, and put to flight his adversaries: some he destroyed or condemned to exile; some—who had wickedly initiated the conspiracy against him—he simply put to death. When these and several other matters had been put in order, which pertained to the honour and correction of the churches of Christ and the Christian populace, the warlike emperor enters the church of St Peter, prince of the apostles, on Christmas day, together with his dukes and magistrates and soldiers; here he is royally robed in purple by Lord Pope Leo; a golden crown is placed on his head and a royal sceptre is given into his hands. He was found worthy this day to receive this distinction, that he should be called 'emperor of the world'—as indeed he was.[183] At the same time ambassadors of the Greeks, sent from Constantinople with magnificent gifts, came to him, asking that he recognize their kingdom and empire.[184] Likewise legates, sent from the Christian populace living in Jerusalem, came to Rome, bearing a silver standard amongst other gifts for the king, and they presented him with keys to the holy places of the Lord's Resurrection and other places, earnestly requesting that he be their keeper and protector. They asked him that he preserve, rule, and defend the holy monasteries devoted to Christian religion, and that he would rise up with warlike might and royal majesty against peoples attacking them.[185] The kindly king agreed to the blessed entreaties of those who had flocked to him, and said that he was prepared not only to subdue their enemies on land, but even on the high seas, if the need should arise. He understood that 'states would be blessed, if those who were zealous for wisdom ruled them, or if it should happen that their rulers were to pursue wisdom'.[186] He [Charles], arriving in Ravenna, went thereafter back to Aachen, to discuss with his nobles all these matters.

29. In 801, Eadwine, also known as Eda, once an ealdorman of the Northumbrians but then, through the grace of the Saviour of the

---

Olivet and the other from St Saba's. These monks the patriarch of Jerusalem sent to the king with Zacharias. As a sign of his good will they brought along the keys of the Lord's Sepulcher and of Calvary, also the keys of the city and of Mount Zion along with a flag' (ed. Kurze, pp. 112–13; *Carolingian Chronicles*, trans. Scholz, pp. 80–1); cf. discussion by Story in *Carolingian Connections*, p. 114.

[186] Boethius, *De consolatione Philosophiae*, i, pr. iv. 5: 'Atqui tu hanc sententiam Platonis ore sanxisti: beatas fore res publicas, si eas uel studiosi sapientiae regerent uel earum rectores studere sapientiae contigisset' (CCSL xciv. 7); Byrhtferth quotes the same sentence of Boethius below, *HR* iv. 11 (p. 148). Cf. also discussion by Story (*Carolingian Connections*, p. 113), who points out that Alcuin too alluded to this dictum of Plato in a letter written to Charlemagne in 801 (*Ep.* ccxxix); but Alcuin's allusion is a mere paraphrase, whereas here, as throughout the *HR*, Byrhtferth quotes Boethius verbatim, and clearly had a copy of the *De consolatione Philosophiae* at his elbow.

116   HISTORIA REGVM

Dei seruitio roboratus, uelut miles emeritus, diem clausit ultimum in
fo. 68rb conspectu fratrum .xviii. kalendas Februarii. Sepultus | est quoque in
monasterio suo quod appellatur Æt Gegenforda honorifice in ecclesia.[187]

His temporibus Earduulf rex Northanhymbrorum duxit exercitum
contra Cenuulfum regem Merciorum propter susceptionem inimicorum eius. Qui et ipse congregans exercitum secum aliarum promouit
auxilia prouinciarum plurima.[188] Longa inter eos expeditione facta,
tandem cum consilio episcoporum ac principum Anglorum ex utraque
parte pacem inierunt per gratiam regis Anglorum.[189] Factaque firmis-
simae pacis concordia inter eos, quam sub iureiurando in euangelio Christi
ambo reges confirmauerunt, Deum testem atque fideiussorem interpo-
nentes, ut in diebus eorum, quamdiu uita potirentur praesenti et regni
essent infulis suffulti, pax firma ueraque inter eos amicitia inconcussa
et inuiolata persisteret. Contigit in illis esse completum quod legitur,

> Gratius astra nitent, ubi Nothus
> desinit imbriferos dare sonos;
> Lucifer ut tenebras pepulerit,
> pulchra dies roseos agit equos.[190]

'Astra splendebant gratius': hoc est, principes gaudebant profusius,
dum reges pacem dabant inter se clementius. 'Nothus' uentus est
calidus qui solet 'imbriferos dare sonos'. 'Vt dies roseos agit equos'; id
est, totius regni status exultabat dum serena redierunt tempora illius
aeui mortalibus, gratia Domini largiente, qui tempestatibus et coruscis
praestat quietudinis serenitatem:

> Et numeris elementa ligat, ut frigora flammis,
> arida conueniant liquidis, ne purior ignis
> euolet, aut mersas deducant pondera terras.[191]

Eodem anno Hathuberht, Lundoniae ciuitatis antistes, uitae huius
contempsit tempora; et paulo post magna pars uici ipsius repentino
igne consumpta est.[192]

---

[187] Neither Abbot Eadwine nor his monastery at Gainford is known from another source
(cf. *PASE*, s.vv.); he is possibly identical with the *Eduini* recorded among the 'Nomina abbatum'
in *LVD* (ed. Sweet, p. 156, line 89). Gainford (Co. Durham) lies six miles west of Darlington.

[188] Eardwulf's expeditionary force against Coenwulf of Mercia is not recorded in *ASC*, so
the present annal is the only record of this significant event; see Stenton, *Anglo-Saxon
England*, p. 94, and *WB Encyc.* pp. 114–15, s.v. 'Coenwulf' [S. D. Keynes]: 'Coenwulf had
suffered the indignity in 801 of being invaded by Eardwulf, king of the Northumbrians, but
peace was soon re-established between them.'

[189] It is not clear what is meant by *regis Anglorum*, or who could have been the king who
brokered the peace between the kings of Mercia and Northumbria. Whitelock comments:

PARS TERTIA 117

world, an abbot confirmed in the service of God, like a veteran soldier breathed his last in the presence of his monks on 15 January. And he was honourably buried in his monastery called Gainford.[187]

At this time Eardwulf, king of the Northumbrians, led an army against Cenwulf, king of the Mercians, because he had given asylum to his enemies. In assembling his army, he also took with him auxiliary troops from other provinces.[188] Having completed a long expedition among them [the Mercians], with the advice of the bishops and leaders of the Angles, they agreed at last upon a peace involving both parties through the mediation of the king of the Angles.[189] When the harmony of an enduring peace had been established between them, which both kings confirmed by swearing on a gospelbook of Christ, calling God as their witness and surety that during their lifetimes, for as long as they remained in this present life and were sustained by the insignia of rule, a firm and true peace would last between them with unshakable and inviolate friendship. What is written happened to be fulfilled in them,

> The stars shine more kindly when the south wind
> ceases to produce its rain-bearing blasts;
> as when the Day-Star has driven away the shadows,
> the glorious day leads out its rosy horses.[190]

'The stars were shining more kindly': that is, princes rejoiced more abundantly when kings established peace among themselves more gently. 'Nothus' is the hot wind which usually produces rain-bearing roars. 'As the day drives rosy horses': that is, that status of the entire realm rejoiced when peaceful times of that age returned for mortals, through the grace of the Lord's abundance, Who provides the serenity of peace in place of storms and lightning bolts:

> And He binds the elements with numbers, so that cold with flames,
> dryness will harmonize with liquid, so that a purer fire
> does not fly away, or great weight submerge the earth.[191]

In the same year Heathoberht, bishop of the city of London, scorned the temporal duration of this life; and shortly thereafter, a great part of that same place was consumed by a sudden fire.[192]

'A mysterious reference, probably an error for "king of the angels"' (*EHD*, p. 276, n. 1); but this suggestion is most implausible.

[190] Boethius, *De consolatione Philosophiae*, iii, met. i, lines 7–10 (CCSL xciv. 37–8).

[191] Ibid., met. ix, lines 10–12 (CCSL xciv. 52); Byrhtferth has replaced the transmitted *Tu* of the first line with *Et*.

[192] Neither the death of Bishop Heathoberht nor the London fire is known from any other source; on Heathoberht, see Keynes, 'Bishops', p. 546.

<PARS QVARTA>

fo. 68rb 1. Anno 'dccii. ab incarnatione dominica, Brihtric Occidentalium
fo. 68va <Saxonum>^b rex, qui eidem | genti decem et septem annis nobilis-
sime praefuit, defunctus est; cuius imperium et regnum post eum
Ecgberht, ex regali illius gentis prosapia, suscepit ac tenuit.[1]

Rex autem Brihtric Occidentalium Saxonum accepit sibi in coniugi-
um^c Eadburgam,^d quae erat filia regis Merciorum nomine Offa, qui
uallum magnum inter Britanniam atque Merciam, id est de mari usque
ad mare, facere imperauit. Cumque filia regis esset, multis suffulta
honoribus, miris se extollebat ambitionibus; quae more paterno tyran-
nice uiuere coepit, et omnem hominem exsecrari, sicque ut omnibus
esset perosa, non solum ducibus et magistratibus, uerum etiam cunctis
populis. Omnes religiosos uiros ad regem semper accusare non cessauit, et ita maledicta uirum suum constrinxit blanditiis, ut illos quos
accusare coepit, aut uita aut regno priuaret; et si a rege impetrare non
posset, ueneno eos clam disperdere^e non distulit. Erat eodem tempore
quidam praediues adolescens, praeamabilis^f regi praedicto ^get carus;^g
quem cum accusare uellet ad regem et minime praeualeret, ueneno
ipsum ipsa maleuola necauit.^h De quo ueneno cum ipse rex inscienter
gustasset, periit. Neque etiam illa uenenum regi proposuerat dare sed
puero; quem princeps ducum praeoccupans, ambo necis poculum
biberunt, ambo gustu amarissimo perierunt.[2] Quo ex hoc saeculoⁱ perempto ^juenefica illa nequissima timore perterrita^j fugiendo ultra mare
est egressa, cum innumerabilibus thesauris, regem adiens Francorum
famosissimum Carolum. Ad quem cum ante solarium astaret et regi
deferret munera preciosa, sic est eam affatus: 'Elige, Eadburg, quem
uelis,^k me aut filium meum, qui mecum in solario astat.' At illa sine
fo. 68vb deliberatione stulte respondit, dicens: | 'Si mihi optio daretur, filium
tuum magis eligerem quam te, quia iunior esse uidetur.' Cui rex

---

iv.1 ^{a–a} *suppl. ed.*   ^b *suppl. ed.*   ^c *over* in coniugium *C*² *adds* uel in matrimonium   ^d Earburgam *C*   ^e *C*² *adds* scilicet necare   ^f *over* prae- *C*² *adds* scilicet ualde   ^{g–g} *add. C*¹   ^h scilicet extinxit *C*²   ⁱ uel scelere *C*²   ^{j–j} *suppl.*
*C*¹ *at foot of col. 68*va *(linked by a* signe de renvoi*)*   ^k *add. C*¹

---

[1] *ASC*, s.a. 802 (800): 'In this year King Brihtric and Ealdorman Worr died, and Ecgberht
succeeded to the kingdom of the West Saxons' (trans. Whitelock, p. 38); cf. 'Ramsey Annals',
s.a. 800: 'Obiit Bryhtric rex, et Echbert regnat' (p. 42). Beorhtric was king of the West Saxons
from 786 to the time of his murder in 802; see Keynes, 'Rulers', p. 534. From this point
onwards, Byrhtferth abandons his annalistic source(s), and turns to Asser's *Vita Ælfredi* for
his account of King Alfred and the kingdom of the West Saxons.

PART IV

1. In the year of the Lord's Incarnation 802, Brihtric, king of the West Saxons, who had presided supremely over that nation for seventeen years, died; following him Ecgberht, from the royal line of that people, assumed and held the realm and kingdom.[1]

Now Brihtric, king of the West Saxons, took as his wife Eadburg, who was the daughter of the king of the Mercians named Offa, who ordered a great rampart to be built between Britain and Mercia, that is, from sea to sea. And since she [Eadburg] was the daughter of a king, attended by so many honours, she vaunted herself with amazing ambitions; she began to behave like a tyrant after the model of her father, and to abominate all men, to the point that she became detestable to everyone, not only ealdormen and judges, but even all the populace. She did not cease from accusing men of religion before the king [Brihtric], and the cursed woman so controlled her husband with flattery that she could deprive either of life or of rule those whom she began to accuse; and if she could not obtain this from the king, she did not hesitate to kill them secretly with poison. At that same time there was an extremely wealthy young man, a favourite of the aforesaid king and dear to him; when she wished to accuse him before the king and did not succeed, this same wicked woman killed him with poison. When the king himself tasted this poison unknowingly, he died. She had not intended to give the poison to the king, but to the young man; the leading ealdorman, anticipating this, drank together with the young man the deadly chalice, and both of them perished from the bitter draught.[2] When the king [Brihtric] had departed from this world, that wicked poisoner, overcome with terror, set out in flight for lands across the sea, taking with her innumerable treasures, and arrived before Charles, the famous king of the Franks. When she stood before him on the terrace [of the palace] and handed over to the king the precious gifts, he spoke to her thus: 'Choose, Eadburg, whom you wish: either me or my son, who is with me here on the terrace.' And she replied stupidly, without reflection, saying: 'If the choice were given to me, I should choose your son rather than you, because he seems to be

---

[2] The account of Eadburg, daughter of King Offa of Mercia, and her marriage to King Beorhtric (and his poisoning) is taken from Asser, *Vita Ælfredi*, c. 14 (ed. Stevenson, pp. 12–13; trans. Keynes and Lapidge, pp. 71–2). On Offa's Dyke, mentioned here by Asser (and Byrhtferth), see Fox, *Offa's Dyke*, and, for more recent bibliography, *WB Encyc.*, pp. 348–9 (M. Worthington).

HISTORIA REGVM

Carolus ita respondisse fertur: 'Si me eligeres, haberes filium meum, sed quia illum elegisti, nec me nec illum propitium habebis.' Contulit tamen illi propter improbitatem eius optimum monasterium, in quo, deposito saeculari habitu, sub specie hypocrissima indumento sanctimonialium assumpto perpaucis fungebatur annis; sicut enim *l*execrabilis et*l* flebilis ipsa nequiter*m* et irrationabiliter in propria uixit regione, ita multo nequius, *n*miserabilius et*n* irrationabilius in terra aliena uixisse deprehenditur.

> Æstas (ut quidam ait) Cererem feruida siccat,
> remeat pomis grauis autumnus,
> hiemem defluus irrigat imber.[3]

Sed huius pessimae reginae mentem nec pulchritudo aestatis, nec algor hiemis ualuit a libidine cohibere. Namque interstitio*o* peracto, dum quae sancta erant exerceret, ut quidam aestimabant, a quodam suae propriae gentis ignobili uiro constuprata est.

> Cedat inscitiae nubilus error,
> cessent profecto mira uideri.[4]

'Mulierem', inquit, 'in adulterio deprehensam'.[5] Nihil itaque est quod admirere; 'nichil occultum quod non sciatur'.[6] Post haec, praecipiente magno Carolo imperatore, proiecta est cum magno mentis taedio *p*et angore*p* a suo sancto monasterio: quae in paupertate et miseria uitae suae tempora uituperabiliter ad finem perduxit. Quae ad ultimum uno seruulo comitata, cotidie mendicans per domos et per ciuitates atque castella, in Pauia miserabiliter obiit.[7]

2. Defuncto rege glorioso Bryhtrico, occidentalis regni suscepit post ipsius obitum regnum et imperium Ecgberht rex, qui ex regali illius gentis prosapia exortus, diadema totius regni capiti imposuit, maximo sceptro redimitus.[8] *a*Erat enim strenuissimus uir et potens; multaque regna suo subiecit imperio. Regnauit annos .xxxvi. Et*a*

---

l-l add. *C*[1] *m* add. *C*[1] *n-n* add. *C*[1] *o* uel paruo tempore add. *C*[1] *p-p* add. *C*[1]

iv.2 *a-a* added by *C*[1] at foot of col. 68*vb* (with a signe de renvoi)

---

[3] Boethius, *De consolatione Philosophiae*, iv, met. vi, lines 27–9 (CCSL xciv. 85).

[4] Ibid., met. v, lines 21–2 (CCSL xciv. 79). Note that Byrhtferth had quoted these very same two lines earlier, in *HR* iii. 27 (above, p. 112).

[5] John 8: 3 ('adducunt autem scribae et Pharisaei mulierem in adulterio deprensam').

[6] Matt. 10: 26 ('nihil...occultum quod non scietur').

PARS QVARTA

younger.' King Charles is said to have replied to her: 'If you had chosen me, you would have had my son; but since you chose him, you shall have neither me nor him at your convenience.' Yet in spite of her impudence he granted to her an excellent monastery in which, having put aside her worldly dress, she assumed with extreme hypocrisy the garb of a nun, in which she functioned for a very few years; but just as this execrable and pitiable woman lived wickedly and unreasonably in her homeland, so she is understood to have lived even more wickedly, wretchedly, and unreasonably in a foreign land.

> A hot summer dries out the crop (as someone said),
> autumn returns heavy with fruit,
> the pouring rain floods the winter.[3]

But neither the beauty of summer, nor the chill of winter, was able to restrain the impulses of this worst of queens. For after a certain period, when she was still performing her holy duties, she was debauched, as certain people assumed, by a man of low birth from her own people.

> Let the dark error of ignorance depart,
> let wonders straightway cease to seem so![4]

'A woman', he says [in other words], 'taken in adultery.'[5] And there is nothing here which you would admire; 'nothing hidden which is not known'.[6] After these things, at the command of the emperor Charlemagne, she was cast with great disgust and mental anguish from her holy monastery; she passed the [remaining] time of her life in poverty and misery deplorably up to its end. In the end, accompanied by one mere servant, begging by day at homes and in cities and towns, she died wretchedly in Pavia.[7]

2. When glorious King Brihtric was dead, King Ecgberht took up the rule and government of the western kingdom in his place; being descended from the royal line of that people, he placed the diadem of the entire realm on his head, and was adorned by a great sceptre.[8] For he was a mighty and extremely energetic man; he subjected many

---

[7] The account of Eadburg's departure from England, her experience with Charlemagne, and her eventual disgrace and death in Pavia is from Asser, *Vita Ælfredi*, c. 15 (ed. Stevenson, pp. 13–14; trans. Keynes and Lapidge, p. 72); see discussion by Story, *Carolingian Connections*, pp. 110–11. The story of Eadburg is known only from Asser, and is not found in Continental sources.

[8] The succession of King Ecgberht (802–39) was recorded in the entry in *ASC*, s.a. 802 (800), cited above, n. 1. On Ecgberht, see Keynes, 'Rulers', p. 534.

HISTORIA REGVM

122

*b*Ecgberhto successit Ætheluulfus filius eius potentissimus;*c* cui successit filius eius Æthelbaldus; deinde frater suus Æthelberhtus; post quem frater suus Æthelredus; post hunc frater eorum Ælfredus.[9] Denique Ætheluulf habuit ex coniuge sua nobili .iiii. filios,[10] scilicet Æthelbaldum et Æthelberhtum et Æthelredum et Ælfredum,*b* *d*qui omnes sibi inuicem in regnum successerunt.*d*[11]

fo. 69ra

3. Anno dominicae incarnationis .dcccxlix. exortum est lumen e tenebris: Ælfredus rex Anglorum natus est in regali uilla quae ab Anglis Vuanetinge appellatur. Cuius genealogia tali serie contexitur: Ælfred rex filius erat Ætheluulfi regis, qui fuit Ecgberhti, qui fuit Alchmundi, qui fuit Affa, qui fuit Eoppa, qui fuit Ingild. Ingild et Ine fratres fuerunt. Ine rex famosissimus erat per totius fines gentis Anglorum; qui occidentalium regionum regna regaliter regebat, et peractis in regno plurimis annis Romam perrexit, relinquens patriam et regnum praesens*a* ut cum Christo possideret <illud>*b* aeternum, quod ei concessit diuinae maiestatis imperium. Hii fuerunt filii Coenredi, qui fuit Ceoluuold, qui fuit Cuda, qui fuit Cuduuine, qui fuit Ceauulin, qui fuit Cinric, qui fuit Creoda, qui fuit Cerdic, qui fuit Elesa, qui fuit Geuuis, a quo Britones totam illam gentem Geuuis nominant, qui fuit Brand, qui fuit Belde, qui fuit Vuoden, qui fuit Frithuuald, qui fuit Frealaf, qui fuit Fridupulf, qui fuit Geta, quem iam dudum pagani pro deo uenerabantur.[12] Cuius Sedulius poeta insignis mentionem faciens in Pascali carmine, ita exorsus est:

---

b–b added by C at foot of col. 68*cb* (with a signe de renvoi)   *c* add. C*l*   *d–d* add. C*l*

iv.3   *a* praesentem C   *b* suppl. ed.

---

[9] The complicated story of the succession of King Æthelwulf (839–58) by his son Æthelbald (855–60) and his brothers Æthelberht (860–5) and Æthelred I (865–71) is set out concisely by Keynes, 'Rulers', pp. 534–5. The information could have been gleaned from *ASC*, s.aa. 839, 855, and 866, but more likely derived from a copy of the West Saxon genealogical regnal list like that edited by David Dumville from seven manuscripts: 'þa feng Æðelwulf his sunu to...ond ða feng Æþelbald his sunu to rice...þa feng Æðelbyrht his broþur to...þa feng Æðered his broðor to rice...þa feng Ælfred hyra broþer to rice' ('The West Saxon genealogical regnal list', pp. 24–5).

[10] That Æthelwulf fathered the four named sons is clear from the previous sentence, translated from a copy of the West Saxon genealogical regnal list; see also Keynes, 'Rulers', pp. 534–5.

[11] Byrhtferth's original text had no annal-entry for the period 802 to 849. In order to fill this chronological gap, the later (Durham) scribe C² added three entries at the foot of col. 68*va*, mostly pertaining to the see of Lindisfarne:

Anno .dccciii. Hibaldus episcopus obiit, et Egbertus ei successit.

Anno .dcccxxx. Celnodus consecratus est episcopus, et Felgildus abbas obiit, et Egredus episcopus factus est.

Anno .dcccxlvi. Eanbertus episcopatum suscepit.

PARS QVARTA 123

kingdoms to his rule. He reigned for thirty-six years. And Æthelwulf, his mighty son, succeeded Ecgberht; his son Æthelbald succeeded him [Æthelwulf]; then his brother Æthelberht; after him his brother Æthelred; after him their brother Alfred.[9] And so Æthelwulf had by his noble wife four sons,[10] namely Æthelbald and Æthelberht and Æthelred and Alfred, who all succeeded to the kingdom in turn.[11]

3. In 849, a light arose from the shadows: Alfred, king of the English, was born on the royal estate which is called Wantage by the English. His genealogy is threaded together in this way: King Alfred was the son of King Æthelwulf, the son of Ecgberht, the son of Ealhmund, the son of Eafa, the son of Eoppa, the son of Ingild. Ingild and Ine were brothers. Ine was a most famous king throughout all the territories of the English people; he ruled the realm of the western kingdom royally, and having spent many years on the throne he went to Rome, abandoning his fatherland and temporal kingdom so that he might possess that eternal [kingdom], which the command of the divine majesty granted to him. These were the sons of Coenred, the son of Ceolwold, the son of Cutha, the son of Cuthwine, the son of Ceawlin, the son of Cynric, the son of Creoda, the son of Cerdic, the son of Elesa, the son of Gewis, from whom the Britons name the whole of that race 'Gewisse', the son of Brand, the son of Bældæg, the son of Woden, the son of Frithuwald, the son of Frealaf, the son of Frithuwulf, the son of Geat, whom the pagans worshipped for a long time as a god.[12] The distinguished poet Sedulius mentions him in his poem *Carmen paschale*, speaking as follows:

For the first of these entries, cf. *ASC* D(E), s.a. 803: 'In this year Hygbald, bishop of Lindisfarne, died on 25 May, and Egbert was consecrated in his place on 11 June' (trans. Whitelock, p. 39). For the second, cf. *ASC*, s.a. 833 (for 830): 'In this year Ceolnoth was elected bishop and consecrated, and Abbot Feologild died' (trans. Whitelock, p. 41). Feologild was briefly archbishop of Canterbury in 832 (elected 25 April, consecrated 9 June, died 30 August); it is not known where he was abbot before his election to Canterbury. Ceolnoth was elected to Canterbury on 29 June 833, consecrated 27 August, and died in 870; see Keynes, 'Bishops', p. 543. Ecgred became bishop of Lindisfarne in 830 and died in 845 (Keynes, ibid. p. 565). Eanberht succeeded Ecgred as bishop of Lindisfarne in 845, and died in 854: Keynes, 'Bishops', p. 565.

[12] Byrhtferth has supplied the first sentence of this paragraph ('Anno dominicae...lumen e tenebris') by way of introducing the life of King Alfred; otherwise the genealogical information is taken nearly verbatim from Asser, *Vita Ælfredi*, c. 1 (ed. Stevenson, pp. 1–2; trans. Keynes and Lapidge, p. 67), save that the sentence describing King Ine (*Ine rex famosissimus...maiestatis imperium*) is Byrhtferth's addition, with a characteristic example of Byrhtferthian polyptoton, that is, wordplay based on distinct but etymologically related forms of a word (*regionum regna regaliter regebat*); on Byrhtferth's delight in polyptoton, see *Byrhtferth: Lives*, ed. Lapidge, pp. lix–lx, and Introduction, above, pp. xxxvii–xxxviii. Byrhtferth will have known of King Ine's pilgrimage to Rome from Bede, *HE* v. 7. 3.

124   HISTORIA REGVM

Cum sua Gentiles studeant figmenta poetae
grandisonis pompare modis tragicoque boatu
ridiculoue Getae seu qualibet arte canendi,[13] etc.

Qui Geta fuit Cetuua, qui fuit Beauu, qui fuit Selduua, qui fuit Heremod,
qui fuit Itermod, qui fuit Hatra, qui fuit Vuala, qui fuit Beduuig, qui fuit
Sem, qui fuit Noe, qui fuit Lamech, qui fuit Matusalem, qui fuit Enoch,
qui fuit Malaleel, qui fuit Canaan, qui fuit Enos, qui fuit Seth, qui fuit
Adam primi hominis.[14]

fo. 69rb   Mater uero regis Ælfredi Osburg appellata est, quae erat religiosa
nimium femina nobilisque ingenio, quam nobilitatem exornauit pru-
dentia mentis. Erat quoque pater eius Oslac uocitatus, qui fuit pin-
cerna Ætheluulfi regis deuotus atque fidelissimus. Ortus enim fuit de
Gothis et Iutis, de semine <scilicet>^c Stuf et Vuihtgar, duorum
fratrum.[15] His sic praelibatis iam pro posse, suspectum exsequamur
negotium suscepti operis.

Anno Dominicae incarnationis .dcccli., natiuitatis Ælfredi tertio,
Ceorl <Domnaniae>^d comes pugnauit contra Danos, et Christiani uictoriam de inimicis adepti sunt. Dani quoque hiemauerunt in insula
quae uocatur Scepige, id est, 'insula ouium'.[16] Eodem anno magnus
exercitus paganorum uenit cum trecentis quinquaginta nauibus in
ostium Tamensis fluminis. Qui Doroberniam, id est, Cantuariorum
ciuitatem, depopulati sunt, et Berhtuulfum Merciorum regem cum
omni exercitu suo, qui ad proeliandum contra illos uenerat, in
fugam uerterunt.[17] Post haec audaciores Dani effecti; exercitus omnis
ipsorum ad Suthrige est congregatus. Quod audiens bellipotens
Ætheluulfus rex <Occidentalium>^e Saxonum, congregauit et ipse
exercitum copiosum, et filius suus Æthelbaldus cum eo in loco qui
dicitur Aclea, id est, 'in campo quercus'. Cumque decus Angligenae
gentis armis splendesceret resultantibus, diutissime pugnauerunt

---

^c *suppl. ed. (from Asser)*   ^d *suppl. ed. (from Asser)*   ^e *suppl. ed.*

[13] The mention of *Geta* (OE *Geat*) in the regnal list reminded Asser of the mention of
Geta by Caelius Sedulius, *Carmen paschale* i. 17–19 (CSEL x. 16), and Byrhtferth repeated
(but abbreviated) Asser's quotation. The Geta mentioned by Sedulius was a character in
the Roman comedies of Terence, and has nothing whatsoever to do with the Anglo-Saxon
ancestor Geat.

[14] Byrhtferth's verbatim quotation of Asser, *Vita Ælfredi*, c. 2 (ed. Stevenson, pp. 3–4;
trans. Keynes and Lapidge, p. 67) continues; the final words *primi hominis* are Byrhtferth's
addition, and he has managed to mangle a number of the names in the regnal list; see discussion in Keynes and Lapidge, *Alfred the Great*, pp. 228–9, n. 4.

[15] The words *Mater…duorum fratrum* are quoted from Asser, *Vita Ælfredi*, c. 2 (ed.
Stevenson, p. 4; trans. Keynes and Lapidge, p. 68), with some embellishment (for Asser's

PARS QVARTA 125

Since the pagan poets seek in their fictions
to swagger either in high-flowing measure, or in the wailing of
tragedy's speech,
or with comedy's absurd Geta, or by means of any sort of verse
whatever,[13] etc.

Geat was the son of Tætwa, the son of Beaw, the son of Sceldwa, the
son of Heremod, the son of Itermon, the son of Hathra, the son of
Hwala, the son of Bedwig, the son of Sem, the son of Noah, the son of
Lamech, the son of Mathusalah, the son of Enoch, the son of Malaleel,
the son of Canaan, the son of Enos, the son of Seth, the son of Adam
the first man.[14]

Now the mother of King Alfred was called Osburh, a most religious
woman and noble by birth, whose mental intelligence adorned her
nobility. Her father was named Oslac; he was the devoted and faithful
butler of King Æthelwulf. Oslac was sprung from the Goths and Jutes,
from the line, that is, of Stuf and Wihtgar, two brothers.[15] Having
explained these things to the best of my ability, let us follow the business
of the work at hand.

In the year of our Lord 851, the third of Alfred's life, Ceorl, ealdorman of Devon, fought against the Danes, and the Christians achieved
victory over their enemies. The Danes also wintered on the Isle of
Sheppey, that is, the 'island of sheep'.[16] In the same year a great Viking
army, with three hundred and fifty ships, arrived in the mouth of the
river Thames. They ravaged Canterbury, that is, the city of the Kentish
people, and put to flight Berhtwulf, king of the Mercians, with all his
army who had come to do battle against them.[17] After these [events] the
Danes became bolder; their entire army mustered in Surrey. Hearing
of this, the warlike king of the West Saxons, Æthelwulf, himself assembled a large army, and his son Æthelbald with him, in the place called
Aclea, that is, the 'field of the oak'. And when the glory of the English
people stood there gleaming with their bristling weapons, the English
fought at length with the Danes, fighting valiantly because they saw

---

simple *nobilis et genere* Byrhtferth has pompously written *quam nobilitatem exornauit prudentia mentis*).

[16] The words *Anno Dominicae incarnationis .dcccli. . . . 'insula ouium'* are quoted from Asser,
Vita Ælfredi, c. 3 (ed. Stevenson, pp. 4–5; trans. Keynes and Lapidge, p. 68), with some
Byrhtferthian rewording (e.g. Asser's words *victoriam habuerunt* have been replaced by
Byrhtferth's *uictoriam de inimicis adepti sunt*).

[17] The words *Eodem anno . . . in fugam uerterunt* are quoted from Asser, *Vita Ælfredi*, c. 4
(ed. Stevenson, p. 5; trans. Keynes and Lapidge, p. 68).

126 HISTORIA REGVM

Angli cum Danis, fortiter repugnantes quia uiderunt atrociter regem bellare ipsorum; ideo fortiores hostibus facti sunt in bello. Cumque diutissime uiriliter decertarent, et acerrime animoseque ex utraque parte pugnatum esset, maxima pars paganae multitudinis funditus deleta atque occisa est, ita ut numquam in aliqua regione in una die ante nec post tanti occubuerunt in | morte. Christiani uero ipso die uictoriam honorifice tenuerunt, et loco funeris dominati sunt, grates reddentes Domino in hymnis et confessionibus.[18]

fo. 69va

4. Anno Dominicae incarnationis .dccclii. Æthelstanus rex et Alchhere comes magnum paganorum exercitum inuenerunt in Cantia, in loco qui dicitur Æt Sandwic, quem ibidem Deo auxilium concedente prope occiderunt, et ex nauibus eorum nouem rapuerunt, ceteri per fugam terrore perculsi fugerunt.[19]

Anno Dominicae incarnationis .dcccliii., natiuitatis Ælfredi quinto, Burhred Merciorum rex per nuntios deprecatus est Ætheluulfum Occidentalium Saxonum regem ut ei auxilium conferret, quo mediterraneos Brittones, qui inter Merciam et mare occidentale habitabant, dominio suo subdere posset, qui contra eum frequenter reluctabantur. Rex autem Ætheluulf legatione eius accepta exercitum mouit, stipendia[a] distribuit, cum Burhredo rege intrepidus ad bellum exiit. Mox ut ingressus est ad gentem illam deuastandam, cepit occidit subdiditque regi Burhredo, qui gratias agens dimisit eum cum gaudio ad propria remeare.[20]

Eodem anno Ætheluulfus rex filium suum Ælfredum cum magno nobilium militum agmine constipatum Romam transmisit. Quo tempore beatus papa Leo apostolicae sedi praeerat; qui praefatum infantem ordinans unxit in regem, et in filium adoptionis sibimet accipiens confirmauit, et ad patriam atque ad patrem cum benedictione sancti Petri apostoli direxit.[21]

Ea tempestate Alchhere comes et Vuada cum Cantuariis et Suthrigiis contra paganorum exercitum duriter pugnauit in insula quae Saxonica

---

iv.4 [a] *over* stipendia *C adds* uel spolia

[18] This passage (*Post haec audaciores...hymnis et confessionibus*) has been adapted from Asser, *Vita Ælfredi*, c. 5 (ed. Stevenson, pp. 5–6; trans. Keynes and Lapidge, p. 68), with some additions by Byrhtferth (the introductory clause *Post haec audaciores Dani effecti*; the clause *fortiter repugnantes...uiriliter decertarent*; and the final clause *grates reddentes... confessionibus*).

[19] The wording *Anno Dominicae...fugerunt* has been taken from Asser, *Vita Ælfredi*, c. 6 (ed. Stevenson, p. 6; trans. Keynes and Lapidge, p. 69), with some Byrhtferthian additions

PARS QVARTA   127

their king fighting ferociously; for that reason they became stronger than their enemies in battle. And when they had fought fiercely and vigorously on both sides for a long time, a great part of the Viking horde was utterly destroyed and killed, so much so that never on one day, before or since, in any place, did so many men succumb to death. The Christians honourably gained the victory and were masters of the battlefield, giving thanks to the Lord in their hymns and confessions.[18]

4. In the year of the Lord 852, King Æthelstan and Ealdorman Alchhere came upon a great army of Vikings in Kent, in the place called Sandwich; with God granting assistance they nearly slaughtered them, and they carried off nine of their ships, and the remainder, struck with fear, got away in flight.[19]

In the year of the Lord 853, the fifth of Alfred's life, Burgred, king of the Mercians, sent messengers to Æthelwulf, king of the West Saxons, asking him for help, so that he could subject to his authority the inland Welsh, who were living between Mercia and the western sea, and who were continually struggling against him. After receiving this legation King Æthelwulf mounted an army, distributed rations, and went fearlessly into battle with King Burgred. As soon as he entered [Wales] in order to destroy that race, he seized, killed, and subjected it to King Burgred; who, giving thanks, joyously allowed him to return home.[20]

In that same year King Æthelwulf sent his son Alfred, surrounded by a great retinue of noble soldiers, to Rome. At that time the blessed Pope Leo was ruling the apostolic see; he anointed the aforesaid child as king, and confirmed him as his adoptive son, and sent him back to his homeland and his father with the blessing of the apostle St Peter.[21]

At that time Ealdorman Ealhhere and Wada, together with the men of Kent and Surrey, fought stoutly against the Viking army on the

---

(e.g. the words *terrore perculsi*); and note that Byrhtferth has assigned this event to 852, whereas in Asser it is assigned to the same year (*eodem quoque anno*) as the previous event, namely 851. The event is similarly assigned to 851 in *ASC* (Asser's source): trans. Whitelock, p. 43.

[20] This paragraph has been taken nearly verbatim from Asser, *Vita Ælfredi*, c. 7 (ed. Stevenson, pp. 6–7; trans. Keynes and Lapidge, p. 69).

[21] This paragraph has been taken from Asser, *Vita Ælfredi*, c. 8 (ed. Stevenson, p. 7; trans. Keynes and Lapidge, p. 69), save that the words *et ad patriam... Petri apostoli direxit* are Byrhtferth's addition.

128 HISTORIA REGVM

lingua Tened dicitur, Britannico sermone Ruim appellatur. Primitus Christiani uictoriam habuerunt, sed prolongato diu proelio ex utraque fo. 69ᵛᵇ parte, plurimi corruerunt, multique | in flumine suffocati sunt et occisi, inedicibilis multitudo! Duces uero praedicti ambo ibidem occubuerunt pro gentis suae liberatione. Ætheluulfus rex gloriosae potestatis ipso anno, post festiuitatem sanctae resurrectionis Christi, filiam suam Burhredo regi Merciorum tradidit cum magna gloria, ut regibus mos est, in uilla quae dicitur Æt Cippanhama; quo nuptiis peractis reginae praecepit nominis dignitatem.[22]

Anno Dominicae incarnationis .dcccliiii. Vulfhere archiepiscopus pallium suscepit, et Earduulf suscepit episcopatum Lindisfarnensem.[23]

5. Anno .dccclv., natiuitatis praephati regis septimo, paganorum exercitus tota hieme in insula Scepige hiemauerunt.[24] Quo tempore Ætheluulfus rex decimauit totum regni sui imperium pro redemptione animae suae et antecessorum suorum. Ipso uero anno cum magno honore ad limina principis apostolorum profectus est, habens secum Ælfredum, eo quod illum magis diligeret quam ceteros. Susceptus est rex Anglorum ab apostolico uiro decenter, quo moratus est anno integro, orationibus et elemosinis insistens diligenter.[25] Eo quoque ad patriam reuertente, filio suo Æthelbaldo et Scirburnensi Ealhstano episcopo et plurimis aliis perosus erat.[26] Vixit ergo Ætheluulfus rex clementissimus annis duobus postquam Romuleas adire sedes coepit. Qui inter alia praesentis uitae bona et studia regalis operis, de suo transitu praemeditatus est, ne filii sui post obitum suae uitae disceptarent, epistolam satis eleganti compositione composuit, quae omnia quae sui iuris erant distribuit. Per omnem haereditatem suae terrae semper in decem manentibus*a* unum pauperem aut indigenam uel peregrinum cibo et potu siue uestimento iussit adiuuari uel pasci pro se et pro omnibus successoribus suis. Romam quoque pro redemptione animae

---

iv.5 *a* corr. ed. (from Asser), mansis C

---

[22] This paragraph has been taken from Asser, Vita Ælfredi, c. 9 (ed. Stevenson, pp. 7–8; trans. Keynes and Lapidge, p. 69), with some characteristic Byrhtferthian additions such as the phrase inedicibilis multitudo (on Byrhtferth's use, indeed abuse, of the adjective inedicibilis, see Byrhtferth: Lives, ed. Lapidge, p. xlvii, and Introduction, above, p. xxv).

[23] The receipt of the pallium by Wulfhere, archbishop of York (854–92 or 900), and the election of Eardwulf to the see of Lindisfarne in 854 are not recorded in either Asser or ASC, and are known only from this present passage in Byrhtferth; see Keynes, 'Bishops', pp. 562, 565.

[24] This sentence has been taken from Asser, Vita Ælfredi, c. 10 (ed. Stevenson, p. 8; trans. Keynes and Lapidge, p. 69).

PARS QVARTA 129

island which in the Saxon tongue is called Thanet, but in Welsh is called *Ruim*. Initially the Christians had the victory; but as the battle was prolonged on both sides, many fell, and many were drowned and killed in the river—an indescribable multitude! The aforementioned ealdormen both died for the liberation of their people. In the same year, after the feast of the resurrection of Christ [Easter], Æthelwulf, the king of glorious authority, gave his daughter to Burgred, king of the Mercians, with great ceremony, as is the custom with kings, on the [royal] estate called Chippenham; when the ceremony was concluded, she assumed the distinction of the name of queen.[22]

In the year of the Lord's incarnation 854, Archbishop Wulfhere received the pallium, and Eardwulf succeeded to the bishopric of Lindisfarne.[23]

5. In 855, the seventh of the aforesaid king's life, the Viking army stayed for the entire winter on the Isle of Sheppey.[24] At this time King Æthelwulf freed the tenth part of his whole kingdom [from every royal tribute] for the redemption of his soul and those of his predecessors. In the same year he travelled in great state to the threshold of the prince of the apostles [St Peter's, Rome], having with him Alfred, because he loved him more than his other [sons]. The king of the English was honourably received by the pope; he remained there for an entire year, devoutly occupied in prayers and alms-giving.[25] When he returned from there to his homeland, he was greatly detested by his son Æthelbald and by Ealhstan, bishop of Sherborne, and by a number of others.[26] This merciful King Æthelwulf lived for two years after he set out for the Roman see. Amidst the bounties of this present life and his concerns over royal business, he reflected on his own passing, [and] so that after the ending of his life his sons should not squabble among themselves, he composed a letter in fairly elegant style, which distributed all the possessions which were in his jurisdiction. He ordered that for every ten hides throughout all his hereditary land one poor man, whether a native or foreigner, should be assisted or nourished with food and drink or clothing on his own behalf and that of his successors. He ordered that three hundred mancuses should be taken to Rome for

---

[25] The words *Quo tempore Ætheluulfus... insistens diligenter* have been adapted from Asser, *Vita Ælfredi*, c. 11 (ed. Stevenson, pp. 8–9; trans. Keynes and Lapidge, pp. 69–70), with some Byrhtferthian additions (e.g. the words *orationibus et elemosinis insistens diligenter*).

[26] The words *Eo quoque ad patriam reuertente... perosus erat* have been abbreviated from Asser, *Vita Ælfredi*, c. 12 (ed. Stevenson, pp. 9–10; trans. Keynes and Lapidge, p. 70).

HISTORIA REGVM

130

fo. 70ʳᵃ suae trecentas mancusas*b* portari praecepit: centum | ad limina sancti Petri, specialiter ad emendum oleum, et centum ad honorem sancti Pauli, centum uniuersali papae apostolico.[27]

Defuncto igitur Ætheluulfo rege glorioso, filius eius Æthelbald contra Iesu Christi interdictum et Christianorum traditionem, ac contra omnium paganorum consuetudinem, thorum patris sui ascendens, Iuditham Caroli Francorum regis filiam cum magna infamia in matrimonium duxit, effrenisque duobus et dimidio annis Occidentalium Saxonum post nobilissimi patris sui obitum imperii gubernacula rexit.[28]

Anno .dccclx., natiuitatis Ælfredi clitonis insignis duodecimo, Æthelbald defunctus est atque in Scireburna sepultus. Quo ablato e saeculo, Æthelbyrht ipsius frater has prouincias suo regno adiunxit, hoc est, Cantiam et Suthrigam, Suthsexam quoque cum omnibus uillis et territoriis, ut iustum erat. In ipsius quoque regni statu magnus paganorum exercitus de mari adueniens, Vuintoniam ciuitatem hostiliter inuadens depopulatus est. Exercitus uero praedictus cum reuerteretur cum ingenti praeda ad naues, Osric dignissimus dux Hamtunensium cum suis populis aduenit, et Ætheluulf comes insignis cum Bearrocensibus uiriliter occurrit cum inmenso exercitu, consertoque proelio pagani passim trucidantur ab Anglis, suffultis a spiritibus angelicis. Cumque diutius hostes dirissimi stare nequirent prae uulneribus, cadebat crudeliter perplurima multitudo—alii per latibula densarum ueprium se abdentes,*c* nonnulli muliebriter fugam arripientes.*d* Angli uero loco funeris fortuna arridente[29] dominati sunt.[30] Æthelbyrht itaque rex quinque annis regnum sibi commissum pacifice et amabiliter

fo. 70ʳᵇ atque honorabiliter | gubernauit, qui cum magno suorum principum, episcoporum, omniumque populorum dolore uiam uniuersitatis adiit; relinquens terreni regni monarchiam, alterius coepit esse particeps.

---

b in left-hand margin C¹ notes mancusa continet .xxx. denarios   *c* addentes C
d arripentes C

---

[27] The words *Vixit ergo Ætheluulfus...papae apostolico*, containing the description of King Æthelwulf's testamentary deposition and his scheme of taxation to provide what subsequently came to be called 'Peter's Pence', is adapted from Asser, *Vita Ælfredi*, c. 16 (ed. Stevenson, pp. 14–16; trans. Keynes and Lapidge, pp. 72–3, with n. 37), with the insertion of certain distinctively Byrhtferthian phrases, such as *Romuleas...sedes* (cf. Lapidge, 'The early sections', p. 104 = *ALL* ii. 324, and Introduction, above, p. xxxi), and the polysyllabic superlative *clementissimus*.

[28] This paragraph is taken nearly verbatim from Asser, *Vita Ælfredi*, c. 17 (ed. Stevenson, p. 16; trans. Keynes and Lapidge, p. 73).

PARS QVARTA 131

the redemption of his soul: one hundred for the church of St Peter, especially for the purchase of holy oil; and one hundred in honour of St Paul; [and] one hundred for the universal apostolic pope.[27]

When the glorious King Æthelwulf was dead, his son Æthelbald, against the prohibition of Jesus Christ and Christian dignity, and [even] contrary to the practice of pagans, climbed into his father's bed and in great disgrace married Judith, the daughter of Charles [the Bald], king of the Franks; and for two and a half lawless years after the death of his noble father he controlled the government of the kingdom of the West Saxons.[28]

In 860, the twelfth year of the distinguished prince Alfred's life, Æthelbald died, and was buried in Sherborne. When he had been removed from this world, his brother Æthelberht annexed the following areas to his realm, that is, Kent and Surrey and Sussex, together with all their estates and territories—as was only right. During his tenure of the kingdom a great army of Vikings, arriving from the sea, aggressively attacked and laid waste the city of Winchester. When this aforesaid army was returning to the ships with immense booty, Osric, the worthy ealdorman of Hampshire, came there, together with his people, and Æthelwulf, the distinguished ealdorman, with the men of Berkshire, an immense army, courageously opposed [them]; when battle was joined, the Vikings were killed on all sides by the English, [who were] sustained by angelic spirits. And when the savage enemies could no longer stand on their feet because of their wounds, a mighty multitude fell cruelly to the ground—some of them hiding themselves in the recesses of dense brambles, some taking to flight like women. With fortune smiling on them,[29] the English were masters of the battlefield.[30] And so Æthelberht governed the kingdom entrusted to him peacefully, in a kindly and honourable fashion, for five years; then he went the way of all flesh, accompanied by the great lamentation of all his ealdormen, bishops, and people. Abandoning the monarchy of his earthly realm, he began to be a member of the other [realm]. He was buried next to his

---

[29] The phrase *fortuna arridente* (derived ultimately from Juvenal, *Sat.* vi. 605–6: 'stat Fortuna improba noctu / arridens') is used frequently by Byrhtferth: see *VSO* i. 2, v. 11 and *VSE* iii. 3 (*Byrhtferth: Lives*, ed. Lapidge, pp. 14 with n. 36, 172, and 258 respectively), and below, *HR* iv. 11.

[30] The words *Anno .dccclx....dominati sunt* are from Asser, *Vita Ælfredi*, c. 18 (ed. Stevenson, pp. 17–18; trans. Keynes and Lapidge, pp. 73–4), with various Byrhtferthian additions, such as the phrase *fortuna arridente*, discussed in the previous note.

132   HISTORIA REGVM

Sepultus est igitur iuxta fratrem suum in Scireburnam, quo exspectat consolationem futurae resurrectionis.[31]

6. Anno .dccclxiv. pagani hiemauerunt in insula quae appellatur Tened, quae circumdatur undique maris flumine. Qui firmum cum Cantuariis pepigerunt foedus, quibus Cantuarii pecuniam pro foedere seruato reddere promiserunt. Interea tamen Dani uulpino more noctu clam castris erumpentes, foedereque dirupto, et promissionem pecuniae spernentes, paucis diebus extiterunt quieti. Sed (o nefas!) totam orientalem plagam Cantiae gentis depopulati sunt. Sciebant maiorem pecuniam se furtiua praeda quam pace adepturos, quod et factum est.[32]

Sequenti uero anno, hoc est .dccclxvi., natiuitatis autem Ælfredi decimo octauo, Æthelred frater Æthelbyrti regis Occidentalium Saxonum regni gubernacula suscepit. Eodem anno magna paganorum classis de Danubia[a] Britanniae fines introiit, et sic ad regnum Orientalium Anglorum, quod Saxonico dicitur eloquio Eastengle, hiemauit, ibique ipse copiosus exercitus equestris factus est, equitantes et discurrentes hac illac, praedam diripientes enormem, non parcentes uiris uel feminis uel uiduis nec uirginibus.[33]

His diebus Ælfredus clito iugi meditatione coepit diuinis imbui doctrinis, qui miro[b] patris matrisque amore supra omnes fratres suos ab ipsis diligebatur cunabulis. Crescente denique illo corpore in puerili aetate, forma ceteris suis fratribus decentior uidebatur, uultuque insignis renitebat et uerbis refulsit egregiis. Ceruino quoque desiderio fo. 70va aestuabat[34] | sui cordis penetralia suffundi, et thalamum pectoris sacris litteris imbui. Sed (pro dolor!) parentum ac nutritorum incuria illiteratus permansit usque ad duodecimum suae aetatis annum. Saxonica quoque poemata gloriosus adolescens et futurus rex die noctuque discere studuit; eratque docilis, in arte uenatoria industrius, in omni peritia incomparabilis.[35] Cum ergo quadam die eius dignissima genetrix,

---

iv.6   [a] *C¹ adds* ducibus *in marg., followed by several words which have been erased*   [b] *C¹* (*on an erasure*)

---

[31] The words *Æthelberht itaque rex...futurae resurrectionis* have been taken from Asser, *Vita Ælfredi*, c. 19 (ed. Stevenson, p. 18; trans. Keynes and Lapidge, p. 74), with some Byrhtferthian embellishment, such as the words *quo exspectat consolationem futurae resurrectionis*.

[32] This paragraph has been taken nearly verbatim from Asser, *Vita Ælfredi*, c. 20 (ed. Stevenson, p. 18; trans. Keynes and Lapidge, p. 74), with some rearrangement of clauses, and the addition of the interjection *o nefas*.

[33] This paragraph has been adapted from Asser, *Vita Ælfredi*, c. 21 (ed. Stevenson, pp. 18–19; trans. Keynes and Lapidge, p. 74); but to Asser's brief explanation that the pagan army thereupon took to horseback (*equester factus est*) Byrhtferth has added the verbose

PARS QVARTA 133

brother in Sherborne, where he awaits the consolation of the future resurrection.[31]

6. In 864 the Vikings wintered on the island called Thanet, which is surrounded on all sides by the flow of the sea. They concluded a firm treaty with the men of Kent; the men of Kent undertook to give them money to ensure that the treaty was kept. Meanwhile, however, the Danes, secretly breaking out of their camp by night like stealthy foxes, broke the treaty and, spurning the promise of money, remained quiet for a few days. But—O the disgrace of it!—they laid waste the entire eastern district of Kent. They knew they could get more money from stolen booty than from peace; which was indeed the case.[32]

In the following year, that is 866, the eighteenth year of Alfred's life, Æthelred, the brother of King Æthelberht, took over the government of the kingdom of the West Saxons. In the same year a great Viking fleet from the Danube entered the territory of Britain, and thence wintered in the kingdom of the East Angles, which in Saxon speech is called 'Eastengle'; and there an abundant force of cavalry was assembled, with them riding and chasing here and there, snatching an enormous amount of booty, nor sparing men or women or widows or virgins.[33]

In these days Prince Alfred began with continual meditation to be instructed in divine learning: he was loved with the intense love of his father and mother, more than all his brothers, from the very cradle. As he grew in bodily stature during childhood, he was seen to be more attractive in appearance that the rest of his brothers; his shining face revealed him as someone special, and he gleamed with his outstanding speech. He burned with hart-like desire[34] to have the inner recesses of his heart and the secret chamber of his breast flooded and instructed with sacred letters. But (alas!) through the neglect of his parents and guardians he remained ignorant of letters until the twelfth year of his life. The glorious young man and future king applied himself by day and night to learn Old English poems; and he was teachable, energetic in the pursuit of hunting, incomparable in every skill.[35] When one day his worthy mother was showing him and his brothers a certain English

---

explanation that they rode everywhere (*equitantes et discurrentes hac illac*), plundering the region and not sparing men or women or widows or virgins.

[34] Cf. Ps. 41 (42): 2 ('quemadmodum desiderat cervus ad fontes aquarum, ita desiderat anima mea ad te Deus').

[35] The words *His diebus Ælfredus clito...peritia incomparabilis* have been adapted by Byrhtferth from Asser, *Vita Ælfredi*, c. 22 (ed. Stevenson, pp. 19–20; trans. Keynes and Lapidge, pp. 74–5), with much verbal embellishment.

134 HISTORIA REGVM

sibi et fratribus suis quendam Saxonicum poematicae artis librum ostenderet, ait eis: 'Quisquis, carissimi filii, uestrum istum potuerit codicem citius discere, dabo ei ipsum.' At ille, diuina inspiratione instinctus, et pulchritudine principalis litterae exhilaratus, ita matri respondit, 'Verene', sic ait matri suae, 'dabis?' Ad haec illa arridens et gaudens atque affirmans, 'Dabo', inquit, 'dabo'. Mox autem tulit librum de manu suae genitricis, magistrum adiit, libellum ostendit, et legit praeceptore ostendente. Post spatium non longi temporis uenit ante praesentiam dilectae matris, librumque memoriter recitauit.[36] Ipsa uero grates immensas reddit saluatori[c] gratiae, agnoscens gratiam Dei esse in mente iuuenis.[37] Post haec, inflammatus diuini amoris desiderio, psalmos perplurimos cursumque diurnum, id est, celebrationes horarum, didicit ipse deuotus, quos in uno uolumine congregatos die noctuque in sinu suo inseparabiliter portabat.[38] O felix hominum genus! O rex prudens! gestas gestantem sapientiae claues uehis; sapientiam diligis, sapiens eris, faciens iudicium et iustitiam in terris. O clerici, attendite et uidete regem in sinu librum deferre die noctuque; uos uero nec legem Dei scitis nec scire uultis. Praecipue idem, rex factus, lugebat filium suum, id est animum, quod liberalibus non fuerat[d] artibus instructus.[39]

fo. 70vb   7. Anno .dccclxvii., natiuitatis Ælfredi regis undeuicesimo, praedictus paganorum exercitus de Orientalibus Anglis ad Eboracam ciuitatem migrauit, quae in aquilonali ripa Humbrensis fluminis sita est.[40] Eodem tempore maxima inter Northanhymbrorum populos discordia erat succensa, et apte, quia qui odium diligit odium inueniet.[41] His diebus Northanhymbrorum gens legitimum suae gentis regem, Osbyrht uocitatum onomate, de regno hostiliter expulerunt, et tyrannum quendam nomine Ælla super apicem regni constituerunt. Venientibus super regnum paganis, consilio diuino et optimatum

---

  [c] saluatoris C   [d] C[1] adds uel -rit *(i.e.* fuerit*)*

[36] The words *Cum ergo quadam die...memoriter recitauit* have been taken from Asser, *Vita Ælfredi*, c. 23 (ed. Stevenson, p. 20; trans. Keynes and Lapidge, p. 75), with some minor additions (such as the adverb *memoriter*).

[37] These words (*Ipsa uero...mente iuuenis*) are an addition by Byrhtferth, and have been influenced by Aldhelm, prose *De uirginitate*, c. 1: 'immensas Christo...impendere grates curaui' (MGH, *AA* xv. 229), a work with which Byrhtferth was intimately familiar (see Lapidge, *The Anglo-Saxon Library*, p. 267, and Introduction, above, p. lxxi).

[38] The words *Post haec...portabat* have been adapted from Asser, *Vita Ælfredi*, c. 24 (ed. Stevenson, p. 21; trans. Keynes and Lapidge, p. 75).

[39] The final sentences of this paragraph, including the apostrophes to the king's wisdom and the characteristic Byrhtferthian polyptoton (*gestas gestantem*) are Byrhtferth's addition to

PARS QVARTA

135

book of verse, she said to them: 'Whichever of you, my dear sons, can most quickly learn this book [by heart], I shall give it to him.' And Alfred, touched by divine inspiration and excited by the beauty of the book's opening letter, replied to his mother: 'Will you truly', he said to his mother, 'give it?' To this [question] she said, smiling and rejoicing and confirming: 'I will give it', she said, 'I will give it.' He immediately took the book from the hand of his mother, went to his teacher, showed him the little book, and read it with his teacher showing him how. After the passage of no great length of time, he came into the presence of his beloved mother, and recited the book to her from memory.[36] She gave mighty thanks to the Saviour of Grace, recognizing that the grace of God was present in the mind of the young man.[37] After this, enflamed by desire for divine love, he devotedly learned a good number of psalms and the daily *cursus*, that is, the liturgical celebration of the Hours, which, collected in one book, he carried around continually by day and night in his bosom.[38] O the blessed race of men! O what a wise king!— you convey one bearing the cherished keys of wisdom! You love wisdom: you shall be wise, passing judgement, and doing justice on earth. O you clerics, pay attention and watch the king carrying a book in his bosom by day and night—but you neither know, nor wish to know, the law of God. This man, once made king, particularly mourned for his son, that is, his soul, because he had not been instructed in the liberal arts.[39]

7. In 867, the nineteenth year of the life of King Alfred, the aforesaid Viking army went from East Anglia to the city of York, which is situated on the northern bank of the river Humber.[40] At that time a great dispute had been kindled among the peoples of Northumbria, and appropriately, since whoever loves hatred will find hatred.[41] In these days the Northumbrian people had viciously expelled the legitimate king of that nation, Osberht by name, and had installed at the kingdom's summit a tyrant named Ælle. With the pagans arriving in the kingdom, the dispute had been calmed down, by divine providence

Asser's narrative, as is his outburst against the laziness of clerics (*O clerici, attendite...*), which is very much in the spirit of his recurrent outbursts against the laziness of clerics in his *Enchiridion*: cf. i. 3, lines 2–5, i. 4, lines 3–6, iv. 2, lines 10–13 (ed. Baker and Lapidge, pp. 46, 52, 232 respectively), and discussion by Lapidge, 'The early sections', pp. 111–12 = *ALL* ii. 331–2, and Introduction, above, pp. xxxiv–xxxv.

[40] This sentence is taken verbatim from Asser, *Vita Ælfredi*, c. 26 (ed. Stevenson, p. 22; trans. Keynes and Lapidge, p. 76).

[41] Cf. perhaps Ps. 35 (36): 3 ('quoniam dolose egit in conspectu eius ut inveniatur iniquitas eius ad odium').

136 HISTORIA REGVM

adminiculo discordia illa sedata est. Rex uero Osbyrht et Ælla, adunatis uiribus congregatoque exercitu, Eboracum adeunt oppidum. Quibus aduenientibus classica multitudo confestim fugam arripiunt; quorum fugam et pauorem Christiani cernentes, fortiores ipsis inuenti sunt. Pugnatum est satis crudeliter ex utraque parte, quo ambo reges occubuerunt. Reliqui uero, qui euaserunt, pacem cum Danis pepigerunt.[42] Ipso autem anno Ealhstan Scireburnensis ecclesiae episcopus uiam et uitam deseruit temporalis saeculi, postquam episcopatum per annos quinquaginta honorabiliter rexerat, qui in pace ecclesiae requiescit, sepultus decenter in sede sui episcopatus.[43]

Anno .dccclxviii., Ælfredi regis uicesimo, uxorem accepit de Mercia, nobilem scilicet genere, filiam Æthelredi Gainorum comitis, qui cognominabatur ab Anglis Mucel, eo quod erat corpore magnus et prudentia grandaeuus.[44] Ea tempestate praedictus paganorum exercitus Northanhymbros reliquit, Snotingaham pessimo aduentu uisitauit et fo. 71ᵃ adiit; quae ciuitas Britannico sermone Tiguocebauc interpretatur, | Latina interpretatione 'speluncarum domus' dicitur. Quo in loco hospites insidiosi eodem anno hiemauere, quorum aduentus omnibus populis satis erat ingratus. Audiens autem eorum aduentum armipotens rex Merciorum, Burhred appellatus, et omnes optimates, consilium habuit cum suis comitibus et commilitonibus et omni populo sibi subiecto, qualiter inimicos bellica uirtute exsuperaret siue de regno expelleret. Direxit et nuntios ueloci cursu ad Ælfredum insignissimae uirtutis uirum, et ad Æthelredum fratrem eius, ut ei fraternum ostenderent adminiculum, quo possent uictrici fortitudine eos debellare. Quod ipsi quasi intrepidi leones agere non distulerunt.[45] Tunc incitus Ælfredus rapidis coepit praeceptis exercitum congregare, illud corde tenus recordans:

> Numquam diues agit, qui trepidus, gemens,
> sese credit egentem.[46]

Nequaquam potens uir agit quod desiderat, qui trepidus constat, et qui se putat egentem, id est miserum, si agat quod optat uiriliter

---

[42] The words *Eodem tempore ... cum Danis pepigerunt* are taken nearly verbatim from Asser, *Vita Ælfredi*, c. 27 (ed. Stevenson, pp. 22–3; trans. Keynes and Lapidge, p. 76).

[43] This sentence has been taken from Asser, *Vita Ælfredi*, c. 28 (ed. Stevenson, p. 23; trans. Keynes and Lapidge, p. 77), with the substitution of *in sede sui episcopatus* for Asser's *in Scireburnan*.

[44] This sentence has been taken, with drastic abbreviation, from Asser, *Vita Ælfredi*, c. 29 (ed. Stevenson, pp. 23–4; trans. Keynes and Lapidge, p. 77); the gloss on OE *mucel* (*eo quod erat corpore magnus et prudentia grandaeuus*) is Byrhtferth's addition.

PARS QVARTA 137

and with the support of the leading men. But King Osberht and Ælle, having combined their forces and assembled an army, proceed to the city of York. On their arrival, the sea-borne horde [of Vikings] immediately takes to flight; seeing their flight and fear, the Christians were found to be braver. Very cruel fighting took place on either side, in which both kings died. The remainder [of the Northumbrians] who escaped made peace with the Danes.[42] In the same year Ealhstan, bishop of the church of Sherborne, abandoned the way and the life of this temporal world, after he had honourably ruled the bishopric for fifty years; he rests in the peace of the church, buried fittingly in the seat of his bishopric.[43]

In 868, the twentieth year of the life of King Alfred, he took a wife of noble kin from Mercia, the daughter of Æthelred, ealdorman of the *Gaini*, who was nicknamed by the English 'Mucel' [i.e. 'huge'], because he was of large bodily stature and ancient in wisdom.[44] At that time the aforesaid army of Vikings left the Northumbrians and went to Nottingham, [which they] visited with evil attendance; the city is called *Tiguocebauc* in Welsh, or 'house of the caves' in Latin. In this place the deceitful guests wintered that year; their arrival was very unwelcome to all local people. Hearing of their arrival the warlike king of the Mercians, named Burgred, and all his noblemen, took counsel with his ealdormen and thegns and all the people subject to him, as to how he could conquer the enemies by military force, or drive them from the kingdom. And he sent messengers on a swift course to Alfred, a man of outstanding strength, and to Æthelred his brother, asking that they offer him fraternal assistance so that they could conquer them with victorious force. They, like fearless lions, did not hesitate to act.[45] Then Alfred, provoked [to action], began with rapid commands to assemble an army, remembering in the depths of his heart, that

> A rich man never acts who is fearful, mournful,
> believing himself to be in need.[46]

In no way does the powerful man accomplish what he desires who is fearful, and who thinks himself needy, that is wretched, if he is to

---

[45] The words *Ea tempestate...non distulerunt* have been expanded, with much verbal embellishment, from Asser, *Vita Ælfredi*, c. 30 (ed. Stevenson, pp. 24–5; trans. Keynes and Lapidge, p. 77); in particular, the phrase used here of King Burgred, *armipotens rex*, is characteristically Byrhtferthian: see above, *HR* iii. 28, and below, iv. 10, as well as *VSO* iii. 10 and *VSE* iii. 4, with discussion by Lapidge, 'The early sections', p. 104 = *ALL* ii. 324, and Introduction, above, p. xxviii.

[46] Boethius, *De consolatione Philosophiae*, ii, met. ii, lines 19–20 (CCSL xciv. 21).

138 HISTORIA REGVM

decertando. Frater eius simili succensus furore <erat>;ᵃ usque ad Snotingaham perueniunt, parati aduersus temptamina stare. Pagani uero, munitione arcis muniti, bellum promittunt, acies struunt, numerosum exercitum ostendunt, sed tremebundi, claris cernentes uisibus Christianum populum in centenis et millenis⁴⁷ milibus aduersariis resistere, sacris ducibus exhortantibus.⁴⁸ Tandem per gratiam omnipotentis Domini cessauit uentus turbinis, sedata sunt corda iniquorum, pacem rogantes et foedus a Christianis, acsi ipsi tali propitio Christo mente exorarent.

> Rapidos, rector, comprime fluctus,
> et quo caelum regis immensum,
> firma stabiles foedere terras.⁴⁹

Facta est inter reges et paganos pax, et segregati ab inuicem, sicut oues ab hedis sequestrantur.⁵⁰

8. Anno .dccclxix., aetatisᵃ uero Ælfredi uicesimo primo, praephatus exercitus rursum ad gentem Northanhymbrorum profectus est, fo. 71ʳᵇ ibique anno integro permansit, | debacchans et insaniens, occidens et perdens perplurimos uiros ac mulieres.⁵¹

Sequenti uero anno, dum solis iubar mundi perlustraret orbes, et annus aduenisset .dccclxx. ab incarnatione Domini, tunc refulsit tempus quo Ælfred rex uicesimum primum habuit annum. Danorum uero enormis multitudo, et, ut ita dicam, legionum cateruae congregatae sunt, ita ut multa uiderentur milia affore, et sicut de mille in uiginti myriadasᵇ excreuissent. Peruenit dehinc per Merciam in Orientales Anglos, et in ciuitate quae dicitur Theodford intrepidus hiemauit.⁵² Rex autem Eadmundus ipsis temporibus regnauit super omnia regna Orientalium Anglorum, uir sanctus et iustus, sicut finis eius sanctissimae uitae probauit euentus. Eodem uero anno rex praedictus

---

iv.7 ᵃ *suppl. ed.*

iv.8 ᵃ *read* natiuitatis (*with Asser*)? ᵇ *Cⁱ adds in marg.* una miriada est .xx. milia

---

⁴⁷ Cf. 2 Kgs (2 Sam.) 18: 4 ('egrediebaturque populus per turmas suas centeni et milleni').

⁴⁸ This sentence (*Pagani uero...exhortantibus*) is Byrhtferth's addition to Asser's narrative, with characteristic Byrhtferthian three-member asyndeton (*bellum promittunt, acies struunt, numerosum exercitum ostendunt*: see *Byrhtferth: Lives*, ed. Lapidge, p. lviii, and Introduction, above, p. xxxviii), preceded by an example of Byrhtferthian polyptoton (*munitione arcis muniti*: ibid. pp. lix–lx).

⁴⁹ Boethius, *De consolatione Philosophiae*, i, met. v, lines 46–8 (CCSL xciv. 12).

⁵⁰ Cf. Matt. 25: 32 ('separabit eos ab invicem sicut pastor segregat oves ab hedis').

PARS QVARTA

139

accomplish what he hopes by fighting manfully. His brother was fired by similar rage; they proceed to Nottingham, ready to stand against the challenges (of battle). But the Vikings, protected by the fortification of the citadel, promise battle, draw up their battle-lines, show off their numerous army, but are fearful, seeing with clear sight the Christians in their hundreds and thousands[47] of thousands opposing them, with their holy leaders urging them on.[48] At length, through the mercy of the omnipotent Lord, the blast of wind dropped, the hearts of the wicked Vikings were soothed into seeking peace and a treaty from the Christians, as if they had themselves prayed to merciful Christ with such an intention.

> Ruler, restrain the rushing waves,
> and with that treaty by which you rule the mighty heavens,
> secure the steadfast earth.[49]

Peace was established between the kings and the Vikings, and they were separated, just as sheep are separated from goats.[50]

8. In 869, the twenty-first year of the life of Alfred, the aforesaid army set out again for the nation of the Northumbrians, and remained there an entire year, raging and rioting, killing and destroying many men and women.[51]

But in the following year, when the brilliance of the sun had illuminated the globe of the world, and the year 870 from the incarnation of the Lord had arrived, then shone the time when King Alfred had his twenty-first year. An enormous multitude of Danes and, so to say, throngs of legions were assembled, so that they seemed to number thousands and thus had grown from a thousand to twenty thousand. It passed thereafter through Mercia into East Anglia, and wintered fearlessly in the city which is called Thetford.[52] King Eadmund at that time ruled over all kingdoms of the East Angles, a saintly and just man, as the events at the end of his holy life proved. In that same year the said king fought fiercely and bravely with his men against the Viking army

---

[51] The first part of the sentence (*Anno .dccclxix....permansit*) is taken nearly verbatim from Asser, *Vita Ælfredi*, c. 31 (ed. Stevenson, p. 25; trans. Keynes and Lapidge, p. 77); the remainder of the sentence (*debacchans...mulieres*) is Byrhtferth's colourful addition.

[52] The first two sentences of this paragraph are taken from Asser, *Vita Ælfredi*, c. 32 (ed. Stevenson, pp. 25–6; trans. Keynes and Lapidge, p. 77); but note that Byrhtferth (or a subsequent scribe) has introduced a chronological error into Asser's date-reckoning: Asser (c. 31) gave 869 as the twenty-first year of Alfred's life, and 870 as the twenty-second (c. 32), whereas in the present text both 869 and 870 are given as Alfred's twenty-first year.

140   HISTORIA REGVM

contra ipsum exercitum atrociter et uiriliter cum suis pugnauit. Sed quia misericors Deus eum praesciuit per martyrii coronam ad caelestis gloriae coronam peruenire, ibidem gloriose occubuit.[53] De cuius passionis honore libet aliqua historiae nostrae inserere,[54] ut sciant et agnoscant filii hominum quam terribilis est Christus Filius Dei in consiliis hominum,[55] et quam glorioso triumpho exornat quos hic passionis titulo excruciat, ut illud impleatur, 'Non coronatur quis nisi legitime certauerit.'[56] Rex autem Eadmundus imperium Orientalium Anglorum suscepit deuotus, quod et tenuit dextra forti potentiae, Deum omnipotentem semper adorans ac glorificans, pro omnibus bonis suis quibus usus fuerat. Eodem anno quo rex et martyr insignis per coronam martyrii supernae felicitatis gaudia subiit, Ceolnoth archiepiscopus Doroberniae ciuitatis uiam ueritatis adiit; qui in eadem ciuitate est sepultus a clericis.[57]

9. Anno Dominicae incarnationis .dccclxxi., natiuitatis Ælfredi gloriosi regis Saxonum | uicesimo secundo, exosae memoriae paganorum exercitus Orientales Anglos deseruit; qui regnum Occidentalium Saxonum adiit, ueniens ad uillam regiam quae dicitur Æt Redingum, in meridianam Tamensis fluminis ripam, in illa plaga quae nuncupatur ab incolis ipsius patriae Bearrocscire. Tertio uero die quo ibi aduenerunt inimici Anglorum, comites eorum cum magna multitudine in parte illius fluminis equitauerunt, praedamque immensae multitudinis acceperunt.[58] Quidam autem ex ipsis uallum inter Tamense et Cynetan flumina facere studuerunt; sed consilium eorum et opus Danorum dissipatum est per auxilium Anglorum, ut impleretur in eis illud scolastici:

fo. 71ᵛᵃ

> Quamuis se Tyrio superbit ostro,
> comet et niueis lapillis,
> inuisus tamen omnibus pollet.[59]

---

[53] This brief mention of King Edmund of East Anglia derives from Asser, *Vita Ælfredi*, c. 33 (ed. Stevenson, p. 26; trans. Keynes and Lapidge, p. 78).

[54] Byrhtferth is evidently referring to the *Passio S. Eadmundi* by Abbo of Fleury (*BHL* 2392; *Three Lives of English Saints*, ed. Winterbottom, pp. 67–87); but in spite of what he says, no excerpts from Abbo's work have been incorporated into the text of his *Historia regum*, which suggests either that Byrhtferth forgot to include them or that they have been omitted by a later redactor, either Symeon or the Durham scribe of CCCC 139.

[55] Cf. Ps. 65 (66): 5 ('Venite et videte opera Dei terribilis in consiliis super filios hominum').

[56] 2 Tim. 2: 5 ('nam et qui certat in agone non coronatur nisi legitime certaverit').

[57] The report of the death of Archbishop Ceolnoth is taken from Asser, *Vita Ælfredi*, c. 34 (ed. Stevenson, p. 26; trans. Keynes and Lapidge, p. 78).

PARS QVARTA 141

itself. But because merciful God had foreseen that through the crown of martyrdom he would arrive at the crown of heavenly glory, he [Eadmund] died there gloriously.[53] It is fitting to insert into our history some details concerning the distinction of his martyrdom,[54] so that the sons of men may know and recognize how terrifying is Christ the Son of God in the counsels of men,[55] and how He adorns with glorious victory those whom He tortures here in the name of martyrdom, so that the saying may be fulfilled: 'No one is crowned unless he shall legitimately have struggled.'[56] King Eadmund devoutly accepted the rule of the East Angles, which he maintained with the strong right arm of authority, always worshipping and glorifying omnipotent God, on behalf of all the bounties which he had made use of. In the same year in which the king and martyr entered the joys of heavenly bliss through the crown of martyrdom, Ceolnoth, archbishop of the city of Canterbury, entered the way of truth; he was buried in the same city by his clergy.[57]

9. In 871, the twenty-second year of the life of Alfred, the glorious king of the Saxons, the Viking army of hated memory left the East Angles; it came into the kingdom of the West Saxons, arriving at the royal estate which is called Reading, on the south bank of the river Thames, in that district which is called Berkshire by the residents of this country. On the third day after the enemies of the English arrived there, their earls, accompanied by a great horde, rode out in the vicinity of the river, and acquired an immense amount of booty.[58] Some of them attempted to build a rampart between the rivers Thames and Kennet; but their plan and the work of the Danes was aborted through the help of the English, so that the words of the scholar was fulfilled in them:

> Although he revels in Tyrian purple
> and adorns himself with snow-white jewels,
> yet he remains hated by everyone.[59]

---

[58] The first sentences of this paragraph derive from Asser, *Vita Ælfredi*, c. 35 (ed. Stevenson, pp. 26–7; trans. Keynes and Lapidge, p. 78). The chronological error continues: Asser records 871 as the twenty-third year of Alfred's life, whereas here in Byrhtferth it is the twenty-second.

[59] Boethius, *De consolatione Philosophiae*, iii, met. iv, lines 1–3 (CCSL xciv. 44). Note that Byrhtferth has substantially altered the wording of Boethius, replacing *superbus* in Boethius with *superbit*, *comeret* with *comet*, and *uigebat* with *pollet*. To judge from Bieler's *apparatus criticus*, these variant readings are not recorded elsewhere, and are perhaps the result of Byrhtferth's faulty memory.

142   HISTORIA REGVM

Et illud:

> Quis illos igitur putet beatos,
> quos miseri tribuunt honores?[60]

Cumque peruersi raptores uiriliter operibus desudarent, aduenit protinus Ætheluulf Bearrocensis regionis incliti uigoris dux, cum suis agminibus centuriatus, et trilicis thoracis[61] circumdatus. Cernens autem multitudinem barbarorum princeps Christianorum populorum, dixit suis: 'Horum numerosus est exercitus, sed tamen est spernendus. Qui si aliquando contra nos aciem struens ualentior incubuerit, noster quidem dux, qui Christus est, fortior illis est.' Obuiant denique Christiani Danis, confidentes in tuitione Christi nominis; dux praephatus suos hortatur praecipue ut resisterent aduersariis, constitutus cum suis inclitis legionibus in loco qui appellatur Englafeld. Vbi dimicatum est satis atroci bello, quo ex utraque parte ceciderunt uulnerati multi et occubuerunt. Occubuit ibidem quidam princeps Danorum cum magna multitudine sui exercitus; ceteris fuga elapsis, Christiani uictoriae palmam adepti*a* sunt, et loco funeris dominati sunt.[62]

fo. 71ᵛᵇ   **10.** His ita peractis, post, bis binis dierum curriculis expletis, rex praepotens Æthelredus ac frater eius Ælfred adunatis exercitibus copiosis, ut regum est potestas et uirtus, ad Readingum uenerunt, desiderantes aut gloriose uiuere in regno, aut in bello occumbere pro Christo. Cumque armipotens rex Æthelred cum fratre dilectissimo ad portam arcis peruenissent, caedendo et prosternendo hostes ante et retro, pagani e contra caedebant, hostica rabie resistentes. Sed (heu pro dolor!) uictoriam eo die inimici Anglorum assumebant. Ætheluulfus quoque \<dux\>*a* Bearrocensis, qui prius ut leo fremuit in bello, tunc cum ceteris fidelibus occubuit in Christo.[63] Quo dolore et uerecundia Anglorum populus commotus, auxilium implorabant angelorum ut eis dignarentur impendere adminiculum diuini adiutorii. Iterum enimuero post quatuor dies contra praephatos inimicos exercitum commouent,

---

iv.9   *a* C^2 adds in- *(i.e.* indepti*)*

iv.10   *a*   *suppl. ed.*

---

[60] Ibid. lines 7–8.

[61] Cf. Prudentius, *Psychomachia* 125–6 ('prouida nam uirtus conserto adamante trilicem / induerat thoraca humeris'); the same Prudentian phrase is used below, *HR* iv. 13.

[62] This paragraph recording the victory of Ealdorman Æthelwulf at Englefield is taken from Asser, *Vita Ælfredi*, c. 35 (ed. Stevenson, p. 27; trans. Keynes and Lapidge, p. 78); Byrhtferth has amplified Asser's account by inserting words of Æthelwulf's speech to his men on the eve of battle (*Horum numerosus . . . fortior illis est*).

PARS QVARTA 143

And that:

> Who therefore would think blessed
> the honours which wretches grant?[60]

And while the wicked robbers were vigorously intent on their work, Æthelwulf, the ealdorman of the district of Berkshire, [a man] of outstanding energy, arrived, accompanied by his troops and protected by a three-layered breastplate.[61] On seeing the horde of barbarians, the leader of the Christian peoples said to his followers: 'Their army is numerous, but it is to be scorned. For if at some point it should press strongly, drawing up its battle-line against us, our leader, who is Christ, is stronger than them.' At length the Christians engaged the Danes, trusting in the protection of the name of Christ; the aforesaid ealdorman, drawn up with his excellent legions in the place called *Englafeld*, urges his men specifically to resist their adversaries. Fighting took place there in a very violent encounter, so that on either side many fell down wounded and died. A certain leader of the Danes died there, together with a great number of his army; with the remainder having escaped in flight, the Christians achieved the palm of victory, and were masters of the field of slaughter.[62]

10. When these events had taken place, after the passage of four days, the mighty King Æthelred and his brother Alfred, having combined their abundant forces, in accordance with the authority and power of kings, came to Reading, desiring either to live gloriously in their kingdom, or to die for Christ in battle. And when the warlike King Æthelred with his beloved brother arrived at the gate of the stronghold, hacking down and killing the enemies before and behind, the Vikings for their part were hacking away, resisting with hostile fury. But, alas (the shame of it!), on that day the enemies of the English achieved the victory. And Æthelwulf, the ealdorman of Berkshire, who had earlier roared like a lion in battle, died in Christ along with others of the faithful.[63] The English people, moved with sadness and shame, begged the assistance of the angels, that they would deign to offer them the support of divine aid. And once again, after four days, they muster their army against the aforesaid enemies, take up their arms, [and] station their legions in the place called *Æscesdun* [Ashdown], which can

---

[63] The report of the second encounter at Reading, and the death of Ealdorman Æthelwulf, is taken from Asser, *Vita Ælfredi*, c. 36 (ed. Stevenson, pp. 27–8; trans. Keynes and Lapidge, p. 78). For the characteristically Byrhtferthian formulation *armipotens rex*, see above, n. 45.

144 HISTORIA REGVM

arma arripiunt, statuunt legiones in loco qui dicitur Æscesdun, quod
Latine 'mons fraxini' potest reuerenter interpretari. Ibi autem totis
uiribus et plena uoluntate ad proelium prodeunt uiri famosi, ad bella
fortissimi. Dani quoque, ut sunt astuti, in duas se turmas diuidentes
uiriliter pugnauere[b] cum suis; habebant et ipsi duos reges multosque
duces. Qui cauta ratione utentes, mediam partem exercitus duobus
regibus concedebant, dimidiam uero omnibus ducibus. Quod Angli
cernentes constituunt et ipsi duas turmas, et construunt machinas et
machinatorum propugnacula. Ælfred autem rex promptissime cum
suis legionibus procedit ad bellum, sciens procul dubio non in multitudine hominum affore uictoriam, sed in Dei miseratione et misericordia. Rex quoque Æthelred in tentorio erat in oratione constitutus,
missam et 'quae Dei sunt' sollicite audiendo.[64] Quae sancta mysteria
regi et Christiano populo multum proficiebant, uti in sequentibus
ostendetur.

fo. 72ra   Decreuerant ergo Christiani populi et Angli deuotissime, audacter
committere contra inimicos bellum; et ut Æthelred rex fortissimus
principum contra legiones dimicaret cum suis myriadis, unus uidelicet
rex Anglorum contra duos Danorum. Ælfred uero rex cum suis
ducibus et commilitonibus, satrapis et populis, debuit contra omnes
paganorum duces belli sortem sumere, ut decretum est. Quibus res
publica utrisque regibus et populis sat satis bene complacuit. Quibus
ita firmiter ab utraque parte dispositis, cum rex Æthelred in oratione
diutius moraretur, et pagani parati ad locum diri certaminis citius
aduenissent, Ælfred tunc secundus in regno non potuit hostiles diutius
acies sufferre, nisi eos aut bello superaret aut morte. Repente uero,
consternatus animo,[65] irruit super aggregatas multitudines Danorum
cum sacris agminibus Anglorum:[66] uenit autem rex praecinctus armis
et orationibus; qui intuitus exercitum fratris satis eleganter esse ordinatum, quasi Iudas bellicosus processit ad bellum.[67] Dimicatum est uirili
intentione ab utrisque partibus, quo in loco ceciderunt quinquageni et

---

[b] pugnare C

---

[64] The words *Quo dolore et uerecundia . . . sollicite audiendo* are based on Asser, *Vita Ælfredi*,
c. 37 (ed. Stevenson, pp. 28–9; trans. Keynes and Lapidge, pp. 78–9), with some Byrhtferthian
alterations (Byrhtferth refers to *Angli* in lieu of Asser's *Christiani*, for example) and additions, such as the clause *auxilium implorabant . . . diuini adiutorii.* The phrase *quae Dei sunt* is
biblical (Matt. 16: 23; Mark 8: 33; Luke 20: 25).
[65] The expression *consternatus animo* is biblical (1 Macc. 3: 31, 4: 27); Byrhtferth had used
it previously at *HR* iii. 16 (above, p. 82, with n. 101).
[66] The words *Decreuerant ergo . . . agminibus Anglorum* are based on Asser, *Vita Ælfredi*,
c. 38 (ed. Stevenson, pp. 29–30; trans. Keynes and Lapidge, p. 79), with substantial

PARS QVARTA
145

respectfully be translated into Latin as 'hill of the ash'. And there the renowned men, mighty in battle, opposed [the enemy] with all their might and with total commitment. The Danes also, since they were clever, splitting themselves up into two groups, fought bravely with their men; for they had two kings and many earls. Implementing a cautious plan, they allocated half of the army to the two kings, the other half to all the earls. Seeing this, the English themselves divided into two groups, and they construct battle-engines and defences against such engines. King Alfred proceeds swiftly into battle with his legions, knowing without doubt that victory does not lie in the number of [fighting] men, but in the pity and mercy of God. King Æthelred, too, was to be found in his tent deep in prayer, listening attentively to mass and to 'things which pertain to God'.[64] These holy mysteries were of great benefit to the kings and the Christian populace, as will be revealed in what follows.

The Christian peoples, and most particularly the English, had therefore decided boldly to engage in battle with the enemies; and as Æthelred, the mighty king, would fight against the legions of the earls with their thousands—one king of the English, that is, against two [kings] of the Danes. But King Alfred, along with his ealdormen and soldiers, thegns and peoples, had to take his chances against all the war leaders of the Vikings, as had been decided. This state of affairs was entirely satisfactory to both kings and peoples. When they were securely drawn up on either side, and King Æthelred was being detained at length in his prayers, and the Vikings had quickly advanced in readiness to the place of dire combat, then Ælfred, second in line to the throne, could no longer tolerate the enemy battle-lines, unless he were either to overcome them in battle or in death. Suddenly then, in mental rage,[65] he fell upon the assembled multitudes of Danes with the venerable throngs of the English:[66] for the king arrived protected by weapons and prayers; having seen the army of his brother elegantly marshalled, he proceeded into battle like another warlike Judas [Maccabeus].[67] Fighting took place on both sides with brave involvement, and men fell in their fifties and hundreds and also

---

amplification by Byrhtferth (e.g. in lieu of Asser's *cum suis cohortibus*, Byrhtferth wrote *cum suis ducibus et commilitonibus, satrapis et populis*).

[67] The comparison of a brave king to Judas Maccabeus is used again by Byrhtferth in *VSO* iv. 13: 'uelut alter Iudas prouocatus ad bellum' (*Byrhtferth: Lives*, ed. Lapidge, p. 128); the image is based on 1 Macc. 2: 66, 3: 1–22, etc. On the topos, see Dunbabin, 'The Maccabees as exemplars'.

146 HISTORIA REGVM

centeni necnon milleni. Qui pro patriis legibus et patria ceciderunt, perducti sunt, ut credi libet, ad patriam aeternae felicitatis. Alii uero ad eum perducti sunt, de quo dictum est: 'Ipse est caput omnis iniustitiae'.[68] Reges autem non solum uerbis populum constantem hortabantur, uerum etiam armis hostes bellica uirtute prosternabant. Tandem Dani, uidentes suorum corruisse sociorum agmina, turbati sunt, admirati sunt, commoti sunt, timorque inmensus apprehendit eos.[69] Erant enim diuino perculsi Dani timore infra cordis cubicula, impetus Anglorum diutius non ferentes in ipso concilio. Qui opprobriosam[e]

fo. 72[rb] arripientes fugam, laxatis gladiis dextras | dederunt, pacemque petierunt. Extendentes reges gladios uix sedauerunt populum bellicantem. Fugerunt hac illac ignobile uulgus, quos per totius diei horas Angligenus persecutus est populus. Multa milia prostrata sunt in illa die; quorum interitum pii reges cernentes, gloriam dixerunt Deo immensam qui eis talem ipso die contulit uictoriae palmam. Cecidit quoque ibi Bagsecg[d] rex et hi duces cum eo, dux Sidroc ueteranus comes, de quo illud aptatur, 'Inueterate dierum malorum.'[70] Corruit ibidem dux Sidroc iunior, atque Osbern dux militiae, duxque Frana, duxque Harald cum suis agminibus; qui latam et spatiosam uiam arripientes descenderunt in profundum laci.[71] 'Viam disciplinae nescierunt, nec intellexerunt semitas eius; a facie illorum longe facta est.'[72]

11. Bello peracto glorioso, reges et omnis populus inmenso repletus est tripudio, uidentes Danorum fugam et Anglorum constantiam. Post quatuordecim dierum excursum, rex Æthelred praestantissimus, ignorans annum iubilei habere remissionem,[73] adiutus fidelissimo auxilio fratris sui, coadunauit exercitum, congregauit spolia, diuisitque arma et dona perplurima suis commilitonibus.[74] Sciebant pro certo ipsi

---

[e] opprobosam C   [d] Bergsecg C

[68] The source of this quotation is uncertain; but cf. Tertullian, *De idololatria*: 'quod si caput iniustitiae idololatria est' (CSEL xx. 32). Byrhtferth was obviously referring to Satan; but if he was in fact recalling and misapplying the passage of Tertullian, he may by implication have been intending to chastize the idolatry of the pagan Vikings.

[69] Cf. Luke 1: 65 ('factus est timor super omnes vicinos') and 5: 26 ('et stupor apprehendit omnes').

[70] Dan. 13: 52.

[71] Byrhtferth's account of the battle of Ashdown is based on Asser, *Vita Ælfredi*, c. 39 (ed. Stevenson, pp. 30–1; trans. Keynes and Lapidge, pp. 79–80), with much Byrhtferthian amplification such as the three-member asyndeton (*turbati sunt, admirati sunt, commoti sunt*).

[72] Cf. Baruch 3: 20–1 ('viam autem disciplinae ignoraverunt, neque intellexerunt semitas eius, neque filii eorum susceperunt eam; a facie ipsorum longe facta est').

PARS QVARTA 147

thousands. Those who died for the fatherland and its laws were taken, as is permissible to believe, to the fatherland of eternal bliss. But others were taken to him of whom it is said: 'He is the head of all iniquity.'[68] Not only did the kings exhort their faithful people in words, but with weapons they slaughtered the enemies in warlike strength. At length the Danes, seeing that hordes of their colleagues had fallen, were disturbed, were astonished, were moved, and a mighty fear seized them.[69] For the Danes had been struck with fear within the recesses of their hearts, not being able to withstand for long the onslaught of the English in that same engagement. Taking to ignominious flight, they held out their right hands, having dropped their swords, and sought peace. The [English] kings, holding up their swords, were scarcely able to calm their warlike peoples. The ignoble horde fled here and there; the English people pursued them for the duration of a whole day. Many thousands were slaughtered on that day; the devout [English] kings, observing their death, expressed their immense gratitude to God, Who that same day granted to them the palm of victory. King Bagsecg fell there, and these earls with him: Earl Sidroc the Elder, of whom that saying can be applied, 'O ancient man, [grown old] in evil days'.[70] Earl Sidroc the Younger fell there, and Earl Osbern, leader of the troops, and Earl Frana, and Earl Harald with his troops; taking to the wide and spacious road they descended into the depths of the lake [of Hell].[71] 'They knew not the way of discipline, nor did they understand its ways; it is far from their face.'[72]

11. When this glorious battle was over, the kings and the entire populace were filled with immense joy on seeing the flight of the Danes and the constancy of the English. After the passage of fourteen days, the outstanding King Æthelred, being unaware that the year has the remission of the Jubilee,[73] aided by the most faithful assistance of his brother, assembled his army, heaped up the spoils, and divided up the weapons and a great many gifts among his soldiers.[74] For the leaders of the people knew for certain that states 'would be blessed, if those who

---

[73] References to the 'remission of the year of the Jubilee' as a metaphor for entry into the eternal life are frequent in Byrhtferth: see above, *HR* ii. 12 (with n. 37), and *VSO* i. 6: 'sumere ab eo iubelei anni remissionem' (*Byrhtferth: Lives*, ed. Lapidge, p. 26), and discussion by Lapidge, 'The early sections', p. 111 = *ALL* ii. 331, and Introduction, above, p. xxviii.

[74] The account of the meeting of Æthelred and Alfred two weeks after the battle of Ashdown, for the purpose of dividing the spoils of battle, is not found in Asser, at least not in the text of Asser as it has come down to us. In the *Vita Ælfredi*, c. 40, Asser relates instead that 'after fourteen days', Æthelred and Alfred came together to engage the Vikings at Basing (ed. Stevenson, p. 31; trans. Keynes and Lapidge, p. 80).

148   HISTORIA REGVM

principes populorum, 'beatas fore res publicas, si eas uel studiosi sapientiae regerent, uel si earum rectores studere sapientiae contigisset'.[75]

Congregati sunt rursum ad bellum Angli atque Dani; quibus cum durissimum esset illatum robur, pagani uictoriam prope assumpserunt. Eodem uero anno rex Æthelred, plenus aetate et perfectus in bonitate, post perpetrationem insignium bellorum, futurae uitae et perpetui regni felicitatem coepit uidere, cum rege saeculorum 'in terra uiuentium'.[76]

Subtracto ab hoc saeculo rege praedicto, mox Ælfredus a | ducibus et a praesulibus totius gentis eligitur, et non solum ab ipsis, uerum etiam ab omni populo adoratur, ut eis praeesset 'ad faciendam uindictam in nationibus, increpationes in populis'.[77] Adepto regni gubernaculo totius gentis, semper bellicosus refulsit et uictor in omnibus bellis, fortuna arridente[78] Christoque faciente.[79] Rebellauit contra eum praedictus exercitus satis acerrime, qui Anglorum intuentes austeritatem, et suam cognoscentes imbecillitatem, terga in fugam uerterunt. Sed (proh dolor!) per audacitatem persequentium reuersi rursum ad proelium sunt prouocati, capientes uictoriae munus, et loco funeris sunt dominati.[80] Ipso quoque anno Saxones cum isdem paganis pacis concordiam pepigerunt, ea ratione ut ab eis discederent.

12. Anno Dominicae incarnationis .dccclxxii., natiuitatis Ælfredi regis uicesimo tertio, praephatus paganorum exercitus Londoniam adiit, ibique hiemauit; cum quo Mercii pacem pepigerunt.[81]

Anno .dccclxxiii., natiuitatis autem Ælfredi regis Anglorum uicesimo quarto, saepe memoratus exercitus Londoniam deserens ad Northanhymbrorum regionem profectus est, ibique hiemauit; cum quo iterum Mercii pacem pepigerunt.[82]

Anno Dominicae incarnationis .dccclxxiiii., natiuitatis autem Ælfredi regis Anglorum uicesimo quinto, supra memoratus exercitus Lindissem

---

[75] Boethius, *De consolatione Philosophiae*, i, pr. iv. 5: 'Atqui tu hanc sententiam Platonis ore sanxisti: beatas fore res publicas, si eas uel studiosi sapientiae regerent uel earum rectores studere sapientiae contigisset' (CCSL xciv. 7). Byrhtferth quoted this aphorism earlier in the present work (*HR* iii. 28; above, p. 115 with n. 186).

[76] The death of King Æthelred is narrated in Asser, *Vita Ælfredi*, c. 41 (ed. Stevenson, pp. 31–2; trans. Keynes and Lapidge, p. 80); Byrhtferth has recast the narrative in his own distinctive wording, such that the words *plenus aetate... in terra uiuentium* replace Asser's simple *viam universitatis adiens*. The phrase *in terra uiuentium* is biblical: Ps. 26 (27): 13 ('Credo videre bona Domini in terra viventium'), 141 (142): 6 ('tu es spes mea, portio mea in terra viventium').

[77] Ps. 149 (150): 7 ('ad faciendam uindictam in nationibus, increpationes in populis').

[78] For the Byrhtferthian phrase *fortuna arridente*, see above, *HR* iv. 5 with n. 29.

[79] The accession of King Alfred is narrated by Asser, *Vita Ælfredi*, c. 42 (ed. Stevenson, p. 32; trans. Keynes and Lapidge, pp. 80–1); Byrhtferth retains some of Asser's wording

PARS QVARTA 149

pursued wisdom ruled them, or if it happened that their rulers were to pursue wisdom'.[75]

The English and the Danes were again drawn up for battle; when unshakeable strength was granted them [the Danes], the Vikings very nearly achieved victory. In that same year King Æthelred, advanced in age and complete in goodness, after his participation in these outstanding battles, began to look towards the bliss of a future life and of the perpetual realm, with the King of Ages 'in the land of the living'.[76] When this aforementioned king had been taken from this world, Alfred is immediately elected by the ealdormen and thegns of the entire people, and is adored not only by them, but also by the entire populace, so that he would lead them 'in wreaking revenge against the pagans, in rebuking those peoples'.[77] Having assumed the government of the entire nation, he shone out as the warlike victor in all battles, with fortune smiling on him,[78] and with Christ accomplishing it.[79] The aforesaid army rebelled very savagely against him; seeing the rigour of the English, and recognizing their own weakness, they turned their backs in flight. But (alas!), because of the recklessness of those pursuing them, they turned around, having been provoked into fighting, and grasping the benefit of victory, they were dominant on the field of slaughter.[80] In that same year the Saxons made peace with the Vikings, on condition that they would depart from them.

12. In the year of the Lord's incarnation 872, the twenty-third year of King Alfred's life, the aforesaid army of Vikings went to London, and wintered there; the Mercians made peace with them.[81]

In 873, the twenty-fourth year of King Alfred's life, the frequently mentioned army, leaving London, set out for the territory of the Northumbrians, and wintered there; once again the Mercians made peace with them.[82]

In the year of the Lord's incarnation 874, the twenty-fifth year of King Alfred's life, the above-mentioned army left the province of

---

(cf., for example, *quod nimium bellicosus et victor prope in omnibus bellis erat*), but much of the account is Byrhtferthian amplification.

[80] The wording *terga in fugam uerterunt...sunt dominati* is taken nearly verbatim from Asser, *Vita Ælfredi*, c. 42 (ed. Stevenson, p. 33, lines 25–8; trans. Keynes and Lapidge, p. 81).

[81] From Asser, *Vita Ælfredi*, c. 44 (ed. Stevenson, p. 34), with the usual chronological dislocation (Asser's *nativitatis Ælfredi regis vigesimo quarto* has become *natiuitatis Ælfredi regis uicesimo tertio*).

[82] From Asser, *Vita Ælfredi*, c. 45 (ed. Stevenson, p. 34; trans. Keynes and Lapidge, p. 81), with the usual chronological dislocation (Asser's *nativitatis Ælfredi regis vigesimo quinto* has become *natiuitatis Ælfredi regis uicesimo quarto*).

HISTORIA REGVM

prouinciam deseruit, Merciam adiit, et in Hrepadun hiemauit. Burhredum quoque Merciorum regem de regno depulerunt, et ad Romam exire compulerunt uicesimo secundo regni sui anno. Qui postquam Romam adierat, non diu uixit saeculo, quoniam peruenit ad eum qui est uera uita, sepultusque honorifice est in ecclesia sanctae Mariae genitricisque Domini nostri Iesu Christi semper uirginis, exspectans
fo. 72ᵛᵇ eius aduentum secundum, | quando bonis iusta praemia largiter concedit, malis dira dispensat supplicia. Dani quoque post huius expulsionem regnum Merciorum suo dominio subdiderunt. Commendauerunt illud cuidam militi ipsius gentis nomine Ceoluulfo, ea ratione ut quando uellent, rursum absque dolo absque malo haberent.⁸³

Anno Dominicae incarnationis .dccclxxv., natiuitatis autem Ælfredi regis uicesimo sexto, praedictus exercitus Hrepadun deseruit, seseque in duas partes diuisit. Vna pars cum Halfdene ad regionem Northanhymbrorum secessit, ᵃet eam uastauit,ᵃ et hiemauit iuxta flumen quod dicitur Tyne, et totam gentem suo dominatui subdidit, et Pictos atque Stretcluttenses depopulati sunt.⁸⁴

Earduulfus episcopus et abbas Eadredus, de Lindisfarnensi insula corpus sancti Cuthberti tollentes, per nouemᵇ⁸⁵ annos ante faciem barbarorum de loco ad locum fugientes, cum illo thesauro discurrerunt.⁸⁶

Altera quoque pars ipsius classis cum Gutthrum et Oscytel et Amund, regibus paganorum, ad locum qui dicitur Grantabric peruenit, ibique hiemauit.⁸⁷ Rex uero Ælfred nauali proelio confortatus

---

iv.12   ᵃ⁻ᵃ *add. Cⁱ*   ᵇ *over* nouem *C²* writes septem

---

⁸³ From Asser, *Vita Ælfredi*, c. 46 (ed. Stevenson, pp. 34–5; trans. Keynes and Lapidge, p. 81), with the usual chronological dislocation (Asser's *natiuitatis Ælfredi regis vigesimo sexto* has become *natiuitatis Ælfredi regis uicesimo quinto*).

⁸⁴ From Asser, *Vita Ælfredi*, c. 47 (ed. Stevenson, pp. 35–6; trans. Keynes and Lapidge, p. 82), with the usual chronological dislocation (Asser's *natiuitatis Ælfredi regis vigesimo septimo* has become *natiuitatis Ælfredi regis uicesimo sexto*).

⁸⁵ The original scribe of C wrote *nouem* here, but the later annotator (C²) altered this number to *septem*, which agrees with the figure given in the *Historia de sancto Cuthberto*, c. 20 (see following note). It is not clear whether this interpolated sentence on St Cuthbert formed part of Byrhtferth's original text, or whether it is the contribution of a later redactor (Symeon or a later Durham scribe). There is no vocabulary characteristic of Byrhtferth in this sentence.

⁸⁶ This mention of Bishop Eardwulf and Abbot Eadred and the removal of the relics of St Cuthbert from Lindisfarne has been introduced—by Byrhtferth, or Symeon, or a later Durham redactor—into Asser's narrative (c. 47). Asser does not mention this event, and the source for the information is not certainly known. However, there is a very similar report in the *Historia de sancto Cuthberto*, c. 20: 'Eodem quoque tempore bonus episcopus Eardulfus et

PARS QVARTA

Lindsey, went to Mercia, and wintered in Repton. They drove Burgred, the king of the Mercians, from his kingdom, and forced him to go to Rome in the twenty-second year of his reign. After he had gone to Rome, he did not live long in this world, since he departed to Him Who is the true life, and was honourably buried in the church of St Mary, mother of our Lord Jesus Christ, ever Virgin [S. Maria in Sassia], awaiting His second coming, when He bountifully distributes just rewards to the good [and] dispenses dire punishments to the evil. After his expulsion, the Danes subjected the kingdom of the Mercians to their dominion. They entrusted it to a certain soldier of that nation [the English] named Ceolwulf, on the condition that whenever they wanted, they would have it back without deceit or malice.[83]

In the year of the Lord's incarnation 875, the twenty-sixth year of King Alfred's life, the aforementioned army abandoned Repton and divided itself into two parts. One part departed with Halfdan for the district of the Northumbrians, and laid waste to it, and wintered next to the river called the Tyne, and subjected all the people to their domination; and they devastated the Picts and the inhabitants of Strathclyde.[84]

Bishop Eardwulf and Abbot Eadred, taking the body of St Cuthbert from the island of Lindisfarne and fleeing from place to place for nine years[85] before the face of the barbarians, travelled about with that treasure.[86]

The other part of that same army, with Guthrum and Oscytel and Amund, kings of the Vikings, arrived at the place which is called Cambridge, and wintered there.[87] But King Alfred, taking comfort in naval warfare, came upon six (Viking) ships on the high sea; fighting

---

abbas Eadred tulerunt corpus sancti Cuthberti de Lindisfarnensi insula et cum eo errauerunt in terra, portantes illud de loco in locum per septem annos' (ed. Johnson South, p. 58). Excepting the discrepancy concerning the *Wanderjahre* (nine years according to the original scribe of C, against the *Historia*'s seven: see previous note), the accounts are very similar; the problem is that the date of the *Historia de sancto Cuthberto* is uncertain (see Johnson South, ibid. pp. 25–36, who inclines to date the text to the mid-11th c.). It is questionable, therefore, whether the *Historia de sancto Cuthberto* was in existence when Byrhtferth was writing; but cf. discussion in the Introduction (above, p. lxxii) to the effect that the *Historia de sancto Cuthberto* was known to Ælfric of Winchester and Eynsham, Byrhtferth's exact contemporary. On balance, it is perhaps more likely that this notice (and others concerning St Cuthbert: see below, nn. 91, 109) was interpolated either by Symeon or a later Durham scribe; and note that Symeon in his *LDE* treats Bishop Eardwulf and the removal of St Cuthbert's relics at some length (*LDE* ii. 5, ii. 6; ed. Rollason, pp. 94–5, 100–3). Eardwulf was bishop of Lindisfarne from 854 until his death in ?899 (Keynes, 'Bishops', p. 565); according to the *Historia de sancto Cuthberto*, c. 13, Eadred was abbot of Carlisle.

[87] Byrhtferth now returns to Asser, *Vita Ælfredi*, c. 47 (ed. Stevenson, pp. 36–8; trans. Keynes and Lapidge, p. 82) for the account of the Viking army's wintering in Cambridge.

HISTORIA REGVM

sex naues inuenit in mari, cum quibus fortiter debellans, unam cepit, ceteri fugerunt timore perculsi.[88]

Anno Dominicae incarnationis .dccclxxvi., natiuitatis autem Ælfredi regis uicesimo septimo, praephatus exercitus nocte de Grantabric exiens, castellum quod dicitur Werham intrauit. Quorum subitum aduentum rex Saxonum praenoscens, foedus cum eis pepigit, ea conditione ut ab eius regno discederent, obsides accipiendo. Ipsi uero more solito obsides et iuramenta non seruantes, nocte quadam foedere dirupto ad Exancestriam diuerterunt, quod Britannice dicitur Cairuuisc, Latine 'ciuitas aquarum'.[89]

13. Anno Dominicae incarnationis .dccclxxvii., natiuitatis autem fo. 73ra Ælfredi duodetricesimo, | exercitus ipse nefandus Exancester dereliquit, Cippanham regiam uillam adiit, ibique hiemauit. Ælfred uero rex his diebus magnas sustinuit tribulationes et inquietam uitam agebat uel durabat.[90] Rex Ælfredus apto confortatus oraculo per sanctum Cuthbertum,[91] contra Danos pugnauit, et sicut quo ipse sanctus iusserat tempore et loco, uictoria potitus est, semperque deinceps hostibus terribilis et inuincibilis erat, sanctumque Cuthbertum praecipue honori habuerat. Qualiter hostes uicerit paulo post, hic legitur.

Eodem denique anno Inguar et Healfdene cum bis denis ac ternis nauibus, de Demetica regione in qua hiemauerant egressi, ut lupi feroces, post multas ibi Christianorum strages patratas, post combustiones coenobiorum, ad Domnaniam enauigauerunt, et ibi a regis ministris fortissimis cum mille ducentis uiris occisi sunt ante arcem Cynuit, quia in eadem arce perplurimi regis famuli, ut dictum est, se concluserant causa refugii.[92] Rex autem Ælfred in Domino Deo confisus, cum paucis agminibus stipatus, fecit arcem in loco qui appellatur Æthelingaige, in quo habitans cum suis commilitonibus hostes frequenter infatigabiliter

---

[88] The account of Alfred's naval battle, and his capture of a Viking ship, is from Asser, *Vita Ælfredi*, c. 48 (ed. Stevenson, p. 36; trans. Keynes and Lapidge, p. 82).

[89] Abbreviated from Asser, *Vita Ælfredi*, c. 49 (ed. Stevenson, pp. 35–6; trans. Keynes and Lapidge, p. 82–3), with the usual chronological dislocation (Asser's *natiuitatis Ælfredi regis vigesimo octavo* has become *natiuitatis Ælfredi regis uicesimo septimo*). Byrhtferth's Latin gloss on Welsh *Cairuuisc* is not found in Asser, who has *Cairuuisc Latine quoque civitas Exae* (ed. Stevenson, p. 38: 'the city of the Exe'); possibly Byrhtferth's copy of Asser had the corrupt reading *civitas aquae*, which Byrhtferth reproduced as *ciuitas aquarum*; in any event, his etymology is mistaken.

[90] This sentence is taken from Asser, *Vita Ælfredi*, c. 52 (ed. Stevenson, p. 40; trans. Keynes and Lapidge, p. 83); but whereas Asser had assigned this chapter to 878 and to the thirtieth year of Alfred's life ('Anno Dominicae incarnationis .dccclxxviii., nativitatis autem Ælfredi regis trigesimo'), Byrhtferth assigns it to 877 and the twenty-eighth year of Alfred's life, thus compounding the error which underlies his chronological entries. The transmitted

PARS QVARTA 153

manfully with them, he captured one; the remainder fled, struck with terror.[88]

In the year of the Lord's incarnation 876, the twenty-seventh year of King Alfred's life, the aforesaid army, setting out from Cambridge by night, entered the fortified town of Wareham. The king of the Saxons, acknowledging their arrival, made a treaty with them, on the condition that they depart from his kingdom, after receiving hostages. The Vikings, not keeping the hostages and oaths in their usual manner, broke the treaty and went one night to Exeter, which in Welsh is called *Cairuuisc*, in Latin the 'city of the waters'.[89]

13. In the year of the Lord's incarnation 877, the twenty-eighth year of Alfred's life, the unspeakable army left Exeter, went to the royal estate of Chippenham, and wintered there. But King Alfred experienced great tribulations in these days, and lived—or endured—a very troubled life.[90] King Alfred, comforted by means of a fitting prophecy from St Cuthbert,[91] fought against the Danes, and at whatever time and place the saint had ordered him, he achieved victory, and ever thereafter he was terrifying and unconquerable, and held St Cuthbert in especial respect. How he overcame his enemies shortly thereafter, is here explained.

And so in that very same year Ivar and Halfdan, with twenty-three ships, set out like savage wolves from the region of Dyfed where they had wintered, after having perpetrated there the slaughter of many Christians and the burning of many monasteries, and sailed for Devon, and there, in front of the stronghold of *Cynuit* [Countisbury], they were killed, together with 1,200 men, by the courageous agents of the king, because many of the king's thegns, so it is said, had shut themselves up for safety.[92] King Alfred, trusting in the Lord God, accompanied by very few troops, constructed a fort in a place which is called Athelney; residing there with his soldiers, he frequently [and] tirelessly

---

text of Asser is unstable at this point (see Keynes and Lapidge, pp. 246–7, n. 94), and it is possible that the chronological dislocation was present in Byrhtferth's exemplar, the result of an omitted chapter.

[91] The report of Alfred's vision of St Cuthbert is not found in Asser; it is, however, narrated at length in the anonymous *Historia de sancto Cuthberto*, cc. 16–17 (ed. Johnson South, pp. 54–6), which raises again the question of when the *Historia* was composed, and whether a version of it could have been known to Byrhtferth; see above, nn. 85–6. The vision is also narrated by Symeon of Durham, *LDE* ii. 10 (ed. Rollason, p. 110), which perhaps makes it more likely that the account of Alfred's vision is a later Durham interpolation, and did not form part of Byrhtferth's original *HR*.

[92] The words *Eodem denique anno…causa refugii* are taken nearly verbatim from Asser, *Vita Ælfredi*, c. 54 (ed. Stevenson, p. 43; trans. Keynes and Lapidge, pp. 83–4).

154 HISTORIA REGVM

contriuit ab arce. Hoc egit tempore resurrectionis Domini nostri Iesu Christi; qui egressus ab arce, uiribusque susceptis, post, septem uidelicet septimanis dierum et monade, hoc est quinquaginta diebus suppletis, uenit ad petram Ecgberhti, quae est in orientali parte saltus qui Anglico eloquio dicitur Mucelpudu, Latine uero 'magna silua', Britannico more, Coitmaur.[a] Ibi ergo obuiauerunt regi dilectissimo omnes accolae Sumortunenses ac Vuiltunenses, necnon Hamtunenses, uisoque laetati sunt immenso cordis tripudio, quasi rediuiuum ipsum suscipientes.[93] Post tertium uero diem uenit cum immenso exercitu ad locum qui dicitur Edderandun, quo iuxta immensas paganorum phal-

fo. 73[rb] anges | inuenit, paratas cum densa multitudine ad bellum. Exorto solis iubare limpidissimo,[94] rex et omne decus suae plebis induerunt se bellicis ornatibus, scilicet trilici thoraca fidei, spei caritatisque Dei.[95] Hi exsurgentes a solo audacter prouocabant incelebres ad bellum, de clementia conditoris sperantes, securi ac uallo muniti astantis regis, cuius uultus ut angeli splendentis refulsit. Commiserunt ergo bellum per longa tempora diei utrique populi, quorum uoces et collisiones armorum per longa terrarum spatia audita sunt.[96]

Cernens igitur speculator insignis desuper penetral sui terreni regis desiderium, concessit ei angelicae potestatis suffragium. Is denique potitus uictoria hostes suos prostrauit,[b] gratias reddens summo saluatori cum cordis laetitia. Cumque ibidem rex cum suis legionibus arrideret, inimici qui remanserant ipsius magnis eiulatibus deflerent; ob famis et frigoris austeritatem atque tanti regis timorem, rogant pacis clementiam qui eam semper impugnabant. Promittunt obsides, et iuramenta in dextris extendunt. Auscultans haec omnia rex, suatim motus clementia concedit cuncta petita. Rex uero ipsorum, Gutthrum onomate, Christianum se uelle fore testatus est; qui sub manu piissimi regis in baptismatis purgatione regaliter susceptus est. Tinctus est idem Gutthrum[c] baptismate salutis cum aliis uiris electis triginta, quem rex Saxonum in filium adoptionis accepit. Qui postquam baptizatus est duodenis noctibus cum ipso mansit in magna gloria, cui

---

iv.13   [a] coitmapur C   [b] *after* prostrauit C *adds* cum   [c] Guderum C

[93] The words *Rex autem Ælfred…ipsum suscipientes* are taken nearly verbatim from Asser, *Vita Ælfredi*, c. 55 (ed. Stevenson, pp. 44–5; trans. Keynes and Lapidge, p. 84).

[94] Aldhelm, prose *De uirginitate*, c. 4: 'et exorto limpidissimi solis iubare' (MGH, *AA* xv. 231).

[95] The phrase *trilici thoraca*, adapted from Prudentius *Psychomachia* 125–6, was used earlier by Byrhtferth, *HR* iv. 9 (above, p. 142, with n. 61).

PARS QVARTA 155

harassed his enemies from the fort. He did this at the time of the resurrection of our Lord Jesus Christ [i.e. Easter 877]; setting out from the fort, and acquiring [additional] forces, he subsequently, after seven weeks of seven days each plus one more, that is, after fifty days, came to 'Ecgberht's Stone', which is in the eastern part of [Selwood] Forest, which in English is called *Muceluudu*, in Latin 'the great wood', in Welsh *Coit Maur*. All the inhabitants of Somerset and Wiltshire and Hampshire met their beloved king there, and having seen him they were filled with immensely heartfelt joy, treating him as one restored to life.[93] After the third day he came with his immense army to the place called Edington, next to which he found the mighty hordes of Vikings, ready for battle in their great numbers. When the clear light of day had dawned,[94] the king and all the glory of his people armed themselves with warlike weaponry, that is, with the three-layered breastplate of faith, hope, and charity.[95] Rising up from the ground they boldly called the disreputable [Vikings] to battle, hoping for the mercy of the Creator, secure and protected by the palisade of the upright king, whose face shone as if that of a shining angel. Both peoples engaged in battle for long periods of the day; their shouts and the clash of their weapons were heard across wide distances of land.[96]

The eminent Examiner, observing from above His inner sanctum the intentions of the earthly king, granted to him the assistance of angelic power. He [Alfred], gaining the victory at last, devastated his enemies, returning thanks to the Highest Saviour with heartfelt joy. And when the king with his legions was smiling there, the enemies who remained were weeping with great outbursts; because of the harsh suffering of hunger and cold, and their fear of so mighty a king, they who were always repudiating [it] now beg the clemency of peace. They promise hostages, and swear oaths with their right hands. The king, listening to all this, moved by mercy as was his wont, grants all their requests. But their king, named Guthrum, professed that he wished to be a Christian; he was royally received in the purification of baptism at the hand of the devout king. This same Guthrum was anointed in the baptism of salvation together with thirty of his chosen men; the king of the Saxons received him [Guthrum] as his adoptive son. After he had been baptized, Guthrum remained with him for twelve nights in great

---

[96] Byrhtferth's account of Alfred's victory at the battle of Edington is based on the first part of Asser, *Vita Ælfredi*, c. 56 (ed. Stevenson, pp. 45–6; trans. Keynes and Lapidge, pp. 84–5), but Byrhtferth has recast the narrative in his own words, incorporating quotations from Aldhelm and Prudentius.

156 HISTORIA REGVM

spiritualis pater multa et inedicibilia largitus est dona, ac omnibus qui Christianitatis fidem perceperunt.[97]

14. Anno Dominicae incarnationis .dccclxxix., natiuitatis Ælfredi regis uicesimo octauo, praedictus paganorum exercitus de Cippanham, ut promiserat, consurgens Cirencestre adiit, quae Britannico | appellatur elogio Cairceri, ibique per unius anni cursum mansit.[98] Ipso quoque anno immensus uenit paganorum exercitus de ultramarinis climatibus in Tamensi fluuio: qui adunatus est supradicto cuneo, complices effecti, quod prauorum est.[99] Eclypsis solis inter nonam et uesperam facta est eodem anno.[100]

Anno Dominicae incarnationis .dccclxxx., natiuitatis autem Ælfredi regis gloriosi uicesimo nono, saepe memoratus paganorum exercitus a Cirencestre egressus ad Orientales accessit Anglos;[101] ipsamque regionem diuidentes inhabitare coeperunt. Pagani qui in Fulanhame hiemauerant, Britannicam deseruerunt insulam, Franciamque uisitare coeperunt, pessima agnitione, quo uno anno permanserunt.[102]

Anno Dominicae incarnationis .dccclxxxi., natiuitatis autem Ælfred regis tricesimo, praephatus exercitus equis ascensis in Francorum finibus deuenit, quod mirabile uideri potest—quod uisibiles hostes contra tam fortem bellicosumque populum auderent insurgere. At tunc feroces Franci, inuicta fortitudine, a castellis et oppidis et ciuitatibus atque turribus uiriliter progredientes, more leonum succensi sunt ira, uidentes nefarias sceleratorum potestates emergere, gaudio laetitiaque exultare malos, iacere bonos terrore prostratos, innocuos flere, nocentes exultare. Inito consilio prudenti, audaces Franci bellum iniere durissimum cum paganis. Finito proelio Franci cum triumpho reuersi sunt; pagani equis acquisitis hac illac equitabant.[103]

His diebus plurima in eadem gente monasteria concussa sunt ac desolata. Nam et fratres coenobii sanctissimi Benedicti, ipsius reliquias

---

[97] The words *Cumque ibidem rex…fidem perceperunt* are based on the latter part of Asser, *Vita Ælfredi*, c. 56 (ed. Stevenson, pp. 46–7; trans. Keynes and Lapidge, p. 85).

[98] From Asser, *Vita Ælfredi*, c. 57 (ed. Stevenson, p. 47; trans. Keynes and Lapidge, p. 85), with further chronological dislocation (Asser's *nativitatis Ælfredi regis trigesimo primo* has become *natiuitatis Ælfredi regis uicesimo octauo*).

[99] From Asser, *Vita Ælfredi*, c. 58 (ed. Stevenson, p. 47; trans. Keynes and Lapidge, p. 85).

[100] The notice of the solar eclipse is taken nearly verbatim from Asser, *Vita Ælfredi*, c. 59 (ed. Stevenson, p. 48; trans. Keynes and Lapidge, p. 85, with n. 118). The problems raised by Asser's dating of this eclipse are discussed at length by Schove and Fletcher, *The Chronology of Eclipses*, pp. 196–200, who conclude: 'All solar eclipses recorded in the British Isles and Europe under years 874 to 880 really refer to the total solar eclipse of 878 Oct. 29' (p. 196). The eclipses of 879 were not visible.

PARS QVARTA 157

honour; the spiritual father bestowed many indescribable gifts on him, and on all those who adopted the Christian faith.[97]

14. In the year of the Lord's incarnation 879, the twenty-eighth of the life of King Alfred, the aformentioned Viking army got up and went, as it had promised, from Chippenham to Cirencester, which in Welsh speech is called *Cairceri*, and remained there for the course of a year.[98] In the same year an immense army of Vikings came from overseas territories [and sailed] up the river Thames; they joined up with the aforementioned contingent, having become accomplices, as is the way with wicked men.[99] In that same year an eclipse of the sun took place between noon and evening.[100]

In the year of the Lord's incarnation 880, the twenty-ninth of the life of glorious King Alfred, the frequently mentioned army of Vikings, setting out from Cirencester, went to East Anglia,[101] and, dividing up this district, they began to settle there. The Vikings who had wintered at Fulham left the British Isles and began to afflict France, where they remained for a year, with their foul presence.[102]

In the year of the Lord's incarnation 881, the thirtieth of the life of King Alfred, the aforesaid army took to horseback within the bounds of France: which could be seen as marvellous—that these visible enemies would dare to rise up against so mighty and warlike a people. And so the Franks, with their unconquerable bravery, setting out boldly from strongholds and towns and cities and fortresses, were enraged by anger like lions on seeing the unspeakable forces of the miscreants emerging, and [seeing] these evil men exulting in joy and happiness, and [seeing] good men prostrate with terror, innocents weeping, and the wicked rejoicing. Having taken wise advice, the daring Franks initiated a very severe battle with the Vikings. At the end of the battle, the Franks returned in triumph; the Vikings, having acquired horses, rode about here and there.[103]

In these days a number of monasteries among this same people were attacked and abandoned. The monks of the monastery of the most holy

---

[101] From Asser, *Vita Ælfredi*, c. 60 (ed. Stevenson, p. 48; trans. Keynes and Lapidge, pp. 85–6), with a chronological dislocation now of three years (Asser's *nativitatis Ælfredi regis trigesimo secundo* has become *natiuitatis Ælfredi regis uicesimo nono*).

[102] From Asser, *Vita Ælfredi*, c. 61 (ed. Stevenson, p. 48; trans. Keynes and Lapidge, p. 86).

[103] The account of the Vikings in Francia and the Franks' valiant resistance is based on Asser, *Vita Ælfredi*, c. 62 (ed. Stevenson, p. 48; trans. Keynes and Lapidge, p. 86), but has been greatly expanded by Byrhtferth, with the continuing chronological dislocation of three years (Asser's *nativitatis autem Ælfredi regis trigesimo tertio* has become *natiuitatis autem Ælfredi regis tricesimo*).

158 HISTORIA REGVM

a tumulo quo locata fuerant immensa pulchritudine secum auferentes, hac illac discurrebant.[104]

fo. 73vb Anno Dominicae incarnationis .dccclxxxii., natiuitatis autem Ælfredi gloriosi regis tricesimo primo, paganorum exercitus suas naues per flumen quod dicitur Mese in Francigenae gentis regionem pertraxit, et ibi hiemauit uno anno.[105] Eodem denique anno, Ælfred rex Saxonum, audacissimus ducum, nauali proelio suffultus, contra paganicas naues in mari congressus est. Ex quibus ipse aequiloquus^{a}[106] duas potenti uirtute naues exsuperauit, occisis omnibus qui in eis erant. His exsuperatis, principum princeps grates reddidit dignas sospitatis auctori. Quid deinde gestum sit referre libet. Principes duarum nauium post haec cum omnibus sociis ualde uulnerauit; qui, depositis eneruiter armis, curuis poplitibus precibusque supplicibus dedere se regi magno, quamdiu scintillula uitalis caloris eis arrideret.[107]

15. Sequenti anno, hoc est .dccclxxxiii., natiuitatis uero Ælfredi famosissimi regis tricesimo secundo, ipse nec nominandus exercitus naues suas per flumen quod appellatur Scald pertraxit, ibique uno mansit anno.[108] ^{a}Guthred ex seruo factus est rex, et sedes episcopalis in Cuncecestra restauratur.^{a}[109]

Anno Dominicae incarnationis .dccclxxxiiii., natiuitatis denique Ælfredi famosissimi regis tricesimo tertio, indignissimus exercitus in duas se turmas segregauit. Vna quidem in Orientalem Franciam perrexit, altera ad Britanniam ueniens, Cantiam adiit ciuitatem^{b} quae Hrofeceaster dicitur. Ante huius portam castellum pagani fecerunt,

---

iv.14 ^{a} equilocus C

iv.15 $^{a-a}$ add. C^{l} (interlined) ^{b} suppl. ed. (from Asser)

---

[104] Fleury was sacked and burned by the Vikings in 865, and not re-established as a Benedictine monastery until 930. The Viking attack on Fleury is not mentioned by Asser, and may have been known to Byrhtferth from Abbo of Fleury, who spent the years 985–7 teaching at Ramsey.

[105] Taken nearly verbatim from Asser, Vita Ælfredi, c. 63 (ed. Stevenson, p. 49; trans. Keynes and Lapidge, p. 86), with the continuing chronological dislocation of three years (Asser's nativitatis Ælfredi regis trigesimo quarto has become natiuitatis Ælfredi regis tricesimo primo).

[106] The word aequiloquus ('speaking justly', hence probably simply 'just') is not attested in classical Latin. It is interpreted in DMLBS p. 42, s.v. 'aequilocus', to mean 'evenly matched', but this is simply a guess from context. The word was conceivably coined by Asser.

[107] The words Eodem denique anno ... caloris eis arrideret have been taken from Asser, Vita Ælfredi, c. 64 (ed. Stevenson, p. 49; trans. Keynes and Lapidge, p. 86), with much Byrhtferthian embellishment.

PARS QVARTA 159

St Benedict [i.e. Fleury], removing his relics from the tomb of immense beauty where they had been deposited, travelled around here and there.[104]

In the year of the Lord's incarnation 882, the thirty-first of the life of the glorious King Alfred, the Viking army drew up its ships into the river which is called the Meuse, further into the territory of the Frankish people, and wintered there for a year.[105] In the same year Alfred, king of the Saxons, most valiant of leaders, well equipped for naval combat, attacked the Viking ships on the high seas. Of these the just king[106] overcame two ships with mighty force, having killed all those who were in them. Having overcome them, the leader of leaders gave worthy thanks to the Author of his delivery. It is appropriate to report what happened thereafter. After this [engagement] he had severely wounded the captains of the two ships, with all their companions; they, weakly laying down their arms, on bended knee and with earnest supplication, gave themselves up to the great king, for as long as there still glowed within them a tiny little spark of vital life.[107]

15. The following year, that is 883, the thirty-second year of the life of the famous King Alfred, that unspeakable army drew up its ships into the river called the Scheldt, and remained there a year.[108] Guthred, formerly a slave, was made king; and the episcopal see at Chester-le-Street is restored.[109]

In the year of the Lord's incarnation 884, the thirty-third year of the life of the famous King Alfred, the despicable army divided itself into two bands. One set off for eastern Francia; the other, arriving in Britain, went to Kent, and to the city which is called Rochester. The Vikings made a fort before the gate [of Rochester]; but they could not capture the city, because the citizens of that city defended themselves bravely,

---

[108] Abbreviated from Asser, *Vita Ælfredi*, c. 65 (ed. Stevenson, p. 49; trans. Keynes and Lapidge, p. 86), with the continuing chronological dislocation of three years (Asser's *nativitatis Ælfredi regis trigesimo quinto* has become *natiuitatis Ælfredi regis tricesimo secundo*).

[109] The reference is apparently to Guthfrith I, Scandinavian king of York, who reigned from 883 until 895 (see Keynes, 'Rulers', p. 526, and *LDE*, ed. Rollason, pp. 122–3, n. 78, and 127 n. 86); but note that this same ruler is named Guthred (as here) in the *Historia de sancto Cuthberto*, c. 13, where St Cuthbert, appearing in a dream to Eadred, abbot of Carlisle, tells him to go to the army of the Danes and to 'a certain young man named Guthred son of Hardacnut, the slave of a certain widow' (ed. Johnson South, p. 52); this same Guthred is then subsequently described as king (ibid. c. 19a, ed. Johnson South, p. 58). The same dream, with reference to King Guthred, is described by Symeon of Durham, *LDE* ii. 13 (ed. Rollason, pp. 124–6); and the restoration of the see of Chester-le-Street is similarly described by Symeon, *LDE* ii. 13 (ed. Rollason, pp. 122–4), all of which makes it likely that this report concerning Guthred was interpolated into the text of Byrhtferth by Symeon, and did not form part of his original design.

HISTORIA REGVM

nec tamen ciuitatem expugnare potuerunt, quia ciues illius ciuitatis se uiriliter defenderunt, quoadusque defensor totius regni Ælfred rex cum magno exercitu superuenit. Adueniente subito rege, ad naues suas Dani confestim confugiunt, concussi terrore, relicta sua arce et equis*c* quos de Francia secum adduxerant, necnon captiuis*d* quos de Francia de eadem gente ceperant.[110] Eodem tempore et anno, ipse armipotens rex classem suam de Cantia | plenam bellatoribus in Orientales direxit Anglos. Cumque ad ostium Sture fluminis adueniret, confestim tredecim naues paratae ad bellum paganorum obuiauerunt eis, qui hinc inde acriter pugnantes, pagani omnes occisi, omnesque naues cum omni pecunia eorum captae sunt. Qui autem fugere poterant ex Danis, cateruatim congregauere undique naues, consertoque nauali proelio cum Anglis, ubi dormiebant somno inerti, occisi sunt, inermis multitudo;[111] quibus illud aptatur congruenter quod legitur: 'Multi claudent uisus cum aspicere deberent.'[112]

Ipso nemphe anno magnus exercitus paganorum de Germania in regionem Antiquorum Saxonum superuenit, contra quos, adunatis undique bellicis uiris, iidem Saxones atque Frisones uiriliter atque fortiter pugnauere, in quibus duobus bellis Christiani populi, diuinae pietatis clementia concedente, uictoriam habuere.[113]

Ea tempestate sanctissimae memoriae praesul Marinus uniuersitatis uiam arripuit, transmittendo spiritum unde prius uenerat. Is denique scolam Saxonum in Romana urbe pro amoris affectu benignissimi regis Ælfredi constituit ab omni tributo <liberam>,*e* qui etiam multa dona ipsi transmisit, inter quae dedit illi partem sanctissimae crucis, in qua Dominus noster Iesus Christus pro uniuersali hominum salute pependit.[114]

Nati sunt ergo regi filii et filiae satis perspicui ac decore formae, quorum quarumque nomina hic sunt deflorata: Eaduuard et Ætheluueard, Æthelflæd et Æthelgifu atque Ælfthryth. Eaduuard uero filius regis, et Ælfthryth*f* soror eius, semper in curia regis cum magna nutritorum atque nutricum diligentia sunt nutriti. Nam et psalmos et Saxonicos libros et carmina studiose didicere.[115] Ætheluueard itaque,

---

c equos *C* *d* captiuos *C* *e* suppl. ed. *f* ealthrid *C²* on an erasure

---

[110] The words *Anno Dominicae incarnationis .dccclxxxiiii.... de eadem gente ceperant* are from Asser, *Vita Ælfredi*, c. 66 (ed. Stevenson, pp. 49–50; trans. Keynes and Lapidge, pp. 86–7), with a chronological dislocation of three years (Asser's *nativitatis Ælfredi regis trigesimo sexto* has become *natiuitatis Ælfredi regis tricesimo tertio*).

[111] The words *Eodem anno... occisi sunt* are from Asser, *Vita Ælfredi*, c. 67 (ed. Stevenson, pp. 50–1; trans. Keynes and Lapidge, p. 87).

PARS QVARTA 161

to the point that King Alfred, defender of the entire realm, arrived with a great army. On the sudden arrival of the king, the Danes quickly flee to their ships, shaken with fear, having abandoned their fort and the horses which they had brought with them from Francia, not to mention the captives which they had seized in Francia from that same people.[111] At the same time, in the same year, the warlike king [Alfred] sent his fleet loaded with warriors from Kent to the East Angles. When it arrived at the mouth of the river Stour, thirteen ships full of Vikings ready for battle encountered them; with fierce fighting on both sides, all the Vikings were killed, and all their ships, with all their booty, were captured. Those of the Danes who were able to flee assembled ships from all over, and, in a naval encounter with the English, where they [the English] were inert, dozing sleepily, they were killed, an unarmed multitude;[111] concerning them that phrase can appropriately be applied which reads 'Many close their eyes when they ought to be watching'.[112]

In that same year a great army of Vikings arrived from Germany in the territory of the Old Saxons; these same Saxons and the Frisians, having combined their warlike forces, fought bravely and valiantly against them; in two battles the Christian peoples, through the bounty of heavenly mercy, had the victory.[113]

At the same time Pope Marinus of most blessed memory went the way of all flesh, sending on his spirit to whence it had previously come. This [pope] established, free of all taxation, the 'school of the Saxons' in Rome out of deep affection for the kindly King Alfred; he [Pope Marinus] also sent to him [King Alfred] many gifts, among which he gave him a piece of the holy and venerable Cross, on which our Lord Jesus Christ hung for the salvation of all mankind.[114]

To King Alfred were born outstanding sons and daughters, of great beauty, whose names are depicted here: Eadweard and Æthelweard, Æthelflæd and Æthelgifu and Ælfthryth. Now Eadweard, the king's son, and Ælfthryth his sister, were always brought up in the king's court by the attentive care of guardians and nurses. For they eagerly learned psalms and books and poems in English.[115] Æthelweard, his

---

[112] This quotation cannot be identified in the electronic databases.

[113] This paragraph is quoted nearly verbatim from Asser, *Vita Ælfredi*, c. 69 (ed. Stevenson, p. 52; trans. Keynes and Lapidge, p. 87).

[114] This paragraph is quoted nearly verbatim from Asser, *Vita Ælfredi*, c. 71 (ed. Stevenson, pp. 53–4; trans. Keynes and Lapidge, p. 88).

[115] The sentence *Nati sunt ergo...studiose didicere* has been taken, greatly abbreviated, from Asser, *Vita Ælfredi*, c. 75 (ed. Stevenson, pp. 57–9; trans. Keynes and Lapidge, pp. 90–1).

162   HISTORIA REGVM

iunior filius eius, ludis litterariae disciplinae subditus emicuit cum plurimis militum puerulis, nobilibus scilicet et ignobilibus. Æthelflæd, soror | eorum, Æthelredo*g* Merciorum principi in matrimonio copulata est; soror quoque ipsorum Æthelgifu monasticae uitae ferulis subiuncta est. His temporibus fideliter glorioseque regimine rexit ecclesiam Christi Plegmundus archiepiscopus; qui uenerandus uir sapientiae fructibus renitebat,*h* praeditus bis binis columnis, iustitiae uidelicet, prudentiae, temperantiae, fortitudinis. Vuerferthus*i* uero regni sceptra Vuigornensis ciuitatulae eodem tempore purpurabat deuotissimo cordis ingenio. Qui imperio regis iussus atque expetitus librum dialogorum Gregorii in Saxonicam linguam euertit, aliquando sensum ex sensu elegantissime interpretatus est. Æthelstanum quoque et Þeruulfum sacerdotes insignes de Mercia ad se inuitarat, eo quod hi praestantius atque perfusius in diuinae legis eruditione pollebant. Hos praecipuo amoris honore dilexit, honorauit; quorum doctrina et eruditione magnificatus est rex pacificus super omnes reges terrae.[116]

16. Anno Dominicae incarnationis .dccclxxxvi., natiuitatis uero Ælfredi regis gloriosi tricesimo quinto, nec nominandus exercitus Danorum iterum in Occidentalium Francorum regionem uenit; qui applicuerunt in flumine quod Sigene*a* dicitur, Parisium quoque ciuitatem adiit ibique hiemauit: transitum pontis ciuibus prohibuit. Sed Deo adminiculum ueri auxilii concedente, et ciuibus uiriliter se protegentibus munitionem irrumpere non potuit.[117] Eodem tempore rex Anglorum post incendia urbium stragesque populorum, Londoniam permaximam ciuitatem honorifice restaurauit et habitabilem fecit, quam Æthelredo praecipuo duci Merciorum commendauit seruandam. Omnes uero Angli et Saxones qui prius ubiubi erant dispersi cum paganis, aut a captiuitate liberati, uenerunt sponte ad regis praesentiam, sponte se suo dominio*b* inclinantes. Ipse autem, ut erat clementissimae mentis, cunctis indulsit patrocinium suae benignitatis.[118]

---

g Eadredo *C*   *h* renidebat *C*   *i* Warfridus *C*
iv.16   *a* insigne *C*   *b* domino *C*

---

[116] The words *His temporibus... omnes reges terrae* have been taken, with some abbreviation and some embellishment, from Asser, *Vita Ælfredi*, c. 77 (ed. Stevenson, pp. 62–3; trans. Keynes and Lapidge, pp. 92–3). That Archbishop Plegmund was endowed with the fourfold columns of the Four Cardinal Virtues (justice, wisdom, moderation, and strength) is a Byrhtferthian topos: *Enchiridion* iv. 1, lines 37–9: 'Quaternarius perfectus est numerus et quattuor uirtutibus exornatus: iustitia uidelicet, temperantia, fortitudine, prudentia' (ed. Baker and Lapidge, p. 198 with commentary at pp. 340–1; cf. also *VSO* iii. 8 and *VSE* i. 9 (*Byrhtferth: Lives*, ed. Lapidge, pp. 68 and 220 respectively). For Byrhtferth's use of the verb

PARS QVARTA

163

younger son, when subjected to games of literary learning, shone out in the company of many other children of soldiers, both noblemen and commoners. Æthelflæd, their sister, was joined in matrimony to Æthelred, ealdorman of the Mercians; and their sister Æthelgifu was suborned to the rules of the monastic life. At this time Archbishop Plegmund faithfully and honourably governed with his rule the church of Christ [at Canterbury]; this venerable man shone out with the fruits of wisdom, endowed by twice-two columns, namely of justice, wisdom, moderation, strength. And Werferth at the same time adorned through the devout genius of his heart the sceptres of the little city of Worcester. Ordered and requested by the command of the king, he turned the book of *Dialogues* of Gregory into the English tongue, sometimes elegantly translating sense for sense. He [Alfred] had also invited the priests Æthelstan and Werwulf from Mercia to [come to] him, for the reason that these two men excelled outstandingly and abundantly in knowledge of divine learning. He loved [and] honoured them with the distinct esteem of love; through their teaching and erudition the peaceful king was glorified above all kings of the earth.[116]

16. In the year of the Lord's incarnation 886, the thirty-fifth year of the glorious King Alfred's life, the unspeakable army of the Danes came again into the district of the western Franks; they anchored in the river Seine, advanced to the city of Paris, and wintered there: they forbade the citizens passage across the bridge. But with God granting the help of genuine assistance, and with the citizens bravely protecting themselves, they [the Vikings] could not breach the fortifications.[117] At the same time the English king, after the conflagrations of cities and the slaughter of peoples, restored the great city of London and made it habitable [again]; he entrusted it to Æthelred, the outstanding ealdorman, for safekeeping. And all the Angles and Saxons, who previously had been scattered everywhere with the Vikings, or had been redeemed from captivity, came willingly into the king's presence, willingly subjecting themselves to his authority. And he, since he was of the most merciful disposition, granted to all of them the patronage of his kindness.[118]

---

purpurare, 'to adorn', see above, *HR* ii. 12 (p. 36). The final words of the paragraph are modelled on 3 Kgs (1 Kgs) 10: 23 ('<u>magnificatus</u> est ergo rex Salomon <u>super omnes reges terrae</u>').

[117] The words *Anno Dominicae incarnationis .dccclxxxvi.... irrumpere non potuit* are from Asser, *Vita Ælfredi*, c. 82 (ed. Stevenson, pp. 68–9; trans. Keynes and Lapidge, p. 97), with the continuing chronological dislocation of three years (Asser's *nativitatis Ælfredi regis trigesimo octavo* has become *natiuitatis Ælfredi regis tricesimo quinto*).

[118] The words *Eodem tempore...suae benignitatis* are from Asser, *Vita Ælfredi*, c. 83 (ed. Stevenson, p. 69; trans. Keynes and Lapidge, pp. 97–8).

164 HISTORIA REGVM

fo. 74va Anno Dominicae incarnationis .dccclxxxvii., natiuitatis autem Ælfredi incliti regis tricesimo sexto, supradictus exercitus Parisium ciuitatem relinquens uenit ad Sigene, deinde ad ostium fluminis quod Materre nominatur, exhinc ad locum qui <dicitur>^{c} Cazei, id est uilla regia, peruenerunt: in quo loco hiemauerunt integro anno. Sequente uero sane anno in ostio fluminis quod appellatur Iona intrauerunt, non sine magno regionis damno, et illic morati sunt uno anno.[119] Ipso denique tempore Ælfredus rex Saxonum, diuino instinctus munere, legere et interpretari sacros apices potuit.[120] Erat itaque multis tribulationibus huius mundi afflictus, quamuis in regia foret potestate constitutus. Nam etiam de Ierosolima ab Elia^d patriarcha epistolas et dona illi diuersa directa uidimus et legimus.[121] Qualiter dilatauit regni sui imperia, et renouauit urbium moenia, atque ciuitatum munitiones roborauit quae erant dirutae, et quae non erant fecit, quis urbana facundia suffultus possit labiis exultationis edicere? Sancta quoque loca qualiter^e ditauit ornamentis et regalibus donis, quis enuntiet?[122] Perturbatus erat frequenter animo contra principes et pentecontarchos[123] et omne genus peruersorum, quoniam ipsi noluerunt eum sequi in studiis quibus ipse desudabat. Sed tamen ille solus, diuino suffultus amminiculo, regni gubernacula, uelut praecipuus gubernator nauim suam, hoc est, uitam suae gloriosae mentis ad portum pacifici paradisi studuit transferre. Solebat frequenti memoria hoc retinere quod canitur,

> Quidquid uolet perhennem
> cautus ponere sedem,
> stabilisque nec sonori
> sterni flatibus Euri,[124]

Et infra:

fo. 74vb
> quam tenet ruinis^f
> miscens aequora uentus.

---

^{c} *suppl. ed. (from Asser)* ^{d} el *C* ^{e} qualibet *C* ^{f} *after* ruinis *C adds* huius saeculi status

---

[119] The words *Anno Dominicae incarnationis .dccclxxxvii .... sunt uno anno* are from Asser, *Vita Ælfredi*, c. 84 (ed. Stevenson, p. 71; trans. Keynes and Lapidge, p. 98), with some abbreviation and with the continuing chronological dislocation of three years (Asser's *nativitatis Ælfredi regis trigesimo nono* has become *natiuitatis Ælfredi regis tricesimo sexto*).

[120] This sentence has been drastically abbreviated from Asser, *Vita Ælfredi*, c. 88 (ed. Stevenson, pp. 73–4; trans. Keynes and Lapidge, pp. 99–100).

[121] Abbreviated from Asser, *Vita Ælfredi*, c. 91 (ed. Stevenson, pp. 76–7; trans. Keynes and Lapidge, p. 101). The transmitted reading *ab El* in C was convincingly emended by Stevenson to *ab Elia*, that is, the presents were sent by Elias, patriarch of Jerusalem (*c*.879–907) to King Alfred.

PARS QVARTA
165

In the year of the Lord's incarnation 887, the thirty-sixth year of the distinguished King Alfred's life, the aforementioned army, abandoning the city of Paris, came down the Seine, and then to the mouth of the river named the Marne, and thence they arrived at the place called Chézy, that is, a royal estate; in this place they wintered for a whole year. In the following year they entered the mouth of the river Yonne, not without great damage to the region, and stayed there for a year.[119] At that same time Alfred, king of the Saxons, prompted by divine assistance, could read and translate sacred writings.[120] He was afflicted by many tribulations of this world, even though he was established in royal authority. For we have seen and read that he received letters and gifts sent to him from Jerusalem by the patriarch Elias.[121] As to how he extended the dominions of his realm, and renewed the ramparts of towns, and strengthened the fortifications of cities which had been demolished, and which no longer existed, who sustained by urbane eloquence could possibly express with the lips of exultation? As to how he enriched holy places with ornaments and royal gifts, who shall say?[122] He was frequently troubled in his mind against leaders and captains[123] and all kinds of perverse [men], because they did not wish to follow him in the pursuits at which he exerted himself. But yet he alone, sustained by divine assistance, sought to transfer the governance of his reign, as an outstanding pilot his ship, that is, the life of his distinguished mind, to the port of a peaceful paradise. He used frequently to retain in his memory that which is sung [in verse]:

> Whosoever should wish
> cautiously to establish a permanent and stable home,
> [one] not to be demolished
> by the blasts of the south-east wind,[124]

And, further on,

> [a home] which the wind occupies,
> churning up the waves [of the sea].

---

[122] Asser describes the wonderful works of reconstruction undertaken by Alfred (*Vita Ælfredi*, c. 91), but the formulation—*quis urbana facundia suffultus possit...edicere?...quis enuntiet?*—is characteristically Byrhtferthian; see discussion by Lapidge, 'The early sections', pp. 107–8 = *ALL* ii. 327–8, and Introduction, above, p. xxxix.

[123] An ostentatious graecism ($\pi\epsilon\nu\tau\eta\kappa\text{o}\nu\tau\acute{\alpha}\rho\chi\text{o}\varsigma$), meaning 'captain (of fifty men)', which Byrhtferth probably lifted from Aldhelm, prose *De uirginitate*, c. 20 (*MGH, AA* xv. 249); it is not in the text of Asser at this point.

[124] Boethius, *De consolatione Philosophiae*, iii, met. iv, lines 1–4 (CCSL xciv. 44); but note that the transmitted text of Boethius reads *quamuis* against Byrhtferth's erroneous *quidquid*.

166 HISTORIA REGVM

Tu conditus quieti,
felix robore ualli,
duces serenus aeuum,
ridens aetheris iras.[125]

Haec spirituali indagine secum rex piissimae mentis reuoluens, inedicibilibus bonitatum fructuum actibus redolebat. Diebus solemnibus festis quanta munera suis episcopis et ducibus atque militibus contulit, quis enarret? Tunc pauperes iubilando exultabant; tunc orphani et uiduae nimio gaudio cordis applaudebant. Nouerat illud scholastici: 'Tunc est pretiosa pecunia cum translata fuerit in alios; largiendi usu desinit possideri.'[126] Coepit denique assidue non solum episcopos aetherea claritate nitentes admonere, ut populi delicta corrigerent, et uulgarem stultitiam castigando acrius coercerent; et non solum pastores admonuit populorum, uerum etiam ducibus et dilectissimis ministris praecepit, ut semetipsos ad communem totius regni utilitatem sapientissime suppeditarent.

17. Fecerat idem rex monasterium praepulchrum in loco qui dicitur Æthelingaige, <cui>[a] uicina occidentali limite arx munitissima praephati regis imperio et operatione consita est. In quo coenobio diuersi generis monachos undique congregauit, et in eodem loco collocauit.[127] Aliud quoque constituit monasterium iuxta orientalem portam ciuitatis quae Sceftesburg appellatur, satis habitationi sanctimonialium habile, in quo filiam suam Æthelgyfu deuotam Deo uirginem abbatissam constituit. Tanta enim dona et possessiones ambobus concessit monasteriis, ut sufficeret eis ad uictum et ad uestitum quamdiu uita comes afforet.[128]

18. His quae supra retulimus pleniter firmiterque peractis, saepe
fo. 75ʳᵃ nominatus | rex Ælfredus solito suo more intra suae mentis thalamum coepit sagaci ingenio pertractare, et pertractando ruminare illud quod in diuinis scriptum est litteris. 'Si', inquit, 'recte offeras, et recte non diuidas, peccasti.'[129] Et illud medullitus est praemeditatus quod ait Salomon sapientissimus regum: 'Cor sane regis in manu Domini est

---

iv.17 *ᵃ suppl. ed.*

---

[125] Boethius, *De consolatione Philosophiae*, ii, met. iv, lines 17–22 (CCSL xciv. 26). Note that the transmitted text of Boethius here reads *Quamuis tonet* ('although [the wind] thunders'), whereas Byrhtferth has corrupted this to *Quam tenet* (translated accordingly).

[126] Boethius, *De consolatione Philosophiae*, ii, pr. v. 5 (CCSL xciv. 26).

[127] The description of Athelney is abbreviated from Asser, *Vita Ælfredi*, c. 92 (ed. Stevenson, pp. 79–80; trans. Keynes and Lapidge, pp. 102–3).

PARS QVARTA 167

You, settled in calm,
content with the strength of your rampart,
spend your time peacefully,
smiling at the rage of the weather.[125]

Turning these things over with spiritual reflection, this king of devout mind abounded in the inexpressible deeds of the fruits of goodness. As to what great gifts he granted to his bishops and ealdormen and thegns on solemn feast days, who shall describe? At such times poor people rejoiced in exultation; orphans and widows then celebrated with extreme joy in their hearts. He knew that saying of the scholar, 'Money is precious when it is distributed to others; through its distribution it ceases to be owned'.[126] At length he began not only to urge his bishops, shining with heavenly brightness, to correct the sins of the people and sharply to constrain the people's stupidity by chastizing them; and he warned not only these pastors of the people, but even commanded the ealdormen and his favourite thegns wisely to address themselves to the common benefit of the entire kingdom.

17. He had constructed an attractive monastery in the place called Athelney, near to which a fortified citadel was built at the command and execution of the aforesaid king. He assembled in this monastery many kinds of monks from everywhere, and established them in this same place.[127] He also built another monastery near the eastern gate of the town which is called Shaftesbury, entirely suitable for the occupation of nuns, in which he established his daughter Æthelgifu, a virgin devoted to God, as abbess. He granted such great gifts and possessions to both monasteries as would suffice them for food and clothing as long as life remained.[128]

18. When these things which we have fully and faithfully described had been achieved, the oft-mentioned King Alfred began in his usual way to consider in the recesses of his heart, and in so considering to ruminate, on that which is written in divine Scripture. 'If', it says, 'you rightly offer, and do not rightly divide, you have sinned.'[129] And he meditated inwardly on that which Solomon, wisest of kings, said: 'The

---

[128] The description of Shaftesbury is abbreviated from Asser, *Vita Ælfredi*, c. 98 (ed. Stevenson, p. 85; trans. Keynes and Lapidge, p. 105).

[129] The quotation is from the Vetus Latina translation of Gen. 4: 7 (God speaking to Cain), as quoted by Augustine, *De ciuitate Dei* xv. 7: 'Si recte offeras, recte autem non diuidas, peccasti' (CCSL xlviii. 460).

168 HISTORIA REGVM

omnipotentis.'[130] Censum quoque suum trifarie diuisit, ita ut istic libet praetitulari: primae partis sectionem sui census, bellatoribus annualiter largitus est; secundam, operatoribus quos ex multis gentibus aggregauerat; tertiam, aduenis undique ad se uenientibus, sciens illud cordetenus, 'Hilarem datorem diligit Deus.'[131] Erat enimuero in multis et in multiphariis tribulationum stimulis constitutus, quamuis in regia esset potestate subthronizatus.

[130] Cf. Prov. 21: 1 ('cor regis in manu Domini quocumque voluerit inclinabit illud').
[131] 2 Cor. 9: 7.

PARS QVARTA

king's heart is in the hand of the Almighty.'[130] He divided his revenue into three parts, as may be spelled out as follows: the first part of his revenue he gave annually to his warriors; the second part, to the labourers whom he had assembled from many nations; and the third part, to foreigners coming to him from everywhere, knowing in the depths of his heart that 'God loves a cheerful giver'.[131] But he was troubled by the goads of many and multifarious tribulations, even though he was enthroned in royal authority.

APPENDIX I

The Annals 888–957

Part IV of Byrhtferth's *Historia regum* ends with an entry drawn from Asser for 887 (c. 86), in fact the last annal-entry in Asser which is based on a text of the *Anglo-Saxon Chronicle*. The end of the *Historia regum* is followed immediately in CCCC 139 by a set of annals for the years 888–957 (fos. 75[ra]–76[ra]), which appear in context to be an intentional continuation of Byrhtferth's work. Interestingly, at one point (below, s.a. 890), the annalist refers specifically to what has previously been stated in Byrhtferth's *Historia regum*: *sicut superius legitur*, referring to *HR* iv. 13. But were these additional annals composed by Byrhtferth?

Previous editors have considered the annals for 888–957 to be a simple continuation of the preceding text, and hence to be the composition of the same anonymous author. In the editions of Petrie and Hodgson-Hinde, the annals follow on from the end of (what I designate) Part IV without a break, or any indication that the annals mark a new beginning. As we have seen, Thomas Arnold referred to the anonymous author of the additional annals as 'the Cuthbertine', on the strength of references to St Cuthbert in these additional annals against the years 899, 925, and 934.[1] But Peter Hunter Blair rightly observed of these additional annals (888–957) that 'the individual entries are written with an economy of words and a simplicity which provides a striking contrast with the preceding parts of the *Historia Regum*. Nowhere do they show any trace of those stylistic features which have been found to be characteristic of sections 1–5 [*scil*. Parts I–IV in the present edition]'.[2] I share the opinion of Peter Hunter Blair. The terse, telegraphic style of the annals 888–957 shows none of the flamboyant verbosity characteristic of Byrhtferth, as I have described it in previous pages (above, pp. xxiv–xxviii). Of polysyllabic adjectives and adverbs construed in the superlative, there is not a single example, nor a single example of an adjective in *-bilis* or an adverb in *-iter*. Not a single one of Byrhtferth's favourite phrases appears in these additional annals. Not a single one of the rhetorical tropes used to excess by Byrhtferth

---

[1] *Symeonis Monachi Opera Omnia*, ed. Arnold, ii, p. xvii.

[2] Hunter Blair, 'Some observations', pp. 105–6.

172 APPENDIX I

(hyperbaton, polyptoton, paronomasia, asyndeton, and erotema) is found in them.

The annals 888–957 are, like most surviving sets of annals, largely concerned with recording deaths and murders. In order to describe the death of a king or bishop, the author of the additional annals uses the simple expression *obiit*: *obiit Ethelswith* (888), *Guthrum rex obiit* (890), *Eboracensis episcopus Wlfhere obiit* (892), *Elfredus rex obiit* (899), *Eardulfus quoque episcopus... obiit* (899), *Ethelstanus rex obiit* (939), *Ouuel rex Brittonum obiit* (951). The only variation to this plain formula occurs when the death of Edward the Elder is recorded as *Edwardus rex mortuus est* (922), or when a king has been murdered (*Brehtsige occisus est* (902), *Niel rex occisus est* (914), *Edmundus rex occisus est* (948)). Byrhtferth's treatment of the deaths of kings and bishops may be seen in the annals for 732–801, which form Part III of his *HR*, and which are comparable to the additional annals in their concern with deaths and murders. In the course of the annals in Part III, Byrhtferth uses the plain expression *obiit* some eleven times and *mortuus est* once; but he typically describes the death of a king or bishop by means of a verbose circumlocution.[3] The following list will give some idea of Byrhtferth's practice:

ad supernae ciuitatis gaudia subleuatus (iii. 3)
pro meritis supernis allectus ciuibus (iii. 3)
caelestium donorum consecutus est praemia (iii. 3)
poli culmina conscendit pro meritis (iii. 3)
episcopus diem clausit ultimum (iii. 5)
antistes migrauit ad Dominum (iii. 5, iii. 7)
episcopus subleuatus est in regionem uiuentium (iii. 6)
ad caelestia migrauit (iii. 7)
translatus sit ex hoc mundo ad celsitudinem aeternae uisionis (iii. 7)
de Ægypto huius saeculi translatus est (iii. 7)
translatus est ad alterius uitae contemplationem (iii. 8)
uiam sanctorum patrum est secutus (iii. 9)
ex hoc saeculo migrauit (iii. 11)

---

[3] Peter Hunter Blair identified the use of 'a wide variety of bombastic circumlocutions' to describe the deaths of individuals as a salient feature of (what I designate) Part III of the *Historia regum*, and went on to comment: 'It is evident that a determined attempt has been made to achieve literary effect and to depart from the monotony of an annalistic chronicle recording isolated events' ('Some observations', p. 97). The author of the additional annals (888–957) made no attempt whatsoever to 'achieve literary effect'.

THE ANNALS 888–957

ex hac uita subtractus est (iii. 12)
hanc uitam dereliquit (iii. 12)
de hac mortali carne migrauit ad uerae lucis perennitatem (iii. 12)
feliciter spiritum emisit ad superos (iii. 13)
de hoc instabilis uitae cursu migrauit ad consortium electorum (iii. 14)
diem Domini uidere desiderauit, cui et concessum est (iii. 14)
ex huius uitae naufragio subtrahitur (iii. 15)
ex uoragine huius coenulentae uitae eripitur (iii. 15)
uectigal morti dedit (iii. 15)
migrauit ex hoc saeculo ad aeternae salutis gaudium (iii. 16)
ex hac luce migrauit ad aeternae lucis perennitatem (iii. 17)
huic uitae modum fecit (iii. 18)
ad supernam feliciter migrauit patriam (iii. 19)
ergastulum huius laboriosae uitae deseruit (iii. 19)
optata percepit munera alterius uitae (iii. 19)
ex 'rapidis flatibus' huius saeculi spiritum emisit (iii. 20)
ex hac lucis tenebrositate transmigrauit ad uerae lucis beatitudinem
    (iii. 21)
ex hac luce migrauit ad Dominum (iii. 23)
uitae huius tempora contempsit (iii. 24)
diem suscepit ultimum (iii. 27)
diem uidit ultimum (iii. 27)
diem clausit ultimum (iii. 29)
uitae huius contempsit tempora (iii. 29)

Although there is a certain amount of repetition, it is clear that
Byrhtferth devoted considerable ingenuity in coining expressions to
describe the death of an individual. By contrast, the author of the
additional annals contented himself with plain *obiit*. In order to
describe the devastation wrought by armies, the annalist of 888–957
sometimes uses striking vocabulary: for example the verbs *infringo* (*Rex
Sihtricus infregit Deuennport* (920)) and *irrumpo* (*irruperunt et uastauerunt Dunbline* (912), *Rex Inguald irrupit Eboracum* (919)). Neither
of these verbs was ever used by Byrhtferth. In short, there are no
grounds whatsoever for thinking that the annals 888–957 were composed by Byrhtferth. Finally, a decisive argument against Byrhtferth's
authorship is chronological: the last annal (957) refers to King Æthelred
'the Unready' (978–1016) as the 'father of King Edward (the Confessor)'
(1042–66), which suggests that this annal could not have been composed before 1042 at the earliest: by which time Byrhtferth had been
silent for many years, and was probably dead.

174 APPENDIX I

The question remains, however: when and where were these annals appended, and what is their relationship to Byrhtferth? The sources drawn on by the annalist present a confusing picture. A number of annals appear to be translated from a version of the *Anglo-Saxon Chronicle* (annals for 888, 890, 893, 894, 899, 902, 906, 910, 914, 919, 927, 933, 934, 939, 941, 948, 950, 955, 956), but it is not clear which version of the *Chronicle* is in question: sometimes the wording most closely resembles that of the D-version, which was apparently produced at either York or Worcester (906, 910, 939, 950, 956); at other times, it resembles that of the E-version, or 'Peterborough Chronicle' (910, 914, 927, 933, 941, 955); and at yet other times, the entries agree almost verbatim with the F-version, a Latin text of the *Chronicle* written at Canterbury (888, 899, 919, 948), but derived from an archetype very similar to that which lies behind the E-version. On a few occasions (894, 900, 902), the annalist's wording resembles that of the Latin *Chronicon* of Æthelweard, itself based on a (lost) version of the *Anglo-Saxon Chronicle*. And finally a couple of entries repeat material found in the Irish *Annals of Ulster* (912, 951), but how the annalist was able to consult (or understand) annals composed in Irish is totally unclear. In short, the annalist's use of earlier annal collections throws no light whatsoever on where he was working.

Other entries may point to a place of origin in northern England. Numerous entries refer to Northumbria in general (890, 941, 943, 945, 948, 950, 952, 953) and some to York in particular (892, 900, 919, 939, 941). Significantly, a number of entries relates to St Cuthbert and the community of St Cuthbert, housed at Lindisfarne until 875, but during the period after 883 at Chester-le-Street, before eventually being located at Durham in 995. Several such entries have their closest parallel in the *Historia de sancto Cuthberto* (899, 925, 934); one entry, which has no parallel elsewhere and preserves information not found elsewhere, concerns Lindisfarne (941). The sum of this evidence suggests that the annals for 888 to 957 were compiled somewhere in Northumbria, conceivably at York, or perhaps more likely at Durham, where the entire corpus of materials in CCCC 139 appears to have been assembled.

In printing these annals, I reproduce the twelfth-century orthography of CCCC 139, rather than attempting to restore the (presumed) orthography of Byrhtferth's own day, as I have attempted to do with the *Historia regum*.

THE ANNALS 888–957   175

[888] Anno Dominicae incarnationis .dccclxxxviii. Beocca princeps fo. 75ʳᵃ
Romam detulit elemosinam regis Ælfredi. Illo itinere obiit Ethelsuith,
soror eiusdem regis, et sepulta est in Pauia.[4]

[890] Anno .dcccxc. Beornhelm abbas elemosinam regis Elfredi et
Occidentalium Saxonum Romam pertulit. Eodem anno Guthrum rex
Northanhymbrorum obiit.[5] Hunc, sicut superius legitur,[6] rex Ælfredus ele-
uauit de baptismate et uocauit eum Ethelstan. Quo anno prefatus exercitus
a Sigene perrexit Sanlaudan, quod est situm inter Britanniam et Galliam.
Sed a Britonibus in fugam uersi, plures in amne proximo submersi sunt.[7]

[891] ᵃAnno .dcccxci. Heathured suscepit episcopatum.ᵃ[8]

[892] Anno .dcccxcii. Eboracensis episcopus Wlfhere obiit, anno sui
archiepiscopatus .xxxix.[9]

[893] Anno .dcccxciii. Orientales Saxones et Northumbrenses obsides
dederunt, et iurauerunt regi Elfredo fidelitatem | contra predictos fo. 75ʳᵇ
paganos, qui iam in Angliam reuersi fuerant.[10]

ᵃ⁻ᵃ *entered at foot of column a, with* signes de renvoi, *by a later hand*

---

[4] The last year in which Asser depends on (a version of) the *Anglo-Saxon Chronicle* is 887,
which—probably not by coincidence—is the last year of Alfred's life described by Byrhtferth
in Part IV. The present annal-entry for 888 is from *ASC*, s.a. 888 (A): 'In this year Ealdorman
Beocca took to Rome the alms of the West Saxons and of King Alfred. And Queen Æthelswith,
who was King Alfred's sister, died, and her body is buried in Pavia' (trans. Whitelock, p. 53).
The statement that Æthelswith was with Beocca on the journey to Rome (*illo itinere*) is not
included in the A-text of *ASC*, but is stated explicitly in the F-version of *ASC*: 'et Æðelspyð
soror Alfredi regis obiit in itinere Rome, et sepultum est corpus illius in Pavia' (ed. Baker,
p. 75). Similar information is contained in *Chronicle of Æthelweard*, ed. Campbell, p. 47.
[5] From *ASC*, s.a. 890: 'In this year Abbot Beornhelm took to Rome the alms of the West
Saxons and of King Alfred. And the northern king, Guthrum, whose baptismal name was
Æthelstan, died' (trans. Whitelock, p. 53).
[6] The cross-reference is to *HR* iv. 13 (above, p. 154). The cross-reference implies that these
annals were originally intended as a sort of appendix to the four parts of Byrhtferth's *HR*.
[7] Also from *ASC*, s.a. 890: 'And the same year the Danish army went from the Seine to
St. Lô, which lies between Brittany and France; and the Bretons fought against them and had
the victory, and drove them into a river and drowned many of them' (trans. Whitelock, p. 53).
Similar information is found in Æthelweard, *Chronicon* (ed. Campbell, p. 47).
[8] No bishop of this name and approximate date is listed in *PASE*, s.v. 'Hathored'. However,
there was an earlier bishop of Lindisfarne named Heathured, who died in 830 (Keynes, 'Bishops',
p. 565); and since this annal was added after the event by a later scribe (see *app. crit. ad loc.*), one
wonders whether an entry relating to this earlier Heathured has been inserted here by mistake.
[9] Cf. *ASC*, s.a. 892 (F): 'Hic etiam obiit Wlfherus Norðanhymbrorum archiepiscopus' (ed.
Baker, p. 77). Keynes ('Bishops', p. 562) gives the year of this Wulfhere's accession as 854.
[10] Whitelock remarks (*EHD* i. 277, n. 4): 'Under 893 and 894 are brief entries taken from
a correctly dated copy of the [Anglo-Saxon] Chronicle.' For the present annal (893), see
ASC, s.a. 893: 'In this year...the Northumbrians and the East Angles had given King Alfred
oaths, and the East Angles had given six preliminary hostages' (trans. Whitelock, p. 55). Note
that the annalist here mistakenly describes as 'East Saxons' (*Orientales Saxones*) the peoples
whom the chronicler calls 'East Angles' (*Eastengle*).

176   APPENDIX I

[894] Anno .dcccxciiii. Exercitus predictus qui obsedit Exancestre
uastauit omnia circa Cissacestre. Sed non multo post ab his qui erant
in ciuitate in fugam uersi sunt, multi occisi et multe ex nauibus eorum
capte.[11] Hoc anno Guthred rex obiit.[12]

[899] Anno .dcccxcix. Elfredus rex obiit cum regnasset[b] annis
.xxviii.; cui filius Edwardus successit,[13] diligenter a patre admonitus ut
precipue sanctum Cuthbertum honoraret.[14] Eardulfus quoque episcopus in Cunceceastre obiit, quo corpus sancti Cuthberti transtulerat,
cum quo per .ix. annos ante paganorum exercitum multo cum labore et
penuria de loco ad locum fugerat.[15] Huic Cuthbertus in episcopatum
successit.[16]

---

[b] regnassed C

---

[11] *ASC*, s.a. 894: 'And when the Danish army which had besieged Exeter turned home-
wards, they ravaged up in Sussex near Chichester, and the citizens put them to flight and
killed many hundreds of them, and captured some of their ships' (trans. Whitelock, p. 56).

[12] This entry reports the death of Guthfrith I, Scandinavian king of York (883–94): see
Keynes, 'Rulers', p. 526, and Æthelweard, *Chronicon*, s.a. 895: 'Transeunte etiam anni unius
decursu obiit et Guthfrid, rex Northanhymbrorum, in natalitia sancti Bartholomaei, apostoli
Christi [24 Aug.]; cuius mausoleatur Euoraca corpus in urbe in basilica summa' (ed.
Campbell, p. 51). In northern sources, however, this same king is named Guthred (not
Guthfrith): see *HSC*, c. 13 (ed. Johnson South, p. 52, with commentary at pp. 87–9), and
Symeon of Durham, *LDE* ii. 13 (ed. Rollason, pp. 122–7, esp. 122 n. 78). Interestingly,
Byrhtferth (*HR* iv. 15) refers to this same king as Guthred: 'Guthred ex seruo factus est rex,
et sedes episcopalis in Cunceceastra restauratur' (above, p. 158).

[13] The death of King Alfred after a reign of twenty-eight years is given in *ASC*, but against
the year 901 (F): 'Rex Ælfredus obiit, et filius eius Edpardus suscepit regnum. Ælfredus
regnauit .xxviii. annis' (ed. Baker, p. 77). The correct date of Alfred's death, and the succession of Edward, is given in Æthelweard, *Chronicon* (ed. Campbell, p. 51).

[14] The statement that Edward was admonished by his father (Alfred) to honour
St Cuthbert is not found in southern English tradition; but note *HSC*, c. 18: 'Ammonuit
etiam filium suum Eadwardum qui ibi erat, quod si uellet esse fidelis Deo et sancto Cuthberto,
non ei esset timendum de inimicis suis' (ed. Johnson South, p. 56), as well as Symeon of
Durham, *LDE* ii. 10: Cuthbert, appearing in a vision to King Alfred, states that if the king
and his sons were faithful to him, he would protect him; and thus it transpired: 'Vbi de hos-
tibus uictoria Aelfredus potitus, per filium suum Edwardum regalia dona transmisit sancto
Cuthberto' (ed. Rollason, p. 112).

[15] According to the *Historia de sancto Cuthberto*, c. 20, Eardwulf became bishop of
Lindisfarne in 854. In 875 he and his community abandoned Lindisfarne and eventually settled in Chester-le-Street (*Cunceceastre*) in 883, after seven years' wandering, taking the relics
of St Cuthbert with them (*portantes illud de loco in locum per septem annos*): *HSC*, ed. Johnson
South, p. 58. In the same chapter of *HSC*, it is stated that Bishop Eardwulf died at the same
time as King Alfred (*Eo tempore obiit rex Elfredus et Eardulfus episcopus*). The figure of nine
years' wandering given in the present annal is found in no other source, and *.ix.* should probably be emended to *.vii.*

[16] The annalist (or the scribe of C) has mistakenly written *Cuthbertus* for *Cuthheardus*, for
we know from both *HSC* and Symeon of Durham that the successor of Eardwulf was named
Cuthheard: see *HSC*, c. 21 ('Cutheardus episcopalem cathedram apud Cunceceastre accepit':
ed. Johnson South, p. 58), and Symeon of Durham, *LDE* ii. 16: 'In cuius [*scil*. Eardulfi] loco
Cutheardus...cathedram episcopalem suscepit regendam' (ed. Rollason, p. 128).

THE ANNALS 888–957   177

[900] Anno .dcccc. Ethelbald ordinatus est in episcopatum Eboracensis ęcclesię.[17]

[901] Anno .dcccci. Osbrith regno pulsus est.[18]

[902] Anno .dcccci. Brehtsige occisus est.[19]

[906] Anno .dccccvi. Rex Edwardus necessitate compulsus pacem firmauit cum Orientalibus Anglis et Northymbrensibus.[20]

[910] Anno .dccccx. Angli et Dani pugnauerunt apud Teontanhole.[c] Rex Edwardus Londoniam et Oxnaforda et que ad ea pertinent suscepit; quo anno multa piratarum manus circa Sabrinam flumen crudeliter uastando grassata est, sed ibi citius tota pene interiit.[21]

[912] Anno .dccccxii. Reginwald[d] rex et Oter comes et Osuulf[e] Cracabam irruperunt et uastauerunt Dunbline.[22]

---

[c] Teontanbole *C*   [d] Reingwald *C*   [e] Osuul *C*

---

[17] The ordination of Æthelbald as archbishop of York is not reported in *ASC*; but Æthelweard, *Chronicon*, s.a. 900, records the ordination as having taken place in the same year as King Edward's coronation: 'In eodem anno Æthelbald in Lundonia arce praesulatum sumpsit Euoracae urbis' (ed. Campbell, pp. 51–2); cf. Keynes, 'Bishops', p. 562.

[18] The identity of this Osbriht, and the kingdom from which he was expelled, is unknown; *PASE* s.v. states simply 'king or nobleman, fl. 901' (evidently derived from the present annal).

[19] According to *ASC*, s.aa. 904 (A), 905 (BCD), Brihtsige was the son of the ætheling Beornoth, and was killed, fighting on the Danish side, at the battle of the Holme. According to Æthelweard, *Chronicon*, the 'battle of the Holme' took place in late 902 (ed. Campbell, p. 52). But since, according to the 'Mercian Register' (*ASC*, trans. Whitelock, p. 60), the battle involved the Danes and the men of Kent, the location of 'Holme'—a very common place-name—is presumably to be sought in East Anglia, Suffolk, or Norfolk. Ekwall (*DEPN*, p. 246) identifies the site of the battle as Holme Hale, near Swaffham in Norfolk.

[20] Apparently derived from *ASC*, s.a. 906 (CD): 'And that same year the peace was established at Tidingford, just as King Edward decreed, both with the East Angles and the Northumbrians' (trans. Whitelock, p. 60), describing the 'peace of Tiddingford' (near Leighton Buzzard, Bedfordshire).

[21] This entry is apparently derived from *ASC*, s.a. 910 (DE): 'In this year the English army and the Danish army fought at Tettenhall [in the outskirts of present-day Wolverhampton]... and King Edward succeeded to London and Oxford and to all the lands which belonged to them; and a great naval force came hither... and ravaged greatly by the Severn, but they almost all perished afterwards' (trans. Whitelock, p. 62).

[22] This event is not recorded in other Anglo-Saxon sources; but what is apparently the same event is recorded against the year 918 in the *Annals of Ulster*, s.a. 918.4: 'The foreigners of Loch dá Chaech, i.e. Ragnall, king of the dark foreigners, and the two jarls, Oitir and Gragabai, forsook Ireland and proceeded afterwards against the men of Scotland. The men of Scotland, moreover, moved against them and they met on the bank of the Tyne in northern Saxonland... The Scotsmen routed the three battalions which they saw, and made a very great slaughter of the heathens, including Oitir and Gragabai. Ragnall, however, then attacked the rear of the Scotsmen, and made a slaughter of them' (ed. MacAirt and MacNiocaill, p. 367). The names of the jarls, given here in Irish orthography, correspond to ON Ottar and Kraka-bein, 'crow-foot', and *Dunbline* here refers to Dunblane (Perthshire), not Dublin (see also *EHD* i, ed. Whitelock, p. 278).

178   APPENDIX I

[914] Anno .dccccxiiii. Niel rex occisus est a fratre Sihtrico.[23]

[919] Anno .dccccxix. Rex Inguald irrupit Eboracum.[24]

fo. 75ᵛᵃ   [920] Anno .dccccxx. Rex Sihtricus infregit Deuennport.[25]

[923] Anno .dccccxxiii. Edwardus rex mortuus est, relinquens imperium filio suo Æthelstano.[26]

[925] Anno .dccccxxv.ᶠ Wigredus episcopus consecratur ad episcopatum sancti Cuthberti.[27]

[927] Anno .dccccxxvii. Ethelstanus rex de regno Brittonum Gudfridum regem fugauit.[28]

[933] Anno .dccccxxxiii. Rex Ethelstanus iussit Eadwinum fratrem suum submergi in mare.[29]

ᶠ .dccccv. C

---

[23] Cf. *ASC*, s.a. 921 (E): 'In this year King Sihtric killed his brother Niall' (trans. Whitelock, p. 68), and the *Annals of Ulster*, s.a. 919.3: 'The heathens won a battle against the Irish at Duiblinn in which fell Niall Glúndub son of Aed, king of Ireland, in the third year of his reign' (*EHD* i, ed. MacAirt and MacNiocaill, p. 369).

[24] The transmitted form *Inguald* is an error, perhaps scribal, for *Ragnuald*, to judge from entries in *ASC*, s.a. 923 (DE): 'In this year King Ragnald won York' (trans. Whitelock, p. 68), and *ASC* s.a. 923 (F): '.dccccxxiii. Her Regnold cing gewann Euorwic. Rex Regnoldus deuicit Eboracam' (ed. Baker, p. 78). Keynes ('Rulers', p. 526) notes that Ragnald I, Scandinavian king of York (and son of Ívarr the Boneless) acceded to the throne in 919, and submitted to King Edward in 920.

[25] The information that King Sihtric destroyed Davenport is apparently not recorded elsewhere. Davenport is the name of an area near Hale (Greater Manchester).

[26] *ASC*, s.a. 924 (925 (F)): 'In this year King Edward died and his son Æthelstan succeeded to the kingdom' (trans. Whitelock, p. 68).

[27] The consecration of Wigred as bishop of St Cuthbert (at Chester-le-Street) is recorded by Symeon of Durham, *LDE* ii. 18: 'Tilredus... defunctus est et in eius locum Wigredus eligitur episcopus et consecratus' (ed. Rollason, p. 134, with n. 101: 'Wigred may have been bishop at Chester-le-Street from 925 until around 942, but the dates are uncertain'; so also Keynes, 'Bishops', p. 565).

[28] *ASC*, s.a. 927 (E): 'In this year King Æthelstan drove out King Guthfrith' (trans. Whitelock, p. 69).

[29] *ASC*, s.a. 933 (E): 'In this year the atheling Edwin was drowned at sea' (trans. Whitelock, p. 69). The present annal is unique in stating that Edwin was drowned on Æthelstan's orders ('iussit... submergi'), and one would like to know the source of this information. The fullest account of Edwin's drowning is contained in the *Gesta abbatum S. Bertini Sithensium*, because Edwin was honourably buried at Saint-Bertin, in return for which Æthelstan granted the monastery at Bath as well as many gifts in remembrance of his brother's death: 'Quos [*scil.* monachos Sithienses] rex Adalstenus benigne suscipiens, monasterium quod dicitur Ad-Balneos eis statim concessit, ob id maxime, quia frater eiusdem incliti regis Edwinus rex in monasterio sancti Bertini fuerat tumulatus. Siquidem anno Verbi incarnati 933 idem rex Edwinus, cum, cogente aliqua regni sui perturbatione, hac in maris parte ascensa navi vellet devenire, perturbatione ventorum facta navique collisa, mediis fluctibus absortus est. Cuius corpus cum ad litus esset devectum, Adalolfus comes, quoniam propinquus ei carnali consanguinitate erat, cum honore sumens, ad Sancti Bertini monasterium detulit tumulandum. Post cuius mortem frater eius Adalstanus plurima huic loco in eius elemosina direxit exenia, et ob id eiusdem monasterii monachos amabiliter suscepit ad se venientes' (MGH, *SS*

THE ANNALS 888–957
179

[934] Anno .dccccxxxiiii. Rex Ethelstanus cum multo exercitu Scotiam tendens,[30] ad sepulcrum sancti Cuthberti uenit, illius patrocinio se suumque iter commendauit, multa ac diuersa dona que regem decerent ei obtulit et terras, eterno igni contradens cruciandos quicumque ei aliquid ex his subtraxerint.[31] Deinde hostes subegit, Scotiam usque Dunfoeder et Vuertermorum terrestri exercitu uastauit, nauali uero usque Catenes depopulatus est.[32]

[937] Anno .dccccxxxvii. Ethelstanus rex apud Wendune pugnauit, regemque Onlafum cum .dc. et .xv. nauibus, Constantinum quoque regem Scotorum et regem Cumbrorum, cum omni eorum multitudine, in fugam uertit.[33]

[939] Anno .dccccxxxviiii. Æthelstanus rex obiit,[34] cui frater suus Edmundus in regnum successit, quo anno rex Onlaf primo uenit

---

xiii. 629; *EHD* i, trans. Whitelock, pp. 346–7). The piety shown by Æthelstan concerning his brother's death does not square easily with the allegation that it was he who ordered it. One would wish more enlightenment on the 'political unrest' (*aliqua regni sui perturbatione*) which preceded the drowning.

[30] *ASC*, s.a. 934: 'In this year King Æthelstan went into Scotland with both a land force and a naval force' (trans. Whitelock, p. 69).

[31] Once again, the account of Æthelstan's detour to Chester-le-Street and his many gifts to the shrine of St Cuthbert are not recorded in southern sources, but fully described in Durham sources such as the *Historia de sancto Cuthberto*, c. 26 (ed. Johnson South, p. 64, with commentary at pp. 108–10) and esp. Symeon of Durham, *LDE* ii. 18 (ed. Rollason, p. 136). These gifts included the finely written copy of Bede's *uitae* of St Cuthbert (prose and verse) which survives as CCCC 183; see Keynes, 'King Æthelstan's books', pp. 180–5, and Rollason, 'St Cuthbert and Wessex'.

[32] On Æthelstan's expedition into Scotland, see above, n. 30. Of the places mentioned in the text, the most certainly identifiable is modern Caithness (here *Catenes*). *Dunfoeder* is thought to correspond to Dunnottar, located on a rocky headland on the NE coast of Scotland, some 15 miles south of Aberdeen (and 2 miles south of Stonehaven), and the site of an imposing castle: see A. O. Anderson, *Early Sources of Scottish History*, pp. 395–7 (but what the element *-foeder* represents, in what language, is unclear to me). Most problematical is the mention of *Vuertermorum*. In the Andersons' edition of *Adomnan's Life of Columba*, pp. 32–5, they associate the element *Vuerter-* with the *Verturiones*, a Scottish tribe mentioned by Roman historians (*-morum* is presumably from OE *mor*, 'moor'). But the precise location of this 'moor' is unknown.

[33] From a parallel entry in *ASC*, s.a. 937, we know that Æthelstan's battle at *Vuendun* (as it is named here) corresponds to what the Anglo-Saxon chronicler describes as the battle of *Brunanburh*; Æthelweard in his *Chronicon* names it as *Brunandun* (ed. Campbell, p. 54); and Symeon of Durham, *LDE* ii. 18 reports: 'apud Weondune, quod alio nomine Æt Brunnanwerc uel Brunnanbyrig appellatur' (ed. Rollason, p. 138, with n. 105, where some of the many identifications are discussed). In spite of many inspired guesses, the location of this important battle is quite unknown. For suggested identifications, see Campbell (ed.), *The Battle of Brunanburh*, pp. 57–80, and, more recently, Livingston (ed.), *The Battle of Brunanburh*, as well as Wood, 'Searching for *Brunanburh*'. The *Anglo-Saxon Chronicle* mentions Æthelstan's defeat of King Olaf and of Constantine (king of the Scots), but no other source has the precise detail that Olaf fled with 615 ships.

[34] Æthelstan's death is recorded against the year 940 in *ASC* (trans. Whitelock, p. 70).

180 APPENDIX I

Eboracum; deinde ad austrum tendens, Hamtonam obsedit.[35] Sed nihil ibi proficiens, uertit exercitum ad Tameweorde, et uastatis omnibus per circuitum, dum rediens ad Legraceastre perueniret, occurrit ei rex Edmundus cum exercitu.[36] Nec erat pugna difficilis, quoniam duo archiepiscopi, Oda[g] et Wlfstan, placatis alterutrum regibus, pugnam sedauerant. Pace itaque facta, terminus utriusque regni erat Wetlingastrete. Edmundus ad | australem plagam, Onlaf ad aquilonalem, regnum tenuerunt.

fo. 75[vb]

[941] Anno .dccccxli. Onlaf, uastata ecclesia sancti Balteri et incensa Tiningaham,[37] mox periit.[38] Vnde Eboracenses Lindisfarnensem insulam depopulati sunt,[39] et multos occiderunt. Filius uero Sihtrici nomine Onlaf regnauit super Nortanhymbros.[40]

[943] Anno .dcccxliii. Northumbri regem suum Onlaf de regno expulerunt.[41]

[945] Anno .dcccxlv. Edmundus rex, expulsis duobus regibus, regnum obtinuit Nortanhymbrorum.[42]

[948] Anno .dcccxlviii. Edmundus rex occisus est et frater eius, Edredus, regnum suscepit, cultor iustitię et pietatis. Moxque

---

[g] Odo C

---

[35] No other source mentions that Olaf came first to York, or that, turning south, he beseiged Northampton (here *Hamtona*).

[36] *ASC*, s.a. 943 (D) explains that, 'In this year Olaf took Tamworth by storm' (trans. Whitelock, p. 71). Then, in the same entry, we are told that 'King Edward besieged King Olaf and Archbishop Wulfstan in Leicester' (trans. Whitelock, ibid.). But no other source, *ASC* included, mentions that two archbishops, Oda and Wulfstan, brokered a peace between Olaf and Edmund, and that Watling Street became the border of both kingdoms, with that of Edmund to the south, and Olaf to the north. *ASC* (s.a. 943) reports that King Edmund stood as sponsor to the baptism of Olaf, but this detail is not mentioned by our annalist.

[37] Balthere was an anchorite at Tyninghame (East Lothian); his death in 756 is recorded in the *Annales Lindisfarnenses*, and commemorated in Alcuin's poem on the saints of York (MGH, *PLAC* i. 198–200 (lines 1318–86)). The hermitage of Balthere was on Bass Rock, an offshore island a few miles from Tyninghame, as Alcuin relates. On Balthere, see *Historia de sancto Cuthberto*, c. 4 (ed. Johnson South, p. 46, with commentary at p. 80), and Symeon of Durham, *LDE* ii. 2 (ed. Rollason, p. 80 with n. 6), together with Blair, 'A handlist', p. 513. Olaf's destruction of the church of Tyninghame is not recorded in any other source.

[38] The death of Olaf is recorded in *ASC*, s.a. 942 (EF): 'In this year King Olaf died' (trans. Whitelock, p. 71).

[39] This sack of Lindisfarne by the (Viking) men of York is not recorded elsewhere.

[40] This is Olaf I Cuarán (941–4), son of Sihtric II Caech (920/1–927). Olaf I was baptized by King Edward in 943, but driven from the kingdom in 944, and thereafter became king of Dublin. See the *Annals of Ulster*, s.a. 945.6: 'Blacair gave up Áth Cliath and Amlaíb succeeded him' (ed. MacAirt and MacNiochaill, p. 393), and Keynes, 'Rulers', p. 526.

[41] *ASC*, s.a. 944: 'In this year King Edmund reduced all Northumbria under his rule, and drove out two kings, Olaf, Sihtric's son, and Ragnald, Guthfrith's son' (trans. Whitelock, p. 71).

[42] This entry continues the information given above, s.a. 943.

THE ANNALS 888-957

Northumbriam circuiens totam possedit; sed post iuratam ei fidelitatem Northymbrenses quendam Danum,[43] Eiricum, preficiunt*h* regem.[44]

[950] Anno .dccccl. Eadredus rex uastata Northymbria cum iam rediret, Northymbrenses erumpentes extremos exercitus regis peremerunt. Statuit rex reducto exercitu prouinciam delere penitus, sed indigene, abiecto quem constituerant rege, Eadredum citius muneribus placarunt.[45]

[951] Anno .dccccli. Ouuel rex Brittonum obiit.[46]

[952] Anno .dccccli. Defecerunt hic reges Nortanhymbrorum; et deinceps ipsa prouincia administrata est per comites.[47]

[953] Anno .dcccclii. Comes Osuulf suscepit comitatum Nortanhymbrorum.[48]

[955] Anno .dcccclv. Eadredo rege defuncto, successit Eadwinus, filius Edmundi, qui ante eum regnauit.[49]

[956] Anno .dcccclvi. Beatus Dunstanus abbas ab Eadwino expellitur.[50]

---

h prefaciunt *C*

---

[43] *ASC*, s.a. 948 (F): 'Hic Edmundus rex occisus est, et Edredus frater eius regnauit pro eo et statim accepit totam Norðhumbriam in potestatem propriam, et Scotti ei iusiurandum fecerunt quod quicquid uellet facerent' (ed. Baker, p. 81); *ASC*, 948 (E): 'In this year King Edmund was stabbed to death, and his brother Eadred succeeded to the kingdom, and immediately reduced all Northumbria to his rule; and the Scots swore oaths to him that they would agree to all that he wanted' (trans. Whitelock, p. 72).

[44] *ASC*, s.a. 952 (F): 'Hic Nordhumbreni pepulerunt regem Anlaf...et receperunt Yric, filium Haroldi' (ed. Baker, p. 81). Eric Blood-axe was the son of Harold Fairhair, king of Norway: Keynes, 'Rulers', p. 527.

[45] *ASC*, s.a. 948 (D): 'In this year King Eadred ravaged all Northumbria, because they had accepted Eric as their king...Then the king became so angry that he wished to march back into the land and destroy it utterly. When the councillors of the Northumbrians understood that, they deserted Eric and paid to King Eadred compensation for their act' (trans. Whitelock, pp. 72–3).

[46] *Annales Cambriae*, in *Nennius*, ed. Morris, s.a. 950 (p. 91): 'Higuel rex Brittonum obiit'; cf. *Annals of Ulster*, s.a. 950.2: 'Hywel, king of Wales, dies' (ed. MacAirt and MacNiochaill, p. 395).

[47] The last Scandinavian king of York was Eric Blood-axe, who was killed at Stainmore in 954 (Keynes, 'Rulers', p. 527); the present entry places the event two years too early. Among the *comites* ('earls', in this context) was Oswulf, mentioned in the following annal.

[48] Oswulf was the high reeve of Bamburgh (Keynes, 'Rulers', p. 527); but he did not take charge of the earldom of Northumbria until after Eric Blood-axe had been killed (in 954).

[49] *ASC*, s.a. 955 (E): 'In this year King Eadred died...and Eadwig, Edmund's son, succeeded to the kingdom' (trans. Whitelock, pp. 73–4).

[50] *ASC*, s.a. 956 (D): 'And in the same year Abbot Dunstan was driven across the sea' (trans. Whitelock, p. 74).

182   APPENDIX I

[957] Anno .dcccclvii. Mortuo Eadwino, frater eius Eadgarus successit in regnum, qui magne deuotionis extitit erga Dei cultum, ideoque
in pace et honore, seruientibus sibi octo regibus, regnum tenuit .xvii.

fo. 76ʳᵃ annis.[51] | Post quem filius eius Eadwardus regnauit, qui dolo nouercę
suę interfectus, Scestonie requiescit.[52] Cui successit frater suus
Ethelredus,[53] pater Eadwardi regis quem susceperat ex Emma.[54]

[51] Events of many years are collapsed in this entry. Edgar only became king of all England
after the death of Eadwig (*ASC*, s.a. 959). Against the year 973, *ASC* (D) reports that 'the
king took his whole naval force to Chester, and six kings came to meet him, and all gave him
pledges that they would be his allies on sea and land' (trans. Whitelock, p. 77). However, John
of Worcester, in his Chronicle, records against 973 that Edgar came to Chester and received
there the formal loyalty of *eight* sub-kings: 'Legionum Ciuitatem appulit, cui subreguli eius
.viii. . . . occurrerunt et quod sibi fideles et terra et mari cooperatores esse uellent, iurauerunt'
(ed. Darlington and McGurk, p. 422). John of Worcester's statement closely resembles that
of the present annalist.

[52] Again, John of Worcester Chronicle, s.a. 978, provides the closest parallel to this report
concerning Edward, king and martyr (the *Anglo-Saxon Chronicle* does not mention the
involvement of Edward's stepmother in the murder): 'Rex Anglorum Eadwardus iussu
nouerce sue Ælfthrythe regine . . . a suis iniuste occiditur' (ed. Darlington and McGurk,
pp. 428–30). The fullest account of the murder of Edward the Martyr is given by Byrhtferth,
VSO iv. 18. According to the *Anglo-Saxon Chronicle* (s.a. 978 (D)), Edward was buried first at
Wareham; his remains were subsequently translated to Shaftesbury (*Scestonia*) by Ealdorman
Ælfhere in 979. This translation is described by John of Worcester, Chronicle, s.a. 979 ('ad
Sceaftesbyrig est delatum et honorifice tumulatum': ed. Darlington and McGurk, p. 430). It
is also described by Byrhtferth (*VSO* iv. 19), who characteristically omits to mention where
the body was translated to. The translation is treated in detail by Keynes, 'King Alfred the
Great and Shaftesbury Abbey', esp. pp. 48–55 ('Shaftesbury and Edward the Martyr').

[53] Æthelred 'the Unready' (978–1016).

[54] The notice that Æthelred's son by Emma was 'King Edward'—that is, Edward the
Confessor (1042–66)—cannot have been written before 1042, the year in which Edward
became king, and rules out any possibility of Byrhtferth's involvement in the compilation of
these annals (utterly inconceivable on stylistic grounds).

APPENDIX II

The Hexham Interpolations

At two points in Part III of the *Historia regum*, where Byrhtferth has mentioned the deaths of Bishops Acca (iii. 6) and Alchmund (iii. 18) of Hexham, a copyist—writing it would seem at Hexham itself—has interpolated extensive accounts of the cult of these two important bishops as it was practised at Hexham.[1] References to external events in the interpolations enable them to be dated to later than 1113 (in the case of Bishop Acca) and to a period later than the bishopric of Æthelwine of Hexham, 1056–71 (in the case of Bishop Alchmund); they date, in other words, from at least a century and a half later than the time when Byrhtferth was composing his *Historia regum*, and have nothing whatsoever to do with his original composition. I have therefore removed the two interpolations from the text of *HR*; they are printed here for their relevance to the transmissional history of *HR*; in printing them, I reproduce the twelfth-century orthography of CCCC 139, rather than attempting to restore the (presumed) orthography of Byrhtferth's own day.

I. INTERPOLATION IN *HR* III. 6 (CONCERNING ACCA, BISHOP OF HEXHAM)

Dueque cruces lapidee mirabili celatura decoratę positę sunt, una ad caput, alia ad pedes eius [*scil.* Accae]. In quarum una, quę scilicet ad caput est, litteris insculptum est, quod in eodem loco sepultus sit. De quo loco, post annos plusquam .ccc. depositionis suę, a quodam presbytero diuina reuelatione translatus est, ac in ecclesia intra feretrum condigno honore positus est; ubi usque hodie in magna ueneratione habetur. Ob cuius sanctitatis meritum omnibus demonstrandum casula et tunica et sudarium que cum sanctissimo eius corpore in terra posita erant, non solum speciem sed etiam fortitudinem pristinam usque in hodiernum | diem seruant. Inuenta est etiam super pectus eius tabula lignea in modum altaris, facta ex duobus lignis, clauis argenteis coniuncta, sculptaque est in illa scriptura hęc: 'ALMĘ TRINITATI AGIE SOPHIE SANCTĘ MARIĘ'. Vtrum uero reliquie in ea positę fuerint, uel

fo. 60ᵛᵇ

fo. 61ʳᵃ

---

[1] The two interpolations were identified and discussed by Hunter Blair, 'Some observations', pp. 87–90.

184   APPENDIX II

qua de causa cum eo in terra posita sit, ignoratur. Attamen absque
rationabili deuotionis causa, summe uenerationis cultu cum sancto
eius corpore nequaquam esse condita creditur. Vestimenta uero eius
predicta fratres eiusdem Hagustaldensis ęcclesię aliquotiens populo
monstrare solent, a quo cum omni deuotione deosculantur.

Plurima uero miracula de sancto Acca etiam uulgo narrantur, que
omnia scripto explicare perlongum est. Aliqua tamen de illis memorie
breuiter commendare libet, uidelicet quam mirabiliter ac terribilier
aduersarios suos, pacem ecclesię in qua requiescit infringere tempt-
antes, uel ipsam ęcclesiam funditus euertere molientes, crebro coher-
cuerit, et qualiter reliquias de corpore suo furtim auferre uolentibus
sepius obstiterit. Fuit frater quidam in prefata Hagustaldensi ecclesia,
Aldredus nomine, qui nunc in Christo requiescit, uir ueracissimus et
morum probitate conspicuus, sed et in scripturis sanctis bene eruditus,
qui tale miraculum de sancto Acca in semetipso patratum fratribus
eiusdem ecclesie narrare solebat. Cum ipse adhuc esset adolescens,
nutrireturque in domo fratris sui cuiusdam presbyteri, qui sepefatam
Hagustaldensem regebat ecclesiam, antequam donatione uenerabilis
memorię Thomae secundi Eboracensis archiepiscopi[2] canonicis regu-
laribus (qui ibidem usque hodie Deo seruiunt) tradita esset, placuit
eidem fratri suo ossa reuerenda sancti Acce adhuc cum puluerę corpo-
fo. 61ʳᵇ ris mixta separare, | separatimque in theca quam in hoc parauerat
recondere. Prolatas ergo uenerabiles reliquias super altare sancti
Michaelis in australi porticu ecclesie situm deposuit, ibique ossa de
puluere collegit et in syndone munda inuoluta in theca recondidit, et
dum eam in chorum ubi stare debebat deferret, porticum illam, cum
reliquiis quae remanserant, predicto fratri suo tuendam delegauit. Qui
solus ibi remanens, cepit intra se cogitare, quia magna munera etiam
precelsa quelibet ecclesia se ditatam crederet, si uel unum de ossibus
tam gloriosi confessoris haberet. Proposuit ergo ad altare accedere et
perquirere si forte aliquid de minutis ossibus in puluere relictum
inuenire posset, quod penes se reponens alicui ecclesię ad honorem Dei
et sancti Accę donaret. Sed id irreuerenter perpetrare non ausus, prius
humi procumbens septem penitentiales psalmos deuote cantauit,[3]
Deum exorans quatinus tale furtum ei non displiceret, quod non sac-
rilega mente sed pię deuotionis et uenerationis gratia facere cogitabat.

---

[2] The reference is to Thomas II, archbishop of York (1108–14); Hexham was gifted to
canons regular in 1113 (see Hunter Blair, 'Some observations', p. 88).
[3] The Seven Penitential Psalms: Pss. 6, 31 (32), 37 (38), 50 (51), 101 (102), 129 (130), and
142 (143).

THE HEXHAM INTERPOLATIONS

Post hanc orationem se erigens, quod proposuerat explere temptabat. Cumque hostio interioris porticus in qua erant uenerandę reliquię, appropinquasset, ecce subito calor quidam, quasi ignis uaporantis de ore clibani ardentis, ei obuius fuit, eumque magno timore perculsum retroire coegit. Ille uero credens hoc ei ideo contigisse, quod cum minori deuotione quam deberet tantam rem assequi uellet, solotenus iterum prostratus, multo uberiores et deuotiores preces quam antea fecerat Domino fudit, quatinus quod deuote desiderabat digne adhipisci ualeret. Post aliquantum itaque interuallum surgens, cum timore et reuerentia magna ad hostium porticus accessit, | sed multo ardentiore calore quam antea de illa egrediente repercussus est. Quo facto intelligens non esse uoluntatem Dei ut aliquid de reliquiis sancti Acce furtim asportaret, tertio id temptare non ausus est.

Sed et aliud miraculum de eodem Deo dilecto confessore non est silentio pretereundum, quod multi qui usque hodie supersunt per reliquias eius patratum esse testantur. Cum uenisset ad prefatam Hagustaldensem ecclesiam quidam canonicus regularis et sacerdos, scilicet Edricus, qui illuc primus canonicorum a uiro uenerabili Thoma archiepiscopo missus est, inuenit aceruum de terra congestum iuxta maius altare quod infra cancellos ecclesię erat, quem inde auferre uolens, effodere eum cepit. De quo cum aliquam partem fodisset, repperit thecam ligneam non admodum magnam. Quam aperiens, inuenit duo sigilla plumbea, insculptis litteris quid intus continerent intimantia. In quorum altero scriptum erat, quod de sancto Acca reliquię intro haberentur. Mox ergo illud confringens, inuenit puluerem cineri simillimum, nonnullaque ossa de sancto eius corpore pulueri immixta; quae inde tollens, in honestiori theca reposuit. Erat tunc temporis paupercula quedam sanctimonialis femina in ipsa uilla, quam predictus frater pro simplicitate eius et innocentia uitę oppido diligebat. Ista multo tempore extiterat ceca, ita ut ad ecclesiam et ubicumque necesse ire habebat, semper ab alio duceretur. Quadam die repente uenit in cor fratris praefati talis cogitatio, ut unum de ossibus illis quae nuper inuenerat in aqua benedicta abluere deberet, mulierique de ipso lauacro dare, ut inde oculos suos lauaret, si forte Deus, meritis sancti confessoris | sui Accę intercedentibus, lumen oculorum hoc uenerando lauacro ei restituere dignaretur. Fecitque ille quod diuino instinctu ammonitus, sicut postea claruit, faciendum cogitauerat. Abluensque unum de ossibus in aqua benedicta, mulieri dedit, precipiens ei quatinus de illa oculos suos lauaret. Quę cum ita fecisset, quasi post duarum horarum spatium per merita et intercessiones sancti Accę uisum recepit.

186   APPENDIX II

Fuit alter quidam homo pauper in eadem uilla cuius guttur intercutaneo morbo in tantum intumuerat, ut nec loqui nec manducare posset. In cuius ore cum idem frater de ipsa aqua parum infudisset, repente post unius horę spatium disrupta est cutis ex inferiori parte tumoris, sicque exeunte tumore sanatus est.

Qualiter uero Malcholmus rex Scottorum[4] ab inuasione pacisque uiolatione ęcclesię Hagustaldensis, sancto Acca ceterisque sanctis qui in ea requiescunt meritorum suorum presidiis illam conseruantibus, cohercitus sit, silentio tegere nimis impium est. Licet enim uulgo etiam notissimum sit, tamen ne penitus cum tempore a memoria hominum transeat, notitię posteriorum scripto tradendum est. Malcholmus igitur rex Scottorum, homo scilicet ferocissimus mentemque bestialem gerens, Northumbrensem prouinciam crebra irruptione misere deuastare solebat, plurimosque de illa uiros et mulieres captiuos in Scotiam deducere. Qui cum quadam uice cum numerosiore solito exercitu fines prouintię illius eam deuastaturus ingressus fuisset, prouinciales eius aduentum audientes, fere omnes ad ecclesiam Hagustaldensem cum rebus suis quas secum portare poterant sub protectione sanctorum in illa quiescentium confugerunt. Quod ut Malcolmus comperit, proposuit illo pergere, omnesque qui eo confugerant expoliare, ipsamque ecclesiam | funditus euertere. Quod audiens presbyter eiusdem ęcclesię, perrexit obuiam ei, ammonuitque illum ne tantum nefas in sanctos Dei ecclesię illius patronos committere presumeret. At ille eius spernens monita, eum a se cum iniuria proiecit. Qui ad ęcclesiam festinato rediens, omnes qui ibidem confugerant in commune exhortatus est, gloriosos sanctos Dei, sub quorum presidium confugerant, instanter deprecari, quatinus illos solita pietate sua a tam immani hoste Scottisque bestiis crudelioribus protegere dignarentur. Et fecerunt ita. Nocte uero sequenti cum idem presbyter pre tristicia in soporem decidisset, apparuit ei uir quidam uultu et habitu uenerandus, qui ab eo sciscitabatur quasi ignorans causam tantę tristicię. Cumque pro hostium imminentium seuitia se pauere respondisset, ait illi: 'Ne timeas, quoniam, antequam illucescat, rete meum in fluuium mittam, per quod omnino Scottorum transitus impedietur.' Hęc cum dixisset, euanuit. Mane autem facto, inuentus est amnis qui Tyna dicitur, absque pluuiarum inundatione et uentorum uiolentia, in tantum excreuisse, ut absque nauis amminiculo minime transiri posset. Preterea eadem nocte et die sequenti tanta repente nebula accidit, ut maxima pars

fo. 62ra

---

[4] Malcolm III ('Canmore'), king of Scots from 1058 to 1093; his invasion of Northumbria is recorded in *ASC*, s.a. 1079 E.

THE HEXHAM INTERPOLATIONS 187

exercitus supradicti regis per tenebras dispersa a se inuicem dilabere-
tur, ita ut plures ad aquilonem, multi ad orientem, nonnulli quoque ad
meridiem, aperte miraculo diuino confusi per intercessionem sanctorum Hagustaldensis ęcclesię, cum magna festinatione tenderent. Rex
uero Malcolmus cum illa particula exercitus sui que cum eo remanserat
ueniens, omnem transmeandi copiam sibi negatam uidit. Resedit ergo
supra ripam fluminis, expectare uolens donec aqua diminueretur
ut transire posset. Sed cum tribus diebus expectasset, aquamque
absque omni | pluuię amministratione cotidie magis ac magis crescere   fo. 62ʳᵇ
uideret, tam euidenti miraculo perterritus, cum magna festinatione recessit. Sicque ab eius crudelitate omnes qui ad prefatam
Hagustaldensem ecclesiam confugerant, meritis sanctorum in illa
requiescentium erepti sunt. Sed nunc ad historicam narrationem pre-
termissam redeamus.

2. INTERPOLATION IN *HR* III. 18 (CONCERNING
ALCHMUND, BISHOP OF HEXHAM)

De quo loco post annos plusquam .ccl. diuina reuelatione translatus est   fo. 64ʳᵃ
[*scil.* Alchmund] hoc modo. Tempore illo fuit quidam Dregmo[5] in ter-
ritoria Haugustaldensis ęcclesię, Deum ualde | timens et elemosinarum   fo. 64ʳᵇ
operibus, prout sibi facultas suppeditabat, haut segniter deditus, ac per
omnia a comprouincialium moribus uita discordans. Erat enim mirę
simplicitatis et innocentię homo, ac erga sanctos Dei deuotionis et uenerationis immensę. Quapropter eum omnes uicini sui in magno honore
habebant, illumque uerum Dei cultorem appellabant. Huic itaque
quadam nocte in stratu suo quiescenti apparuit quidam uir pontificali
infula decoratus, uirgamque pastoralem in manu tenens. Cum qua
eum pulsans, sic ait illi: 'Surge, uade et dic Alfredo filio Westueor,[6]
presbytero Dunelmensis ęcclesię, quatinus plebe coadunata territorii
Haugustaldensis transferat corpus meum de loco illo ubi sepultus
sum, ac intra ecclesiam in honestiori loco reponat. Dignum est enim
illos uenerationem ab omnibus in terris accipere, quos Rex regum
dignatus est in caelis stola glorię et immortalitatis induere.' Quem cum
ille interrogasset: 'Domine, tu quis es?', ille respondit: 'Ego sum

---

[5] This Dregmo is not apparently recorded in any other source.

[6] On Alfred, son of Westou, see Symeon of Durham, *LDE* iii. 7 (ed. Rollason, pp. 160–6).
According to Symeon of Durham, Alfred lived in the days of Bishop Æthelwine of Hexham
(1056–71).

188 APPENDIX II

Alchmundus ęcclesię Haugustaldensis episcopus, qui eidem loco quartus post beatum Wilfridum gratia Dei prefui. Corpus uero meum iuxta predecessorem meum uenerandę memorię sanctum Accam episcopum positum est. Ad quod transferendum tu quoque cum presbytero simul adesto.' Hec cum dixisset, disparuit.

Mane autem facto, homo ille cum magna festinacione ad prefatum presbyterum perrexit; quicquid uidisset, quodue mandatum ei deferre iussus esset, per ordinem ei indicauit. Qui letus admodum effectus, conuocauit plurimam populi multitudinem, | rem notam eis faciens, diemque statuit quo uenerabiles reliquias transferrent. Die ergo statuta presbyter prefatus ad sepulchrum accedens, illud a terra denudari precepit. Quod cum factum esset, adiuuante se uiro illo cui reuelatio facta fuerat, populorum turbis hinc inde stantibus, ueneranda ossa de tumulo collegit, lintheoque inuoluta ac in scrinio recondita super feretrum collocauit. Et quia pro tanta ueneratione diei sacrosanctas hostias Domino offerendi hora transierat, posuerunt eum nocte illa in porticu sancti Petri ad orientem plagam ipsius ęcclesię Haugustaldensis, sequenti die cum canticis et hymnis et missarum solempniis in ecclesiam illum transferre statuentes.

Nocte uero illa predictus sacerdos, excubias circa uenerabiles reliquias cum clericis suis celebrans, ceteris alto sompno depressis, accedens ipse scrinium aperuit, unumque de minutis ossibus, partem uidelicet digiti unius, clanculo auferens penes se reposuit, cupiens illud ęcclesię sancti Cuthberti Dunelmensi ad honorem Dei et sancti Alchmundi conferre. Luce itaque terris reddita, ad transferendum corpus almificum plurima populi multitudo conuenit. Cumque iam hora tercia appropinquaret, iubente presbytero, manus apponentes feretrum leuare conati sunt; sed illud mouere minime ualebant. Repulsis igitur his qui primi accesserant, iudicatisque quasi indignis tanti patris reliquias suis humeris deferre, accesserunt alii, qui sicut et priores casso labore defecerunt. Deinde aliis et aliis se ingerentibus, a nullo penitus moueri ualebat. Animo uero | consternati seseque mutuo intuentes omnes qui aderant, mirabantur rei nouitatem stupentes. Tunc sacerdos, illius reatus se ipsum causam esse nesciens, exhortatus est omnes Deum deprecari, quatinus illis reuelare dignaretur pro qua culpa hoc eis contigisset. Et factum est. Illis autem in ecclesia pernoctantibus, Deumque pro iam dicto negotio exorantibus, apparuit iterum sanctus Alchmundus eidem homini, cui prius apparuerat, forte tunc infra ecclesiam irruente subito sopore pregrauato, et cum aliquantum seuero uultu ait ad eum: 'Quid est quod facere uoluistis? Putastis menbris desectum me in ecclesiam referre, in qua Deo et sancto Andree apostolo eius integro corpore et

THE HEXHAM INTERPOLATIONS

spiritu seruiui? Surge ergo, et contestare coram omni populo ut corpori meo citius restituatur quod inconsulte inde ablatum est, alioquin me de loco in quo nunc sum nullatenus mouere poteritis.' Et cum hec dixisset, ostendit ei manum suam medietate unius digiti carentem. Facta autem die, uir ille in medio populi astans, quid sibi nocte illa reuelatum fuisset uniuersis propalauit, uehementi uerborum inuectione multari dignum esse indicans quicumque hoc facere presumpsisset. Tunc sacerdos se deprehensum cernens, in medium prosiluit, et qua de causa quaue intentione hoc perpetrasset, omnibus patefecit. Restituensque sancto Alchmundo quod pie deuotionis gratia ei abstulerat, congrua satisfactione ueniam ilico impetrauit. Et accedentes clerici qui aderant, absque ulla ui leuauerunt eum, ac in ęcclesia transtulerunt .iiii. nonas Augusti, ubi usque hodie a fidelibus condigno honore ueneratur, ad laudem et honorem Domini nostri Iesu Christi.

BIBLIOGRAPHY

Abbo Floriacensis Quaestiones Grammaticales, ed. A. Guerreau-Jalabert (Paris, 1982).

Abbots of Wearmouth and Jarrow, ed. C. Grocock and I. N. Wood (OMT, 2013).

Adams, J. N., 'A type of hyperbaton in Latin prose', *Proceedings of the Cambridge Philological Society*, n.s. xvii (1971), 1–16.

Adomnan's Life of Columba, ed. A. O. and M. O. Anderson (London and Edinburgh, 1962).

Ælfredi Regis Res Gestae, ed. Matthew Parker (London, 1574).

Æthelwulf, *De abbatibus*, ed. A. Campbell (Oxford, 1967).

Aird, W. M., 'An absent friend: The career of Bishop William of Saint-Calais', in Rollason, Harvey, and Prestwich, eds., *Anglo-Norman Durham*, pp. 283–97.

Aldhelmi opera, ed. R. Ehwald (MGH, *AA*, xv; Berlin, 1919).

Aldhelm: The Poetic Works, trans. M. Lapidge and J. L. Rosier (Cambridge, 1985).

Alfred the Great, *Asser's Life of King Alfred and Other Contemporary Sources*, trans. S. Keynes and M. Lapidge (Harmondsworth, 1983).

Anderson, A. O., *Early Sources of Scottish History, A.D. 500 to 1286* (2 vols.; Edinburgh, 1922; repr. with bibliographical supplement by M. O. Anderson, Stamford, 1990).

Anderson, M. O., *Kings and Kingship in Early Scotland* (1973; 2nd edn. with introduction by N. Evans, Edinburgh, 2011).

The Anglo-Saxon Chronicle: A Revised Translation, ed. D. Whitelock with D. C. Douglas and S. I. Tucker (London, 1961).

The Anglo-Saxon Chronicle: MS F, ed. P. S. Baker (The Anglo-Saxon Chronicle, viii; Cambridge, 2000).

Annales regni Francorum 741–829, ed. F. Kurze (MGH, *Scriptores rerum Germanicarum*; Hanover, 1895).

Annales Rerum Gestarum Ælfredi Magni, auctore Asserio Menevensi, ed. F. Wise (Oxford, 1722).

The Annals of St Neots with Vita Prima Sancti Neoti, ed. D. N. Dumville and M. Lapidge (The Anglo-Saxon Chronicle, xvii; Cambridge, 1985).

The Annals of Ulster (to A.D. 1131), ed. S. MacAirt and G. MacNiocaill (Dublin, 1983).

Anthologia Latina sive Poesis Latinae Supplementum, ed. A. Riese, i: *Carmina in codicibus scripta* (2 vols.; 2nd edn.; Leipzig, 1894–1906).

Arator, *Historia apostolica*, ed. A. P. McKinlay (CSEL lxxii; Vienna, 1951).

Asser's Life of King Alfred together with the Annals of St Neots Erroneously Ascribed to Asser, ed. W. H. Stevenson (Oxford, 1904; repr. 1959).

BIBLIOGRAPHY

Augustine, *Enarrationes in psalmos*, ed. E. Dekkers and J. Fraipont (CCSL xxxviii; Turnhout, 1956).

Baker, D., 'Scissors and paste: Corpus Christi, Cambridge MS 139 again', in D. Baker, ed., *The Materials, Sources and Methods of Ecclesiastical History* (Studies in Church History, xi; Oxford, 1975), pp. 83–123.

Beda: Storia degli inglesi, ed. M. Lapidge, trans. P. Chiesa (2 vols.; Milan, 2008–10).

Bede's Ecclesiastical History of the English People, ed. R. A. B. Mynors, trans. B. Colgrave (OMT, 1969; rev. repr. 1991).

Bede's Latin Poetry, ed. M. Lapidge (OMT, 2019).

Blair, J., *The Church in Anglo-Saxon Society* (Oxford, 2005).

—— 'A handlist of Anglo-Saxon saints', in A. Thacker and R. Sharpe, eds., *Local Saints and Local Churches in the Early Medieval West* (Oxford, 2002), pp. 495–565.

Boethius, *Philosophiae consolatio*, ed. L. Bieler (CCSL xciv; Turnhout, 1984).

Bourgain, P., 'Abbo Floriacensis abb.', in L. Castaldi and V. Mattaloni, eds., *La trasmissione dei testi latini del medioevo / Mediaeval Latin Texts and their Transmission*, vi (Florence, 2019), pp. 3–31.

Bremmer, R. H., 'The Germanic context of "Cynewulf and Cyneheard" revisited', *Neophilologus*, lxxxi (1997), 445–65.

Brooks, N., 'The creation and early structure of the kingdom of Kent', in S. Bassett, ed., *The Origins of Anglo-Saxon Kingdoms* (Leicester, 1989), pp. 55–74.

Bullough, D., 'Alcuin and the kingdom of heaven: Liturgy, theology, and the Carolingian age', in U.-R. Blumenthal, ed., *Carolingian Essays: Andrew W. Mellon Lectures in Early Christian Studies* (Washington, DC, 1983), pp. 1–69.

Byrhtferth of Ramsey, *The Lives of St Oswald and St Ecgwine*, ed. M. Lapidge (OMT, 2009).

Byrhtferth's Enchiridion, ed. P. S. Baker and M. Lapidge (Early English Text Society, s.s. xv; Oxford, 1995), pp. 2–248.

Byrhtferth's Northumbrian Chronicle: An Edition and Translation of the Old English and Latin Annals, ed. C. R. Hart (Lewiston, NY 2006).

Caesarius of Arles, *Sermones*, ed. G. Morin (CCSL ciii; Turnhout, 1953).

Cambridge, E., 'Archaeology and the cult of St Oswald in pre-Conquest Northumbria', in Stancliffe and Cambridge, eds., *Oswald*, pp. 128–61.

Campbell, A., *Old English Grammar* (Oxford, 1959).

—— ed., *The Battle of Brunanburh* (London, 1938).

Carley, J. C., 'More pre-Conquest manuscripts from Glastonbury Abbey', *Anglo-Saxon England*, xxiii (1994), 265–81.

Carolingian Chronicles: Royal Frankish Annals and Nithard's Histories, trans. B. W. Scholz (Ann Arbor, MI, 1972).

Cassiodorus, *Expositio psalmorum I–LXX*, ed. M. Adriaen (CCSL xcvii; Turnhout, 1958).

BIBLIOGRAPHY 193

Castaldi, L., and V. Mattaloni, eds., *La trasmissione dei testi latini del medioevo / Mediaeval Latin Texts and their Transmission (Te.Tra)*, vi (Florence, 2019).

Chadwick, H. M., 'Vortigern', in N. K. Chadwick, ed., *Studies in Early British History* (Cambridge, 1954), pp. 21–33.

Chadwick, N. K., 'Bede, St Colmán and the Irish abbey of Mayo', in N. K. Chadwick, ed., *Celt and Saxon: Studies in the British Border* (Cambridge, 1963), pp. 186–205.

Charters of Christ Church, Canterbury, ed. N. Brooks and S. E. Kelly (Anglo-Saxon Charters, xvii–xviii; 2 vols.; Oxford, 2013).

Charters of St Augustine's Abbey, Canterbury, and Minster-in-Thanet, ed. S. E. Kelly (Anglo-Saxon Charters, iv; London, 1995).

Charters of Selsey, ed. S. E. Kelly (Anglo-Saxon Charters, vi; London, 1998).

Chiesa, P., and L. Castaldi, eds., *La trasmissione dei testi latini del medioevo / Mediaeval Latin Texts and their Transmission (Te.Tra)*, iii, iv (Florence, 2008–12).

Chronica Magistri Rogeri de Houeden, ed. W. Stubbs (Rolls Series; 4 vols., London, 1868–71).

The Chronicle of Æthelweard, ed. A. Campbell (London and Edinburgh, 1962).

The Chronicle of Ireland, trans. T. M. Charles-Edwards (2 vols, Translated Texts for Historians, xliv; Liverpool, 2006).

The Chronicle of Melrose Abbey: A Stratigraphic Edition, ed. D. Broun and J. Harrison (Woodbridge, 2007).

Chronicon Abbatiae Rameseiensis, ed. W. D. Macray (Rolls Series; London, 1886).

Cramp, R. J., *County Durham and Northumberland* (Corpus of Anglo-Saxon Stone Sculpture, i; Oxford, 1984).

Crawford, S. J., 'Byrhtferth of Ramsey and the anonymous Life of St Oswald', in *Speculum Religionis: Being Essays and Studies in Religion and Literature from Plato to von Hügel* (Oxford, 1929), pp. 99–111.

Cubitt, C., *Anglo-Saxon Church Councils, c.650–c.850* (London and New York, 1995).

Dubois, J., and J.-L. Lemaitre, *Sources et méthodes de l'hagiographie médiévale* (Paris, 1993).

Dumeige, G., *Nicée II* (Histoire des conciles oecuméniques, iv; Paris, 1978).

Dumville, D., 'The Anglian collection of royal genealogies and regnal lists', *Anglo-Saxon England*, v (1976), 23–50.

—— 'The Corpus Christi "Nennius" ', *Bulletin of the Board of Celtic Studies*, xxv (1974), 369–80.

—— 'The West Saxon genealogical regnal list: Manuscripts and texts', *Anglia*, civ (1986), 1–32.

BIBLIOGRAPHY

Dunbabin, J., 'The Maccabees as exemplars in the tenth and eleventh centuries', in K. Walsh and D. Wood, eds., *The Bible in the Medieval World: Essays in Memory of Beryl Smalley* (Oxford, 1985), pp. 31–41.

The Early Lives of St Dunstan, ed. M. Winterbottom and M. Lapidge (OMT, 2012).

Edgington, S. B., *The Life and Miracles of St Ivo* (St Ives, 1996).

English Monastic Litanies of the Saints after 1100, ed. N. J. Morgan, iii: *Addenda, Commentary, Catalogue of Saints, Indexes* (Henry Bradshaw Society, cxxiii; London, 2018).

Forsey, G. F., 'Byrhtferth's *Preface*', *Speculum*, iii (1928), 505–22.

Fox, C., *Offa's Dyke: A Field Survey of the Western Frontier-Works of Mercia in the Seventh and Eighth Centuries A.D.* (London, 1955).

Fraser, J. E., *From Caledonia to Pictland: Scotland to 795* (The New Edinburgh History of Scotland, i; Edinburgh, 2009).

Freeman, A., 'Theodulf of Orléans and the *Libri Carolini*', *Speculum*, xxxii (1957), 663–705.

Gneuss, H., 'Die Handschrift Cotton Otho A. xii', *Anglia*, xciv (1976), 289–318.

—— and M. Lapidge, *Anglo-Saxon Manuscripts: A Bibliographical Handlist of Manuscripts and Manuscript Fragments Written or Owned in England up to 1100* (Toronto, 2014).

Gorman, M., 'The glosses of Bede's *De temporum ratione* attributed to Byrhtferth of Ramsey', *ASE* xxv (1996), 209–32.

Gransden, A., *Historical Writing in England c.550 to c.1307* (London, 1974).

Gregory the Great, *Homiliae in Hiezechielem prophetam*, ed. M. Adriaen (CCSL cxlii; Turnhout, 1971).

Gullick, M., 'The hand of Symeon of Durham: Further observations on the Durham Martyrology scribe', in Rollason, ed., *Symeon of Durham*, pp. 14–31.

—— 'The scribes of the Durham Cantor's book', in Rollason, Harvey, and Prestwich, eds., *Anglo-Norman Durham*, pp. 93–109.

Hall, D., 'The sanctuary of St Cuthbert', in G. Bonner, D. Rollason and C. Stancliffe, eds., *St Cuthbert, his Cult and his Community to AD 1200* (Woodbridge, 1989), pp. 425–36.

Hardy, T. D., *Descriptive Catalogue of Materials relating to the History of Great Britain and Ireland to the End of the Reign of Henry VII*, i: *From the Roman Period to the Norman Invasion* (Rolls Series; London, 1862).

Hart, C. R., 'The Ramsey Computus', *English Historical Review*, lxxxv (1970), 29–44.

Die Heiligen Englands: Angelsächsisch und lateinisch, ed. F. Liebermann (Hanover, 1889).

Historia de Sancto Cuthberto: A History of Saint Cuthbert and a Record of his Patrimony, ed. T. Johnson South (Anglo-Saxon Texts, iii; Woodbridge, 2002).

Historiae Anglicanae Scriptores X, ed. R. Twysden and J. Selden (2 vols.; London, 1652).

BIBLIOGRAPHY 195

Hollis, S., 'The Minster-in-Thanet foundation story', *Anglo-Saxon England*, xxvii (1998), 41–64.

Holtz, L., *Donat et la tradition de l'enseignement grammatical* (Paris, 1981).

Hunter Blair, P., 'The *Moore Memoranda* on Northumbrian history', in C. Fox and B. Dickins, eds., *The Early Cultures of North-West Europe (H. M. Chadwick Memorial Studies)* (Cambridge, 1950), pp. 245–57.

—— 'Some observations on the "Historia Regum" attributed to Symeon of Durham', in N. K. Chadwick *et al.*, eds., *Celt and Saxon: Studies in the Early British Border* (Cambridge, 1963), pp. 63–118.

James, M. R., *A Descriptive Catalogue of the Manuscripts of Corpus Christi College, Cambridge* (2 vols.; Cambridge, 1909–12).

John of Worcester, *The Chronicle of John of Worcester*, ed. R. R. Darlington and P. McGurk, ii: *The Annals from 450 to 1066* (OMT, 1995); iii: *The Annals from 1067 to 1140*, ed. McGurk (OMT, 1998).

Jones, C. A., '*meatim sed et rustica*: Ælfric of Eynsham as a Medieval Latin author', *Journal of Medieval Latin*, viii (1998), 1–57.

Ker, N. R., *Catalogue of Manuscripts containing Anglo-Saxon* (Oxford, 1957).

—— *Medieval Manuscripts in British Libraries*, ii (Oxford, 1977).

Keynes, S., 'Archbishops and Bishops, 597–1066', Appendix II in *WB Encyc.*, pp. 539–66.

—— *An Atlas of Attestations in Anglo-Saxon Charters, c.670–1066* (Cambridge, 1998).

—— 'The control of Kent in the ninth century', *Early Medieval Europe*, ii (1993), 111–31.

—— 'King Æthelstan's books', in M. Lapidge and H. Gneuss, eds., *Learning and Literature in Anglo-Saxon England: Studies presented to Peter Clemoes on the Occasion of his Sixty-Fifth Birthday* (Cambridge, 1985), pp. 143–201.

—— 'King Alfred the Great and Shaftesbury Abbey', in L. Keen, ed., *Studies in the Early History of Shaftesbury Abbey* (Dorchester, 1999), pp. 17–72.

—— 'Rulers of the English, c. 450–1066', Appendix I in *WB Encyc.*, pp. 521–38.

Kleist, A. J., *The Chronology and Canon of Ælfric of Eynsham* (Anglo-Saxon Studies, xxxvii; Cambridge, 2019),

Lapidge, M., 'Aediluulf and the school of York', in A. Lehner and W. Berschin, eds., *Lateinische Kultur im VIII. Jahrhundert: Traube-Gedenkschrift* (St Ottilien, 1989), pp. 161–78 [repr. *ALL* i. 381–98].

—— 'Aldhelmus Malmesberiensis abb. et Scireburnensis ep.', in Chiesa and Castaldi, eds., *La trasmissione dei testi latini del medioevo*, iv, pp. 14–38.

—— *The Anglo-Saxon Library* (Oxford, 2008).

—— 'Asser Menevensis ep.', in Castaldi and Mattaloni, eds., *La trasmissione dei testi latini del medioevo*, vi, pp. 47–58.

—— 'Beda Venerabilis', in Chiesa and Castaldi, eds., *La trasmissione dei testi latini del medioevo*, iii, pp. 44–137.

—— 'Byrhtferth and the *Vita S. Ecgwini*', *Mediaeval Studies*, xli (1979), 331–53 [repr. *ALL* ii. 293–315].

BIBLIOGRAPHY

—— 'Byrhtferth of Ramsey and the early sections of the *Historia regum* attributed to Symeon of Durham', *Anglo-Saxon England*, x (1981), 97–122 [repr. *ALL* ii. 317–42].

—— 'Byrhtferth of Ramsey and the *Glossae Bridferti in Bedam*', *Journal of Medieval Latin*, xvii (2007), 384–400.

—— 'Byrhtferthus Ramesiensis mon.', in Castaldi and Mattaloni, eds., *La trasmissione dei testi latini del medioevo*, vi, pp. 109–22.

—— *The Cult of St Swithun* (Winchester Studies, iv/2; Oxford, 2003).

—— 'The hermeneutic style in tenth-century Anglo-Latin literature', *Anglo-Saxon England*, iv (1975), 67–111 [repr. *ALL* ii. 105–49].

—— 'Poetic compounds in Late Latin and early Medieval Latin verse (300–900)', in S. G. Bruce, ed., *Litterarum dulcis fructus: Studies in Honour of Michael W. Herren on his 80th Birthday* (Turnhout, 2021), pp. 189–234.

—— 'A tenth-century metrical calendar from Ramsey', *Revue Bénédictine*, xciv (1984), 326–69 [repr. *ALL* ii. 343–86].

Leechdoms, Wortcunning and Starcraft of Early England, ed. O. Cockayne (Rolls Series; 3 vols.; London, 1864–6).

Lendinara, P., 'The *Versus de die iudicii*: Its circulation and use as a school text in late Anglo-Saxon England', in R. H. Bremmer and K. Dekker, eds., *The Transfer of Encyclopaedic Knowledge in the Early Middle Ages: The Foundation of Learning* (Leuven, 2007), pp. 175–212.

Levison, W., *England and the Continent in the Eighth Century* (Oxford, 1946).

Le Liber pontificalis: Texte, introduction et commentaire, ed. L. Duchesne (3 vols.; Paris, 1886–1957).

The Liber Vitae of the New Minster and Hyde Abbey Winchester: British Library Stowe 944 together with Leaves from British Library Cotton Vespasian A. VIII and British Library Cotton Titus D. XXVII, ed. S. Keynes (Early English Manuscripts in Facsimile, xxvi; Copenhagen, 1996).

Liber Vitae: Register and Martyrology of New Minster and Hyde Abbey, Winchester, ed. W. de G. Birch (London and Winchester, 1892).

The Lives of the Eighth-Century Popes (Liber Pontificalis). The Ancient Biographies of Nine Popes from AD 715 to AD 817, trans. R. Davis (Translated Texts for Historians, xiii; Liverpool, 1992).

Livingston, M., ed., *The Battle of Brunanburh: A Casebook* (Exeter, 2011).

Love, R. C., 'Goscelinus Sancti Bertini mon.', in Castaldi and Mattaloni, eds., *La trasmissione dei testi latini del medioevo*, vi (Florence, 2019), pp. 228–64.

—— 'St Eadburh of Lyminge and her hagiographer', *Analecta Bollandiana*, cxxxvii (2019), 313–408.

Madan, F., H. H. E. Craster, R. W. Hunt, and P. D. Record, *A Summary Catalogue of Manuscripts in the Bodleian Library at Oxford*, ii(1) (Oxford, 1922).

Le Martyrologe d'Usuard. Texte et commentaire, ed. J. Dubois (Subsidia Hagiographica, xl; Brussels, 1965).

Meehan, B., 'Durham twelfth-century manuscripts in Cistercian houses', in Rollason, Harvey, and Prestwich, eds., *Anglo-Norman Durham*, pp. 439–49.

BIBLIOGRAPHY 197

Meyvaert, P., 'The authorship of the *Libri Carolini*: Observations prompted by a recent book', *Revue Bénédictine*, lxxxix (1979), 29–57.

Monumenta Historica Britannica; or Materials for the History of Britain, from the Earliest Period, ed. H. Petrie with J. Sharpe (London, 1848).

Murray, A., *Suicide in the Middle Ages* (2 vols., Oxford, 1998).

Nennius: British History and the Welsh Annals, ed. J. Morris (London and Chichester, 1980).

Norton, C., 'History, wisdom and illumination', in Rollason, ed., *Symeon of Durham*, pp. 61–105.

Offler, H. S., 'Hexham and the *Historia Regum*', *Transactions of the Architectural and Archaeological Society of Durham and Northumberland*, n.s. ii (1970), 51–62.

Opera Bedae, ed. J. Herwagen (8 vols.; Basel, 1563).

Page, R. I., 'Anglo-Saxon episcopal lists, part III', *Nottingham Mediaeval Studies*, x (1966), 2–24.

Peden, A. M., ed., *Abbo of Fleury and Ramsey: Commentary of the Calculus of Victorius of Aquitaine* (Auctores Britannici Medii Aevi, xv; Oxford, 2003).

Piper, A., 'The Durham Cantor's book', in Rollason, Harvey, and Prestwich, eds., *Anglo-Norman Durham*, pp. 79–92.

Poetae Latini Minores, ed. E. Baehrens (5 vols.; Leipzig, 1879–83).

Prosper of Aquitaine, *Liber epigrammatum*, ed. A. G. A. Horsting (CSEL c; Berlin and Boston, MA, 2016).

Rollason, D. W., 'The cults of murdered royal saints in Anglo-Saxon England', *Anglo-Saxon England*, xi (1983), 1–22.

—— *The Mildrith Legend: A Study in Early Medieval Hagiography in England* (Leicester, 1982).

—— 'St Cuthbert and Wessex: The evidence of Cambridge, Corpus Christi College MS 183', in G. Bonner, D. Rollason, and C. Stancliffe, eds., *St Cuthbert, his Cult and his Community to AD 1200* (Woodbridge, 1989), pp. 413–24.

—— *Sources for York History to AD 1100* (The Archaeology of York, i; York, 1998).

—— 'Symeon of Durham and the community of Durham in the eleventh century', in C. Hicks, ed., *England in the Eleventh Century: Proceedings of the 1990 Harlaxton Symposium* (Stamford, 1992), pp. 183–98.

—— 'Symeon of Durham's *Historia de regibus Anglorum et Dacorum* as a product of twelfth-century historical workshops', in M. Brett and D. Woodman, eds., *The Long Twelfth-Century View of the Anglo-Saxon Past* (Farnham, 2015), pp. 95–112.

—— ed., *Symeon of Durham: Historian of Durham and the North* (Stamford, 1998).

——, M. Harvey, and M. Prestwich, eds., *Anglo-Norman Durham, 1093–1193* (Woodbridge, 1994).

Schove, D. J., and A. Fletcher, *The Chronology of Eclipses and Comets, A.D. 1–1000* (Woodbridge, 1984).

198   BIBLIOGRAPHY

Sharpe, R., 'Goscelin's St Augustine and St Mildreth: Hagiography and liturgy in context', *Journal of Theological Studies*, n.s. xli (1990), 502–16.

—— J. P. Carley, R. M. Thomson, and A. G. Watson, *English Benedictine Libraries: The Shorter Catalogues* (Corpus of British Medieval Library Catalogues, iv; London, 1996).

Sims-Williams, P., 'Byrhtferth's ogam signature', in T. Jones and E. B. Fryde, eds., *Essays and Poems Presented to Daniel Huws* (Aberystwyth, 1994).

Sisam, K., *Studies in the History of Old English Literature* (Oxford, 1953).

Smith, Thomas, *Catalogus librorum manuscriptorum Bibliothecae Cottonianae / Catalogue of the Manuscripts in the Cottonian Library, 1696*, ed. C. G. C. Tite (Cambridge, 1984).

Stancliffe, C., and E. Cambridge, eds., *Oswald: Northumbrian King to European Saint* (Stamford, 1995).

Stenton, F. M., *Anglo-Saxon England* (3rd edn.; Oxford, 1971).

Stevenson, J., *The Church Historians of England* (5 vols. in 8 pts.; London, 1853–8).

Story, J. E., 'After Bede: Continuing the *Ecclesiastical History*', in S. Baxter, C. Karkov, J. L. Nelson, and D. Pelteret, eds., *Early Medieval Studies in Memory of Patrick Wormald* (Aldershot, 2009), pp. 165–84.

—— *Carolingian Connections: Anglo-Saxon England and Carolingian Francia, c. 750–870* (Aldershot, 2003).

—— 'Charlemagne and the epitaph of Pope Hadrian I', in J. Graham-Campbell and M. Valor, eds., *The Archaeology of Medieval Europe*, I: *Eighth to Twelfth Centuries AD* (Acta Jutlandica lxxxiii; Aarhus, 2007), pp. 444–5.

—— 'Symeon as annalist', in Rollason, ed., *Symeon of Durham*, pp. 202–13.

—— *et al.*, 'Charlemagne's Black Marble: The origin of the epitaph of Pope Hadrian I', *Papers of the British School at Rome*, lxxiii (2005), 157–90.

Stotz, P., *Handbuch zur lateinischen Sprache des Mittelalters* (5 vols.; Munich, 1996–2004).

Symeonis Dunelmensis Opera et Collectanea, ed. J. Hodgson-Hinde (Surtees Society li; Durham and London, 1868).

Symeonis Monachi Opera Omnia, ed. T. Arnold (Rolls Series; 2 vols.; London, 1882–5).

Symeon of Durham: Libellus de exordio atque procursu istius, hoc est Dunhelmensis, ecclesie, ed. and trans. David Rollason (OMT, 2000).

Taylor, H. M. and J. Taylor, *Anglo-Saxon Architecture* (3 vols.; Cambridge, 1965–78).

Thacker, A., 'Membra disjecta: The division of the body and the diffusion of the cult', in Stancliffe and Cambridge, eds., *Oswald*, pp. 97–127.

Three Eleventh-Century Anglo-Latin Saints' Lives, ed. R. C. Love (OMT, 1996).

Three Lives of English Saints, ed. M. Winterbottom (Toronto, 1972).

Two Lives of St Cuthbert, ed. B. Colgrave (Cambridge, 1940).

Wallenberg, J. K., *Kentish Place-Names: A Topographical and Etymological Study of the Place-Name Material in Kentish Charters Dated before the Conquest* (Uppsala, 1931).

BIBLIOGRAPHY
199

White, S. D., 'Kinship and lordship in early medieval England: The story of Sigeberht, Cynewulf and Cyneheard', *Viator*, xx (1989), 1–18.

William of Malmesbury, *Gesta pontificum Anglorum. The History of the English Bishops*, ed. M. Winterbottom (OMT, 2007).

—— *Gesta Regum Anglorum. The History of English Kings*, ed. R. A. B. Mynors, R. M. Thomson, and M. Winterbottom (2 vols.; OMT, 1998).

Wills, J., *Repetition in Latin Poetry: Figures of Allusion* (Oxford, 1996).

Winterbottom, M., 'A "Celtic" hyperbaton?', *Bulletin of the Board of Celtic Studies*, xxvii (1976–8), 207–12.

—— 'The text and transmission of some Bedan texts', *Mittellateinisches Jahrbuch*, lii (2017), 445–59.

Wood, M. 'Searching for *Brunanburh*: The Yorkshire context of the Great War of 937', *Yorkshire Archaeological Journal*, xxxv (2013), 138–59.

Wright, N., 'Gildas's prose style and its origins', in M. Lapidge and D. Dumville, eds., *Gildas: New Approaches* (Studies in Celtic History, iv; Woodbridge, 1984), pp. 107–28.

Wulfstan of Winchester: Life of St Æthelwold, ed. M. Lapidge and M. Winterbottom (OMT, 1991).

Yorke, B., 'The kingdom of the East Saxons', *Anglo-Saxon England*, xiv (1985), 1–36.

INDEX OF QUOTATIONS AND ALLUSIONS

A. BIBLICAL QUOTATIONS AND ALLUSIONS

Genesis			Baruch		
4: 7	166		3: 20–1	146	
25: 8	38		Daniel		
35: 29	38		13: 52	146	
Leviticus			1 Maccabees		
25: 10	6		2: 66	144	
2 Kings (2 Samuel)			3: 1–22	144	
18: 4	138		3: 31	82, 144	
3 Kings (1 Kings)			4: 27	82, 144	
10: 23	162		Matthew		
1 Chronicles			3: 16	20	
23: 1	38		10: 26	120	
29: 28	38		13: 8	6	
Esther			16: 23	36, 144	
2–13	8		24: 7	72	
Job			25: 1–8	86	
24: 19	18		25: 32	138	
Psalms			Mark		
26 (27): 13	148		8: 33	36, 144	
35 (36): 3	134		9: 43	30	
41 (42): 2	132		Luke		
65 (66): 5	140		1: 65	146	
67 (68): 36	112		5: 26	146	
103 (104): 9	112		20: 25	36, 144	
137 (138): 6	14		24: 32	30	
141 (142): 6	148		John		
149 (150): 7	148		8: 3	120	
Proverbs			2 Corinthians		
21: 1	168		9: 7	168	
Song of Songs			2 Thessalonians		
2: 10	20		2: 3	8	
Ecclesiasticus			1 Timothy		
32: 1	32		2: 7	24	
44: 14	94		2 Timothy		
Isaiah			2: 5	140	
11: 2	6				
42: 3	44				

B. SOURCES AND ALLUSIONS IN CLASSICAL AND PATRISTIC AUTHORS (BEFORE AD 700)

Alcimus Avitus			Augustine	
Carmina			*De ciuitate Dei*	
vi. 302	34		xv. 7	166
Arator			xv. 26	6
Historia apostolica			Boethius	
i. 226–7	56		*De consolatione Philosophiae*	

202 INDEX OF QUOTATIONS AND ALLUSIONS

Boethius (*cont.*)

i, met. i, 2	82
i, met. ii, 1–3	22
i, met. v, 46–8	138
i, met. v, 29–36	96
i, pr. iv, 5	114, 148
ii, met. ii, 1–2	88
ii, met. ii, 19–20	136
ii, met. iv, 17–22	166
ii, met. vii, 12–14	22
ii, pr. v, 5	166
iii, met. i, 7–10	116
iii, met. iv, 1–4	140,
164	
iii, met. iv, 7–8	142
iii, met. v, 8–10	82
iii, met. ix, 10–12	116
iv, met. v, 21–2	112, 120
iv, met. vi, 27–9	120

Caelius Sedulius
Carmen paschale

i. 17–19	124

Gregory the Great
Dialogi

ii. 1	26
ii. 3	30

Isidore
Etymologiae

iii. 58	68
iii. 59	68

Juvenal
Saturae

vi. 605–6	130

Pliny
Naturalis historia

ii. 56	68
xx. 247	96

Prosper of Aquitaine
Epigrammata

ciiiA	108
ciiiB	108
ciiiC	108
ciiiD	110

Prudentius
Psychomachia

125–6	142, 154

Vergil
Aeneid

vi. 732	34
viii. 369	38

Georgics

ii. 339	38

C. SOURCES AND ALLUSIONS IN EARLY MEDIEVAL AUTHORS (700–1000)

Abbo of Fleury
Passio S. Eadmundi — 140

Alcuin
Carmina

i. 1318–86	70
i . 1387–92	76
i. 1457–8	78
ix	96

Aldhelm
De uirginitate (prose)

c. 1	134
c. 4	154
c. 19	6
c. 20	164

Enigmata

vi	94

Anglo-Saxon Chronicle D(E)

s.a. 737	62
s.a. 740	62, 64
s.a. 741	64
s.a. 744	64
s.a. 750	66
s.a. 752	66
s.a. 756	68

s.a. 758	70
s.a. 759	70, 74
s.a. 761	70
s.a. 763	72
s.a. 765	74
s.a. 766	74
s.a. 768	76
s.a. 774	78, 80
s.a. 776	82
s.a. 777	82
s.a. 778	82
s.a. 779	82, 84
s.a. 780	84
s.a. 782	84
s.a. 786	86
s.a. 787	88
s.a. 788	88, 90
s.a. 790	90
s.a. 791	90
s.a. 792	92
s.a. 793	92, 94, 96
s.a. 794	98
s.a. 796	100, 102
s.a. 797	104

INDEX OF QUOTATIONS AND ALLUSIONS 203

s.a. 798	104	c. 41	148
s.a. 802	118, 120	c. 42	148
s.a. 803	122	c. 44	148
s.a. 833	122	c. 45	148
Annales regni Francorum		c. 46	150
s.a. 768	76	c. 47	150
s.a. 771	78	c. 48	152
s.a. 772	78	c. 49	152
s.a. 774	80	c. 52	152
s.a. 775	82	c. 54	152
s.a. 796	98, 100	c. 55	154
s.a. 799	110	c. 56	154, 156
s.a. 800	114	c. 57	156
s.a. 801	114	c. 58	156
s.a. 802	114	c. 59	156
Asser		c. 60	156
Vita Ælfredi regis		c. 61	156
c. 1	122	c. 62	156
c. 2	124	c. 63	158
c. 3	124	c. 64	158
c. 4	124	c. 65	158
c. 5	126	c. 66	160
c. 6	126	c. 67	160
c. 7	126	c. 69	160
c. 8	126	c. 71	160
c. 9	128	c. 75	160
c. 10	128	c. 77	162
c. 11	128	c. 82	162
c. 12	128	c. 83	162
c. 14	118	c. 84	164
c. 15	120	c. 88	164
c. 16	130	c. 91	164
c. 17	130	c. 92	166
c. 18	130	c. 98	166
c. 19	132	B. (canonicus)	
c. 20	132	*Vita S. Eadburgae*	
c. 21	132	c. 2	10
c. 22	132	c. 7	18
c. 23	134	c. 10	12, 20
c. 24	134	c. 14	20
c. 26	134	Bede	
c. 27	136	*De natura rerum*	
c. 28	136	c. 39	94
c. 29	136	*De temporum ratione*	
c. 30	136	c. 27	68
c. 31	138	c. 29	94
c. 32	138	*Historia abbatum*	
c. 33	140	i. 1	24, 26
c. 34	140	i. 2	26, 28
c. 35	140, 142	i. 4	24, 28
c. 36	142	i. 5	28
c. 37	144	i. 6	28
c. 38	144	i. 7	24, 28, 30
c. 39	146	i. 8	34

204 INDEX OF QUOTATIONS AND ALLUSIONS

Bede (*cont.*)

i. 9	34	v. 24. 2	24, 54
i. 11	34	*Versus de die iudicii*	42–50
i. 13	36	*HE Continuatio* (I)	
ii. 14	36, 38	s.a. 731	58
ii. 15	38	s.a. 733	58
ii. 16	40	s.a. 734	58
ii. 17	40	*HE Continuatio* (II)	
ii. 18	40	s.a. 731	58
ii. 20	40	s.a. 733	58
ii. 21–3	40	s.a. 735	60
Historia ecclesiastica		s.a. 737	62
		s.a. 739	62
praef. 1	24, 72	s.a. 740	62, 64
i. 14. 2	2	s.a. 745	64
i. 34	24	s.a. 750	66
ii. 2	24	s.a. 753	66
ii. 5. 1	2, 24	s.a. 754	68
ii. 5. 2	2	s.a. 757	70
ii. 5. 3	2	s.a. 758	70
ii. 9	24	s.a. 759	70
iii. 8. 1	2	s.a. 761	70
iii. 12.3	80	s.a. 765	74
iiii. 15. 2	106, 108	s.a. 766	74
iiii. 15. 3	106	*Historia de sancto Cuthberto*	
iiii. 15. 4	106	c. 13	158
iiii. 24. 1	24	cc. 16–17	152
iiii. 26. 1–3	96	c. 20	150
v. 6	66	*Liber pontificalis*	
v. 7. 3	122	Hadrian	98
v. 20. 2	62	Leo III	110
v. 23. 3	52	'Me legat annales'	40–2
v. 23. 4	54	'Metrical Calendar of Ramsey'	
v. 23. 5	54	93–4	104
v. 23. 6	54	'Moore Memoranda'	22, 24
v. 24. 1	58	'West Saxon Regnal List'	122

GENERAL INDEX

Abbo, abbot of Fleury (988–1004) xiii, xxxviii; *Comm. in calculum Victorii* of, xiii n. 2; *Computus* of, xiii; *Passio S. Eadmundi* [*BHL* 2392] of, xiii, lxx–lxxi; *Quaestiones grammaticales* of, xiii n. 3; sojourn at Ramsey Abbey (985–7), xiii, lxxviii

Acca, bishop of Hexham (710–31) liv, lix, lx, lxxxi, lxxxii, lxxxiii, lxxxv, lxxxvi, 40, 54, 62, 64, 84, 88, 183–7, 188

Aclea, battle of 124

Adam, first man, alleged ancestor of King Alfred 124

Adda, early king of Northumbria 22

Ælberht (Æthelberht), archbishop of York (767–80) lxiii, 74, 78, 82

Ælf, son of Ælfwald, king of Northumbria 90

Ælfflæd, queen of Æthelred, king of Northumbria 92

Ælfric, abbot of Eynsham lxxii–lxxiii

Ælfric, archbishop of Canterbury (995–1005) xlvi

Ælfthryth, daughter of King Alfred 160

Ælfwald, king of the East Angles (713–49) lxi, 66

Ælfwald (I), king of Northumbria (778–88) xxxiii, lxiii, 82, 84, 88, 90

Ælfwine, son of Ælfwald, king of Northumbria 90

Ælle, tyrant in Northumbria 134–6

Æscesdun (Ashdown), battle of 142–6

Æt Læte (Otley?) 102

Æthelbald, archbishop of York (900–904/28) 177

Æthelbald, king of Mercia (716–57) lxi, 52, 58, 66, 70

Æthelbald, king of Wessex (858–60), son of King Æthelwulf 122, 124, 128, 130

Æthelbald, thegn of Æthelred, king of Northumbria 82

Æthelberht, bishop of Whithorn, subsequently bishop of Hexham 82, 90, 102, 104

Æthelberht, king of East Anglia 66

Æthelberht, king of Kent (560–616) xliii, 2, 4

Æthelberht, king of Wessex (860–5), son of King Æthelwulf 122, 130

Æthelflæd, daughter of King Alfred 160, 162

Æthelfrith, bishop of Elmham 60

Æthelfrith, king of Northumbria (592–616) 22

Æthelgifu, daughter of King Alfred, abbess of Shaftesbury 160, 162, 166

Æthelheard, abbot of Louth (?) 92

Æthelheard, ealdorman 98

Æthelheard, king of the West Saxons (726–40) lx, 62

Æthelhun, thegn of King Æthelbald of Mercia 67 n. 40

Æthelred, ealdorman in Devon 162

Æthelred, ealdorman in Mercia 136

Æthelred (I), king of Northumbria (774–9, 790–6) lxiv, lxv, 80, 82, 90, 92, 100, 104

Æthelred (I), king of Wessex (865–71) 132, 142, 144, 146

Æthelred and Æthelberht, SS. xix, xxi, xxxvi, xliii, xlvi–li, lxxviii, lxxxiii, 2, 4–16

Æthelred Mucel, ealdorman of the *Gaini* 136

Æthelred 'the Unready', king of England (978–1016) lxvii, 173, 182

Æthelric, early king of Northumbria 22

Æthelstan, king of England (924–39) 178, 179

Æthelstan, king of Kent (839–851/5) under King Æthelwulf 126

Æthelstan, priest in Mercia 162

Æthelswith, sister of King Alfred 175

Æthelthryth, queen of King Æthelwald Moll 72

Æthelwald, bishop of Lindisfarne (721–40) lx, 54, 62

Æthelwald Moll, king of Northumbria lxii, 70, 72, 74

Æthelweard, ealdorman, author of Latin *Chronicon* 174

Æthelweard, son of King Alfred 160–2

Æthelwine, bishop of Hexham (1056–71) 183

GENERAL INDEX

Æthelwine, ealdorman of East Anglia
(962–92), lay-patron of Ramsey
Abbey xiii, xliii–xliv, li
Æthelwulf, ealdorman of Berkshire
130, 142
Æthelwulf, king of Wessex (839–58) lxix,
122, 124, 126, 128
Alberht, abbot of Ripon lxiv, 86, 88
Alchhere, ealdorman 126
Alchmund, bishop of Hexham
(767–81) lxxxi, lxxxii, lxxxiii,
lxxxv, lxxxvi, 74, 84, 187–9
Alchmund, son of King Alchred 112
Alchred, king of Northumbria
(765–74) lxiii, 74, 76, 78, 88
Alcuin lxii, lxiii, 92
Aldfrith, king of Northumbria
(685–705) 24, 38
Aldhelm, abbot of Malmesbury, bishop of
Sherborne (c.706–c.710) lxiv, lxv,
94; Enigmata of, lxxiii; prose
De uirginitate of, lxxi
Aldred, ealdorman, murderer of King
Æthelred of Northumbria 110
Aldred, monk of Hexham 184
Aldwine (Wor), bishop of the Mercians 60
Aldwulf, bishop of Lindsey 66, 74
Aldwulf, bishop of Mayo (Ireland) 86
Aldwulf, bishop of Rochester lx, 52
Aldwulf, ealdorman 82
Alfred, king of the Anglo-Saxons
(871–99) xx, xxxiv, lxxii, 122–68
passim, 175, 176
Alfred Westou, priest of Durham 187
Alric lix, 58, 100
Aluberht, bishop of the Old Saxons
lxiii, 74
Alwig, bishop of Lindsey lix, 58, 66
Amund, Viking king 150
Anglo-Saxon Chronicle lvii, lx–lxv, 174
Annales regni Francorum ('Royal Frankish
Annals') lvii, lxiii–lxv
'Annals of St Neots' lxvi, lxvii, lxviii
'Annals of Ulster' 174
Arator, Christian-Latin poet, Historia
apostolica of xv, xl, xlii–xliii, lvi,
lxxiii, lxxxvi, 56 and n. 63
Arnold, T. xx, xxii, lxxxiv–lxxxv, lxxxvii, 171
Arnwine lx, 64
Asser, Vita Ælfredi of xx n. 28, xxi, xxxvi,
lxv–lxxiii, lxxv, 118–68 passim
Athelney 166
Augustine, St, first archbishop of
Canterbury (597–604/9) 60, 86

B. (canonicus), Vita S. Dunstani [BHL
2342] of xlvi–xlvii;
Vita S. Eadburgae [BHL 2384a]
of, xlv, xlvi–xlvii
Badwulf, bishop of Whithorn 90, 102
Bældæg, ancestor of King Alfred 122
Bagsecg, Viking king 146
Balthere, anchorite 68, 180
Bamburgh 66, 78, 80
Barton 104
Beaw, ancestor of King Alfred 122
Bede (673–735) xix, xxxvi, xxxvii, lix, 2,
22, 24, 52, 54–6, 60, 80, 94;
De natura rerum of, xiv, xxxiii,
lxiv; De temporibus of, xiv;
De temporum ratione of, xiv,
xxxiii, lxi, lxiv; De schematibus et
tropis of, xxxv; Historia abbatum
of, lii–liii, 24–40; Historia
ecclesiastica of, xliii, lii, lv–lvi,
lvii, lviii, lxii, lxiii, lxv, 2, 52, 54,
54–6, 58, 64, 72, 106; Versus de
die iudicii of, liv–lv, lxxiv, lxxxiii,
42–50
Bedwig, ancestor of King Alfred 122
Benedict, founding abbot of
Monkwearmouth–Jarrow 26–30,
34–6, 54
Benedict, St xiii, xxxix, lxxviii; relics of, at
Fleury, 158
Beocca, ealdorman 175
Beonna, king of East Anglia 66
Beorn, ealdorman lxiii, 82
Beornhelm, abbot 175
Beornred, pretender to the Mercian
throne 70
Berhtwald, archbishop of Canterbury
(692–731) lv–lvi, lviii, 52, 58, 60
Berhtwulf, king of Mercia (840–52) 124
Berkshire 140, 142
Billington Moor, battle of 104
Boethius, De consolatione Philosophiae
of lxiv, lxxiv–lxxv
Boniface (Wynfrith), St, martyred
archbishop of the Franks lxi, 68
Bosa, bishop of York 62
Botwine, abbot of Ripon 84
Brand, ancestor of King Alfred 122
Breedon, monastery at 52
Bregowine, archbishop of Canterbury
(761–4) 74
Brihtric (Beorhtric), king of the West
Saxons (786–802) 118
Brihtsige 177

GENERAL INDEX

207

Britons 64, 68
Brorda (Hildegils), *princeps* of the
    Mercians 110
Bückeburg (*Bohuueri*) 82
Burgred, king of Mercia (852–873/4) 126,
    128, 136, 150
Bury St Edmunds lxvii
BYRHTFERTH OF RAMSEY: oblate at
    Ramsey (?) xiv; tutelage under
    Abbo of Fleury xiv;
  corpus of computistical writings
    (incl. Bede and Helperic) xiv;
  Latin style of xvi, xxiii–xliii, 171–4:
    favourite quotations xxxix–xliii;
    irrelevant digressions xxxii–xxxv;
    poeticism xxvii;
    repeated phrases xxviii–xxxii;
    rhetorical constructions xxxv–xxxix:
      asyndeton xxxviii–xxxix;
      erotema xxxix;
      hyperbaton xxxv–xxxvii;
      paronomasia xxxviii;
      polyptoton xxxvii–xxxviii;
      solecism xxvii–xxviii;
      vocabulary xxiv–xxviii;
  writings of:
    Computus xiv–xv, xli, xlii, liv, lxxv
      (*proemium* of [*Comp. proem.*], xiv,
      xxiii);
    Enchiridion xv, xvi, xxiii, xxxiv, xxxv,
      xxxvii, xxxviii, lxxxvi;
    Glossae Bridferti Ramesiensis in
      Bedam xiv, xxxiii;
    Historia regum xvi, xxiii–xliii, 1–169,
      171–4;
    Passio SS. Æthelredi et Æthelberhti
      [*BHL* 2643] xliii–lii, lxxxiii;
    Vita S. Ecgwini [*BHL* 2432] xvi, xxiii,
      xxxviii, xliii, liv n. 135, lxxxvi;
    Vita S. Oswaldi [*BHL* 6374] xvi, xxii,
      xxiii, xxxv, xlii, xlvi, xlvii n. 110,
      lxxiii, lxxxvi

Caelius Sedulius, Christian-Latin
    poet lxxv
Caithness 179
Cambridge 150–2
Canaan, alleged ancestor of King
    Alfred 124
Canterbury lxviii, lxix, 124; St Augustine's
    Abbey at, xlv, xlix, liii, 14; Christ
    Church, xlix, 14, 162
Carloman, king of the Franks lxiii, 76
Catterick (N Yorks) lxii, 72, 76

Ceawlin, ancestor of King Alfred 122
Celestine III, pope (1191–8) lxxvi
Ceolfrith, abbot of Jarrow (685–716) 30,
    34, 38–40, 54
Ceolnoth, archbishop of Canterbury
    (833–70) lxxi, 123 n. 11, 140
Ceolwold, ancestor of King Alfred 122
Ceolwulf, bishop of Lindsey 74, 102
Ceolwulf, king of Mercia (874–9) 150
Ceolwulf, king of Northumbria
    (729–37) lii, lvii, lviii–lix, lxii,
    24, 52, 58, 72
Ceorl, ealdorman of Devon 124
Cerdic, ancestor of King Alfred 122
Charlemagne, king of the Franks lxiii, lxiv,
    lxv, 76, 80, 92, 98, 112–14,
    118–20
Chester-le-Street (Durham) 158, 174, 176
Chézy, Frankish royal estate 164
Chichester 176
Chippenham 128, 152, 156
'Chronicle of Melrose' lxxxii, 65 n. 26
Ciniod (Cynoth), king of the Picts lxiii,
    78, 80
Cirencester 156
Coenhelm: *see* Kenelm, St
Coenred, ancestor of King Alfred 122
Coenred, king of Northumbria
    (716–18) 24
Coenwulf, king of Mercia (796–821) lxv,
    102, 104, 106, 116
Colgu, priest and lector 98
Constantine, king of the Scots 179
Constantinople 114
Corbridge 86
Cotton, Sir Robert (1571–1631) lxv, lxvi
Countisbury (Devon) 152
Crawford, S. J. xvi
Crayke (N Yorks) lxiii, 76
Creoda, ancestor of King Alfred 122
Cutha, ancestor of King Alfred 122
Cuthbert (*recte* Cuthheard) 176
Cuthbert, bishop of Hereford, archbishop
    of Canterbury (740–60) lx, 60, 64
Cuthbert, St, bishop of Lindisfarne
    (685–7) xxii, lxiv, lxxii, lxxix, 90,
    94, 152, 171, 174, 176, 179; relics
    of, 66, 150; retreat on Farne
    Island, lxiv, 96
Cuthfrith, bishop of Lichfield 74
Cuthred, king of the West Saxons lx, lxi,
    62, 66, 68
Cuthwine, ancestor of King Alfred 122
Cyneberht, bishop of Lindsey lix

208 GENERAL INDEX

Cyneheard, murderer of King
    Cynewulf 86
Cynewulf, bishop of Lindisfarne lx, lxi,
    lxiii, 62, 66, 82, 84
Cynewulf, king of the West Saxons
    (757–86) 86
Cynric, ancestor of King Alfred 122
Cynwulf, ealdorman 82

Danes: *see* Vikings
Daniel, bishop of Winchester 52
Desiderius, king of the Lombards 80
Deusdedit, archbishop of Canterbury
    (655–64) l–li, 12, 20, 60
Domneua (Eormenburg), abbess of
    Minster-in-Thanet xlv,
    xlviii, l–li, 16
Doncaster 72
Dracontius, Christian-Latin poet xl, liv
Dregmo, citizen of Hexham 187
Dumbarton, siege of lxi, 68
Dunblane 177
Dunn, bishop of Rochester lx, 64
Dunnottar 179
Durham lxxi, lxxvi, lxxx, 174, 188
Dunstan, St, archbishop of Canterbury
    (960–88) 191

Eadbald, king of Kent (616–40) xlix
    n. 118, 2, 4
Eadberht (*recte* Aldberct), bishop of the
    East Angles 52
Eadberht, king of Northumbria
    (737–58) lxi–lxii, 62, 66, 68,
    70, 76
Eadberht Praen, king of Kent (796–8) 104
Eadburg, queen of King Brihtric, daughter
    of King Offa 118–20
Eadmund, St, martyred king of East
    Anglia xiii, lxx, 138–40
Eadred, abbot of Carlisle lxxii, 150
Eadred, king of England (946–55) 180, 181
Eadweard (Edward the Elder), son of King
    Alfred, king of Wessex
    (899–924) 160, 176, 177, 178
Eadwig, king of England (955–9) 181
Eadwine (Eda), abbot of Gainford 114–16
Eadwine (Edwin), brother of King
    Æthelstan 178
Eadwulf, ealdorman lxiii, 78, 80
Eadwulf, king of Northumbria 64
Eafa, ancestor of King Alfred 122
Ealdwine, bishop of Lichfield 52
Ealdwulf, bishop of Rochester 62, 64

Ealhhere, ealdorman 126
Ealhmund, ancestor of King Alfred 122
Ealhstan, bishop of Sherborne 128, 136
Eanbald (I), archbishop of York
    (780–96) xli, lxv, 82, 84, 102
Eanbald (II), archbishop of York
    (796–808?) 102, 104, 106
Eanberht, bishop of Hexham 112
Eanberht, bishop of Lindisfarne 123 n. 11
Earconberht, king of Kent (640–64) xlix,
    2, 4
Eardwulf, bishop of Lindisfarne 128,
    150, 176
Eardwulf, ealdorman 90
Eardwulf, king of Northumbria
    (796–806) lxv, 100, 104, 110,
    112, 116
Earnred, 'tyrant' lxii, 76
East Anglia, kingdom of 132, 134, 138–40
Eastry (Kent) xlvii, xlix, 14
Ebbi, abbot lxiii, 80
Ecga, ealdorman 82
Ecgberht, archbishop of York (732–66) lvii,
    lviii, lix, lxii, 60, 74
Ecgberht, king of Kent (664–73) xliii,
    xlviii, l, li, 2, 4, 6, 7 and n. 14,
    10–12, 16
Ecgberht, king of the West Saxons
    (802–39) 118, 120
'Ecgberht's Stone' (in Selwood Forest) 154
Ecgfrith, king of Mercia (787–96) lxv, 102
Ecgfrith, king of Northumbria (670–85)
    lxxxix, 24, 28, 30, 32; 'port of', 96
Ecgred, bishop of Lindisfarne 123 n. 11
Ecgric, priest and lector lxiii, 76
Ecgwine, St, founder of Evesham Abbey xvi
Echha, anchorite of Crayke lxiii, 74
eclipses (solar and lunar) lxi, 58, 66–8,
    70, 156
Ecumenical Councils 106–8
Edgar, king of England (959–75) xxxv
Edington (Wilts), battle of 154
Edmund, king of England (939–46) 179
Edric, canon of Hexham 185
Edward 'the Confessor', king of England
    (1042–66) xxi, xxii, 173, 182
Edward 'the Martyr', king of England
    (975–8) 182
Eldon (Durham) 70
Elesa, ancestor of King Alfred 122
Elias, patriarch of Jerusalem 164
Englafeld, battle of 142
English Channel 110
Enoch, alleged ancestor of King Alfred 124

GENERAL INDEX 209

Enos, alleged ancestor of King Alfred 124
Eormenburg: *see* Domneua
Eormenred, brother of King
    Earconberht xlviii–xlix, 2, 4
Eosterwine, abbot of Monkwearmouth
    30–4
Eresburg 82
Eric 'Blood-axe', Scandinavian king of
    York 181
Esc lix 58
Exeter 152, 176

Farne Island 96
Felix, bishop of the East Angles lxxviii
    and n. 190
Feologild, archbishop of Canterbury
    (832) 123 n. 11
Fleury xiii, 158
'Florence' of Worcester: *see* John of
    Worcester
Forthere, bishop of the West Saxons 52
Frana, Viking earl 146
Frealaf, ancestor of King Alfred 122
Freohelm, abbot lxii, 72
Frithuberht, bishop of Hexham lix, 60, 74
Frithuwald, ancestor of King Alfred 122
Frithuwald, bishop of Whithorn lxii, 72
Frithuwald, early king of Northumbria 22
Frithuwulf, ancestor of King Alfred 122
Fulham 156

Gainford (Durham) 116
Geat, ancestor of King Alfred 122–4
George, bishop of Ostia, papal legate to
    England 86
Gesta abbatum S. Bertini Sithensium
    178 n. 29
Glappa, early king of Northumbria 22
Glastonbury, abbey of liii
Goscelin of Saint-Bertin, *Vita, miracula et*
    translatio S. Ivonis [*BHL*
    4621] lxxvi; *Vita S. Mildrethae*
    [*BHL* 5960], xlv
Govan (*Ouania*) 68
Gregory the Great, pope (590–604) 82,
    162; *Dialogi* of, 162
Gullick, M. xix
Guthred (*recte* Guthfrith I), Scandinavian
    king of York 158, 176, 178
Guthrum, Viking king 150, 154, 175;
    baptism of, 154–6, 175

Hadrian, abbot in Canterbury 28
Hadrian (I), pope (772–95) lxiv, 78, 86, 98

Hadwine, bishop of Mayo (Ireland) 76, 78
Halfdan, Viking king 150, 152
Harald, Viking earl 146
Hart, C. R. lxxxv–lxxxvi
Hatfield, synod of lxv
Hathra, ancestor of King Alfred 124
HE Continuatio (I) lvii, lviii, lix
HE Continuatio (II) lvii, lviii, lix–lxii
Headolac, bishop of the East Angles 52
Heardberht, thegn of Æthelred, king of
    Northumbria 82
Heardred, bishop of Hexham 104, 112
Hearrahalch 90
Heathoberht, bishop of London lxv, 116
Heathured, bishop 175
Helperic, *De computo* of xiv
Hemel, bishop of the Mercians 74
Hengest, early king of Kent 2
Herebald, abbot lxi 66
Heremod, ancestor of King Alfred 124
Herewald, bishop of Sherborne 60
Herwagen, Johann xiv
Hexham xvii, 64, 88, 104, 112, 183–9
Hill, James lxvi–lxvii
Historia Brittonum xvii
Historia de sancto Cuthberto lxxi–lxxiii, 174,
    176 n. 15
Historia post Bedam lxxx–lxxxi
Hodgson-Hinde, J. xxi, lxxxiii–lxxxiv, 171
Honorius, archbishop of Canterbury
    (627/31–53) 60
Hun, king of East Anglia 66
Huns (Avars) 98
Hunter Blair, P. xviii, xxii–xxiii, xxxviii, 171
Hussa, early king of Northumbria 22
Hwætberht, abbot of Jarrow 40
Hwala, ancestor of King Alfred 124
Hwita, bishop of Lichfield 60
Hygbald, bishop of Lindisfarne 84, 86,
    102, 104, 123 n. 11
Hywel, king of the Britons 181

Ida, early king of Northumbria lii, 22, 74
Ine, king of the West Saxons (688–726) 122
Ingild, ancestor of King Alfred, brother of
    King Ine 122
Ingwald, bishop of London lxi, 52, 64
Ingwald (*recte* Ragnwald?), Viking king 178
Irene, Byzantine empress lxv
Irminric, early king of Kent 2
Isidore, *Etymologiae* xxxvii, lxi
Itermon, ancestor of King Alfred 124
Iustus, archbishop of Canterbury
    (624–627/31) 60

GENERAL INDEX

Ivar, Viking king 152
Ivo, St xlv n. 100, lxxvi, lxxviii

Jænberht, archbishop of Canterbury
    (765–92) 74, 90
John of Hexham, *Historia .xxv.*
    annorum xviii
John of Worcester, *Chronica* xx, lxvi–lxxi
John Scottus Eriugena xx n. 29
Judith, daughter of Charles the Bald, wife
    of King Æthelwulf 130

Kenelm, St 102
Kent, kingdom of xliii, 104, 126, 130, 132,
    158–60

Lamech, alleged ancestor of King
    Alfred 124
Langres 40
Laurence, archbishop of Canterbury
    (604/9–19) 60
Leicester 180
Leo (III), pope (795–816) lxv, 110–12,
    114, 126
Lerins 26
Leutfrith, bishop of Mayo (Ireland) 78
Liber pontificalis lxiv, lxv
Lindisfarne xxxiii, lxiv, lxxix, 66, 94, 96,
    100, 174, 180
London lxix 72, 104, 116, 148, 162, 177

Macrobius, *Comm. in Somnium Scipionis*
    xiii, xiv
Malaleel, alleged ancestor of King
    Alfred 124
Malcolm III 'Canmore', king of Scots
    (1058–93) 186
Malcolm IV, king of Scots (1153–65) xvii,
    lxxxii
Man, Isle of 92
MANUSCRIPTS:
    Cambridge, CCC 139 xvii–xx, lv n. 138,
        lxxix, lxxx–lxxxi, lxxxvii–lxxxix,
        171
    Cambridge, Trinity College, O. 3. 7
        lxxiv
    Cambridge, UL, Kk. 3. 21 lxxiv–lxxv
    Cambridge, UL, Kk. 5. 16 lii, lviii
    Durham, CL, B. II. 35 xvii
    Durham, CL, B. IV. 24 xix,
        lxxvii–lxxviii
    Durham, CL, B. IV. 25 xvii
    Durham, CL, C. IV. 15 xvii
    Gotha, Forschungsbibliothek, I. 81 xlvi

London, BL, Cotton Augustus ii. 22
    lxvii
London, BL, Cotton Caligula A. xiv, xlv
London, BL, Cotton Cleopatra B xiii,
    xlvii n. 110
London, BL, Cotton Otho A. xii
    [destroyed in 1731] lxvi–lxxi
London, BL, Cotton Rolls II. 16 lxxvii
London, BL, Cotton Tiberius B. iv
    lvii n. 145
London, BL, Cotton Tiberius C. ii lxii
London, BL, Harley 3020 lii–liii
London, BL, Royal 13. A. VI lxxx
London, BL, Stowe 944 xlv
Paris, BnF, lat. 5362 lxxiii
Oxford, BodL, Bodley 285 xlv, lxxvi
Oxford, BodL, Laud misc. 636
    lvii n. 145
Oxford, St John's College 17 xiv, xxxiii,
    xli, liv n. 131, lvi n. 143
Oxford, St John's College 97 lxxx
Mathusalah, alleged ancestor of King
    Alfred 124
'Me legat annales' xl–xli, liii, 40–2
Mechil Wongtune (Middleton?) 70
Meehan, B. xvii
Mellitus, archbishop of Canterbury
    (619–24) 60
Merewalh, king of Mercia 16
'Metrical Calendar of Ramsey' xl, xli–xlii,
    lxv, lxxv
Mildrith, abbess of Minster-in-Thanet xlv,
    xlviii, li, 18–20
'Mildrith Legend' xlv–xlvi, xlviii, xlix, l–li
Minster-in-Thanet, abbey of xlv, xlviii,
    l–li, 18
Moll, ealdorman 110
Monkwearmouth–Jarrow, abbey of xix, lii,
    liii–liv, lxxxiii, 24–6, 28, 30, 54
'Moore Memoranda' lii
More, abbot 110
Mucelwudu (Selwood Forest) 160

Newburgh 68
Niall, king in Ireland 178
Nicaea, Second Council of (787) lxiv, 92
    and n. 133
Noah, alleged ancestor of King Alfred
    124
Northampton 180
Northumbria, kingdom of lii–lxv
Nothhelm, archbishop of Canterbury
    (735–9) lix, lx, 60, 62
Nottingham 136–8

GENERAL INDEX

Octa, early king of Kent 2
Oda, archbishop of Canterbury
    (941–58) 180
Offa, king of Mercia (757–96) lxi, lxv, 70,
    76, 92, 102
Offa, son of Aldfrith lxi, 66
Oiric, early king of Kent 2
Oisc, early king of Kent 2
Olaf I Cuarán, Scandinavian king of York
    (941–4) 179, 180–1
Onuist, kijng of the Picts lxii, 68, 70
Osbald, temporary king of
    Northumbria 100, 110
Osberht, king of Northumbria
    (848/9–862/3) 134–6
Osbern, Viking earl 146
Osbriht, king 177
Osburh, mother of King Alfred 124
Oscytel, Viking king 150
Osgeofu, queen of Alchred, king of
    Northumbria 76
Oslac, butler of King Æthelwulf, father of
    Osburh 124
Oslafa, wife of Eormenred xlix
Osred, king of Northumbria (705–16) 24,
    88, 90, 92
Osred, thegn of King Cynewulf of the West
    Saxons 86
Osric, ealdorman of Hampshire 130
Osric, king of Northumbria (718–29) 24
Oswald, St, bishop of Worcester,
    archbishop of York (961–92),
    founder of Ramsey Abbey xiii,
    xvi, xxii, lvii, lxxv, lxxviii
Oswald, St, martyred king of Northumbria
    (634–42) lxiii, 24; relics of,
    80, 90
Oswine 70
Oswiu, king of Northumbria (651–70)
    24, 26
Oswulf, high reeve of Bamburgh, earl of
    Northumbria 181
Oswulf, king of Northumbria (758–9) 70
Oswulf Cracabam (recte Kraka-bein),
    earl 177
Oter (recte Ottar), earl 177
Oxford 177

Paris 162, 164
Parker, Matthew (1504–75), archbishop of
    Canterbury lxv
Passio SS. Ethelredi et Ethelbricti [BHL
    2641–2] xliii, xlv, lxxvi–lxxvii
Paulinus, bishop of York (627–33) 60

Pavia 80, 120, 175
Pechthelm, bishop of Whithorn 54, 72
Pechtwine, bishop of Whithorn lxiii, 82
Petrie, H. xxi, lxxxi–lxxxii
Picts 54, 64, 100, 150
Pihtel, ealdorman 78
Pincanhale 88, 106
Piper, A. xix
Pippin, king of the Franks lxii, 76
Plegmund, archbishop of Canterbury
    (890–923) xxxiii, 162
Pliny, Naturalis historia xxxiii, lxi, 68
Prosper of Aquitaine, Christian-Latin
    poet lxv, lxxv

Ramsey (Cambs.), abbey of xiii, xliv, lxxvi;
    Liber benefactorum of, xliv
Reading 140, 142
Regino of Prüm, Chronica xvii, xviii
Reginwald (recte Ragnall), Viking king 177
Remigius of Auxerre xxxv, lxxiv
Repton 150
'Resting Places of English Saints' xlv
Richard of Hexham, De gestis regis Stephani
    et de bello Standardii xviii
Ricthryth, abbess, former queen of Oswulf,
    king of Northumbria 86
Ripon 90
Rochester 158
Roger of Howden, Chronica lxxx, lxxxii,
    lxxxix
Rollason, D. xviii, lxxvi
Rome 26, 62, 112, 126, 128, 150, 175

Saint-Lô 175
Sandwich (Kent) 126
Sawley (W Yorks.) xvii, xxxiii, lxiv, 94
Saxons (continental) 78, 80
Sceldwa, ancestor of King Alfred 124
Schola Saxonum (Rome) 160
Scythlesceaster (Chesters?) 88
Seletun (Selby?) 82
Sem, alleged ancestor of King Alfred 124
Sergius, pope (687–701) 38
Seth, alleged ancestor of King Alfred 124
Shaftesbury 166, 182
Sharpe, J. xxi
Sharpe, R. lxxvii
Sheppey, Isle of 124, 128
Sherborne 130, 132, 136
Sicga, ealdorman xxxiii, lxiv, 94
Sidroc the Elder, Viking earl 146
Sidroc the Younger, Viking earl 146
Sigbald, abbot lxiii, 76

212 GENERAL INDEX

Sigeberht, king of the West Saxons lxi, 68
Sigeferth, bishop of Selsey 58
Sigfrid, bishop lix
Sigfrith, abbot of Monkwearmouth 34–8
Sigred, abbot of Ripon 88
Sihtric, brother of King Niall 178
Sockburn (NYorks.) 102
Somerled xvii
Southampton (*Hamwic*) 72
Speusippus, Eleusippus, Meleusippus,
    SS. of Langres 40
Stevenson, Joseph lxxxi n. 197
Stevenson, W. H., editor of Asser lxvii
Story, J. xvii, lviii
Strathclyde 150
Stuf, Jutish ancestor of Osburh, Alfred's
    mother 124
Swæfberht, king of the East Saxons lx, 62
Swithwulf, abbot 78
Syburg 82
Symeon of Durham lxxvii, lxxviii–lxxix;
    *Historia de regibus Anglorum et
    Dacorum*, xviii–xx, xxi, lxxii, lxxix,
    lxxxiii; *Libellus de exordio et
    procursu istius, hoc est Dunhelmensis,
    ecclesiae* xix, lxxii, lxxxix

Tætwa, ancestor of King Alfred 124
Tamworth 180
Tatwine, archbishop of Canterbury
    (731–4) lviii, lix, 52, 58, 60
Tettenhall, battle of 177
Thanet 18, 128, 132; *see also* Minster-in-
    Thanet
Theodore, archbishop of Canterbury
    (668–90) li n. 121, 28, 60
Theodric, early king of Northumbria 22
Thetford 138
Thomas (II), archbishop of York (1108–14)
    lxxxii, 184
Thunor, evil councillor of King
    Ecgberht xlviii, xlix, l–li,
    8–10, 18
Tilberht, bishop of Hexham 84, 86, 90
Tilthegn, prior of Abbot More 110
Torhtmund, ealdorman, murderer of
    Aldred 110
Totta (Torhthelm), bishop of Leicester
    60, 72
Twysden, Sir Roger (1597–1672) lxxxi,
    lxxxii
Tyninghame (ELoth.) 180

Usuard of Saint-Germain, *Martyrologium*
    of xix, lxxviii

Victorius of Aquitaine, *Calculus* xiii n. 2
Vikings xxxiii, lxviii, lxx, 96, 126, 130, 132,
    134, 138, 142–6, 148, 154–6, 160,
    162, 175
Vitalian, pope (657–72) 26
Vulfesuuelle 84
Vuonuualdremere 90

Wada, ealdorman 104, 126–8
Wakering (Essex) xliii–xliv, xlix–l,
    lxxvii, 14
Wales, attacked by Kings Æthelwulf and
    Burgred 126
Walhstod, bishop of Hereford 52
Wanley, Humphrey (1672–1726) lxxvii
Wantage 122
Wareham 152
Wendun (*Brunanburh?*), battle of 179
Werburg, abbess 84
Werferth, bishop of Worcester 162
'West Saxon Regnal List' lxxi
Whalley (Lancs.) 104
Wigred, bishop of St Cuthbert's
    congregation (Chester-le-
    Street) 178
Wihtgar, Jutish ancestor of Osburh,
    Alfred's mother 124
Wilfrid (I), bishop of the
    Northumbrians lx, 62, 64,
    88, 188
Wilfrid (II), bishop of Worcester and
    York lx–lxi, lxxxix, 52, 64
William of Malmesbury, *Gesta regum
    Anglorum* xx; *Gesta pontificum
    Anglorum* xx n. 29
William of Saint-Calais, bishop of Durham
    (1080–96) xviii
Winchester lxix, 72, 130; Old Minster at,
    xxxv
Wirtigirn, early king of Kent 2
Wise, Francis, editor of Asser lxvi, lxvii
Woden, ancestor of King Alfred 122
Woodford 104
Wulfhæth, abbot of Beverley lxiii, 78
Wulfhere, archbishop of York
    (854–892/900) 128, 175
Wulfstan, homilist, archbishop of York
    (1002–23) 180
Wulfstan of Winchester, *Vita S. Æthelwoldi*
    [*BHL* 2647] of lxxiii

York lvi, lvii, lviii, lx, lxii, 64, 72, 90,
    98, 100, 102, 110, 134, 136, 174,
    178, 180
Yvo, St: *see* Ivo, St